D0783491

The author of this important boo
distinguished member of the Lo
reaches, fre

GOVERNMENT OF THE PEOPLE

GOVERNMENT
OF THE PEOPLE

A STUDY IN THE AMERICAN
POLITICAL SYSTEM

BY

D. W. BROGAN

OF THE DEPARTMENT OF POLITICAL SCIENCE,
LONDON SCHOOL OF ECONOMICS

With a Foreword by
PROFESSOR HAROLD J. LASKI

NEW EDITION

IOWA STATE
AMES IA
COLLEGE LIBRARY

HARPER & BROTHERS
PUBLISHERS: NEW YORK

Published in England under the title

The American Political System

PRINTED IN THE UNITED STATES OF AMERICA

1-K

JK268
B786g2

To
MY FATHER AND MOTHER

356439

PREFACE TO NEW EDITION

I

WHEN this book was being written, Mr. Hoover was President of the United States; the Weimar Republic still survived in Germany, though visibly in great danger; the Third Republic survived in France, apparently in no danger at all; and the Second Spanish Republic, a little over a year old, seemed to have reasonable chances of better fortune than the first had had. It is unnecessary to stress the changes that have befallen the world since then, and it is unnecessary to stress the interest of a political system that has passed through those years so little changed in its forms, spirit and personnel as has the political system of the United States. Survival is not the only test of a government, but it is a test all the same, and the American system of government has passed that test. Even in 1932, the American Constitution, the American system of federal government, could claim to be the oldest unchanged system in the world. The "British Constitution" had been more fundamentally altered in 1832 and in 1911, not to speak of the less dramatic changes that had gone on all the time, than had the American Constitution which had gone into effect in 1789. Then there was still a King of France and Navarre, a King of Spain and the Indies, a Venetian and a Dutch Republic, an Emperor in Pekin; a Pope-King ruled in Bologna, a Tsarina in Petersburg and a Shogun in Yedo, not yet Tokio and not yet the residence of the Divine Mikado.

Yet it is still a relevant and emotionally powerful argument in America to quote, as immediately applicable, the words of Washington and Jefferson, or the decisions of the Supreme Court of John Marshall, and to talk of going back to the fundamental principles of the Constitution as exhibited at some date anterior to the present day, back to President Franklin Pierce in the case of Mr. Justice McReynolds, back to the happy days before the New Deal in the case of so many Republican (and Democratic) politicians. Such conservatism has many explanations, but it has one necessary condition: the constitutional system so uncritically worshipped must have been, on the whole, a success. It has survived, it has been admired and almost or quite worshipped by those whom it most affected. And the "People of the United

States," under the Constitution and through the political system of which the Constitution is the core, have waxed strong and prosperous, have defended their own independence and security, and have profoundly affected the history of the world.

This is the basic fact about the American political system: it has neither degenerated into tyranny nor anarchy; it has unified an area the size of Europe, not merely formally but spiritually. It has been far more successful in its combination of local autonomy with central strength than Brazil, Australia or Canada have been. Eleven years ago, one could be more finicky than is wise today; the sad truth which Chesterton enunciated, that the world will never be made safe for democracy since it is a dangerous trade, is truer than ever now. A reluctance to lay rash hands on that "great work of time," the working constitution of the United States, seems, today, more reasonable than it did in 1932. And that not only because the dangers of such a rash course seem more evident, but because the existing political system has proved capable of far more adaptation, of far more effective reforms, than seemed likely when the almost Chinese petrification of the Coolidge era still seemed the normal standard of American government.

It is possible to argue—and to argue rightly—that the changes in the social atmosphere of the United States during the past ten years have been as dramatic and profound as any country that has not passed through an open revolution can show. It is, indeed, difficult for any American, even a Southern Democrat or an Illinois Republican, to think himself back into the boom days of Mr. Coolidge or the gloom days of Mr. Hoover, when the functions of the federal government were so limited that the imposition of the religious taboos of rural America seemed to be the most urgent task and the most serious problem of the administration. In the past ten years, the extensions of the functions of the federal government, the change in the climate of opinion that made those extensions possible, have been as great, at least, as the corresponding changes that marked the period of the Civil War. The survivors of the old order who still dream of a return to the golden days when Mr. Coolidge was simply enunciating an axiom when he said that "the business of the United States is business," recall the stubborn conservatives, like Chief Justice Taney, who hoped by legal decisions to reverse the great revolution that was called the Civil War.

And this spiritual change is reflected in a material change. To return to New York, now, is to be impressed not by the white elephants of speculative capitalism like the Empire State Building, but by the great skyways and bridges that federal money and federal planning made possible. To look on the great bridges across San Francisco Bay under which steamed the ships bearing the wounded from Pearl Harbor is to be reminded of how much has changed since Mr. Hiram Johnson helped to re-elect Wilson in 1916 and helped to destroy his work in 1919. Indeed, most things have changed except Senator Johnson—and the American political system of which he is so typical an ornament. For the great material and psychological changes in American society have been made with astonishingly little effect on the forms, or even on the realities, of the political system which I attempted to describe when prohibition was still part of the Constitution and Mr. Roosevelt was only President-Elect, regarded by many acute critics as a good, easy man, whose dislike of initiative and want of combative energy would make his administration dangerously weak.

There have been changes: one constitutional amendment has been repealed; one has been added. There have been minor but important changes in the federal legal system. There have been interesting modifications in local government in New York City and in state government in Nebraska. Some political figures who loomed large in 1932 are dead; some are in permanent retirement; one or two are or have been in jail; one or two have changed their nominal party affiliations. But how few the changes either in mechanisms or men! Only one quite new political leader of the first rank has appeared, Mr. Wendell Willkie. Only one basic constitutional tradition has been destroyed, the limitation of a President to two terms. American politics have changed far less than American life. Despite Mr. Roosevelt, they have remained largely the politics of horse and buggy days—and it has turned out that the horse and buggy days were in the future as well as in the past.

I have, therefore, felt justified in consenting to a reprint of this book. If I am right, if American politics are still done largely in the same old way and entirely at the same old stand, that makes their study of far greater general interest than it was in 1933. The American impact on Europe and on the world has increased, is increasing and will only be diminished by the choice of the American people. And so the methods by which alone the American people can effectively express its choice are worthy of serious attention.

II

In a democracy, the working of the political system is the business of the parties and the American party system has always been one of the great mysteries of American life for the enquiring stranger. It still is. In 1932, it was possible to believe that one of the two traditional parties, the Democrats, was dying and was bound to die under the pressure for a "real" party of the Left, a party with a common social doctrine, with a leadership agreeing on the same general principles and general attitudes to the problems of modern industrial society.

This belief has proved groundless. The prospects of the progressive third parties have never been bleaker than in the last ten years. There has been an absolute and a still more striking relative falling-off in their voting strength. The Farmer-Labor party in Minnesota, the Non-Partisan League in the Dakotas, the Progressives in Wisconsin, the Socialist and Communist parties in the great cities, have all failed to make the grade. Strongholds like Milwaukee have been lost and if there are a few apparently impregnable positions still held, like Bridgeport, Connecticut, that is more a matter for rejoicing on the Right than on the Left. At best, these splinter parties have a nuisance value and they are far more effective as Democratic than as Republican nuisances. Equally groundless have been the hopes of effective political action by an organized labour movement. There has been a great growth in the formal and in the real strength of American trade unionism, which the feud between the American Federation of Labor and the Congress of Industrial Organizations has not stopped. Some weight should be given to the disastrous results of the application by the most famous American leader of a *condottiere* policy that recalls the careers of Jay Gould or the other great railroad wreckers, more than the policy of labour leaders as we have known them. But even Mr. John L. Lewis could not go on making labour a force that the prudent politician need not take too seriously, if the rank and file had an independent political programme of their own, even the minimum programme of voting for their friends and against their enemies. There has been an increase in the strength of the Left; there has been an increased awareness of the inadequacies of the old agrarian or industrial radicalism for the necessities of our times. But as far as there has been a social movement embodied in a political party, it has been embodied in the Democratic party and, indeed, in one man, the President of the United States. Whether there is in the Democratic party an effective nucleus for a united, progressive party under the old or a new name, will only be decided when the forces of the Left go out to battle under a lesser leader than the incomparable campaigner whom the Democratic party in 1932 made its leader, with so little knowledge of what it was doing.

Nor has the necessity of creating a real conservative party that seemed evident to so many observers after the Republican debacle of 1936, proved to be urgent. The American voter, when he turned to the Right, turned to the old firm. That meant taking over many liabilities, in traditions and in personnel, but it meant taking over even more assets, above all the asset of the unshakable strength of the Grand Old Party in the rural areas of the North and Middle West. When the American farmer is prosperous enough to ride to the polls, he votes Republican. Indeed, the loyalty of so many millions of American voters to the shade of Lincoln and McKinley is one of the greatest safeguards against Fascism, for only in a country in which the conservative forces have no adequate emotional hold on the common man is it necessary to turn to Mussolini, Hitler, or Pétain.

Despite the prophecies of optimists and pessimists, the old two-party system of the United States survives and each party has alike preserved its old character. That is, each party is basically traditional and regional; it is marked off from its rival not by doctrine or class, but by ancestry and geographical distribution of strength. It is true that the Republican party, as a whole, is more conservative than the Democratic party, as a whole, but some sections of the Democratic party in the South are as conservative as any section of the Republican party and more conservative than most sections of it. And many sections of the Republican party in the Middle West are as "progressive" as some important sections of the Democratic party in the North. Again, it is in general true that the Democratic party draws its voting strength more from the poor than from the rich; but not only are there some rich Democrats, but there are millions of lower-income Republicans.

In what has been one of the great themes of American politics in recent years, the foreign policy of the United States, there has been an apparent cleavage on party lines. A decided majority of the Democratic party has supported the policy of Mr. Roosevelt, beginning with the amendment of the Neutrality Act in 1939 down to the last measures adopted before Pearl Harbor. And all of these measures have been opposed by substantial majorities of the Republican members of both houses of Congress. But some of the most determined enemies of the Roosevelt foreign policy have been Democrats like Senators Bennett Champ Clark and Wheeler, while some of the most effective supporters of it have been Republicans inside Congress like Senator Austin or Republican leaders outside it like Mr. Willkie. The congressional support given Mr. Roosevelt by his own party has been largely from those Southern conservative sections most opposed to the rest of his policy, and Republican and independent supporters of the New Deal have, in many cases, been close to Messrs. Wheeler and Lindbergh in all matters affecting foreign and military policy.

Whether the attitude of the Republicans in Congress has been due to an acceptance of the theory that the "business of the Opposition is to oppose," or to a realization that if the United States is to be an active partner in a world reorganization the American voter is more likely to entrust the organization of the partnership to the heirs of Wilson than to the heirs of Harding, matters little.   Even if the isolationist policy of the majority of the Republican members of Congress represents merely an aggregate of personal decisions based on independent judgment of what is good for the United States, this is not proof that the Republican party, as such, has a coherent view of the duties and interests of the United States in the world.   And, of course, the same is true of the Democratic party. There may be a slight trace of fundamental bias and consistency revealed by the analysis of the conduct of the congressional representatives of the two parties since 1939, but it is a trace and no more.

What has changed, however, is the relative strength of the two parties.   The Democrats have carried three presidential and seven congressional elections, although their majorities at each end of the series, 1930 and 1942, were so slight as to be almost unimportant.   Nevertheless, there has been a very great increase of Democratic strength.   The main gains have been in the industrial areas and in the younger age groups.   The apparent stability of the American party structure, as far as the distribution of party strength goes, has been shown to be deceptive.   The signs of a shift in urban party loyalties in the North which the support won by Governor Smith in the great northern cities revealed in 1928, were more than confirmed in 1932.   The shift was, of course, not confined to the cities, but it was most dramatic there—and has proved most lasting there.[1]

It had been customary and right, up to the elections of 1932, to refer to the Democrats as the "minority party."   It would be wrong to call either the Democrats or the Republicans the "minority party" today, if the implication was that the other was the "majority party."   Each is sure of the support of a very large section of the American people, but neither, at the moment, has the right to

[1] The most striking feature of the first Roosevelt landslide was not the proportion of the popular vote or of the vote by states that went to the Democratic candidate.   In both respects, Mr. Hoover in 1928 did better than Mr. Roosevelt in 1932.   What was unprecedented was the area won by counties. "Roosevelt led the poll in 2,721 counties, the greatest number ever carried by a candidate for the presidency.   Of these, 282 had never before been Democratic.   Herein was an indication of change.   However, it is of interest to note that of these 282 counties, only 42 had not been carried by Theodore Roosevelt in 1912 or by Robert La Follette in 1924."   E. E. Robinson, *The Presidential Vote, 1896-1932*, p. 30.   It was in 1936, when there was a positive vote for Mr. Roosevelt rather than a negative vote against Mr. Hoover, that all records were broken.

adopt for itself the old Republican conviction that it automatically represents the normal voting majority of the American people. Each is a minority of the electorate and the millions of independent voters decide the issue, whether by voting or by not voting matters little. It is probable that the Republicans can rely on a larger number of the wholly faithful, who not only vote the straight Republican ticket when they vote, but who do vote. But neither party, outside its unshakable strongholds, can rely with blind confidence on the support of the effective electoral majority. This is a great change since 1932. States like Pennsylvania, that seemed as safely Republican as Georgia is Democratic, are now doubtful. Only a handful of states in the North and in the South have voted for the same party at the last four presidential elections. And none of these states lies west of the Mississippi. The Democratic party, that seemed dead or barely living over a great area, is now alive and formidable over nearly every part of the United States today. On the other hand, the chances of an open abandonment of the Democratic party by the conservative elements in the South that supported Mr. Hoover in 1928 and oppose Mr. Roosevelt today seem less good than they did either in 1928 or in the lowest ebb of Republican fortunes in 1936, when it seemed possible that all conservative forces would be driven together to fight the radicalism of the New Deal. The threat to conservative domination in the South represented by radical Democrats like Senator Black and Senator Pepper does not seem so formidable in 1943 as it did in 1936. The conservative Democrats have now reason to believe that they can keep control of their own states and either impose a conservative candidate on the national Democratic party or accept, with easy resignation, a Republican victory in 1944. The Republican party in the North, the Democratic party in the South, serve the purposes of powerful and resourceful sections of business and politics too adequately to be lightly scrapped. And the weakness of the radical elements in both parties (when Mr. Roosevelt is not running in person) has been demonstrated so completely in 1942 that the Left has few cards to play and as a bluffer starts defeated.[1]

The political race is more open than it was ten years ago. It is less easy to distribute party strength geographically, but the two

[1] I am aware of the argument that the congressional elections of 1942 went the way they did because of discontent with the progress of the war and because the normally New Deal voters did not vote. I find it impossible to believe that it was zeal for the progress of the war that accounted for the results in a state like Illinois, and politicians in America have even less use than politicians elsewhere for voters who do not vote. Their pious opinions, whether confined to their own bosoms or confided to Dr. Gallup, interest him far less than the actual votes cast by possibly less estimable but more energetic citizens.

old parties have not changed in character and have only changed in geographical strength within limits. The tendencies of the election of 1928 in the North have been developed further to the benefit of the Democratic party. The tendencies of the election of 1928 in the South have not developed to the benefit of the Republican party, but they have developed to the benefit of the conservative elements, North and South, of which the Republican party is normally the agent. But no party system has changed so little as the American in the past ten years, and the party system is the indispensable instrument of democratic control of policy in the United States. Only by party decisions, reflected in Congress and in the White House, can American policy be declared or altered. And for the foreign observer there is no more important truth about America to be remembered than this. The United States might be better off with a different party system, but, day dreams apart, what we can expect of the United States is profoundly affected by the internal history of those two illogical and asymmetrical bodies, the Democrats and the Republicans.

‘ III

If the party system has changed little, the constitutional system has changed even less. As will be seen, the one great constitutional innovation attempted by Mr. Roosevelt was defeated; the Supreme Court preserved its formal immunity from pressure. And the distribution of powers between the President and the Congress and the States was not profoundly or even seriously changed. Tendencies that were visible, even obvious, in 1932 were developed. American constitutional history has been one long process of transferring the more important functions of government from the States to the Union; this process has not been halted, but has not been notably accelerated either. There have been few conflicts between the States and the Federal government and none of a novel type.[1]

The unique position assumed by Mr. Roosevelt in the first months of his administration and the unprecedented series of

[1] Despite the fears of the conservatives, the extension of federal power by grants of money, on conditions, to the states, is a necessary evasion of the old distribution of powers between the two governmental machines. Evasion is, perhaps, the wrong word. It is as legitimate a way of achieving ends not foreseen (but not necessarily therefore to be condemned) by the makers of the Constitution as any application of the "necessary and proper" clause by Chief Justice Marshall. To the argument that, by gifts of money, the Federal government bribes the states to give up their legitimate powers, it is a sufficient answer that the states can make the bribe of no effect by resisting temptation. Theirs is, indeed, a very cloistered virtue that is deemed certain to succumb to the first cash offer, if that offer is once permitted to be made. In making

electoral triumphs, culminating in his successful defiance of the taboo against a third term, have led to charges of dictatorship. But these charges do not differ from the charges brought against other energetic Presidents, against Jackson and Lincoln, Theodore Roosevelt and Woodrow Wilson. If the history of the relations between the States and the Union is one of practically uninterrupted growth of federal at the expense of state powers, the history of the relationship between the President and Congress is one of a shifting balance of power. At most, it would be safe to say that there has been a permanent growth in presidential prestige, in the acceptance by the people of presidential leadership—and it is not indisputable that it is safe to go even as far as that. Strong Presidents fight or lead Congress; weak Presidents abdicate before Congress, but without being able to delegate their fundamental powers to Congress. So it is only in the periods of accepted presidential leadership that a coherent national policy is implemented in legislation and in administration.

It follows, therefore, that Congress may be very underrated by the public, written-off as a "rubber-stamp," when it is in fact cooperating with the President to produce and develop a national policy. There is nothing discreditable either to the President or Congress in this collaboration. Some theorists inside and outside Congress talk and write as if close contact between the White House and the Capitol was illegal and indecent, as if legislation and administration had to be the result of some kind of artificial insemination. But the political facts of life are better understood at each end of Pennsylvania Avenue than that. Only a Congress in close relationship to the President and accepting his leadership can carry through a positive programme; and the proud assertions of congressional independence that are made at times like these are merely traditional ways of asserting that a positive programme is not needed at the moment, or that the only programme on which President and Congress can be expected to agree is actively disliked by an important section of one house, or of both.

conditional grants, the Federal government achieves two different objects. It secures a minimum of uniformity between the states and it secures, in return, the use of the police power of the states.

"Thus federal highway construction relies on the state power of eminent domain, as well as on state power to police and protect highways during and after their construction. Also, national protection of forests is supplemented by the power of the states to regulate the conduct of persons entering forests; and the Sheppard-Towner Maternity Act was implemented by the power of the co-operating states to compel birth registration, the licensing of midwives, etc.

"There is, in short, a real wedding of diverse powers on the part of the two governmental centres. *The greater financial strength of the National Government is joined to the wider coercive powers of the states.*" (E. S. Corwin, *Court Over Constitution*, p. 163.)

xvi PREFACE TO NEW EDITION

That Congress under President Roosevelt has seemed to be unduly passive and obedient may be admitted. But that has not been the fault of Congress. The American people, in the first term of President Roosevelt, wanted much done and done quickly. In his second presidential election, they showed that, to an overwhelming degree, they approved of what had been done. The Opposition, in these circumstances, had the *beau rôle* as far as congressional debate was concerned. For the real leader of the dominant party, its spokesman, its counsel before the nation, was the President. With an overwhelming majority in both houses, with overwhelming popular support, the Democratic party in Congress had little reason to want to fight the battles over again to the foregone conclusion of victory in the Senate or the House. But the Opposition, which had no hope of victory but only of delay, which had no effective platform outside Congress, naturally fought its congressional battles as hard as it could. There was given to the people an unfortunate impression that the Democratic majorities had only strength, not arguments, on their side. They seemed to be saying "ditto to Mr. Roosevelt" because they had nothing else to say when, in fact, they had a great deal to say but saw no need to say it. This may have been a mistaken view but it was a natural and defensible view.[1]

For various reasons, of which alleged subservience to the President was only one, the prestige of Congress fell off. Its rules, above all the organization of its committee system, were largely irrelevant to the problems of the day. The work it had to do could not be dramatized, or if it could, what could the run-of-the-mill playwrights of the Capitol do in competition with the Shakespeare of the White House? The working of the locality rule made it plausible to represent Congress as a body which did not and could not be representative of the ablest and most public-spirited Amer-

[1] Inevitably, a great deal of the legislation introduced was highly technical and novel. In the nature of things, only a few Congressmen or Senators could be expert in a given field of legislation. The absurd seniority rule that gives power in committees to the members who have served longest gave no guarantee that the official leaders of the congressional majority would be among these experts. Indeed, since the senior Democrats were mostly from the rural South and the most complicated problems concerned the urban North, there was a probability that, other things being equal, these veterans would be less well fitted for the understanding and exposition of much of the new legislation than were many of the new members. In such circumstances, a great deal depended on the skill and tact with which the Administration's experts set forth the reasons why something had to be done, and why this or that was what had to be done. I give my impression for what little it is worth, that many New Dealers failed to take this duty seriously enough—which was the less defensible since many of them had been college teachers and exposition was their trade.

icans of today. A British critic of Parliament who makes no attempt to get into Parliament, to that extent stultifies himself. But an American critic has the ready answer that he cannot be elected except for the district in which he resides. In an area rich in political talent, like Fairfield County, Connecticut, that means that only one out of a possible score of able and public-spirited Republicans can be elected to Congress. And in Georgia, no Republicans at all, however eminent, can be elected, nor have Democrats any better chance in Vermont. It has become customary to represent Congress as being far behind public opinion, as being timid, short-sighted, selfish. It has been all of these last three things, but that it has really been behind the public seems very doubtful. Indeed, when we see how indifferent to the abilities, the character, the services, even to the name of his Representative, the American voter tends to be, when we see with how little discrimination he rewards and punishes, it is easy to sympathize with the congressional critics of the voters and to agree with their (privately expressed) judgment that the American voter gets a Congress that is more public-spirited, more resistant to pressure blocks, more intelligent, than he deserves. This is certainly just as far as it applies to one of the most numerous and negatively powerful bodies of American citizens, the millions who will do everything for their country but vote.

In any case, we must accept the fact that it is Congress which makes laws as we have to accept the fact that Congress is organized by the two old parties. To underestimate Congress is bad enough; to forget its inalienable constitutional powers is worse. It would be absurd to pretend that Congress legislates of its own free will, uninfluenced by outside organizations, outside interests, outside movements of opinion. Even a King of France, ruling according to his good pleasure, was subject to all sorts of influences, legitimate and illegitimate, and Congress is not, in theory or fact, an absolute monarch. It is possible that, left to itself, Congress would prefer to do nothing. But Congress is not left to itself. We do right, therefore, to look behind the legal façade to the political realities, to the role of lobbies like the United States Chamber of Commerce or the American Federation of Labor, to the National League of Women Voters or the Anti-Saloon League, to popular unofficial leaders of opinion like Father Coughlin or moulders of public opinion like the leading press columnists or the leading radio commentators. We do well, above all, to look to the President of the United States whoever he may be. For not only is he, by his use or neglect of his veto, an important part of the legislative power of the United States, but he is, as a party leader and as the head of the nation, the most important spokesman for or against a proposed

PREFACE TO NEW EDITION

course of action, a proposed programme of legislation, to be found in America. The knowledge that he can make legislation exceptionally difficult, the knowledge that he can make executive action practically impossible, the knowledge that a President's views are always news, this makes it certain that no one, in or out of Congress, is likely to underestimate the role of the President. And the President, both as a party leader and as the embodiment of the executive power of "We, the People of the United States," is unlikely to neglect any useful indication of public opinion, any indication of the weight of any given pressure block. Whether he wishes to swim with or against the tide, he has to know which way it is running, whether it is a spring or neap tide, whether it is the normally languid movement of Florida waters or the gigantic, racing bore that sweeps into Passamaquoddy Bay or round Campobello Island.

But for final, decisive and continued action, the co-operation of Congress is necessary. The President can do a great deal by his own independent authority, especially in war-time, when his always important office of President is doubled in power by his office of Commander-in-Chief. But the United States is not a presidential autocracy tempered by editorials or Gallup polls. Nothing can extrude Congress from its law-making powers, and many things of the utmost importance can only be done by laws. Not only are statutes needed, but treaties are needed. The President cannot commit the United States to a long-term policy; only the United States binding itself by a treaty can do that—and the United States can only bind itself by the constitutional means of a two-thirds vote of the Senate. Failing such a vote, the presidential policy is nullified, or reduced to evasion, or to such limited commitments as his executive powers allow him to make. "Gentlemen's agreements," stern notes from the State Department, impressive public speeches, plebiscites in states like Massachusetts, national polls conducted by private organizations, the support and enthusiasm of the righteous, all are poor substitutes for treaties made "by and with the advice and consent of the Senate," which treaties made "under the authority of the United States, shall be the supreme law of the land."[1]

---

[1] The special character of the treaty-making power is of the greatest importance in view of the role of the Supreme Court. Treaties are valid if made "under the authority of the United States," statutes only if made "in pursuance of" the Constitution. Many things can be done by treaty that cannot be done by statute. The treaty-making power of the Senate is wider than the law-making power of Congress, and for reasons admirably set forth by Justice O. W. Holmes in *Missouri v. Holland* (1920): "Acts of Congress are the supreme law of the land only when made in pursuance of the Constitution, while treaties are declared to be so when made under the authority of the United States.

Yet we must not forget that there are many things that once done cannot be undone, and that a President of the United States in war-time is not indeed a dictator, but is an officer of immense and undefined powers.

The view that the President has a special duty to preserve the authority of the federal government, to take care that no ill befall the Commonwealth, is part of the American political tradition, as much a part as the reverence for the political functions of the Supreme Court which has proved to be so deeply rooted. And the two traditions clash. They clash even when the presidential power is most extended by the existence of a state of war. The "war power" is a vague and undefinable residuum of power on which the President can draw. He can draw on it because in addition to being President of the United States (and so head of all executive departments, civil and military) he is also, by specific constitutional grant, Commander-in-Chief of the Army and Navy. He can draw on it because a state of war creates new rights and duties which arise from the fact that, to the outer world, the United States is a sovereign nation with the belligerent rights of such a nation—and the Supreme Court will not, in a fit of constitutional prudery, alienate these national rights even though, as a consequence, the President is enabled to do many things that otherwise neither he, nor Congress, nor both together could do. And lastly, the war

It is open to question whether the authority of the United States means more than the formal acts prescribed to make the convention. We do not mean to imply that there are no qualifications to the treaty-making power; but they must be ascertained in a different way. It is obvious that there may be matters of the sharpest exigency for the national well-being that an act of Congress could not deal with but that a treaty followed by such an act could, and it is not lightly to be assumed that, in matters requiring national action, 'a power which must belong to and somewhere reside in every civilized government' is not to be found." In many cases, a statute passed by a simple majority of each house is needed to implement the treaty obligations entered into by the United States. A law so passed can deal with matters debarred to the operation of an ordinary statute. That is to say that two-thirds of the Senators voting on a treaty can confer extra powers on simple majorities of both houses on Congress. It is not to be wondered at that the Senate in modern times has not accepted any serious commitments for the United States. Whether such commitments could be unconstitutional is an open question. Historically speaking, no treaty has ever been successfully attacked before the Supreme Court.

But it is not decided that the treaty-making power is unlimited. The limitations are, however, negative. A treaty does not need to be based on an uncontested power of Congress to be valid, but "the Supreme Court has several times said, in so many words, that the authority given to the United States to enter into treaties does not extend" so far as to authorize what the Constitution forbids. (W. W. Willoughby, *The Constitutional Law of the United States*, second edition, volume I, p. 519.) But these negative limitations are usually of little concern to the other high contracting party to a treaty.

power of the President is a source of new rights and duties because
it is still a fact that war is recognized as an emergency, as an
exceptional time, as creating new rights, new duties, as involving
new dangers and new problems, such as no civil crisis can create.
Even a comic opera war, like the war with Spain, has a politico-
legal character marking it off from far more serious internal crises.

In war-time, or in times of military danger, a President can do
things with impunity that he could not do in internal politics.
So Mr. Roosevelt was able to transfer fifty destroyers to Britain in
the black summer of 1940, an act of policy whose consequences
were far greater than those of any executive act performed in the
black spring of 1933. But even when the special legal and emotional force of a state of war or of danger of war is absent, there
is an elasticity in the American system that is hard to fit into the
rigid categories of text-books and decisions.

"It is the American theory that the law, 'by reason of its universality,' as the definition of equity has it, at times operates definitely
against the public interest; and when a public official at such times
sets the law aside, it is flatly impossible to bring him to account
for his illegal action. The common sense of the people holds that,
at such times, scrupulous observance of the law is more blame-
worthy than its defiance.

"Without doubt, this is a dangerous doctrine, but it is incon-
testably American. Indeed, it has already given us occasion for
regret, on more than one occasion. Yet it has worked pretty well
on the whole. There is no convincing evidence, in fact, that it is
more dangerous than a rigid adherence to legal formalism."[1]

It was as Commander-in-Chief that Lincoln freed the slaves,
and even if it was necessary in the eyes of purists to ratify the
Emancipation Proclamation by the thirteenth amendment (which
was also necessary to abolish slavery in the slave states that did not
secede), the only effective invalidation of the Proclamation would
have been a Confederate victory in the war. What General Lee
could not do, could not be done by Chief Justice Taney. And
today Mr. Roosevelt as Commander-in-Chief can do much that he
could not do as President and much that Congress and Court cannot undo. But this quasi-dictatorial power is no invention of Mr.
Roosevelt's; he has not yet done anything comparable to the assumptions of authority by Lincoln. The constitutional practice
of the United States is not enlarged or distorted thereby, no matter
what partisan controversialists may say. And, in most cases, the
attacks on the presidential prerogative have come from critics who
would not have approved of the presidential action even if it had
been ratified by Congress, but who had reason to believe that

[1] Gerald W. Johnson, *Roosevelt*, p. 87 (English edition).

Congress, tied up by its archaic procedure, could not have ratified it. But this again is merely an illustration of the fact that it is to the President and not to Congress that the American people looks for speedy action. All that was said, in St. Louis for example, against the transfer of fifty destroyers to Britain, all the attacks on Mr. Roosevelt's usurpation, was said against Mr. Jefferson when he, with equal boldness, secured the transfer of St. Louis to the United States.

IV

If the bold use of presidential powers in time of crisis is most definitely in the American tradition, the case is more doubtful when it is a question of Mr. Roosevelt's attack on the Supreme Court in the spring of 1937. The case for and against judicial review was made more urgent by the New Deal. The cases involved were far more important to the policy of the United States government and to the American people than were the statutes stricken-down under Harding and Coolidge. The contrast between the view taken of the Constitution by the President, the Congress and the voters on one side and the Court on the other was more dramatic than ever before in American history. Men recalled the destruction of the moral authority of the Court that followed the Dred Scott case when the whole system of judicial review was endangered. Re-elected to the presidency in the most complete electoral triumph of American history, Mr. Roosevelt was faced with what appeared to be the certain refusal of the Court, as then constituted, to permit any of the main features of the New Deal to survive. If it was almost heretical ten or twenty years ago to declare that the Supreme Court was as much a political as a legal body, it was a commonplace by 1937. The extravagant language and the outrageous bias of Mr. Justice McReynolds and of some of the more foolish members of the lower federal courts were more educational than the reasoned dissents of Mr. Justice Holmes and Mr. Justice Brandeis had been. And no dissent of the great twin brethren displayed more hostility to the premises and practises of the Court majority than did the dissent of Mr. Justice (now Chief Justice) Stone in the A.A.A. case. Public opinion was ripe for some remedy and possibly ripe for some drastic remedy.[1]

The remedy proposed by the President was bold in substance and timid in form. Basing its claims to consideration on the slowness and technical inefficiency of the federal courts, and attributing

[1] Senator Wheeler, who strongly opposed the President's plan, introduced a constitutional amendment giving to a two-thirds majority of Congress the right to overrule the Court *after* a congressional election had been held. This proposal has interesting resemblances to the system set up by the Parliament Act of 1911 in England.

these defects to the excessive age of the judges, it proposed to add members to the Supreme Court for each justice over seventy who did not retire, up to a maximum number of six. In his original message, the President did not stress his main and most justifiable motive, the political character of the Court as an upper house appointed by his predecessors and political opponents. The ambiguity turned out to be bad tactics. The technical defects of federal procedure interested no one but lawyers; the threat to "pack" the Court excited not only all conservatives, but many radicals to whom it was most important that there should be no real or apparent threat to the existence of the United States as a "government of laws and not of men."

After months of debate the President was defeated, or was he? His proposed increase in the size of the Court was defeated, but in most other ways he won. The older and more conservative justices began to resign, and resignations and death have made it possible for Mr. Roosevelt to appoint eight out of the nine members of the Court.[1] But even before the personnel of the Court had been reconstituted, the Court had beaten a well-timed retreat. It began to adore what it has burned and to burn what it had adored, or at any rate to refuse to interfere with the incendiary activities of the President and Congress. For the moment the New Deal was safe, but the basic problems of judicial review were left unsettled, the great debate left inconclusive. Yet the limitations of judicial review were made plainer than ever during the years between 1935 and 1937 when the Court, like a new but not self-critical Canute, bade the tides retire. Law was made so uncertain that the rule of law seemed well on the way to producing local anarchy.

The uncertainties produced by the system of judicial veto have always been an obvious evil. And they have seldom been more important than in the years of the New Deal. For what was at issue was the legal validity of great measures of economic planning. The legitimate doubts as to the constitutional force of the new statutes seemed to justify refusal to obey the statutes—and widespread refusal to obey such statutes destroyed what chances they had of working as effective solutions of the economic problems that had brought American society to the edge of chaos by the early spring of 1933.

In the crisis, it was natural and necessary for Congress to try desperate remedies, not scrutinizing too closely its power to act. What Jefferson had written in justification of the unconstitutional purchase of Louisiana from Napoleon applied to the measures

[1] Chief Justice Stone was appointed to the Court as Associate Justice by President Coolidge. Mr. Justice Roberts is the only member of the court who does not owe his present position to Mr. Roosevelt.

adopted by Congress in "the Hundred Days" of the first New Deal session. "The Legislature, in casting behind them metaphysical subtleties and risking themselves like faithful servants," were certainly meeting an urgent public demand and a psychological need. Had the President and Congress waited and debated until they were sure that the Supreme Court, as then constituted, would ratify all the empirical remedies attempted in 1933 they would have provoked a dangerous outburst of popular impatience at the apparent impotence of the government of the United States.

That Congress overstepped its powers was the unanimous opinion of the Court in the N.R.A. cases; that it overstepped them in setting up the Agricultural Adjustment Administration was the opinion of a majority of the Court; that it had also exceeded its powers in creating, by the Wagner Act, the National Labor Relations Board was the opinion of most conservative lawyers and was expected to be the opinion of the Court. The guess turned out to be wrong; the Wagner Act was found constitutional, but, while its status was debated, it was not treated as law by some of the greatest American corporations, which thus set labour an example of disregard for the written law that suited very well the combatant temper of the new militant labour leaders. Mr. Henry Ford and Mr. John L. Lewis were both profoundly American in their readiness to use every legal device to secure their own legal rights and their indifference to the legal rights of others. The belief that the Supreme Court, whatever professions of respect for congressional and presidential prerogatives it might utter, was more likely than not to strike down any "advanced" legislation, was one cause of that bitter and most seditious hostility to the Roosevelt administration which startled and shocked European visitors. The President was not a usurper in the sense that his title was suspect, but he was (so his enemies said) a usurper in that he was perpetually attempting to extend the powers of his office and of the federal government. Against such illegitimate claims, it was the duty as well as the interest and the pleasure of men and corporations to protest. The Courts were the consecrated instruments of these protests and the guarantee that the protests would be effective.

Involved in the whole system of judicial review is the principle that it is the private litigant whose interests are involved who raises the question of constitutionality. If no one cares to protest by the expensive method of litigation, the Courts cannot take the initiative. But of course, in every important controversy, there are interests involved that can afford the luxury of litigation. And the interest of the party which wishes to upset the statute may be far more lively than the interest of its defenders. Indeed the real defender, the government of the United States, might not be for-

mally a party and be only able to be heard as a matter of courtesy.[1]
The Supreme Court, indeed, tried to limit the possible mischiefs
of this system. It denounced suits brought in defence of vague,
general, political interests.[2]   But in subordinate federal courts
it was possible to manœuvre in a fashion that secured respect for
private rights of a certain type at a very considerable cost in
political confusion. And it was the opinion of one of the chief
critics of the Supreme Court (of which he is now a member) that
it was the conduct of the lower federal Courts that manifested
the working of judicial supremacy at "the point of its most reckless,
partisan and irresponsible manifestation—and that while the District courts were sowing the wind, the Supreme Court would reap
the whirlwind."[3]

The whirlwind has not uprooted the system, but it has imposed,
for a time at least, an unwonted modesty on the judges. Thus
the Court in a decision that attracted little interest except from
lawyers (*Erie Railroad Co. v. Tompkins*) reversed the nearly century-old ruling in *Swift v. Tyson*. The Supreme Court suddenly
ceased to build up a uniform federal law in cases where the litigants
were domiciled in different states. This ambition had led to the
creation of two systems of law in many important fields: the law
which federal courts would enforce where the domicile of litigants
differed, and the law which state courts would enforce where both
parties were domiciled in the same state. The political interest of
the case is the revelation of a new temper in the Court. It left the
duty of harmonizing the law to the legislatures of the states; it was
an abdication and, perhaps, a confession of usurpation. The same
spirit has been applied where it is a question of permitting states
to do foolish or harmful things which Congress could prevent, if

[1] The Judiciary Act of August 24th, 1937, one of the minor victories of the
fight over the Supreme Court, changed this.

[2] In *Chicago and Grand Trunk Ry. Co. v. Wellman*, it was laid down that
"The theory upon which, apparently, this suit was brought is that parties
have an appeal from the legislature to the courts; and that the latter are
given an immediate and general supervision of the constitutionality of the
acts of the former. Such is not true. Whenever, in pursuance of an honest
and actual antagonistic assertion of rights by one individual against another,
there is presented a question involving the validity of any act of any legislature,
State or Federal . . . the court must, in the exercise of its solemn duties,
determine whether the act be constitutional or not. . . . It was never the
thought that, by means of a friendly suit, a party beaten in the legislature
could transfer to the courts an inquiry as to the constitutionality of the
legislative act." Cited in W. W. Willoughby, *The Constitutional Law of the
United States*, vol. 1, p. 23 (second edition).

[3] Robert H. Jackson, *The Struggle for Judicial Supremacy*, p. 123. Mr.
Justice Jackson, as Solicitor General, and then as Attorney General, was one
of the chief legal combatants for the New Deal in the courts.

Congress liked. The Court now refuses to do the work of Congress for it. The new Court applies the principle laid down by Justice Holmes, that the People (of the United States or of an individual state) has the right to make its own mistakes, and that it is not the business of the Court either to undo what legislatures have done or to do what they have neglected to do.[1]

Whether the modesty of the Court is being reflected in an increased responsibility in the legislator, who has no longer the easy balm for his conscience that a bad law will be declared unconstitutional, is not subject to proof. But some observers and actors think that it is; that there is more realization of the fact that a constitutional law may be foolish or worse than foolish, a truth concealed from Congress and the People when the Court was most vigorously acting as the guardian of a political minor. The controversy over the Court Bill had one other important consequence. It revealed how completely identified in the American mind were the practice of judicial review and the safeguarding of civil liberties. The more extravagant the expression of this view, the more interesting it was as evidence.[2] That civil liberties are safer in the United States than in England is, at any rate, not obvious, yet the

[1] Holmes wrote to Sir Frederick Pollock in 1910: "I am so sceptical as to our knowledge about the goodness or badness of laws that I have no practical criticism except what the crowd wants. Personally I bet that the crowd, if it knew more, wouldn't want what it does, but that is immaterial." *Pollock-Holmes Letters*, vol. 1, p. 163. Should "criticism" be read as "criterion"?

[2] Thus Mr. William Alfred Eddy, President of Hobart and William Smith Colleges, testifying before the Senate Judiciary Committee, asserted that it would be impossible to teach American government if the Court Bill passed. This teaching "is done in the faith that government is an objective science and today the most vital of the human arts of living. This faith will be jeopardized if the judiciary is robbed of its independence. Why? Students will discover that minorities are without protection, that they must climb on the passing band wagon if they are to participate in government action; that voice and muscle count for more than experience; that academic freedom will be lost in the clamor for conformity. The local courts, of course, will follow the Federal Courts into the discard, and the party will reign supreme, as it does in Germany today." (*Reorganization of the Federal Judiciary Hearings . . . Seventy-Fifth Congress First Session*, p. 1666.) A more objective view of what the courts can and cannot do in the absence of a public opinion that really believes in free discussion is given by Professor Zechariah Chafee, Jr. (*Free Speech in the United States*, p. 563-4.): "The Supreme Court, though much more anxious to support liberty of speech than it was twenty years ago can do nothing to keep discussion open during an emergency. Cases of suppression will get to Washington long after the emergency is over. . . . Above all, the maintenance of open discussion depends on all the great body of unofficial citizens. . . . An atmosphere of open and unimpeded controversy may be made as fully a part of the life of a community as any other American tradition. The law plays only a small part in either suppression or freedom. In the long run the public gets just as much freedom of speech as it really wants."

English courts do not pretend to overrule Parliament when it limits freedom. Parliament can do what it likes with its own, including private liberty. The guarantee is political not legal, but it is as effective as the legal guarantee of the American system.

But this is not to say that, in the United States, the lover of liberty should be indifferent to the power of the courts and to the view they take of their own duties. In all free countries, liberty wears a local costume, and is recognized in that costume, while it may go unrecognized in imported garments. One hundred and fifty years of legal control of legislative and executive action have dressed American liberty in a judge's robe. And, as long as the American people think of liberty in this costume, it would be dangerous to attempt to substitute a new dress for the old.[1]

v

The normal mechanism of national politics has changed little. But in the presidential campaign of 1940 there were two innovations, each so startling that it is hard to decide which would have been the more incredible in 1932. The election of Mr. Roosevelt for a third term broke a tradition as old as the administrations of Washington and Jefferson; and the nomination of Mr. Wendell Willkie by the Republicans brought to the front the darkest horse in the history of the presidency. For Mr. Willkie was not only a very recent convert from the Democratic to the Republican party, but the first public office for which he was an aspirant was the presidency.[2]

In 1936, the century-old rule of the Democratic party that made a two-thirds majority necessary for the nomination was rescinded. This alteration had no importance in 1936 and 1940, but it may well have great importance in 1944 by making it harder for a party minority to block a nomination and to impose a compromise candidate.

At the moment, the great city machines are in a period of

[1] "The restraining power of the judiciary does not manifest its chief worth in the few cases in which the legislature has gone beyond the lines that mark the limits of discretion. Rather shall we find its chief worth in making vocal and audible the ideals that might otherwise be silenced, in giving them continuity of life and expression, in guiding and directing choice within the limits where choice ranges. This function should preserve to the courts the power that now belongs to them, if only the power is exercised with insight into social values, and with suppleness of adaptation to changing social needs." (Benjamin N. Cardozo [later Mr. Justice Cardozo], *The Nature of the Judicial Process*, p. 92.)

[2] Mr. Hoover had not been a candidate for election to any Federal office before his nomination as the Republican candidate in 1928, but he had been an important Federal official under Presidents Wilson, Harding and Coolidge.

decline that may be more ominous for their future than were the transitory and local triumphs of reform in the past. For the decline is national and has more causes than the temporary rigour of public opinion. The immense profits which prohibition made available for every kind of exploitation no longer make municipal or state power so well worth buying or capturing. The old temptation of the utilities to bribe to secure franchises or to avoid regulation (though they have been succumbed to it in fairly recent times in Missouri) has been brought to vanishing point by federal regulation. And the growth of social services has made it harder for the machines to buy support by timely charity. The poor of the great cities now receive, as a right, far more benefits than they ever received as a conditional gift from Tammany Hall or its sister organizations. Then, the rise of real issues in politics has diminished the necessity for artificial stimulation of the voter's interest. In the golden days of Coolidge, personalities and jobs were the staple of politics. Since 1932, there have been great issues and one great national personality to make less necessary and less effective the methods that were necessary, if not edifying, in the days of Pendergast in Kansas City and Len Small in Illinois.

Whatever its causes, the decline of the machines is evident. The third election of Mr. La Guardia as Reform Mayor of New York is almost or quite as extraordinary a phenomenon as the third election of Mr. Roosevelt as President of the United States. Surviving machines, like the Kelly-Nash organization in Chicago, have to be more careful and more representative of public issues than they were in the past. Only in Jersey City, Memphis and a few other strongholds is the old unreconstructed city boss still potent. And although it is harder to be certain that rural machines have been weakened as much as the city machines have been, only in Louisiana has a great state boss appeared, and Huey Long was much more than a mere boss; he was, for good or evil, a great demagogue, a possible national Fascist chief. Politics are now *about* something, a truth probably realized by survivors of a simpler day like Mr. Werner Schroeder, as well as by prophets of the future like Mr. Henry Wallace.

One body which was of great importance when this book was written has lost a great deal of its power. The American Legion is weaker. And it is not only weaker because, in the successful campaign for the bonus which it won in 1936, it may have gone near exhausting the generosity of the public, but because its emotional appeal has now a most serious competitor. For the first time in American history, two great lobbies of old soldiers will soon be in competition. The newer of the two is sure to win. Not only will there be many more real veterans of this than of the last war, but there will be more emotional claims on the American people. In the Solomons, in New Guinea, in North Africa, on all the seas, claims are being created: claims for individual recognition, claims for corporate recognition. Literally as well as metaphorically, the guns of the American army and navy are now "heard round the world."   And although it is too early to see the detailed shape of things to come, a new American Legion, under that or another name, is already conceived if not born.

> "In seeds of laurel in the earth
> The blossom of your fame is blown,
> And somewhere, waiting for its birth,
> The shaft is in the stone."

Even more complete has been the decline of the Anti-Saloon League. With the repeal of the eighteenth amendment, it was thrown back from the simple position of defending the Constitution to converting Congress and the state legislatures to a renewal of the "experiment noble in purpose."   Outside Kansas and the evangelical states of the South, that has so far proved to be an enterprise comparable in difficulty to converting Moslems to Christianity. The religious conflict, of which prohibition was one aspect, has not disappeared. But the distribution of forces has changed. The Catholics, Jews, agnostics and other minority groups are no longer united in opposition to the evangelical majority. Under the influence of a clerical demagogue who puts the most fiery Protestant orators of the dry decade to shame, many American Catholics have committed themselves to an open sympathy with Fascism and anti-semitism that is, to put it no higher, imprudent in a country where they are a minority and not a popular minority. They may in time have to repent their toleration of leaders like Father Coughlin and journals like the Brooklyn *Tablet*, as the militant Protestants have had to repent the lavishing of so many of their assets on the vain campaign to expel the Demon Rum by the id of the secular arm.   This truth is understood by the wiser clerical and lay leaders, but there appears to be no clerical equivalent of Cardinal Gibbons today.

Two great forces in the old politics have not been so much changed as swamped by the development of the New Deal. The old "pork-barrel," at its most lavish, was small change compared with the vast expenditure of public funds that marked Mr. Roosevelt's first two terms. Public works on a colossal scale, relief projects ranging from sweeping up leaves to painting frescoes and producing Congreve, subsidies for colleges and hospitals, loans to students, great integrated schemes like projects of the Tennessee Valley Authority; these made the old "River and Harbor" bills quaint relics of a thrifty and timid past.

But the very magnitude and universality of these schemes weakened their political usefulness.   True, the poor, the disinherited, what Americans call the "underprivileged," were grateful, but not to their local politicians.   It was the President who had taken them off the bread-line.   This helped the Democratic party, or the Administration, but did not necessarily help the local Congressman to dig himself in as much as a tenth of the money spent, in his district, through his congressional diplomacy, would have done. And such was the extent of the programmes, such the disregard of the old political economy, that great schemes were launched in incurably Republican areas, and the mountaineers of Eastern Tennessee received with ready courtesy the bounty of the Democratic administration—and continued to vote for the Republican party as they had done since the days of Parson Brownlow.   There have been, it is true, charges of the use of the federal power of hiring and firing relief workers to win local campaigns, for example in Kentucky during the fight between Senator Barkley and Governor Chandler, but the Hatch Act has made it harder to reap personal harvests of votes from the seed of federal grants.

Something of the same death by excess has come over the Spoils System.   It is true that in the first year of the New Deal, there was almost attained Andrew Jackson's ideal of "a tit for every one of these pigs to suck at."[1]   And the new administration did some very odd things while patronage was being distributed on the good old lines by Mr. Farley, Postmaster-General and party manager.[2]

But the extension of civil service status went on; more and more nominees were fixed in their jobs, the amount of free, political patronage relatively diminished; and the offices still given for purely political reasons were both less numerous and less important than those given for real of presumed administrative competence to carry out the policies of the New Deal.   The spoils system did not disappear, especially in state and local government, but the problems of public administration were now less concerned with keeping the rascals out than with providing for the United States a body

[1] Quoted in C. B. Swisher, *Roger B. Taney*, p. 135.

[2] "In 1933 the new Administration chose James Henry Moyle of Utah as its instrument for freshening the administration of customs. Moyle was then seventy-five years of age."   A. W. Macmahon and John D. Millett, *Federal Administrators*, p. 444.   Mr. Moyle's political services had been zealous. Rather different were the reasons for the appointment of Mr. Frank Bell as head of the Bureau of Fisheries in the Department of Commerce.   Mr. Bell had been private secretary to Senator Dill.   "The Senator was retiring from public life in March, 1933, and was understandably zealous in 'finding a place for one who had been both his aid and his companion, sharing the role of host on numerous fishing trips."   *Ibid*, p. 439.   The new Secretary of Commerce, Mr. Daniel Roper, had played a political role under Secretary of the Treasury (in 1933 Senator) McAdoo that made him sympathetic to such claims.

of administrators, energetic as well as honest, skilled as well as politically neutral. Indeed, it came to be questioned whether neutrality was a good quality. The original administrators of the Tennessee Valley Authority had to declare their faith in the experiment as well as their fidelity to the United States. And in many of the new federal agencies, faith in the project seemed to the political leaders at least as valuable as the tepid loyalty of the bureaucrat not letting his left hand know today what his right hand did, under orders, yesterday.[1] And the old and often blind admiration for the British Civil Service gave way to a critical assessment of the needs of the positive state, a change aided by British critics.[2]

VI

In ten most eventful years, the American political system has changed comparatively little and some of its most dramatic changes have been forced on it from the outside. It was Herr Hitler who both elected Mr. Roosevelt for a third term and nominated Mr. Wendell Willkie in 1940. But this is not the only proof of elasticity that the American system has given. We have only to compare the atmosphere of the United States today with the atmosphere of 1932 or 1922 to see what profound changes are possible even under an apparently rigid constitutional system and conservative

[1] "Neutrality of the public official and continuance in office regardless of the administration in power are correct in theory and practice whenever party labels only are at stake and not fundamental policies or philosophies. Nor should an attitude of indifference, whether dignified by a label of professional spirit or not, be encouraged in the upper administrative corps even if it could be established. Men should not continue or be continued in positions where they will be called upon to advise and administer policies contrary to deeply rooted personal beliefs. The classic view is that though the career public servant is obligated to press forcefully his point of view to his political superior, yet if the superior insists on following another point of view, the civil servant must obey and is apparently expected to remain in his position and administer the decision. Yes, obey he must as any other citizen simply because the decision is that of his government; but if it is a major decision and involves a major point of difference, then the civil servant should not remain responsible for the administration of that decision. He cannot fully execute that policy, and he should not be expected to. Naturally, this assumes that the civil servant has not been won over by his superior's logic and point of view—just overruled. There can be no objection to the employee's continuance in his position if he accepts the philosophy he is to administer." (D. M. Levitan in *Public Administration*, Autumn, 1942.)

[2] "I suspect that the British Civil Service is very nearly the perfect instrument for the negative state. I think that it is yet to be proved that it is, in its present form, adequate for the positive state, particularly for a positive state which requires immense administrative experimentalism if it is to adapt itself to a rapidly changing, perhaps to a revolutionary world." (H. J. Laski, *The American Presidency*, p. 221.)

national tradition. The scope of State and Federal government has been vastly enlarged. The relationship between State and Union has been transformed into an effective partnership. The dangerous strain imposed by the political activities of the Supreme Court has been relieved. And the United States has been provided, in its greatest crisis since 1861, with a chief who may have all the faults his critics impute to him, and yet has that quality which his most bitter enemies in Berlin and Tokio, if not in Chicago, freely credit to him, that power of foresight, of courage, of resolution, by whose presence or absence great political systems live or die.

There have been so few changes in the American system because, for all its defects, for all its inelegancies, it represents a unique success, the extension and maintenance of free institutions over a continental area and the creation at the same time of a national unity that has stood the severest tests. In 1789, the Constitution went into effect; it was designed, so the preamble states, to form "a more perfect union" and to "promote the general welfare." It has done both. The Roman lawyer remembered that *de minimis non curat praetor*. The statesman will not be too ready to condemn or mutilate, in deference to any theory, one of the great living political systems of the world. He will be to its virtues very kind and to its faults a little blind. A political analyst, like myself, has no business to be blind to the faults; but that will matter little as long as the basic truth is remembered, that the American political system has succeeded to a degree that would have surprised the most optimistic of those revolutionary leaders who made the dangerous and novel experiment in 1776 of bringing forth "a nation conceived in liberty and dedicated to the proposition that all men are created equal."

D. W. BROGAN

February 12th (Lincoln's Birthday), 1943

FOREWORD

THE politics of the United States are still in large degree a *terra incognita* even to the informed Englishman. The assumptions of the system are so different, its consequences so divergent, from our own experience, that the application of the standards to which our history accustoms us is rarely a significant adventure.

Mr. Brogan will, I think, be found to have written the most illuminating treatise on American government since the late Lord Bryce's famous volumes of fifty years ago. His pages are not merely distinguished by a wealth of knowledge to which, probably, no living Englishman can pretend ; they have also the power to describe a system in movement, the capacity to grasp the living dynamic which animates an institutional framework, which are among the rarest qualities in political science.

His book, moreover, comes at a singularly opportune time. It has become more important for Englishmen to understand the spirit of American politics than at any period since the Revolution of 1776. An interdependent world has involved our fate with that of the American people in a way, and to a degree, that would have been unthinkable a generation ago. If the adventure of our common interests is to be a profitable one, a real effort to understand the American situation is fundamental. I believe that Mr. Brogan has given us the essential clue to that understanding.

The Constitution he describes is one in which, behind the abstract formulæ, can be discerned a clear effort to protect a certain view of property from invasion by the demands of the multitude. That such an attitude should so long have gone unquestioned is due, I think, above all to two things : it is due, in the first place, to the skill with which, behind the formal façade, the actual working of the Constitution has been adapted ceaselessly to new needs ; and it has been due, in the second place, to the fact that America has genuinely been, to a degree unknown in Western Europe, the land of opportunity for the comparatively humble man. The two causes have, of course, been closely related ; and they explain why, until quite recent times, it has been so largely unnecessary to ask in America those essential questions about the foundations of the State with which we in Europe have been largely concerned. They explain, for example, the curious absence from American political life of a socialist perspective to party action such as has been, with ourselves, one of the motivating forces of political policy.

Recent events have made it probable that this epoch of American history is drawing to a close. The United States have now developed all the typical phenomena of European life. There is an hereditary leisured class, with much the same habits, though on an ampler scale, of a European aristocracy ; there is a strong middle class whose access to favoured positions is becoming increasingly stereotyped ; there is the characteristic proletariat of our great cities ; and there is the historic division between urban and rural interests growing clearly before our eyes. The foreign observer can see without difficulty how the American Constitution could work without undue conflict in an epoch of remarkable growth. His problem is to understand whether the equilibrium it protects can be harmonized with the needs of an era in which, as in our own, the claims of property to a special position in the State are seriously challenged.

Upon this head, I think it will be found that Mr. Brogan's pages contribute a constant illumination. Anyone who reflects upon the European scene will, I think, be tempted to conclude that the sources in which our own security is to be found are still largely to seek in America. The presence of an efficient and neutral civil service, the definite supremacy of the legislature over the judiciary, the allocation of a clear and measureable responsibility to the executive power, a system of local government largely free from the taint of business corruption, party organization which reflects the total economic interests of the community, a method of discovering leadership, especially in the national sphere, which is something more than a lottery, these, I believe, are the main reasons for whatever success our system has had. They represent definite achievements in the art of government which the reader of Mr. Brogan's book will not find it easy to agree America has so far attained. And if it be said, as there is some reason for saying, that the need for them is comparatively new in American experience, the answer, I think, is that the *tempo* of modern change does not make their achievement less urgent. The recent history of Western democracy makes it obvious that their absence, in any serious degree, undermines, to the point of possible destruction, the foundations of constitutional government.

American observers themselves are fully aware of the complexity of the issues that confront them ; and it is worth remarking that a consideration of their social philosophy is one of the most helpful adventures in which an English student of politics

could engage.   Among contemporary figures, I do not know of
men who have seen more profoundly into the issues of our time
than men like Justices Holmes, Brandeis and Cordozo, among
the members of the Judiciary, or Charles Beard, Thorstein
Veblen, Herbert Croly and Felix Frankfurter, among publicists.
Not the least valuable of the many valuable features of Mr.
Brogan's book is that he directs the reader to a literature rich
in analysis of, and comment upon, issues which are common to
both American and European civilization.   He moves amid its
complexities with a sureness of insight that is remarkable.   He
would, I think, agree that anyone who thoroughly understood
the careers of men so different as President Wilson and Senator
La Follette, of Mark Hanna and Eugene Debs ; or who could
explain the underlying assumptions which separate the judicial
opinions of Mr. Justice Brandeis from those, a generation earlier,
of Mr. Justice Peckham ; or who realized the significance of
the literary tradition so magistrally analysed in Parrington's
remarkable work on American ideas—would have clues to the
European scene of inestimable value.   Mr. Brogan has brought
vividly home to me the inescapable fact that it is the minutiæ
rather than the principles of capitalist democracy which separate
America from ourselves.   And by illuminating them both with
so much knowledge and insight he has rendered a high service
to all engaged in the task of meeting its problems.

HAROLD J. LASKI.

THE LONDON SCHOOL OF ECONOMICS AND POLITICAL SCIENCE.

IT is the purpose of this book to describe the working of the American political system as it is to-day. That system has its own history, its own internal coherence, and the main effort of this book has been to depict it as it is, with as little reference as possible to what it might be. Although comparison has not been excluded where it seemed useful, this book is, in only a very minor sense, an essay in comparative government. Indeed, a general background of common political ideas and methods has been taken for granted. No attempt has been made to probe deeply into political ideas and institutions which are common to Great Britain and the United States, or, for that matter, to the whole Western world. The emphasis has been laid, deliberately, on those aspects of the American system which, in their origin or development, are most American. For this reason it has been necessary to introduce more historical matter than may, at first sight, seem in place in a contemporary study. But if we are to reject Seeley's dictum that history is past politics, we have to reverse it in America, for there half at least of politics is past history.

It is inevitable that a study such as this, confined to politics, ignoring the other aspects of government and of the national life, should appear to make an unworthy picture of the United States, for there, as in many other countries, politics are far from being the noblest aspect of the national life, or even of the national government. It is, for example, unfortunate that it should be necessary to devote so much attention to the " pork barrel " and none to the Panama Canal ; a complete section of the book to the " spoils system " and not a page to the Bureau of Standards. But even with the excuse that the subject chosen involves such inclusions and exclusions, there remains the difficulty that to write a book about the institutions of a country other than one's own, is to enter on a dangerous trade. The citizens of the country may well receive the foreigner's criticisms as the Archbishop of Granada did those of Gil Blas, indeed, with an added sense of grievance since, unlike the Archbishop, they have not asked for them. The only excuse I can make for myself is that which the Archbishop made for Gil Blas, a want of sense, not the presence of ill-will, accounts for the many defects of the book and may be some apology for its seeming ungratitude to a country which I admire so much and where, I hope, I still have many friends.

After the apology comes the pleasanter duty of thanking all those who consciously or unconsciously have helped to make this book ; thanks to my father to whom I owe my first knowledge of and interest in American politics ; to Professor Laski who both stimulated me to write it and has consented to usher it into the world ; to the Laura Spelman Rockefeller Foundation for making it possible for me to work in America ; and lastly to my wife who has borne with my typing, with my fondness for clichés and for the manifold defects of method which have added immensely to her secretarial labours. There remain many who cannot be named, especially the numerous Americans on both sides of the Atlantic who have answered my questions, sent me documents and other materials, and endured my expositions of facts and theories. Finally, there are the officials of the libraries of the British Museum, of the London School of Economics, and of the Institute of Historical Research, who not only got me what I asked for, but often told me what it was that I wanted.

D. W. BROGAN.

LONDON, 4th February, 1933.

CONTENTS

GOVERNMENT OF THE PEOPLE

PART ONE

THE CONSTITUTION AND THE COURTS

Lyberties depend on the Silence of the Law.
HOBBES.

Chapter I

THE CHARACTER OF THE CONSTITUTION

THE constitution of the United States has, in a century and a half, acquired all the sanctity of the Twelve Tables in ancient Rome. Framed in the bright light of the eighteenth century, going into effect just as the French Revolution opened, it, in a generation, acquired a patina of age that discouraged the irreverent hands of the renovator. Almost from the start, it was put into the care of a priesthood, the lawyers, who, from time to time, have opened the Sibylline Book, and told the multitude what was the judgment of the ancestors on situations which it is highly improbable that the ancestors had ever forescen. The paradoxes of judicial interpretation and their vast political results are too important to be treated in passing, but the constitution has had a life quite apart from that given it by the lawyers.

The constitution is a brief document, a model of elegant and, in places, artfully ambiguous draughtsmanship. It is a skeleton which custom, the exigencies of party warfare, national emergencies, economic developments, have clothed with flesh and which national faith and love have imbued with life till to-day the constitution is a Frankenstein's monster to whose existence and eccentricities the American people have become so used that it is difficult for most of them to think themselves out of their inherited political atmosphere into the freer and less secure world in which other peoples have to live their political lives.

The American constitution is a specimen of a very rare historical achievement, the stopping of a revolution at the point most convenient for its original sponsors. The dream of all political innovators, the saying to the people thus far and no further, and the inducing of sobriety in the masses stirred out of their usual passivity, was achieved by the ingenious gentlemen whom President Harding called the " founding fathers ". The American Revolution was not, despite such misleading names as the " Boston Tea Party ", the quiet, gentlemanly, Anglo-Saxon remonstrance against illegalities that it appeared to the not wholly disinterested Whig historians. Washington and Franklin were not really on the same side as Rockingham and Burke, nor were Bunker Hill and Saratoga mere substitutes for divisions at Westminster. The Revolution was a revolution and it had all the usual accompaniments of a revolution, violence, demagogy, contempt for vested interests, opportunities given to rancour and greed. It transferred vast amounts of property, upset the balance of classes, and alarmed the original leaders who were quite willing to put themselves into the seats of the mighty, but rapidly developed alarm when rivals continued to stir up the populace.

The substitution of Cabots for Lechmeres was all very well, but the continuance of agitation, the destruction of property rights under cover of law in Rhode Island and North Carolina, the stirring up of class passions with such ominous results as Shay's rebellion in Massachusetts, suggested that the revolution was not yet over—and if it went further its original leaders were pretty sure to fare worse. It is against this background of alarmed revolutionary conservatism that the constitution should be considered. It is, if not a counter-revolutionary document, at any rate a terminus to a revolution. Its sponsors were members of the class called by Albert Vandal, " révolutionnaires nantis ", revolutionaries in possession, and they had no intention of being dispossessed by the Jacobins of their time. The constitution was their way of digging themselves in, of consolidating their personal and class gains. It is, as it was intended to be, a conservative instrument, a happier Directory, a Consulate without a Bonaparte or, to take a closer parallel, it was a spiritual child of the English Revolution of 1688.

It was not primarily as an instrument of centralization that the constitution was suspect. The states were, of course, in command of far stronger loyalties than the puny Union, but they were also possible agents of dangerous social practices, of class legislation, agents of mere democracy, and the fathers regarded mere democracy as certain to be, sooner or later, an instrument of social and economic changes of a deeply revolutionary kind. They had no comforting Liberal illusions that the people could be given all political power, without a danger, or a certainty, that they would rob the rich. The federal constitution attempts to impede this action, by distributing power widely among inharmonious bodies, by creating barriers which, it was hoped, would counter the weight of mere numbers and, finally, by attempting to prevent certain contemporary revolutionary practices from becoming habits.

From its earliest days, then, the constitution, and the government set up under it, have been prizes of war in sectional battles that have usually had a solid core of interest and social passion beneath a more presentable political exterior. The wealthier classes have seen in the constitution a refuge from the cupidity of the multitude, and a means of adding to their own power and prosperity. As class divisions have been sectional divisions, the differences have taken geographical forms, have centred round the powers of the states, but have very seldom been mere exercises in federal theory. At various times, the constitution has been a useful tool to be seized, if only to prevent its use by other people ; it has never been a good tool for action, for its makers feared action in an incurably popular state, but it has shown its temper in the comparative ease with which it has been adapted to the needs of the rich and the astonishing difficulty with which it has been twisted into an instrument of the needs or wants of the poor.

It is difficult to decide between two views of the constitution, each of which has much to be said for it ; the one attributes to the sacred text the power of diverting, with its dead hand, the normal development of the United States and forcing the political life of the nation into narrow and ill-adapted channels ; the other sees little to mark off the American from any other constitution, secs its astonishing flexibility and accepts the glosses of the lawyers and the successful usurpations of the politicians as the equivalent of the freedom slowly broadening down of the English system. Neither school denies all plausibility to the other ; the assertors of rigidity admit some evolution and adaptation and the defenders of the flexibility of the instrument do not deny that the American government is in some degree different from other governments, which are, however theoretically, omnipotent. It is, as Professor H. L. McBain puts it, a difference in degree that is a difference in spirit, " and in government as in most other human institutions the spirit is often the essence ".[1] The spirit of the American constitution is the spirit of the lawyer, sometimes of the lawyer of the old school seeking less the spirit of justice or even of the law than the triumph that comes from winning on

[1] H. L. McBain, *The Living Constitution*, p. 6.

a flaw in the indictment. There has undoubtedly been an immense development of constitutional practice.

" No doctrinal confession in the history of the Church has suffered a more startling metamorphosis in meaning, combined with an unimpaired respect for the letter, than the Fundamental Law of the American Constitution. It is not a coach and four but a heavily loaded freight train that has been driven through some of its clauses." [1]

Yet there have been obstacles that no freight train can drive over ; obstacles that have held up the apparently irresistible rush of popular passion when the point has been reached that no further advance could be made without laying a hand on the Ark. The reverent superstition of the nation has never failed to exert its influence, there has come a time when no ingenuity of interpretation could conceal the fact that, by constitutional means, there was no thoroughfare. This respect for the customs of the ancestors, this inbred respect for legality, has saved the Union from great evils as it has been the shield for decades of what we should deem abuses. It has saved the authority of the presidency at its lowest ebb ; it has preserved the power of the Senate, although that body has defied public opinion and has, at times, forfeited public respect. It has given a little life to the fiction that the rotten-borough of Nevada, created in a moment of political necessity, is the equal of the great common-wealths of New York and Pennsylvania. We should not be surprised that the constitution has been expanded and adapted, that it has been patched and dyed. What should surprise us is the survival of this decidedly old-fashioned garment in this age. It has not been a strait-jacket, or it would long since have been thrown aside, for a nation will always break the law rather than strangle, but it is impossible to believe that the political life of the American people would not have been very different if the constitution had been different, or more easily responsive to the whim of the moment ; that is, assuming that there would have been one American people without the bond of this sacred text.

The rigidity of the American constitution, such as it is, resides in the comparative difficulty of the amending process. There have been only twenty amendments in one hundred and forty-odd years ; the first twelve of these were added almost at once and the others fall into three groups, the three Civil War amendments which were the legal enactment of the results of a great revolution and the five amendments which represent the legal

[1] H. W. Horwill, *The Usages of the American Constitution*, pp. 223-4.

enactment of the popular passions of the reforming generation of Bryan, Roosevelt and Wilson.[1] It will thus be seen that the formal amendment of the constitution has, for whatever reason, been a rare remedy for constitutional difficulties, a remedy only open to exceptionally powerful and determined forces. The only method that has been used has been the submission by two-thirds of each house [2] of amendments that become valid on their ratification by three-fourths of the state legislatures or state conventions. The difference in population between the states is so great that three-fourths of the states may be a minority of the population, and only the theoretically proportional representation of population in the House of Representatives saves the large states from a danger of minority rule, combined with the general understanding that there is a limit to what the large states will stand, law or no law. On the other hand, a very small minority grouped in the small states can veto any alteration in the constitution and prohibition may remain embedded in the text of the eighteenth amendment long after a large majority of the American people has declared against it. That any people should so bind itself is, in these days, a political miracle, but that aspect of the American constitution has not had the attention it deserves because of the still more astonishing phenomenon of the rule of judges, of the arrogation to the Supreme Court of an almost Petrine power of binding and loosing.

[1] The first ten amendments, the " Bill of Rights ", were adopted as a part of an implied bargain made at the time of ratifying the constitution. They all date from 1791. The eleventh and twelfth amendments were adopted to remedy ambiguities in the text in 1798 and 1804. The thirteenth, fourteenth and fifteenth amendments were adopted in 1865, 1868 and 1870. The sixteenth and seventeenth in 1913 ; the eighteenth and nineteenth in 1919 and 1920 ; the twentieth in 1933.

[2] There are, theoretically, two ways of amending the constitution ; that described in the text and another that has been proposed at times but which has proven too bold an enterprise to be undertaken. If the legislatures of two-thirds of the states demand it, Congress must call a convention " for proposing amendments which shall be valid, when ratified by the legislatures of three-fourths of the several States, or by conventions in three-fourths thereof, as the one or the other mode of ratification may be prescribed by the Congress " (Art. V). Only by this method is there a chance of a thoroughgoing reorganization, but no section has felt confident enough in the result of this plunge into Medea's cauldron to recommend so drastic a measure of rejuvenation.

Chapter II

JUDICIAL REVIEW

THE doctrine and practice of judicial review has a *prima facie* reasonableness, especially in a common law country, used to judge-made law. In the great case of *Marbury* v. *Madison*, Chief Justice Marshall laid down the lines of the American system of judicial control of legislation ; since 1803 this extraordinary power has been resented, evaded, attacked, but never overthrown. The courts have waited, have shown prudent regard for the public temper, but have never abated their claims. Marshall based his theory on the necessity of determining the limits of the legislative power of a government working under a written constitution, limiting the powers of the legislature.

" The constitution is either a superior paramount law unchangeable by ordinary means, or it is on a level with ordinary legislative acts, and, like other acts, is alterable when the legislature shall please to alter it. . . . If an act of the legislature, repugnant to the constitution, is void, does it, notwithstanding its invalidity, bind the courts, and oblige them to give it effect ? Or, in other words, though it be not law, does it constitute a rule as operative as if it was a law ? " [1]

Marshall concluded that the courts were bound to inquire into the constitutional authority of a statute and, if they found it unconstitutional, refuse to apply it. It is not to the point, here, to decide whether this was a usurpation or not. The weight of opinion seems to be that it was not. There are, however, political aspects of this practice that deserve note, illusions that should be got out of the way. First of all, it is easy to forget that a great deal of litigation on constitutional points has nothing to do with the federal character of the American system. Even if it were self-evident that the remedy for breaches of a federal code was judicial review, few of the most debated cases of judicial review are concerned with the distribution of powers between the Union and the states. Secondly, it is not self-evident that

[1] *Marbury* v. *Madison* in E. Wambaugh, *A Selection of Cases on Constitutional Law*, p. 30. This case did not, of course, initiate the system, but it underlined it.

the questions which the Supreme Court has to decide are really questions on which a lawyer, however eminent, is better fitted to decide than any other man of equal honesty and intelligence. Many points arise which do depend on legal learning and on the type of acuteness that law training breeds. But many other questions arise which involve, not terms of art, but terms of philosophy. What is a " contract ", or a " combination in restraint of trade " or " property ", are, only in a very narrow sense of the term, legal questions. If narrowly construed they often reduce the legislation, and the courts, to absurdity. Even in America, the people will not consent to have their lives ruled by the last dictum of an English or American judge on an entirely different situation, because there is a verbal identity. So the courts have to expand their terms, " due process ", " unreasonable searches and seizures ", or " life, liberty, or property ", till they acquire the wide and indefinable character of " natural rights ", or similar terms of political philosophy. Once this is done, the decisions of the courts lose their narrow and respectable authority, and become a sort of political casuistry.

" Suppose the Ten Commandments were, after a revolution, accepted by the people of England as their constitution. It would probably be found that the Ten Commandments were not specific enough to give guidance in the myriad activities of modern society. The people of England would have to permit Parliament to pass instrumental legislation to issue orders likely to further the following of the Ten Commandments. But in their anxiety to keep the divine law they would not trust entirely to the judgement of Parliament as to whether its legislation was really instrumental, but might give to the judicial committees of the Privy Council power to veto all legislation that seemed to conflict with these commandments. The parallel need not be taken too literally. As it was framed at the end of the eighteenth century, the words of the American Constitution bear more relation to our material needs than does the Decalogue. But if the judicial committee of the Privy Council had to decide whether a law permitting remarriage after divorce on the grounds of adultery was or was not in contravention of the precept ' Thou shalt not covet thy neighbour's wife ', or whether a capital levy was or was not in contravention of the precept ' Thou shalt not steal ', it would not be fantastic to compare it with the Supreme Court deciding that the regulation of hours of work in bakeries was a deprivation of liberty and property the Constitution did not permit." [1]

[1] K. Smellie, *The American Federal System*, pp. 135-6.

It is only if we regard the Supreme Court as a political body, a third chamber, regulating the acts of the executive and legislature in the light of special principles entrusted to its care that its authority is understandable. The plausible theory of the Marshallian age, that the court must look to the constitution for the authority of any act of Congress has its child by a natural, if illegitimate line of descent in the modern practice of testing legislation by the standard of reasonableness ; of apologizing, as Justice Holmes points out, for recognizing the legitimate authority of states or of the Union by the use of such fig-leaves as the " police power " ; and of taking a stand against or admitting the legitimacy of certain tendencies of legislation. These developments may, as a recent critic suggests, be usurpations even on the constitutional theory of *Marbury* v. *Madison*,[1] but they have the advantage of bringing the judges out into the open and of leading them to make admissions of what they are really doing that may, in the long run, awaken the American people to the true character of judicial control. In the notorious *Adkins* case, Mr. Justice Sutherland, speaking for the majority, defined the rôle of the court in a way that a radical critic could hardly have bettered.

" The liberty of the individual to do as he pleases, even in innocent matters, is not absolute. It must frequently yield to the common good, and the line beyond which the power of interference may not be pressed is neither definite nor unalterable, but may be made to move within limits not well defined, with changing need and circumstance. Any attempt to fix a rigid boundary would be unwise as well as futile. But nevertheless, there are limits to the power, and when these have been passed, it becomes the plain duty of the courts, in the proper exercise of their authority, to so declare." [2]

This plain duty in the case under discussion was not plain to four out of the nine judges and the minority included the very conservative Chief Justice, Mr. Taft.

The effect has been to erect the courts into a third chamber, deciding, not such legal questions as the limits of federal or state jurisdiction, or the carrying out of legal regulations which are essential to make " due process of law " in every country, but the advisability of legislation, its essential justice, its conformity to the " rule of reason ". In whatever legal dress such decisions are clothed, they are, in fact, political decisions. The belief that there is some special non-political wisdom to which, in such

[1] Mr. Louis B. Boudin, *Government by Judiciary*, New York, 1932.
[2] Mr. Boudin from whom I take the citation adds " the announcement that the Court had constituted itself a super-legislature is perhaps plainer than in any other case " (*op. cit.*, vol. ii, p. 484).

cases, the judges learned in the law have recourse and which makes their decisions more impressive, more impartial and worthy of a special kind of respect, is a fiction. There is no reason to believe that a lawyer, as such, is any better judge of the advisability of legislation regulating the hours of labour in factories, the use of private houses as cigar factories, the importance of regulating offensive bill-boards, the undesirability of payment in Pennsylvania mines by the truck system, than any other man of equal intelligence and probity. There is, on the contrary, some reason to believe that the lawyer is *less* fit to pronounce on such matters, for his training makes him unduly conservative of vested interests which have had the sanction of law ; he is prone to attach to the letter of the law a meaning which involves a whole social philosophy without any consciousness of what he is doing, and his technical rules may exclude from the consideration of the court all the really relevant evidence. In the notorious case of *In re* Jacobs, the Supreme Court of New York [1] invalidated a very moderate regulation of domestic cigar-making, as having no connection with public health ; as interfering with property and with liberty. In this decision it committed itself to views on the hallowed character of cigar-making in New York slum houses which, however justifiable, demonstrated that the court was setting its opinion of the desirability of such legislation against that of the people of New York as expressed through their legislature and governor. The court may have been right, but why should such a privilege be conferred on any minority ? While, in general, the Supreme Court of the United States has shown more prudence or less arrogance, it, too, has committed itself to views that can hardly be defended. In the case of *Lochner* v. *New York*, it denied the validity of a New York statute limiting night work in bakeries as being an unjustified extension of the admitted right of states to protect public health. In the most famous of his dissenting opinions, Mr. Justice Holmes pointed out to his colleagues what it was that they were doing ; they were setting up their opinion of what was for the benefit of the health of New York against that of the competent authority, the people of New York, and they were doing that in obedience, not to any precept of the constitution, but in conformity with a social philosophy which might be right or wrong, but which had no especial sanctity and no legal authority. In the disastrously candid judgment delivered by Justice Peckham the legislation was denounced as " mere meddlesome interferences with the right of the individual ". This opinion was quite natural in a Cleveland Democrat and Mr. Peckham, as a citizen of New

[1] In New York the Supreme Court is not the highest court, but to avoid confusion I have called the Court of Appeals by the common title.

York, had every right to be disconcerted at these innovations in legislation, but when Justice Peckham set his opinion of what was proper legislation against the view of the New York legislature, he was guilty of a gross usurpation of power, none the more tolerable for being unconscious. It was not the purpose of the fourteenth amendment, said Justice Holmes in dissenting, to enact " Mr. Herbert Spencer's *Social Statics* ". The court learned its lesson ; it admitted in the Oregon minimum wage case, the brief of Mr. Brandeis which was a treatise on social legislation, backed by evidence of the kind a legislature weighs before enacting a law. The practical improvement was great, but it made even more evident the character of the Supreme Court. It had

" assumed under a somewhat thin disguise the position of an upper chamber which, though it could not originate, could absolutely veto most statutes touching the use or protection of property, for the administration of modern American society now hinges on this doctrine of judicial dispensation under the Police Power ".[1]

It is, at any rate, an advance that the courts are more conscious of their rôle, more ready to admit their social, as apart from their narrowly legal character, than they used to be, and less naïve in their attitude to legislation of which, in their private capacity, they disapprove.

It was bad enough that for forty years Justice Field could stand in the breach devoting himself to the task of persuading his colleagues on the court to join with him in preventing " dangerous changes in the good society " and reminding them that the Supreme Court " ' possesses the power of declaring the law . . . and in that is found the safeguard which keeps the whole mighty fabric of government from rushing to destruction ' ".[2] But while he and his colleagues remained under the impression that in moving " from extremely general statements in the Constitution . . . through almost equally general statements in the Declaration of Independence and through his own individualistic philosophy via the *Wealth of Nations*, to the conclusion that the right to butcher livestock in Louisiana was an inalienable right ",[3] he and they were exercising what could truly be called a judicial function, little hope of rational liberty for the legislator could be entertained.

[1] Brooks Adams, " The American Courts as Legislative Chambers ", in *The Theory of Social Revolutions*, p. 105.
[2] Carl B. Swisher, *Stephen J. Field, Craftsman of the Law*, p. 430.
[3] *ibid.*, pp. 423-4.

It is on the education of the judges in the real nature of their duties, the impressing on them by the force of professional opinion that they are not really deciding legal questions at all, that reforming lawyers base their hopes. Even an American judge may, in very plain cases, be brought to a sufficiently humble frame of mind to be content, like other citizens, with a vote and not to insist on a veto. If that is too much to hope for, he may be brought to realize that he is bound to give to these questions the kind of attention that is expected from a competent legislator. To a European, this programme will seem both modest and excessively hopeful, for the zeal of courts to add to their jurisdiction is a datum of experience, and even in Britain judges are not averse from setting up as censors of political activities of which they disapprove. Nevertheless, some good may come of this education of the judges and the federal courts, at least, occasionally display a surprising degree of modesty.

With state courts it is a very different matter and some of them have reduced legislation to " a guessing contest between the general assembly and the supreme court in which the supreme court has the last guess ".[1]

This extraordinary system has from time to time been violently assailed ; the whole legal basis of judicial review has been attacked and many remedies have been suggested and tried. One reform that has a good deal to be said for it is the refusal to permit the invalidation of statutes by mere majorities of the court or even by tie votes.[2] The spectacle of important congressional legislation being overthrown by votes of five to four has not added to the prestige of the court and the scepticism of judicial infallibility is increased, not only by dissenting opinions that are often more plausible than the judgment, but by the very varying reasons given by majority judges for their decisions. To the reverent mind of Senator Hoar, this revelation of judicial diversity was painful and he wanted to suppress dissenting opinions.

" The recent opinions of the Court in what are known as the Insular Cases have shocked the country and greatly diminished the weight and authority of the tribunal . . . because upon one of the greatest questions of Constitutional law and Constitutional liberty that ever went to judgment, there could be found no single reason for the decision of the Court strong enough to convince any two judges." [3]

[1] F. A. Ogg and P. O. Ray, *An Introduction to American Government*, p. 597. The state criticized is Illinois.
[2] In the event of a tie, the decision of the inferior court is affirmed.
[3] G. F. Hoar, *Recollections*, vol. i, p. 161.

Dissenting opinions and majority decisions put the defenders of judicial review into a very awkward position. It is the first canon of American judicial interpretation that all reasonable doubt of a statute's validity must be resolved in favour of the statute, that the legislature must be considered innocent till it is proved guilty beyond reasonable doubt. A strict adherence to this view would demand unanimity of opinion from the court, for, obviously, there can have been no certainty of invalidity or there would have been unanimity. The two ways round this dilemma are equally inconvenient, for either it must be asserted that the Supreme Court judges are not all impartial, or learned or honest, and such assertions would destroy the whole psychological case for trusting the judiciary, or it must be admitted that there is no body of certain legal science which can be called on to decide the question of constitutionality—if it really is a question of asking, in face of a statute, by what authority ? [1]

When all the difficulties of majority decisions are considered, it is hard to quarrel with states like Ohio, which has provided that her Supreme Court shall not declare any law unconstitutional unless all but one member of the court agree [2] and the only valid objection is the privilege still left to a divided court of affirming the self-contradictory doctrine that a statute is manifestly unconstitutional, when one of its number denies this theoretically undeniable truth.

A more fundamental remedy is to secure that judges appointed shall be of the temper that the majority wants. This remedy has only one drawback, a judge on the bench is very different from a candidate for preferment. Joseph Story was appointed to counter John Marshall and became a confirmed Marshallite and Chief Justice Chase declared unconstitutional

---

[1] An ingenuous defence of majority decisions in constitutional cases is given by Professor W. S. Myers, of Princeton. " The excellence of the Court depends in large part upon the ability of the justices to understand and evaluate the current state of public opinion and keep just abreast of it. . . . When the Court decides by a five to four vote, the case at issue usually is a most contentious one in our public life and our people have not yet had the time or inclination to make up their minds upon it. For this reason and because the justices appreciate the uncertain or even balance of popular opinion their own views likewise *and even unconsciously* reflect this. Therefore a decision by such a narrow majority often may be more of a sign of the real excellence of the judges in *hewing close to the line of real public opinion* than that they are making an unfair, because nearly balanced, decision."—" The Importance of the Judiciary ", in *American Democracy Today* (Princeton, 1924), pp. 103-4.

The italics are mine. Defenders of the legal basis of judicial review might well ask to be saved from their friends !

[2] The Ohio limitation does not apply when the Supreme Court of the State affirms a judgment of the Court of Appeal declaring a law unconstitutional.

legislation, for which, as Secretary of the Treasury, he had been primarily responsible.

" Les Abbés Guiterel [*sic*] de la magistrature américaine ne sont pas plutôt installés sur le banc qu'ils se sentent enveloppés par la grâce sacerdotale et éprouvent le besoin de racheter par l'orthodoxie et la rigidité de leur attitude les concessions au modernisme et les promesses de tolérance qu'il leur a fallu pour obtenir l'investiture." [1]

The immense and uncontrollable powers given to American judges justify the preliminary investigation of a lawyer's judicial philosophy which it is usual to make before his nomination and the refusal of politicians to accept judges whose learning and character may be above suspicion, but whose opinions leave a good deal to be desired. Thus the Senate refused to confirm Mr. Hoover's nomination of Judge John Parker, of North Carolina, because of his hostile attitude to labour unions as exemplified in some of his decisions and the nomination of Chief Justice Hughes was held up for a surprisingly long time by the radical senators.[2]

The federal Supreme Court has been packed on several occasions by the dominant party. It was thus that the Democrats overcame John Marshall and then backed the Jacksonian Chief Justice, Roger Taney ; it was thus that the Republicans threatened to reverse Taney's most famous decision, the *dictum* in the Dred Scott case, and Grant packed the court to upset the inconvenient case of *Hepburn* v. *Griswold*. For such political control of the courts, there is required strong feeling and either a long period of time, an unusually high mortality among the justices, or the creation by Congress of enough judges to carry a measure, the American equivalent of the creation of peers.

In state courts all these remedies have been tried and, in addition, almost all judges are elected for terms less than life ; in a few states they or their decisions are theoretically subject to " recall " by a referendum and the remedy of a constitutional amendment is not so remote as it is in the case of an unpopular decision by the federal Supreme Court. Yet, in the long run, the last word remains with the judiciary which, secure in its fundamental privilege, bides its time.

[1] E. Lambert, *Le gouvernement des juges*, p. 224. This criticism applies especially to state judges, but is not without its bearing on federal judges.
[2] One other source of opposition to the Parker nomination was more political than judicial. The judge had been, as a Republican candidate for governor of North Carolina, an advocate of a " lilywhite " Republican party. This, and other examples of his views on racial questions, mobilized Negro opinion against him.

One consequence, whose inevitability one would have thought axiomatic, has been to drag the courts into politics in a way that elicits constant complaint from American lawyers. Yet nothing can be more natural, or more desirable, in a system which places the courts at the very heart of politics and gives them a final political veto. To complain of political considerations dominating the choice of federal or state judges, is to expect the political authorities to abdicate even more of their legitimate authority than they have done in the past. The results from the point of view of judicial prestige and efficiency have been disastrous, but they have been very natural and only a professional blindness that is truly judicial can conceal this fact from American judges. *Vous l'avez voulu*—John Marshall !

As has been indicated, the Supreme Court has been, in comparison with state courts, a model of discretion and generosity, but even the Supreme Court has had bad falls. One such was the Dred Scott decision, an immediate cause of the Civil War, another, perhaps the least defensible, the performance over the income-tax clauses of the Wilson tariff of 1894. An income tax had been one of the main planks of the Democratic platform in the campaign of 1892. In that campaign the Democrats had won the presidency and both houses of Congress. If ever a party had a mandate, they had. The income tax was an essential part of that programme, because the lowered tariff would, it was imagined, reduce the revenue from the customs. The levy of such a tax was no novelty and it had been upheld by the court after the Civil War. In two cases, the court declared it invalid by majorities of one, and, to make matters worse, a judge who had voted for the tax in the first case, voted against it on the other, a new judge having been appointed in the meantime to uphold the tax. No doubt legal arguments can still be found to defend this outrageous usurpation, but what shreds does it leave of the pretence that the court does not interfere in politics or does not set its opinion against that of the legislature ? [1] If the Democratic party had not been on the point of dissolution, the court might have had reason to repent of its temerity, and had Bryan been elected in 1896, no amount of packing of the court could have been described as uncalled for.

The court guessed right as to the immediate drift of public opinion, and it took nearly twenty years for a constitutional

---

[1] The ranting eloquence with which Joseph Choate adorned his speech against the tax is a commentary on the claim that the court only decides on legal and dispassionate grounds. The peroration would be quite in place in a criminal trial at the Old Bailey before a jury which the counsel for the defence suspected of being open to eloquent noise at least as much as to argument.

amendment to undo the work. Sometimes the court has made a bad guess and has had to bend or break. This was notably the case during and after the Civil War, where the boasted value of the court as a bulwark of freedom in troublous times was put to a test from which it did not emerge with flying colours. During the war, it was ignored by Lincoln when he found it in the way, and after the war, its first sign of independence in the *McArdle* case was the signal for vigorous action by Congress which effectively put the court out of the way till the Republican revolution was over. Apart from this depressed period, the most famous example of defiance of the rulings occurred in the case of the *Cherokee Nation* v. *Georgia* and *Worcester* v. *Georgia*. The Indians and the missionaries got verdicts against Georgia, but the state effectively nullified the legal victory. The same attitude of defiance has been taken up by states which the court has had no means of coercing or has chosen to leave to repentance, but like West Virginia, after years of recalcitrance, they climbed down and the obedience given by American officials and communities to judicial rule is one of the paradoxes of the psychology of that law-worshipping, if not law-abiding, people. But the justices of the court are men and are capable of adjusting themselves to public opinion, if it is powerful and long-lived enough, apart from the effects of the infiltration of new members. In fact, if not in theory, it reverses itself when it has to ; *stare decisis* is all right for such humble bodies as the House of Lords, which can fall back on Parliament to remedy its mistakes, but the Supreme Court must undo its own damage or express its own acceptance of the turn of popular opinion.[1]

The prestige and power of the Supreme Court has, of course, been in great part earned. When one considers the possibilities of aggression, one may wonder at the judges' moderation. In a country where suspicions of corruption, or at any rate of a slack standard of behaviour in officials is common, the Supreme Court has escaped suspicion, which cannot be said for any other office, not even for that of Federal Judge or of Attorney-General or of President. There have been no Macclesfields or even Westburys in American judicial history, and when the political

[1] In the " Insular cases " the awkward problem of adjusting the constitution to the needs of the new imperial rulers of the Philippines, was summed up in the question : " Does the constitution follow the flag ? " The Supreme Court decided that only as much of the constitution followed the flag as did not hamper the bearing of the white man's burden. The decision was given after the country had, in the election of 1900, decided in favour of the imperialistic experiment. Mr. Dooley in the most famous of his *dicta* summed up the decision. " No matter whether the constitution follows the flag or not, th' supreem coort follows th'iliction returns " (*Mr. Dooley's Opinions*, p. 26).

character of the court is borne in mind, there has been very little playing to the gallery with the object of personal advancement. The conduct of McClean before the Dred Scott decision was, in some opinions, not unconnected with presidential ambitions, and there have been one or two other cases, but the court as a whole has been decorous, and as little open to censure as is compatible with a fundamentally bad system. Not so much can be said for the state courts whose powers have often been a good deal in excess of their capacities. Until recent times, these courts were an incubus on the states which could not be thrown off, for if they invalidated a state statute as being contrary to the federal constitution, there was no remedy of an appeal to the federal courts, though there might be strong reason to suppose that the Supreme Court of the United States would take a more generous line than the state court had done.

In general, the state courts have been far more lavish with judicial vetoes than even the most charitable defenders of judicial prerogative find it easy to excuse. They have not only had the " due process " and " contract " clauses of the federal constitution to play with, but, as a rule, equivalent clauses in the state constitutions, and they have managed to do a good deal within these ample limits. The general level of judicial moderation has been low and the state courts have some of their loss of prestige to attribute to their usurpations. It is not the place to discuss the charges of party complicity that have been levelled, such charges as the Supreme Court of Nebraska had to meet when it saved some Republican office-holders from the wrath of the Populists. These charges may have been false, but they are significant of the highly political character of the American state judiciary. There have been other cases when the state judges, if not as disgraceful occupants of the bench as Barnard and Cardozo were in New York in the great days of Erie, were suspect of an undue sympathy with one side or the other in the great social controversies of the time. They might, like the great Chief Justice of Wisconsin, Edward Ryan, find a way for their people's wishes through the legal labyrinth or they might oppose, like the Supreme Court of Pennsylvania, legislation which was possibly unconstitutional and was certainly unpalatable to very powerful interests. Some judges played down to popular applause and catered to the feeling of their states, other risked popular contumely in defence of vested interests which may have had a longer memory or more gratitude than the populace.[1] In such

[1] Mr. Osborne O'Hagan invites us to sympathize with an Illinois judge who earned popular wrath by a decision favouring the meat packers and was not re-elected to the bench. " I trust that the packers did not forget this upright judge " (Osborne O'Hagan, *Leaves from My Life*, vol. i, p. 350).

a system, the law is a good deal less certain and respectable than it should be, as an official learned when he offended a great magnate and was told, " I will bring action to have the very law under which you operate set aside as unconstitutional ; and I will bring the case before my own judge, too ".[1] The discredit into which American judicial methods have fallen is only partly due to the effects of judicial review, but in so far as that system has made American judges politicians, and forced politicians to think of the judiciary as a part of the political system, it has exacted a heavy price for its merits, such as they are.

The final cause of judicial review is the preservation of the rights of minorities, of states, of individuals, against the ever-present danger of the tyranny of the majority. Has judicial review made more secure the rights guaranteed to the American citizen by the constitution ? Has it saved the rights of the states against the Union ? Only in a very limited degree can we answer " Yes ". Certainly, the ordinary rights of the private citizen, in practice, are not more secure in the United States than in other countries, which have no such system of elaborate guarantees. Liberty of the Press, of petition, of public speech, are not particularly secure in some states at any time and in any state at a time of crisis. It may be answered that this is due to the temper of the people, that the tyrannies of the Ku Klux Klan were the work of individuals, the excesses of the Espionage Acts the works of a fever-heated Congress. Yet what are we to think of the educative effect of a century of judicial protection of individual liberty if the result was to make public opinion accept the preposterous tyranny with which, in the war to make the world safe for democracy, the people of America was plagued, three thousand miles from the battle front ? Did England and France, and, for that matter, Germany, behave as badly in their treatment of unpopular minorities ? Whatever else may be said for the American system, it has signally failed to tame the American people's passion for interference, with or without due process of law, with the rights of others. It has been argued, indeed, that it has lessened any initial tolerance and a plausible case can be made out for the thesis. Such rights as the courts do not protect are held on very poor security, whether they be of property or of liberty. The annihilation, without compensation, by the thirteenth amendment, of all slave property, not only in the revolted states, but in the loyal slave states, and by the eighteenth amendment, of the immense investment in breweries, distilleries, saloons, hardly suggest that unpopular forms of property can feel very secure in America, or, to put it at its lowest, that they would have been worse off in countries ruled

[1] C. E. Merriam and H. F. Gosnell, *The American Party System*, p. 125.

by unlimited sovereign parliaments or by absolute monarchs. The record of the " Civil Liberties Union " is a long tale of attempts to make the letter of freedom do the work of the spirit. In this case, as in others, the letter killeth but the spirit giveth life.

The indignation aroused in radical breasts is not always justifiable, but it is understandable when we look at that sphere in which judicial control has been most effective. Liberty, political rights, the necessary guarantees of governmental efficiency may have little help from the courts, but how often has another cause been aided by the lawyers ! The fourteenth amendment was passed, if not planned, to protect the freedmen after the Civil War and as such it was interpreted for ten years, till the court was induced to take up a strong attitude in defence of the corporations fearful of the political reactions that their assault on the old American economic system had provoked. How feeble was the amendment as a weapon to protect the Negro ; how efficient in defence of the ideals of the rich ![1] The contrast has led bitter critics to assail the courts with rather more heat than is justified. It might be argued indeed, that in nothing has the American constitution so met the wishes of its makers, as in its successful shielding of the rich from the consequences of the political power of the poor. That the contract clause, carefully imbedded in the instrument by its makers, should have had a more vigorous life than the " Bill of Rights ", appended to placate the critics, is surely not surprising, but the fundamental weakness of constitutional guarantees of the American kind is their origin in a false, if noble, theory of government. It was in vain that the Massachusetts Declaration of Rights separated the judicial from the legislative and executive powers " to the end it may be a government of laws, and not of men ", for all governments are governments of men ; judicial review only ensures that the men must be lawyers.[2]

This is not to say that the constitution, as interpreted by the courts, has not, at times, saved minorities, or individuals, even Negroes, from the anger of majorities expressed in statute or in more direct action. If we can assume (and it is not certain that we can) that the temper and standards of American legislation would have been as low without judicial review as with it, there is an obvious case for the Bill of Rights. It has been an obstacle to waves of tyranny when all other barriers failed. But

[1] Out of about six hundred cases brought under the amendment, less than thirty have concerned the Negro.

[2] I had imagined that the allusion to the Massachusetts Declaration of Rights had occurred to me spontaneously, but on re-reading Professor H. L. McBain's *Living Constitution*, I find it there on the first page. It is possible that, among much else, I am indebted to that brilliant sketch for this allusion.

it is possible that it would have worked as well had it been merely general counsel from the founding fathers, precepts without judicial sanction. Would it have been less effective if it had merely reminded Mr. Mitchell Palmer that the founder of his party had none of his dread of subversive propaganda or indifference to the rights of leaders of disreputable causes? Would a political reaction, such as stigmatized the Alien and Sedition Acts of 1798, have been less a tribute to the spirit of the constitution than belated protests of lawyers or decisions of the less panic-stricken federal judges? Would not more " Al " Smiths vetoing Lusk Acts in the height of the Red Panic of 1919–20, be more effective and lasting victories of the ideas of the Bill of Rights than an occasional Learned Hand on the federal bench? But all this is guesswork ; in the American situation the courts do at times defend private liberties and rights (other than property rights), and if we are to have judicial review at all, it is as well that there is the Bill of Rights as well as the " contract clause " and the fourteenth amendment.

Yet there is something to be said even against this side of judicial review, for the kind of rights that are protected are rights that can only be effectively protected by a spirit which judicial review does nothing to foster and possibly something to stifle. The Supreme Court will defend the rights of the Catholic minority in the Oregon schools case, but that does nothing to convict Oregon of sin and encourages, not only in Catholics, but in all other groups, that sectional feeling that is one of the banes of American politics. The slow growth of a real national feeling, of the give and take of a healthy commonwealth, of regard for a common consent, not for mere legal victories or majorities, is hindered by the attitude of mind that the recourse to legal, rather than political remedies, reveals. Yet in the present level of American political self-restraint, any suspicious minority may be pardoned for refusing to trust itself to the tender mercies of its fellows, and there is no likelihood that the reform of politics will be so rapid and evident that recourse to judicial review will seem unworthy of good citizens for a long time to come.

But there are two more exclusively political consequences of judicial review that wipe out much of the good the system may do : it encourages irresponsible legislation and it makes political objects too remote, and their attainment too uncertain, to make a healthy interest in politics easy to create or keep alive. The bad habit of relying on the judiciary to remedy the faults of the legislator is not the only cause of the low standard of much American legislation, but it contributes to it. This irresponsibility is possibly more dangerous than the occasional vagaries of unconstitutional legislation could be. Thanks to judicial review, the American legislator is kept permanently in a state of tutelage and he has, naturally, the ways of a child. It is possible that if he were trusted with a man's discretion he might put away childish things. If he did not, would the people not replace him, and if they cannot be trusted to show any passion for justice or liberty, can they be made to cherish either by any number of judicial vetoes ? In all departments of American legislation, the encouragement to irresponsibility bred by judicial review is evident, the delusion that bad legislation does not matter, for if it is unconstitutional it will be nullified, if it is constitutional it cannot be really bad. Left to its own devices, the American people might learn that even if all things are lawful, all things are not expedient, but as it is they remain bound to the law. Even more enervating to sound politics is the uncertainty and remoteness that attaches to any political objective in the nation and the state. We cannot measure this by the number of federal or state acts invalidated, for we have no means of ascertaining the number of laws not passed, or not introduced, or not thought of, because of the possibility of judicial veto ; nor can we assess the damage done to popular interest in politics by the widespread sense of futility that attaches to much legislative activity in America. The damage may be immeasurable and yet its existence certain. The politician and his electors are not the masters of their work or the judges of its limits and desirability. The futility that clings about all legislative chambers that have not a real final authority has sufficient cause for attaching to an American legislature, without the additional support of the consequences of judicial review. The politicians are playing an elaborate game whose rules they did not make and cannot alter, and which they are not even able to master thoroughly, since they are changed from time to time by the judicial masters of the constitution.

It is thus within the limits of the constitution, " as interpreted ", that the politician must work and the forces making for artificiality, for slowness, for piecemeal adjustments rather than thorough schemes of reform or alteration, are powerfully reinforced by a habit of mind which goes very deep and whose ramifications are unseen by most Americans. It is the attitude of the American to the law-making process, the acceptance of the rule of lawyers conceived as being the rule of an objective wisdom above human criticism, that is least comprehensible by the European. Politically, the United States is a new " Country of the Blind " ; along its narrow paths the politicians feel their way, never sure that they will not come suddenly to a dead end, for the guiding principles are feeble threads indeed. At any moment the whole path may have to be retraced and, for reasons that it is hoped are made plain elsewhere, it is hard enough to move American public opinion in any one direction at any time, almost impossible to start it off again on another slow advance, that may end as did the first. This gambling character of a great part of legislation, ranks with legislative irresponsibility as the chief sin against sound politics made easy or inevitable by judicial review. It is naturally hard to get the public to concentrate its attention on the legislative race when the winner may be disqualified for breach of undefined rules, for undefined they are and must be. The American political system is soaked in law, in lawyer's ideas and in the habits of mind bred by attention to the kind of thinking that legal training fosters. It is, of course, possible to think this a merit.

> " The spirit of the work of the Supreme Court permeates every legislative assembly and every important discussion of reforms by legislative action. We largely subject our political thinking to the conception of law, not as an arbitrary edict of power but as governed by the fundamental conceptions of justice." [1]

To most Americans, this influence is a good thing ; it is an example of their fear of the free action of the state and it has, in turn, encouraged that fear. To most Americans it seems obvious that " if either body is to possess uncontrolled omnipotence it should be reposed in the Court rather than in Congress ".[2] But the rest of the world sees no more reason to give the last word to a body of narrow specialists in general politics than it does to give them uncontrolled authority in their own speciality. We shall begin to adopt judicial review only after we have abandoned trial by jury.

There remains a final justification of judicial review, that it is an indispensable organ of control in a federal government. It was from this point of view that Justice Holmes declared that he could imagine a system in which the Supreme Court had no power to invalidate federal statutes, but could not conceive a workable system in which there was no judicial control over the states. This is a point of view that can hardly be confuted in the American system, with no power of remedial legislation such as is entrusted to the parliament of Canada, and with so slow and cumbrous a system of constitutional amendment. Smooth working of the federal system *does* demand some organ of control and adjustment and had the Supreme Court done no more than

---

[1] Charles Evans Hughes (now Chief Justice of the United States), *The Supreme Court of the United States, Its Foundations, Methods and Achievements, An Interpretation,* pp. 241–2.

[2] Charles Warren, *The Supreme Court in American History,* vol. iii, p. 476.

that, it would not have been so powerful a political force. Yet even in this field where legal acumen might seem to be of special value the history of the court, especially in the notorious Dred Scott decision, shows how far from objective are the standards it applies and it is not axiomatic that states' rights would not have been as well preserved by purely political action as by the theoretically impartial operation of judicial decision.

When all allowances are made, the spectacle of the American people living its political life, according to canons laid down in the late eighteenth century to secure the political ideals and the economic rights of the American bourgeoisie, almost beggars credulity. With what complexity of machinery are so many necessary things done, with what almost impassable barriers is the popular will at times confronted, with what self-satisfaction does the average American pride himself alike on his liberty and on his docility under constitutional restraint ! Life cannot be too closely confined, and ways round have been found, but again and again, in this study, we shall come across institutions and practices, which are what they are because of the constitution, and the interpretation of the constitution by judicial review. At moments the barriers give way ; faced with emergencies, the American people holds an extemporary *lit de justice* and ratifies its royal will in an amendment, but for the most part it obeys the voices of the ancestors, the *mos maiorum* as interpreted by the judges ; Hamilton's great beast, the People, may growl, but it does not bite. The ingenious gentlemen who framed and put into operation the American constitution, performed a feat of extraordinary difficulty. In the first ebb of a revolution they hastily proceeded to put a hook into the nose of leviathan and induced him to make a covenant with his new masters, a covenant that the monster has kept till he has forgotten his old liberty and the strength that could break his chain.

PART TWO

THE ORIGIN AND CHARACTER OF THE PARTIES

> Ordinarily, our parties are parties of circumstance, and not of principle ; as the planting interest in conflict with the commercial ; the party of capitalists, and that of operatives ; parties which are identical in their moral character, and which can easily change ground with each other, in the support of many of their measures. . . . The vice of our leading parties in this country . . . is, that they do not plant themselves on the deep and necessary grounds to which they are respectively entitled, but lash themselves to fury in the carrying of some local and momentary measure, nowise useful to the commonwealth.
>
> EMERSON.

Chapter I

THE AGE OF THE DEMOCRATS

DURING the Civil War, Artemus Ward displayed his contempt for Congress by declaring that he would vote, at the next election, for Henry Clay, but what he professed to do in jest, most Americans, to-day, do in earnest. Henry Clay had been dead ten years when the jest was written, but Lincoln has been dead nearly seventy years and millions still vote for him and other millions vote against him. In the name of the immortal principles of Thomas Jefferson, millions support policies that even Jeffersonian subtlety could not have reconciled with the articles of the Jeffersonian creed and Lincoln was scarcely safely buried before his sorrowing party was using his name to carry out policies which he would have fought to the end had he lived. A marked difference between the principle and the practice of the party, the survival of phrases when all meaning has gone out of them, is not confined to America ; " The times have been that, when the brains were out, the man would die " was not written of political parties, but in America this human trait is displayed in forms so remarkable that it is with great difficulty that the observer from another land can see any reason in the system, any method in the madness. It is easy to pile up examples of party divisions that destroy all that we are supposed to mean by party, that union of men who think, more or less, alike concerning the republic. Is the Democratic party the chosen vehicle of those who believe in low tariffs and states' rights? If so, what is the claim to Democratic orthodoxy of the high-tariff Democrats from Pennsylvania or Louisiana or of the southern zealots for the extreme use of federal power to put down drink or sabbath-breaking or drug-taking or fornication? The Democratic orthodoxy of these practical heretics is unquestioned and unquestionable. Is the Republican party devoted to a liberal construction of the constitution, to a bias towards federal authority, to high tariffs and to a kindly Hamiltonian attitude to business? Then what are Eastern "wets" and Western radicals doing in the party? They are at home in it, for American practice and the fundamental American theory accept such anomalies with hardly a protest. It is easier to understate, than to overstate, the doctrinal disunion of American parties, to create the impression that it is merely an exaggerated version of that doctrinal overlapping which marks all parties in all countries. But it is not merely a case of pink shading into red, of left overlapping the centre. In the American system, the right of the Democratic party does not overlap the left, but the right of the Republican party. The radicals of the Republican party are as radical as the radicals of the Democrats, the conservatives as conservative. The parties are names which conceal all the range of potent American political opinion, and if one party were suddenly to be extinguished, there is no shade of opinion in it which would not be represented in the surviving party—and the weight of that opinion in the surviving party would not be much greater or less than in the vanished congeries.

It is natural that the English spectator of the American political system should turn in bewilderment from the paradoxes which it flaunts before him. When all allowance has been made for the constitution, for the federal character of the government, for the colour question, for immigration, there still remains enough of the incomprehensible in American political practice to breed the conviction that American politics are among the things that no fellow can understand and that American parties are as deep mysteries to the stranger as the divisions of the Scottish kirks.

The bewilderment has a simple origin. It is assumed that, because America is undoubtedly a nation, her politics are national, that her parties are national and that the canons of the two-party system of a homogeneous country like England, apply to a country like the United States. It is important—and it is easy—to remember that the United States is a federation, composed of states which still in law and fact detain some part of sovereignty. It is more important—and more difficult—to realize that these states cover an area as great as Europe, with as varied a range of climates and of natural resources. It is still more difficult, and still more important, to realize that these political consequences of differences, would remain if the United States were to become as centralized as France and might not be much less marked and acute if Hamilton had had his way in 1787 and the states had then been reduced to mere departments.

These elementary truths have been concealed behind an elaborate façade of doctrinal difference, the party lines have been assumed to be drawn between the adherents of two different schools of federalism, between two theories of the true character of the constitution, and the party history of the United States has undergone extraordinary distortion in order that facts may fit this ingenuous theory.

The truth has been simpler and less edifying. American parties have flourished as long as they have realized that America is still sectional, that the main business of the federal government is, as it is well described, " the allocating of an economic surplus ".[1] To secure that surplus for one's own section, to make alliances that ensured what one thought was one's share, was the object of the American party leader and his compeer was not to be sought in the parliamentary politician of the Old World, with his doctrinal preoccupations, but in the diplomat partitioning Africa or dividing out spheres of influence in China. The size of the country, the high degree of specialization in economic activity, made it comparatively simple in the earlier days of the republic to build up a combination of interests that was practically foolproof, that united two-thirds of the country against the remaining third. This combination was called the Republican, and then the Democratic party.[2]

The basis of the Democratic party was not the philosophical theory of the state, elaborated, with some useful ambiguity, by Thomas Jefferson. It was not the result of a careful exegesis of the text of the constitution inspired by a fundamentalist belief in its literal inspiration. The real power of the Jeffersonian party came from what Lincoln, who professed to be a Jeffersonian, called the plain people, and the strength of the Jeffersonian party came from the fact, also noted by Lincoln, that God had made many more plain than fancy people.

The Federalist party, to which English sympathies naturally

---

[1] K. Smellie, *The American Federal System*, p. 47.

[2] As an added source of confusion, the modern Republican party in its early days took, for good propagandist reasons, the title of the old Jeffersonian party, as all Presbyterian churches in Scotland profess to be the Church of Scotland. It should be remembered that what was the Republican party up to 1824, reappeared about 1828 as the Democratic party.

go out, was decidedly the party of the " fancy people " or, as the partisans of this point of view put it, " the wise, the good and the rich ".   There were not enough wise, good and above all rich people to rule America, then or now, without the aid of many more or less consciously plain people, so the Federalist party [1] had to think up some scheme of popular appeal which would induce the poor to entrust their interests to their betters and compete, successfully, with Jeffersonian demagogy.   It was a ticklish job and it was more than the Federalists could manage. They had many talents and some virtues, but they were not popular.   They drew too much on New England to be good judges of what less enlightened sections would stomach, and they outdid Aristides by calling themselves " the Just ", constantly, publicly and with a passionate sincerity that annoyed the majority of Americans who could not see sufficient reason for this conviction of virtue.   In the politics of the New England Federalists, there was displayed a great deal too much of the spirit that, in religion, led to an abandonment of old doctrines on the ground that a man who had been born in Boston had no need to be born again.   The rest of the country was full of stubborn men who resented the political superiority of the Federalists and, in a few years, the party was wiped out except in the more conservative parts of New England where Brahminism was endemic. If the New England flavour of the Federalists alienated the commonalty, the economic doctrines of their leader could not win much more support.   Alexander Hamilton is, as near as such things may be, the American Disraeli.[2]   He was a West Indian, he had no American prejudices or loyalties, and never bothered to acquire them.   In the best sense of the term, he was an adventurer.   Like Disraeli, he had an ingenious theory of government where his rivals had only a practice ; unlike Disraeli, he was a confirmed romantic and spent the last part of his short and brilliant life in building castles in the air that were none the less fantastic from being based on a highly " realistic " view of human nature in politics.   Hamilton, of Scottish and French ancestry, and no first-hand knowledge of Europe,[3] was an uncritical Anglophile. He hoped to rebuild the British constitution in America, a fantastic preoccupation which rendered him a useless member of the constitutional convention.   Even he had, gloomily and pessimistically, to abandon any such plans and to devote himself to

[1] The adoption of the name Federalist was calculated to win over support at the cost of clarity of the record, for the original Federalists were those who had opposed the new constitution, as not being federal, but national.

[2] This has been noted by Mr. George Arliss, as well as by me.

[3] Talleyrand said that Hamilton " divined Europe "—as Disraeli divined India.

defending, gallantly and successfully, the new frame of government of which he had so poor an opinion. As Secretary of the Treasury and Washington's most trusted adviser, Hamilton was able to put into practice some of the plans he had formed for the governing of the United States. He held that where is the treasure, there is the heart also, and he attempted to secure that most of the treasure should be firmly attached to the new government. By assuming the debts of the different states, by funding the debt of the old confederation, by indulging in mild protection, he hoped to unite with bonds of gold, the " interests " to the new government. That done, he thought, all was done ; as for the people, " your people is a great beast ".

Like so many hard-headed men, Hamilton was no master of realities, in that respect far inferior to the theorist and idealogue, Jefferson. The plan was all right—we have seen it put into operation by men without a tithe of Hamilton's genius—but what was well within the powers of Nelson Aldrich in the early twentieth century, was far beyond Hamilton in the late eighteenth. It was all very well to study Adam Smith and imitate the younger Pitt ; to fill Congress with business men as Pitt filled the House of Lords ; to encourage manufacturing and shipping and banking ; but there was a world between Philadelphia and London, between Carpenter's Hall and the City, between the English reality and the American dream. The Federalist party was bound up with the life and the prestige of Washington ; it succeeded in damaging his popularity, and, bereft of his sheltering fame, it sank in a few years to schism and decay, surviving as a relic in New England of old prides and old hates, while the direction of American fortunes was entrusted to a party founded on a more optimistic theory and a far more realist practice.

The making and the control of parties in America is, like Napoleon's strategy, " a simple art, all is in the execution of it ". For that task, the flexible and practical mind of Jefferson was far better equipped than the illusion-fed and doctrinaire imagination of Hamilton, but even Jefferson had his difficulties. It was impossible to count on a true national sentiment, north and south, and a policy of interests could only be laid down on the broadest lines. The holders of " real property " might, in the main, be lined up for the Jeffersonian party, the holders of " personal property " be aligned with Hamilton and, in the America of 1800, such a contest could only have one end. America was still a farmer's republic. But things were not so simple as that. Social and sectional prejudice alienated some of the farmers from Jefferson. The great landed magnates of rural New York were Federalists, and so were many of the more thoroughly

Puritan sections of New England. Social prestige was still very largely with the Federalists and there were the differences of temper that made men like John Marshall enemies of popular control and men like his cousin, Jefferson, constitutionally sceptical of aristocratic theories. Even in Federalist New England there were Jeffersonian oases, Vermont and Maine ; towns like Marblehead and Dedham and Jeffersonians of rank and position like Dr. Ames, elder brother of the famous Federalist leader, Fisher Ames. There were even great Jeffersonian ship-owners like the Crowninshields of Massachusetts and the De Wolfs of Rhode Island. There were enough anomalies to make the analysis interesting, but in the main the " line-up " was sectional and the sections were commanded by their chief economic interest, around which the religious and social traditions formed. Where party lines cut too obviously against local interest, the offending party died or, in that locality, modified its creed. No amount of sound doctrine from the leaders of the party in Boston, could make the great landlords in New York oppose internal improvements which promised personal and sectional enrichment, or induce the North Carolina Federalists to oppose, with any zeal, the Louisiana Purchase. The political history of the Louisiana Purchase was, in itself, an acid test of the doctrinal purity of the American parties. The party of strict construction adopted and defended the boldest exercise of presidential prerogative in the early history of the Republic. Beside Jefferson's buying Louisiana from Napoleon, the Hamiltonian glosses of the constitutional text were as nothing. Jefferson felt this and proposed to secure for his conscience an act of indemnity, by having a constitutional amendment passed, but his party would have none of such pedantry, so like Maria Theresia, he wept and took.

As for the New England Federalists, they felt no satisfaction at seeing their arch-enemy act on the principles they had so eloquently preached. A strong federal government, asserting its powers vigorously, was only a doctrine to be admired when that strong federal government was in safe hands :

> " If she be not such to me
> What care I how good she be ? "

The effect of the purchase and of the admission of Louisiana was to increase the precedents of a loose construction of the constitution, but at the expense of strengthening the rival section. Such an upset of the balance of power between the sections was, Josiah Quincy asserted, speaking for his section, a justification for breaking the federal bond. The lesson of the Louisiana Purchase was driven home even more deeply by the War of 1812, a contest whose paradoxes are easily enough resolved into platitudes, if all the official manifestos on either side are discarded. Henry Clay might declaim about seamen's rights, but the sections that supported the war contained no seamen, and the maritime interests were resolved on peace. Whatever excuse there was for war in 1812, there had been a hundredfold in 1807, and even the attack on the United States frigate, *Chesapeake*, in time of peace, could not shake the typical Massachusetts Federalist out of his interested Anglophilism. Indeed, the whole history of the origin, conduct and conclusion of the War of 1812 is an admirable example of the sectional character of American political life. It displays, in rich profusion, the contrast between form and substance that delights the observer. The nominal object of the war was the redressing of the grievances of the American shipowners and sailors, which had arisen from the rigours of the British blockade and the French continental system. The American Government had as good case for war with France as England ; the war with England had just started when its chief ostensible cause stopped ; the section of the country aggrieved had no desire for war ; the war, thus begun, continued when the European conflict was over and was concluded by a lengthy treaty (the Peace of Ghent, 1815) which was farcical in that it made no mention of the ostensible cause of dispute.

The next ten years in politics also partook of a " musical chairs " character. The war party was cheerful, although for no particular reason ; it was still full of its high nationalist doctrine and ready to go great lengths in " Americanism ". Yet the real victor of the war was New England. Her commerce had suffered terribly, but Jeffersonian embargoes and the still more effective British blockade had acted as a hotbed on the infant textile industries of the region. The more far-sighted leaders like Francis C. Lowell were putting their money into cotton mills and wanted a strong federal government that would protect the infant industry. The still-dominant shipping interest had had enough of government aid, which had taken the form of embargoes and war, and was still convinced that nothing good could come out of Washington. While the old views were dominant in New England, that typical lawyer-politician, Daniel Webster, was a free-trader and unrepentant Federalist of the second school, that is, the states' rights school. As wealth and power shifted sides, so did he, till by 1830 he is nationalism incarnate, replying to Hayne's states' rights doctrines with thunderous national rhetoric, relying on the short memories of the public to fail to recall that, fifteen years before, Webster's friends had been planning, at the Hartford Convention, an end of the sacred union, with no audible protest from the eloquent Daniel now come to judge their South Carolina imitators. The darling of South Carolina, John C. Calhoun, had been one of the leading " war hawks " of 1812, had supported the first real protective tariff of 1816, and had only very slowly discarded his earlier nationalist views in response to pressure from his state. The high hopes with which South Carolina and Charleston had looked forward to exploiting their share of the American heritage had faded ; it was apparent that something was wrong with the machinery, and, despairing of getting a share of the dividend, South Carolina decided that there should be no dividend to declare, that the United States should go out of business as a sectional profit-making concern or South Carolina would go out of the United States. Calhoun was not insincere in his change, he was from first to last a servant of his state and section, as was Webster ; he found he had miscalculated the possibilities for his state of a national policy, and so took up a new one. Webster had the same fundamental consistency ; he was a lawyer and his political clients expected him, reasonably, to win cases for them, not to maintain an impossible consistency as a political theorist.

The sudden nationalizing of New England was only one sign among many of a recasting of parties which bore fruit in the " Jacksonian Revolution ". The constantly growing economic and political powers of the West was the key to the situation. Either the South or the North-East would achieve the alliance with the West, and, probably, with the central states, which usually followed the victor.

In the manœuvring between 1824 and 1832 the battle was decided against the North-East. In Andrew Jackson, the old Jeffersonian alliance found a leader and mascot superior to Henry Clay, the western leader of the rival combination. Not only was Jackson a more formidable leader than Clay, but the issues most likely to appeal to the West came more easily to the lips of the Jacksonian leaders. Clay had to appeal to the good, the wise and the rich, to the bankers, manufacturers and merchants and, at the same time, to find something to win over the farmers. The " American system " with its high tariff and the fostering of the home market appealed to many in the West, as it did to the young Abraham Lincoln, but not to enough. The common people, still numerous, still class-conscious, might love Clay as they had never loved any Federalist, but they knew where their real spiritual kinship was, and whatever doubts they had as to where their allegiance lay, were dispelled when Jackson attacked the Wall Street of the day, the Bank of the United States. All the poor, the poor of the towns oppressed by service in the militia, by the severe laws on debts, by the inequalities of political and legal systems ; all the countrymen who wanted cheap and abundant land, to whom the magic virtues of the tariff were not yet apparent ; all the debtors who had reason to dislike banks ; all the plain people who disliked the *grand seigneur* manners of the local rich, went over to Jackson. The Whigs, as the opposition party, with unconscious felicity, called itself, could not compete. It was the party of the rich, of the respectable, and for all the flattery with which it imitated the Jacksonian campaign methods, it was never able to make more than a momentary impression on the common people. From 1828 till the Civil War, with two brief and accidental interludes, the United States was governed by the alliance of South and West, with more emphasis on the West than had been necessary in Jefferson's time, but with a fair balance of interests. The task of Democratic statesmen was to preserve that balance, to find a series of working compromises that would keep the allies on sufficiently good terms with one another to let them present a united front to the enemy. It became at first difficult, then impossible to do this, because the South was tied to a " peculiar institution ", with whose maintenance she was emotionally and economically so bound up that danger or even threat to the institution destroyed all the power of ordinary political prudence.

Once the party lines formed, the advantages of the dominant party were immense. Either the sectional alliance of the dominant party had to break down, temporarily or permanently, or bad luck upset the ruling party to give the minority a chance. In the two victories of the Whigs, the two types of revolt are illustrated. In 1840, Van Buren was made to pay for the panic of 1837, and if the trimmings of the campaign have got most attention, it is probable that hard times cost the Democrats many more votes than hard cider. In 1848, the split in the Democratic party made Taylor President. If Van Buren had not run as an independent, the Democrats, as usual, would have won. What is more important is the reason for the split, it was in fact the thin end of the wedge. What had been a cloud no bigger than a man's hand in 1820, though even then alarming to the far-sighted Jefferson, was now covering the political sky. In 1844 enough anti-slavery Whigs had bolted their party to defeat Henry Clay ; in 1848, enough disgruntled Democrats and anti-slavery men of both parties followed Martin Van Buren in a forlorn hope. A new issue was coming to the front, undoing the bonds of union between South and West which it grew more and more difficult to knit together again. It had been the hope of the early fathers of the republic that slavery was on the way to extinction, and they had grounds for their optimism. Unfortunately, the invention of the cotton gin made slavery profitable and the new generation in the South

had none of the economic pessimism of the fathers and so readily
discarded their moral objections to slavery. By 1820, slavery
was *the* mark of the Southern states and it was obvious that
slavery was not dying peacefully. To the ordinary sectional
interests was added a special interest that had an immense
capacity for attracting loyalty, and the South was not merely
willing to sacrifice the Union, which was easy enough to conceive, but the Democratic and Whig parties and all other sectional
interests, rather than permit any profane hands to be laid on the
divine institution. In the excellence of slavery, in its moral and
political desirability, the South fanatically believed and it was
unwilling to compromise the question. The South was morbidly
sensitive about its peculiar institution, it was conscious that it
was cut off from most of the civilized world by its adherence to
slavery, and though sure that the rest of the world was wrong,
it had none of the calm that comes from security, for the emotional
basis for the intellectual belief in slavery had been too hastily
provided.

So it was that the South, again and again, sacrificed ₁the substance for the shadow. Because the leader of the Democrats,
Martin Van Buren, would not come out for the annexation of
Texas in 1844, the South imposed on the party the first " dark
horse ", Polk. The militant foreign policy of the Democrats
had been doubly sectional on the model of 1812, but despite the
war-cry " 54° 40″ or Fight ", the Oregon boundary question was
compromised as was wise—a war with Britain would have been
absurd—but the North noted that war was made on Mexico,
and a vast accession of territory was made on the south-west. It
might have been Louisiana over again, and have been the cement
of the Democratic party, but the North had no such interest
in the annexation of New Mexico as she had had in the acqui-
sition of the mouth of the Mississippi, and it was suspected that
the South had too much. The rift in the dominant party was
too obvious even for politicians to ignore, and the next ten years
were devoted to expedients designed to postpone the collapse
of that alliance between South and West called the Democratic
party. When the party did collapse, the Union collapsed with it.

The fate of Stephen Douglas illustrates the pathology of
American parties. He saw that the healthy life of the Democratic party, his own ambition, and the Union, depended on a
readjustment of relations between South and West, the repeating
of the work of Jefferson and Jackson in terms of the new conditions. The West, which was his stronghold, needed or wanted,
railroads, ports, free land. The South saw less and less profit
for itself in mere expansion. There was little left of the national
domain into which slavery could profitably expand, and all

Southern politics had come to centre round slavery. The candidate most likely to defend that institution was sure of support from the South, regardless of his party. It was obvious that the Whig party would not long survive the great twin brethren, Clay and Webster. In the South, the Democrats absorbed the more aristocratic Whigs and made a platform which put the defence of slavery before national and party loyalties. It was to unite the West and South that Douglas brought forward the Kansas-Nebraska bill, opening, in theory if not in practice, Kansas to slavery. It was possibly a good bargain' for the West. It removed Southern opposition, opened a new tract to western settlement and might, in happier or saner times, have been the basis of a renewed sectional alliance. But a force had entered politics which was not controllable by mere prudential considerations. All over the North were men in both parties, who regarded slavery as an evil to be tolerated only within the narrowest limits. They were far more numerous and more potent than the Abolitionists, and it was their revolt that made possible the foundation of the Republican party. Douglas may have counted on the gratitude and support of the West, but here was an issue producing a new sectional alignment. The abortive revolts of 1820, 1844, 1848, against the alleged Southern domination, were now eclipsed by a wave of passionate resentment at what seemed a betrayal of the North—and the " North " was a new political entity, embracing all the free states, and not merely the North-East. Yet the election of 1856 seemed to show that mere moral indignation was not enough to build a party on. " The party of moral ideas " went down to defeat with Frémont in 1856, and it seemed that the Democrats had weathered another storm. But the Republicans had luck, leaders and prudence on their side, and they showed masterly propagandist talents in the exploitation of the legend of " Bleeding Kansas ". Only in such an atmosphere of righteous indignation could tempers be kept at the point which would make it possible for the two main sections of the new party, the Whigs and the Free Democrats, to fuse. But more than that was required to build up a party. The old Whigs, Seward, Lincoln, and the rest, had had their party killed under them, there was nowhere else for them to go, but the Democrats who had revolted in 1854 might, like the " Barnburners " of 1848, have gone back. It was desirable to provide a programme which would conciliate all sections. Pennsylvania, " the Keystone State ", had gone for its favourite son, Buchanan, in 1856. It was now to be won over, in the person of its great Boss, Simon Cameron, to liberty and a high tariff. The more obnoxious features of New England righteousness were to be hidden, for the zeal of the foreign voter for Negro freedom was not combined, as was so often the case among the New England Republicans, with horror of alcohol and of profanation of the Sabbath. The West was to be won by the abandonment of all subterfuge, land was to be given to the settler free.

The South did everything to help the Republicans. Fortified by the Dred Scott decision (1857), the South claimed the right to extend slavery through all the territories of the Federal Government, regardless alike of the will of Congress or of the local legislatures : the Territories were the common property of the whole Union and no section could be excluded from their use. This doctrine destroyed the political basis of the Republican party, for that party's central plank was opposition to any extension of slavery in the Territories. It also destroyed the political programme of the Northern Democrats and of their leader, Senator Douglas. He had staked his own and his party's fate on the acceptance of the doctrine of " Popular sovereignty ", as a solution of the slavery question in the Territories. Douglas knew that no federal government dared enforce the full consequences of slavery where the population was hostile or even neutral. The attempts to enforce the undoubted constitutional rights of the South, under the Fugitive Slave Law of 1850, had provoked revolt all over the Northern states. The most devoted unionists and Democrats had, like the Senator in *Uncle Tom's Cabin*, refused to make their fine words vile deeds, had refused again and again to aid, or even to tolerate, the returning of fugitives to bondage. States had backed up this disobedience to Federal authority by resolutions and by laws, unparalleled since the nullification movement in South Carolina, or since the Hartford Convention.

The multiplied exercise of federal authority which would be necessary to enforce slavery in the Territories, would destroy any party in the United States. The South must be content with realities and must put up with slights on its claims, if it wished to keep federal authority in friendly hands. There were some concessions which no northern Democrat could honestly make with any sincere belief in being able to carry them out. The South insisted on its pound of flesh, forced or encouraged President Buchanan to-break with Douglas, thus giving aid and comfort to the doubting and despondent Republicans and, in 1860, insisted on a platform which no Democrat could hope to win on. The Democratic party, after sixty years of success based on its discipline and on its admirable sectional diplomacy, was split in two and ignominiously defeated. The Republicans came into office, if not into power, and a new American party needs the former more than the latter, if it is to hold the mercenary troops who form so large a part of every American political army.

Chapter II

THE AGE OF THE REPUBLICANS

IT has been suggested that American parties are sectional alliances, that the business of party leaders is to make and maintain these alliances, and that success in this task is sufficient to keep a party in power for periods that seem to the English observer fantastically long. There is no swing of the pendulum in American party politics, one party is definitely the majority party and can only be dislodged, temporarily, by ill-luck or ill-discipline and, permanently, by a revolution. The vested interests of the dominant party increase its strength. The spoils system worked and works in favour of the majority party, for it enables that party to maintain a standing army, while the faint hopes of office which the minority party can offer attract only the less competent of the political *condottieri*. Moreover, round the policies and personalities of the dominant party, all kinds of vested interests gather, even the Democrats by the " fifties " had overcome much of their social inferiority and welcomed or received into their ranks adherents from social classes, which, in the early radical days of their party, would have scorned association with the rabble. This was due, in part, to the notoriously steadying effect of office and power on radical parties in all times and countries, but also due to the natural attraction of power for power. The better classes and the rudimentary forms of big business of the time might have preferred to have had dealings with another type of political ruler, but they had to deal with the detainers of political power—no matter what these politicians called themselves, or what subversive principles they preached or even practised.

The acquired assets of the Democrats were not completely dissipated in the gamble of 1860. Lincoln had polled a good deal less than half of the votes cast in the presidential election of 1860, and had the South not seceded, the Democrats would have still controlled Congress. Even secession did not kill the Democratic party in the North. It displayed wonderful power of recovery in 1862, and in 1864, despite the fact that its platform, adopted in August, declaring the war a failure, was palpably false in November, when the election came off,

49

Lincoln's majority was not so great as to reassure nervous party men. If the best the Republicans could do in the flood tide of victory, with eleven states out of the reckoning, was to be measured by the poll of 1864, it was painfully probable that the Republicans would find in 1868 that they had saved the republic for the Democrats. What was most necessary for the new party was time. It must dig itself in, build up its machine with federal offices, solidify the sentiment and reward the zeal of its members. The Morrill Tariff, passed in 1861, thanks to the absence of the Southern members, the Homestead Act of 1863, the increased patronage made possible by the war, the railroads whose building had shifted the interest of the West from New Orleans to New York, were all foundation-stones of a new and artfully planned party fortress, but the party cement required time to set, and time, it seemed, would be denied it.

It can hardly be doubted that a good deal of the reconstruction policy of the Republicans was dictated by this party fear. The defeated southern states showed no sign of a willingness to kiss the rod ; though slavery was gone, the South did not forgive its destroyers, and if a few leading Southerners declared themselves Republicans, most of the Southern leaders began to renew their party ties with the Democrats of the North. The Republicans might have been content to keep the rebel states out of Congress if they could have relied on the support of the North. The great Democratic triumphs of 1867 seemed to menace the Republican party in its own stronghold and it was resolved, for that and for other reasons, to admit the southern states, but only on terms which would make them political assets of the Republican party. This was the political, though not the sole, motive of the fourteenth and fifteenth amendments, and of the orgy of coercion and corruption which, for a few brief but fruitful years, secured Republican control of the federal government and made the republic safe for Republicans.

It is usually asserted that it was the experience of Republican reconstruction which created the " Solid South ". When one remembers the absorption by the Democrats of all politicians in, at any rate, the lower South, before the war, it is hard to believe that the Republicans would have reaped many electoral votes in 1868 or 1872 from an uncoerced South, though doubtless the infamies of the carpet-bag régime stiffened the resolution of the South and prevented the growth of a genuine white Republican party. On the other hand, the enforcement of Negro suffrage and the disfranchisement of so many former rebels secured Republican strength in Congress and, in the critical year, 1876, made possible the securing of the presidency for the Republican party. This was in itself almost worth, from the politician's point of view, all the odium and party hatred earned by the Republican policy. Many Republicans became disgusted with their party ; a few left it ; the discredited Democrats got an issue which more and more won sympathy in the North and the record made by the Republican administrations in the former rebel states defied even the most zealous and skilful apologists for the young " Grand Old Party ". Yet even on this side there were gains, the Republicans were forced by the necessities of the case to use to the utmost the memories of the war as a party asset. It is possible, that in addition to the indisputable advantages of a block of southern states securely in the hands of representatives of the party who were not likely or able to revolt, the sectional feeling which tyranny and outrage bred, with charge and counter-charge following, was almost as valuable a party weapon. " The Bloody Shirt " was a more durable asset than the stolen elections.

In American politics nothing succeeds like success. As year after year went by, with the Republican control of the federal government unshaken, the recruiting of the Democratic party in the northern states grew more difficult. The wise and prudent who sought a political career were forced, over a great part of the Union, to seek it in the Republican party or not at all. The older generation that had known the great days of Van Buren and Douglas might cling to the good old cause. There were plenty of young Democrats, but they tended to be concentrated in special areas, or in the great cities, or to represent special family or personal idiosyncrasies or grievances. All over the North, the rising generation came to think that because Republicans were always in control of the federal government, there was something unnatural and wrong in conceiving them out of it. This view was held in all sincerity by young Republicans like John Hay and by thousands like him. It is even possible, that in their hearts, young Democrats were not quite sure that the young Republicans were wrong in their assumption of divine right. The election of 1876 which marked the great revulsion against " Grantism " gave a popular majority to the Democratic leader, and but for bold and decisive action by the Republicans, would have installed that typical old-fashioned Democrat, Tilden, in the White House. Had Tilden become President, his astonishing adroitness as a political manager, his great business ability and the opportunity of cleansing the government of the accumulated filth of the Grant administration, might have given the Democratic party a coherence and a prestige which would have recalled some of its pristine glory. But in a contest of nerve the Republicans won, and it is not insignificant that the victory went to the party with the worse case, the poorer candidate, and the lesser support ; what the Republicans had, after sixteen years of rule, was the habit of command ; it was the one thing necessary.

When at last the Democrats did get back into office, they had been exiles for twenty-four years. At Cleveland's inauguration there were some figures who suggested Rip van Winkle—men who had sworn never to shave till there was again a Democrat in the White House, and the zealots were not unworthy symbols of the old age of the party and of its inherent feebleness. By 1885 the spectacle of a Democrat in the White House was not so shocking as it would have been in 1877, but it was more surprising and less formidable to the members of the party that was now definitely dominant—almost as dominant as the Democrats had been in the period 1801–61.

There was bred in the Republicans a self-righteousness that was amusing or annoying, but was also useful. Henry Adams might be amused at the Republican fervour of his friend, John Hay, but such faith was catching. To Senator Hoar, the Republican party, whatever its faults since it came into power in 1860, " has been composed in general of what is best in our national life ".[1]   In his speech celebrating the fiftieth anniversary of the party, Hay attributed to it " all the good things of the half-century, except, possibly, the introduction of antiseptic surgery ".[2] Hay might smile at his own oratory, but it was not without its effect and the smiling faith of Hay was a bitter conviction with the rank and file. A Republican government was natural, it could appeal to a general " consumer acceptance " of its wares and could do business with very old stock. The Democrats had no such assets. Outside the South, a Democrat was on the defensive. His faith might be secure, but it was not infectious.[3] It was too much directed to the past, it is still too much directed to the past. Until the present " depression ", the Republican was in the habit of pointing at the United States as at the work of his hands ; the Democrat could only claim the foundations and assert that a much better superstructure would have been put up if the old firm had been left on the job.

Yet the numerical margin between the parties was still small, the Democrats had a popular majority in 1876, in 1884, in 1888 and in 1892, and in the off years they had their share, and more than their share, of congressional power. The surprising strength

[1] G. F. Hoar, Recollections, vol. i, p. 200.

[2] W. R. Thayer, The Life and Letters of John Hay, vol. ii, p. 381.

[3] Vice-President Marshall said : " There are a great many things which I believe that I know are not so ; for instance, I believe that the Democratic party is always right " (Recollections of Thomas M. Marshall, p. 481). A Republican would have been tempted to omit the qualification in his testimony of faith.

in votes of the minority party but serves to underline its weakness in real power ; outside the South, the Democrats had only the plain people on their side, and some of the more delicate-stomached of the fancy people. The real masters of America were, by now, nearly all in the Republican camp, and those who were Democrats did all they could to reduce the difference to one of names. The great and growing business interests of the country had come down decidedly on one side of the fence.

The Republican party had, in the generation after the war, an advantage that the Democrats had lacked in their palmiest days. They combined all the practical power and authority of the dominant party with the social prestige that had gone in the past to the dissentient minority. Right and Might, the great twin brethren, had joined hands to save and preserve the Union and to keep the republic safe. To men of the generation of Senator Hoar, the canonization of the founders of the party had nothing absurd in it, these were men who had wrought the great deliverance from slavery, disunion, free-trade, and at the head of them was the martyr, Lincoln. That Lincoln was bitterly opposed by the most Republican section of his party in his life-time, that his party discarded his policy and impeached the tactless successor who attempted to carry it out as they would certainly have opposed and might have impeached Lincoln him-self, had he lived, were considerations of no weight in face of the immediate growth and profitable use of the Lincoln legend. The blood of the martyr was the seed of the new church and the dead Lincoln did for his party what St. Louis did for the House of France, he gave it a useful odour of sanctity that for long overpowered less agreeable smells.

The Democrats had little to offer in competition. Had Stephen Douglas lived, with his popularity and his prestige in the party, the Democrats might have bided their time and harvested some share of political fruits of the war, especially after the Republican party had shown signs of disintegration on the reconstruction question. But lacking Douglas, they lacked a national leader. They found themselves forced more and more into hostility to the Union cause or into lukewarmness in support of the government. Despite the active support given to the war by most Northern Democrats, the party in 1864 was unable to resist the temptation to gamble on the probable failure of the war ; it nominated General McClellan on a platform drawn up under the influence of the most notorious Northern pacifist, Clement Vallandigham. It was as if the French " left " had staked their electoral fortunes on a platform drawn up by M. Caillaux, and headed by General Sarrail just before the collapse of the German front. The fortune of war was against the

Democrats and the Republicans were entitled to the credit of not having despaired of the republic when their opponents were willing to abandon the cause. It became an axiom of the Republicans that while not all Democrats were traitors, all traitors were Democrats, the burden of proof was laid on the Democrats.

The Democrats wriggled under the charge, but were not happy in their efforts to refute it. Against General Grant, in 1868, they nominated Horatio Seymour, despite his war record, and, in 1872, Horace Greeley, who, during the war, had gone round like a weathercock from the position of Horatio Bottomley to that of Mr. Ramsay MacDonald, and had sacrificed a great deal of his remaining popularity by going bail for the arch-traitor, Jefferson Davis. It was a preposterous nomination and did nothing to restore the party's prestige in the nation. The Democrats still remained the party of treason. Republicans never allowed the charge to be forgotten, the more skill they showed in " waving the bloody shirt ", the more the party loved its leaders. It was his infernal debating skill in reviving bitter war memories that made the " Plumed Knight ", James J. Blaine, the idol of the Republican rank and file. He had plenty of rivals, but no equals, in the art of recalling the war atrocities and the agonies of the gallant Republican soldiers who had suffered at Democratic hands in the terrible years when the nation was being saved by the soldiers on the battlefield and by Mr. Blaine in Congress.

In addition to the general bad repute of the Democrats, in some sections the war had been very decidedly a civil war, with all its bitterness. In the border states there were great numbers of Democrats and many of them were sympathizers with their southern brethren. Republicans bred in border communities in Illinois, Missouri, Kentucky never forgot the iniquities of their opponents, and in such areas as " Bloody Williamson County ", Illinois, it is sometimes suspected that the Civil War is not yet over. It was from his heart that " Uncle Joe " Cannon, the famous Speaker of the House of Representatives, wrote :

" You youngsters of the second generation to whom the Civil War is tradition only, can have no idea of the efforts made by the disloyalists of the North to discredit and defame the President, to embarrass and hamper him at every turn. Nothing was too small or too dastardly for them to do." [1]

Over great areas, the Democratic party practically died out. It came to spasmodic life when there was some split in the

[1] *Uncle Joe Cannon*, by L. White Bushey, p. 107.

dominant party, there were " fusions " even in Maine, but to be a Democrat was odd and almost disgraceful in rural America, wherever there was no special block of settlers connected with the party by family ties. When the nomination of Blaine, in 1884, forced the respectable Republicans to ask themselves if they would support the ticket, the strain of conscience was terrible. Many believed Blaine a dangerous man and a rogue and believed Cleveland an honest and a capable man, yet could not bring themselves to vote the Democratic ticket. A man of the world like Andrew D. White, who had reason to admire Cleveland, forced himself to defend Blaine as he had forced himself to believe and tried to make others believe that Grant's administration was a glory, not a disgrace. Mark Twain and his Hartford friends were oddly excited at the prospect of having to refuse to vote for Blaine, and with surprise at their own daring, worked themselves up to vote for Cleveland.[1] There were thousands of honest men who hated having to palliate Blaine's sins, and who trusted Cleveland, but were terrified that a Democratic victory would mean repudiation of the National Debt or the assumption of the Confederate debt, the re-enslaving or the massacre of the Negroes, the undoing of the work of Lincoln and Grant and the putting into high places of unconverted rebels who would betray their trust, as Cobb and Floyd had betrayed theirs in 1860. Cleveland's administration did a good deal to make this view appear fantastic, but the attempt of the President to return the captured rebel flags to the South was a godsend to such Republicans as Governor Foraker. Was it not what one would expect from a Democrat who had not fought in the war and who was continually vetoing in sarcastic terms pension bills for the saviours of their country ?

The Democrats who remained faithful to their party in the solid Republican states were zealots of the old school. The praises of the unterrified Democracy of Vermont, who voted gallantly and hopelessly for their party, were sung in other parts of the Union, and the most famous Vermont Democrat of modern times bore with him into the Republican party the tell-tale name of George Brinton McClellan Harvey.[2]

In other sections of the country, the Democrats might be more numerous, but they had no easy life. In that part of

[1] Mark Twain was a Southerner and had been, for a few farcical weeks, a Confederate soldier, but he had taken on a protective colouring from his New England associates in more than literary matters.

[2] The most famous modern Vermonter told us that in his home town " there were about two hundred and fifty qualified voters, not over twenty-five of which were Democrats " (Autobiography of Calvin Coolidge, p. 22). We are told that West Branch, Iowa, where Mr. Hoover spent his boyhood, had only one Democrat.

Southern Illinois called "Egypt", it was by no means easy walking for Silas Bryan and his fellows.

"All sorts of dignitaries of the party of Andrew Jackson, including even judges and former state Senators, like the Hon. Silas Bryan himself, were arrested wholesale and held without trial for months, only to be released just as arbitrarily without exoneration. Less prominent Democrats were simply taken out and flogged by bands of ' Union Regulators ', or warned to leave the country." [1]

Can we wonder that in a Republican state like Nebraska, the son of Judge Bryan fought the good fight for the party and that William Jennings Bryan was always a Democrat, and to the end the idol of that Western wing of the party which, like his father, had gone through fire in the name of Andrew Jackson?

In the great cities there were always Democrats. There the pressure of Republican majorities could more easily be avoided than in the intolerant countryside ; there the local authorities might be friendly ; and there the party could always put on a bold front. Chief stronghold of the party in the North was New York. For sixty years Tammany Hall had marshalled the voters for Aaron Burr's party and no politician in the state of New York could afford to disregard the great block of votes invariably cast, or, at least, counted, for the sacred principles of Jefferson and Jackson. When party fortunes were at their lowest, leaders like James Brooks could find a refuge in New York City from disapproving voters elsewhere and when federal or state supplies ran low, there were always the riches of the city to keep the hungry in line. Though the votes of New York were not to be despised, they were not an unmitigated benefit to the Democrats. Tammany had no sweet reputation and it was an old complaint that the fortunes of the greatest city and state in the Union were ruled by exploiters of ignorant foreign voters. The dislike of the Tammany clientèle was increased by the failure of all attempts to divorce the Irish and other foreign voters from the sinful machine. Individuals might profit, but the Democratic party was in Irish eyes the only trustworthy ally of the sea-divided Gael. Every wave of feeling against the immigrants had been resisted by the Democrats and the opposing party, whatever it called itself, had, since Hamilton's time, been the home of " nativist " sentiments. For a Catholic Irishman to be a Whig or a Republican was as disgraceful as for a Catholic in the Falls Road of Belfast to be a Unionist, or for a Vendéen to be a " bleu ", or a Protestant in Nîmes to be a " blanc ".

[1] Paxton Hibben, *The Peerless Leader*, p. 26.

The Civil War had its confusing side, for thousands of Irishmen fought in the Northern as well as in the Southern armies, for reasons not directly connected with any American cause, but the great draft riots of 1863, with their accompaniments of murder and arson were, in the eyes of most Americans, an indelible Irish disgrace, the betrayal, in the hour of its greatest need, of the adopted country of the rioters. To the rioters, and their political allies, it was unfortunate, but it was the only available means of protest against a levy they believed was infamously designed to weigh especially heavily on the great Democratic city and against a system of conscription that exempted the rich who could buy a substitute and so permitted Messrs. Morgan, Rockefeller, Depew and many another less illustrious, to buy the leisure to look after their own business, while the less fortunate inhabitants of the Bowery and the Five Points were shipped off to battle in Virginia.[1]

All foreigners had suffered from Whig hostility and the Germans had enrolled themselves in the Democratic party almost as uniformly as had the Irish, but the slavery issue and the influence of such leaders as Carl Schurz had won over most of them to the Republican side. As long as the issue of freedom was at stake, the Germans were faithful to the Republicans, but they were less reliable when it was a question of keeping the jobs safe and were too prone to follow such errant spirits as Carl Schurz out of the party and in again, when the less doctrinaire Americans held their noses and voted a straight ticket. Moreover, an issue that had caused a great deal of trouble in the early days of the Republican party, had an awkward way of coming alive again. The sudden conversion of the Evangelical churches from faith to works, and the consequent insistence on the " liquor question ", had caused a wave of prohibition to sweep over the New England states, and such parts of other states as had been settled from New England. There was an ebbing of the tide in the decadence of moral feeling that followed the Civil War, but the consciences of the Anglo-Saxon Republicans were

[1] There have always been plenty of Irish Republicans, especially in states where no political career is open to a Democrat. But in the main, the Irish have remained constant to the party that welcomed them. A. D. White was told by an Irish Republican that the penalty of his defection had been ostracism and that " Irishmen really cared more for the Democratic party than they did for the Catholic Church " (*Letters of Goldwin Smith*, p. 476). In Chicago, we are told, " most of the people in this ward wud die befure they'd be buried by a Raypublican undertaker " (*Mr. Dooley's Opinions*, p. 172) and, in modern times, the only candidate of the North Dakota Non-Partisan League who insisted on running as a Democrat instead of as a Republican, was a Mr. Casey. The clean sweep of 1932 has projected a number of little-known bearers of Irish names into high office in the West.

always liable to stirrings which involved legislation or administration that led to an exodus of indignant beer-drinking Germans
from the party. The same cause would have led to an Irish
secession, if there had been any Irish to secede, for both peoples
were financially involved in generous treatment of the liquor
trade. There were exceptions all over the country, but in the
North a dealer in liquor was more at home among the Democrats
and the " temperance " vote was usually Republican. As views
on drink in America follow religious and racial affiliations as
much as tastes and principles, the drink question was a potent
ally of the Democrats among the unregenerate Germans and
Irish.

If slavery had died in the war, the political forces bred by the
institution were given a new lease of life. All the seceded states
learned that their worst apprehensions as to the iniquities of
Republican rule had fallen far short of the reality and when the
last " carpet-bag " governments were overthrown in 1877, the
South was united as never before and convinced that no decent
man could be a Republican. The few Southerners of the white
race who clung to the Republican party were not merely misguided, they were regarded as traitors who were willing to see
their states bankrupt, their pride destroyed and their women
defiled, to earn some dirty money as federal officials. A disinterested Republican was so rare and so unaccountable that
it was hard to decide whether he were a fitter occupant of a
museum or an asylum. The eleven states of the old confederacy
from 1880 on, voted the Democratic ticket with a military discipline that was the envy of other sections ; there was something
attractive in the spectacle of the formal rite of election going
forward as if it had meaning. Round the unbreakable square
of the " Solid South ", the Democratic skirmishers of the North
manœuvred in their unequal battle. Out of the fifteen slave
states, four had stayed in the Union and so had not been " recon-
structed ". In Missouri, Kentucky, Maryland and Delaware, it
was not infamous for a man to be a Republican, but it became
more and more pointless. These states had not so much stayed
in the Union as had been kept in it. In Missouri, there was the
memory of the stirring days of 1861 to keep alive the natural
hostility of country areas against sinful St. Louis, and when the
leading Republicans of the state bolted the party in 1872, Missouri was ready to rejoin her Southern sisters and became an
appendage of the Solid South. Kentucky, in 1865, it was
unkindly said, was furious at not having seceded in 1861, and
resolved to punish the Republicans. Her experience of Federal
rule during the war had embittered vast numbers of all parties,
and the state which had so long supported the Whig banner in

the old days, now went over to the Democrats. So it was in Maryland where Baltimore reversed the rôle of St. Louis, and where Republican feeling, such as it was, was rural, and in tiny Delaware, the great family power of the Bayards, then without a rival, did its work.

This was the basis of Democratic strength in the trying generation after the war, when the party was slowly coming to life again, the Solid South, the Catholics, the friends of free drinking, or as the Reverend Mr. Burchard put it, with more force than tact, it was "the party of Rum, Romanism and Rebellion".

By 1880, the political geography of the United States had taken regular form. Outside the former slave states, the Republican party was normally dominant in federal and usually in state elections. It was the party of the clergy, of the colleges, of the business men, of the older racial stocks, of all the people who regarded themselves and were regarded by others as the "better elements". The Democrats were confined to the towns or to special areas of the country which had been settled from the South and were in sympathy with the South, the lower counties of Illinois, the southern half of Indiana. In the mountain areas of some Southern states, there had been few slaves and the mountaineers who had been Democrats turned Republican during and after the war, while the plains turned Democrat after being largely Whig.[1] Thus eastern Tennessee and Kentucky elected Republican congressmen, though they could not keep their states out of the Democratic column at presidential elections. In normal times, New England was solidly Republican and so were states which had a large New England element in their population without a Southern counterpart. Such were Iowa, Minnesota, Wisconsin, in general the upper tier of western states. The middle states were divided. Pennsylvania was wedded to the tariff party and whatever she might do in local or congressional elections, could be relied on to vote for a Republican president. New York and its dependency, New Jersey, were doubtful, usually Democratic in local politics, and worth courting by both sides in national elections, for their votes were almost decisive and their character hard to foresee. Along with New York ranked the two great doubtful middle-western states, Ohio and Indiana, both full of hereditary Yankee Republicans and Southern Democrats, both full of adroit politicians and both willing to raise their market price by judicious coquetry. The greater part of the population of the United States voted in presidential years for or against the Union cause in the Civil

[1] In North Carolina, the mountains had been Whig, not Democratic, before the war and became, and have largely remained, Republican.

War. But there were enough doubtful cases, enough open-minded men ready to forswear Ephraim and his idols, for ideal, or other considerations, to make presidential elections closely contested and the weight of small sections very great. As has been pointed out, the numerical difference between the two parties between 1876 and 1896 was small. The fighting was confined to the doubtful states and the small section which was independent or venal. To persuade the doubtful voters of New York and buy those of Indiana was the secret of Empire.

In this battle the Democrats were outclassed. What they lacked was not numbers but prestige, money, and a secure basis of sectional co-operation. In the contest for hereditary votes, the Republicans had, on the whole, the best of it. There were enough " rockribbed " Republican states in the North to offset the " Solid South ", and in the doubtful states, Union sentiment was stronger than the old Democratic tradition. Money plays a great part in American elections, as in all elections, and the Republicans had far more money than the Democrats. There were many rich Democrats, but they tended, like the Belmonts in New York, to represent the older financial dynasties, and the new millionaires were as to the old, as the house of Morgan to the house of Belmont. The longer the Republicans controlled the federal government, the firmer grew the politico-economic structure that benefited by their rule. The railroads, the protected industries and all their hangers-on, grew stronger than the importers and the shipowners. Apart from the influence of the tariff, and of definite legislation, the favours of the government to corporations, to banks, to rising lawyers, naturally gave present or future financial power to the Republicans. Both parties avoided " issues ", but if issues should arise, the odds were that the Republicans could stand their unwelcome intrusion better than could the Democrats. So it proved in the critical years from 1888 to 1896.

President Cleveland threw down the gauntlet in 1888 by attacking the existing high tariff and so precipitated a fight that in the long run broke his party. At once it rallied to the Republicans the threatened industries, and many which were not directly threatened, but disliked disturbance, and money poured into the party chest. The revision of the tariff upward—undertaken by the Republicans in 1890—resulted in the greatest congressional defeat in American history up to that time, yet the return of the Democrats to power in 1892, even if it seemed to enthusiasts like Vachel Lindsay's father, the end of the Republican party, was really the end of the laboriously reassembled Democratic party. The election of 1884 had shown that the party had overcome some of its handicaps and had, in certain circles in the East, become respectable again, but the mere issue of purity in government was not enough to keep a party going. The tariff issue appealed to the old sectional alliance of West and South and had a successful reform gone through early in 1893, and had good times continued, there might have been a chance for the Democrats to dig themselves in.

The great financial panic of 1893 burst and tore both parties to pieces. In their fury and rage, the populace had already begun to hanker after strange gods and the million votes given to the Populist candidate in 1892, had been the equivalent of the contemporary election of Keir Hardie to the House of Commons. The fighting force of the Democrats was in the hungry and angry multitude who howled against the tariff and its child the trusts; in the steel-workers who had been shot down by Carnegie's mercenaries at Homestead, and in the embittered farmers who had taken the advice of Mrs. Lease, the " Kansas Pythoness ", to " raise less corn and more hell ". But the control of the party was in far different hands. Cleveland had no understanding of what was " getting under the skin " of his western followers. He was an eastern Democrat with little to distinguish him from a Republican but his views on tariffs and on the crimes of Jeff Davis. A financial crisis overtook his administration a few weeks after inauguration, and Cleveland had to decide whether he should placate Main Street or Wall Street. The men whom he most admired advised one way. His friend, manager, and " angel ", William Whitney, was a Wall Street man of the deepest dye. The intellectuals and " Mugwumps " of the East, to whom he thought he owed his election, were all of the most severe economic orthodoxy. The West wanted to meet the crisis by continuing inflation. Cleveland decided to follow his natural bent, to let Morgan save the country, or at any rate, the banks, and to force through the repeal of the Sherman Silver Act which was emptying the treasury and the country of gold.

Strangely enough, the adoption of the official remedy did not immediately restore good times, and it was in a country prostrate under a panic that Cleveland tried to return to the programme of his party. He proposed to reform the tariff. For reasons explained elsewhere, the resulting Tariff bill was a parody of Democratic professions. Cleveland let it become law without his signature, but it was noticed that he could manage to get the bankers' will done, but could not get his party programme through. The sole result of the Wilson Act, that was any consolation to the party, was the institution of an income tax, a reform welcomed by the hungry all over the land. Again the rich were heard, for the Supreme Court in two remarkable decisions found reasons for preventing the red ruin and the breaking up of laws which they were assured, by such eminent lawyers as Joseph Choate, would follow an income tax. It was obvious that the rascal multitude had made a poor choice when it elected Grover Cleveland. The disappointment of the " silverites " and of the low-tariff men, and the continuance of bad times, resulted in the choice of a Republican House of Representatives in 1894, but prosperity did not return, and discontent boiled more than ever. Horrid things happened all over the Union, but some idea of the trouble and confusion that had been caused can be gathered from the fact that the Populists had been able to endanger Democratic supremacy in the Solid South. The cleavage went so far that the Negroes were encouraged to vote ! By their aid the Republicans captured the state government in North Carolina and, still more extraordinary, the regular Democrats of Alabama called on the black voters to aid them in their fight against the Populists : *Flectere si nequeo superos Acheronta movebo.* In the rest of the Union things were no better. All over the West, and from debtors everywhere, came the cry for the " free and unlimited coinage of silver at the ratio of 16 to 1 ". While Cleveland held to his course, with his party loathing him, the Republicans, while doing their best to play up the tariff as a remedy, dared not come out against silver. The candidate they chose, McKinley, was not sound on the money question, a " sound money plank " was got into the platform with difficulty and it was hoped to fight on the tariff and keep out of a controversy in which it was impossible to do what all American party managers try to do, please all important sections in the party. But the initiative was taken out of their hands, for Ex-Congressman Bryan told the Democratic Convention that they should not crucify mankind upon a cross of gold. That, in those times, incendiary statement, was so much to the liking of the Convention that Bryan was given the nomination and the whole campaign was fought on the currency question. Cleveland had been ignored at the Convention, to all intents and purposes read out of the party, and he hoped and worked for the election of McKinley. He encouraged the bolt of the " Gold Democrats " that was designed to make assurance doubly sure, and many Democrats went further and openly supported McKinley. Others adopted the attitude of Senator David Hill of New York who announced, " I am a Democrat still, very still."

Business, regardless of its party affiliations, rallied to McKinley. His manager, Mark Hanna, assessed the banks, the great insurance companies and all forms of threatened wealth, and raised a fund far beyond the dreams of John Wanamaker and far beyond what the silver magnates put up for Bryan. "The roller-tops" and the "bucket shops", as Vachel Lindsay put it, won. Bryan was defeated, and the irreparable fissure in the Democratic party revealed.

Following a western leader and a western cause, the party had been wiped out in the East, all the careful nursing at the hands of such varied attendants as Senators Hill and Gorman, Messrs. Cleveland and Whitney, was undone. The party was now, in the eyes of the best people, as low and dangerous as it had been in 1864 or 1868, and the conviction that only the Republican party could be trusted, was more firmly rooted in the mind of Big Business than ever. For the first time since 1876, the Republicans had carried former slave states ; three of the border states, united to the Democrats by the Negro peril, had gone over to Republicanism.[1] The incessant war for sectional control of the party had been won by the West, and the result had been a rout. On the other hand, Bryan was a far more popular and effective leader than Cleveland. He was able to win the nomination in 1900 with a new issue, "Anti-imperialism", an issue less sectional than that of 1896, but he was defeated again. In 1904, the eastern section seized control and put forward Alton Parker, but the results were not encouraging, for Roosevelt not merely defeated Parker, he overwhelmed him. Bryan, in 1908, was again beaten, but made a far better showing than Parker.

It was obvious that the point of view represented by Bryan was the point of view that got the votes, but that it did not get enough votes to beat what had come to be a great Republican majority. Gone were the narrow victories of the "'70s" and "'80s". Majorities were now in seven figures, not in odd thousands. The Democratic party had been forced to take a side, to fight on sectional issues, and it was inevitably beaten. The Republican party successfully avoided alienating either East or West ; it kept most of its own natural members and won all the doubtful—and many Democrats who were annoyed because their party had made a decision. The Democrats lost more by bidding for conservative support than they did by giving Bryan his head, but either way they lost.

The Republicans played "the middle against the ends" too long ; there was behind the upheavals of Bryanism, a growing feeling that the West was making a very bad bargain with the East, that she got fine words and immortal principles, while the East got tangible advantages. The Roosevelt administration

[1] These deserters were Kentucky, Maryland and Delaware, all states which were traditionally Whig and had been forced into the Democratic party by the war.

banked the fires down below, without, at the same time, outraging the vested interests of the East beyond endurance. Roosevelt's chosen successor, Taft, was soon, in appearance or reality, a mere tool of the " Old Guard ", of the senatorial oligarchs of whom Nelson Aldrich was the most striking and odious example, and whose agent in the lower house was the despotic Speaker, " Uncle Joe Cannon ". In 1910, the Democrats, for the first time since 1892, carried a Congressional election. It was obvious that unless the split between East and West were healed, the Republican party was going to be split open as the Democratic party had been in 1896, with Taft as Cleveland. A President can force his own renomination, yet it was as certain as such things can be, that Taft could not be re-elected. Roosevelt was back from his lion-hunting trip and went after the nomination, to the annoyance of Senator La Follette who had cast himself for the Bryan of this Republican schism. With Roosevelt, the Republicans might win, with Taft they would probably lose ; but the refusal of the party managers to permit the nomination of Roosevelt showed too plainly where the heart of the G.O.P. was. The decision to keep out Roosevelt made a Democratic victory practically certain, but the Republican leaders thought that they could handle the problems of a Democratic administration better than they could those presented by the passing of the Republican machine under radical control.

The Democrats could win if they could keep united, but could they keep or rather become united ? Had the resentful West any more in common with the discredited Eastern wing than it had had in 1896 or 1904 ? The Eastern wing did not dare to put forward another Parker, what they wanted was a " sound " Westerner, but they were faced by the fact that, as had been true for the last twelve years, the fighting force of the party was in the West and its chief was still Bryan. The nomination was the reflection of this situation. It was a Bryanite victory, if not a victory for Bryan, and in the election it was seen that the Convention had chosen the winning emphasis, for Taft ran a bad third to Wilson and Roosevelt. The fight was between the two " progressive " candidates. Wilson was elected, but by a minority vote, and by fewer votes than Bryan had got in any of his three campaigns. The voting strength of the party was still radical, still with the " Great Commoner ", and for once the American people was of the mind of the Bryanites. The lesson of 1912 was driven home again in 1916. The Republicans won in the East, even defeating Wilson in his own state of New Jersey, but the West and the Middle West, despite the formal progressiveness of Mr. Hughes, knew where the Republican party affections really were and elected Wilson.

After the European War there was the *débâcle* of 1920. No Democratic candidate could have made head against the passionate longing of the American people to draw its skirts away from the filth in Europe, to undo most of what America had done and to restore the golden days of " normalcy ". They would have elected anybody the Republican machine threw at them, and they did elect Warren Harding. The Democrats were swept out everywhere, even the " Solid South " suffered its first breach, for Tennessee went for Harding. Cox carried only the remaining ten Confederate states. On what foundations should the party rebuild ? That was the great issue of the Convention of 1924, and it was undecided then and is undecided still. With the Republicans there had been no dubiety ; the professionals may have disliked accepting Mr. Hoover, but there has been no faltering in the implicit faith in the alliance with Big Business.

The Democrats have had the opportunity of choice. In 1924 they refused to decide, they ran a compromise candidate and he made no show in the East, carried the Solid South and ran behind the dissident Republican, Senator La Follette, in the West. The Republicans had every reason to be satisfied. Twenty years before they had gathered in a whole tier of normally Democratic states and had on the whole kept their gains. They had turned nominal Democratic states like New York into Republican states, and had undone such temporary losses as the loss of the silver-mining states in 1896. They had played their hand too openly and had been punished by eight years of Democratic rule, but their time had come again and their opponents had failed, even more openly than usual, to secure that fusion of interests and sentiments that is the only route to success. The events of 1928 seemed to make the ruin of the Democrats merely a matter of time. The struggle of 1924 was avoided and the superficially united party nominated Governor Smith. So much attention was concentrated on the candidate's religion and on his " wetness ", that it was insufficiently noticed that Governor Smith was the representative of the Eastern section that had run Cleveland and Parker, that the nomination was a return to a party emphasis that had been discredited since 1904, that the implied promise of the nominee was that New York and Massachusetts should do for him what California and Ohio did for Wilson in 1916. The gamble did not come off, worse than that it carried further the breach made in the southern citadel in 1920. Now it was not merely Tennessee, but Virginia, North Carolina, Texas, Florida, that went Republican.

The rebuke to the Parker nomination in 1904 was nothing to this.

But the implications of the Smith campaign really belong to a discussion of the future of both parties, and for the moment attention must be given to the effects of certain changes in the strength of party sections.

Chapter III

THE PRESENT DISTRIBUTION OF
PARTY STRENGTH

THE main lines of party strategy in the United States are laid down for a generation at a time, and, despite brief alterations of the map, there is normally little hope of remaking the main political frontiers. Discontent with a policy, or a candidate, will express itself by abstention from the polls, not by a desertion to the other side. It is within states, and in the doubtful states, that the slow movements of sectional, class and racial alignments show themselves, and, of recent years, the movements have been unusually rewarding to the student. The Democratic party went to the depths in 1920, but in 1924, the anti-Republican vote cast for the Democrat, Davis, and the Progressive, La Follette, was a much better share out of the votes than had been achieved in 1920. The trust of the populace in the Republican party was no longer quite so widespread, but it was obvious that the Democrats could not count on a united front against the Republicans and though there was no likelihood of another third party movement in 1928, there was grave doubt if all who had voted for La Follette would again register their distrust of the Eastern control of the Republican party by voting for the Democratic nominee. Yet if Western discontent could not be capitalized, where were the rueful Democrats to get votes? The nomination of Governor Smith provided a new if not totally unexpected answer : in the great urban areas which were growing instead of in the rural areas which were decaying, among the sections of the population which had no emotional fixation on the Republican party, and which could be seduced by appeals to interests, resentments and emotions that the Republicans would find it hard to satisfy. Governor Smith carried the war into Africa and, despite his defeat, he frightened the Republicans very badly, for he showed how vulnerable they had become—he was an Agathocles if not a Scipio.

Governor Smith's success was scored with remarkable uniformity in the cities, or, more exactly, in the cities whose population was largely of " non-Nordic " origin. New York, Jersey City,

67

Boston, Chicago, Detroit, Saint Paul, San Francisco : in Indiana
he ran behind normal party strength in such an " Anglo-Saxon "
county as Delaware—the county whose capital is "Middletown",
but ahead of it in the great city of Indianapolis. The states
he carried outside the faithful remnant of the Solid South,
Rhode Island and Massachusetts, are among the most highly
industrialized and least Anglo-Saxon states in the Union. What
is the significance of this achievement ? It is too early yet to
dogmatize, but if Governor Smith lost heavily on account of
his religion and origin, he undoubtedly gained heavily among
the new immigrants of the great industrial towns, the Italians,
the Jews, the Poles, the French-Canadians who followed the
Irish in the campaign to prove that in America there were to
be no half-citizens, no *perioeci*.

In the South, the ice also began to break, to the profit of
the Republicans. It is so often assumed that a devotion to
Protestantism and Prohibition accounted for the defection of so
many states of the Solid South in 1928 that it has not been
noticed enough what parts of these states broke away from the
old party allegiance. It was not the ignorant superstition-ridden
denizens of the " Hookworm and Bible Belt " who left the
Democratic party in fear of rum and Rome. If this section
had deserted, the Democrats might have lost Mississippi, South
Carolina, perhaps Louisiana, but the states they did lose were
the least backward, least evangelical of all the South : North
Carolina, Texas, Florida, Virginia. And in all these states it
was the cities, in the main, which carried the day for Mr. Hoover.
Even in the states which stayed loyal to the Democratic party
it was the newly industrialized areas which supported Senator
Heflin and the other " Hoovercrats ".

It was the distribution of the new Republican vote that was,
from the party point of view, most encouraging to those who
hoped to see the birth of that long-hoped-for child, a respectable
" Lily White " Republican party in the South. The old sectional interests had long been changing, it was absurd to let
traditions bred in a very different world dictate policy and, to
do the leaders of these sections justice, it very seldom was allowed
to do more than enforce a nominal adherence to the principles
of Calhoun or Jackson. In fact, the areas that went over to
Mr. Hoover in 1928, had been, for decades past, Republican in
all but name. They have become industrialized, and business
in the South, like business everywhere, is Republican at heart
Party associations, historical traditions, made it convenient for
Senator Simmons of North Carolina to call himself a Democrat
but in everything but name he was the ally of the Senators from
Pennsylvania, the incarnations of Republican orthodoxy, as critics

had pointed out with some heat long before the Senator justified their worst suspicions by turning " Hoovercrat ". No doubt, the Senator would still have been sound on white supremacy and careful to call the Civil War, the "War between the States", but no other barriers would have stood between him and his spiritual home. Governor Smith's religion and his liquor policy were as heaven-sent an opportunity to the crypto-Republicans of the South as the Kansas-Nebraska bill had been to the disconsolate Whigs of 1854 whose party had incontinently vanished.

It is true that the break-up of the Solid South had been long overdue in the opinion of the prophets. The Mahone-Riddleberger alliance in Virginia, in the " '80s ", had seemed to some to mark the end of one-party dominance in the Old Dominion. The alarm spread among the possessing classes by the capture of the party machine by demagogues of the Tillman type, seemed to indicate that they would seek a home in the Republican ranks, but the terror of black company was too much for the overthrown gentry. As late as 1926, a leading North Carolina manufacturer, Mr. Charles A. Cannon, had to refuse the Republican nomination for the United States Senate, since he could not desert the White man's party in state politics, no matter how thoroughly he sympathized with the Coolidge régime in national affairs. Yet the forces that rallied against " Fergusonism " in Texas in 1924 and enabled the Republican candidate for governor, Professor George C. Butte, to make so good a showing had more permanently formidable strength behind them than the Ku Klux Klan supplied, for in " Jim " Ferguson they saw a revival of the old agrarian demagogy of "Jim " Hogg, a most unwelcome phenomenon in days when Texas was becoming increasingly hospitable to business. But the opportunity of casting off the traditional yoke seemed to have come in 1928 and the temptation to " rat " must have dazzled even more politicians than those who succumbed to it. What had been done in 1896 for the Border States, might have been done for the wealthier states of the South and the incorrigibly Democratic and poverty-stricken states, like the Federalist states of New England, left to themselves in dignified impotence. If the Solid South had really died, we should have been on the eve of very interesting developments, for without a Solid South there would have been no Democratic party as we know it, and the Republicans need a Democratic party.

For once luck deserted the Republicans and their allies, the " Hoovercrats ". Had the Hoover administration been a success, Senators Simmons and Heflin, and their allies, clerical and lay, with the prestige of having broken the dominance of the official party in the South, might have passed gracefully into the Republican camp, or at least won control of the local nominating machinery. But fate has been against them. The financial smash that befell the United States upset Bishop Cannon's political as much as his speculative plans. The orthodox Democrats who felt themselves betrayed and menaced by the Hoovercrats, laid their plans to punish the rebels at all costs. It did not cost very much, for by the time the primary elections came off in 1930, it was almost fatal to have been a Republican in Kansas, much more to have been a traitor Democrat in the South. The renegades were routed, sound party men came in in their place and a lesson was read to mutineers that it will take a long time to forget. The defeat of Senator Heflin in Alabama by Mr. Bankhead was not of much intrinsic importance except with those sections of the electorate who would see anybody, even the Pope, in the White House rather than a " nigger-loving " Republican. But the defeat of Senator Simmons was a very different matter. A veteran and a master of politics, only the sternest sense of duty or unshakable confidence in the future of Republican-Democracy, or both, could have made him take the risk, and his defeat will scare all but the boldest. Yet it is impossible not to speculate what would have been the result if the Republican administration had continued to shower prosperity on a grateful country. Should we have come to regard Senator Simmons as a forward-looking man and the still faithful adherents of the orthodox Democracy as modern successors of the Democrats in the North who did not get on the Republican band-wagon while there was time, or the Southern politicians like Hugh White, who backed Clay instead of Jackson ?

The earthquake of 1928 was followed, after the premonitory quiverings of 1930, by the even more widespread disturbance of 1932. It seems possible that the old order in American politics, the " line-up " that has lasted since the end of the Civil War, or of Reconstruction, is at last changing and that the time is ripe for a recasting of parties on new lines. The argument against change, that it was attempting the impossible to loosen the hold of party loyalty on the American voter, is far less forceful than it was twelve or even four years ago. The old parties, with their avoidance of issues, their purely historical justification, their incapacity to give or to suffer leadership, have long been an affront to the intelligence of such Americans as still hanker after the comparatively rationalized English system. To Professor Paul Douglas, writing before the recent landslide, it seemed that :

"The Republican party has a definite place and a real function to perform. It represents the conservative element and the propertied classes. There is room for one such party. But there is not room for two." [1]

To President Nicholas Murray Butler, contemplating the fragments of the G.O.P. left after its greatest electoral defeat, the need seems to be for a new party to act as a receiver of both the old parties.

In the face of such an upheaval as that of 1932, prophecy is especially ungrateful, but it seems to be not unlikely that both academic prophets of doom, in reporting the imminent deaths of the old parties, are grossly exaggerating the import of the facts. Both Mr. Douglas and Mr. Butler look forward to parties which shall be national and not sectional ; shall be based on a general policy and not on an accumulation of sectional bargains. There is no immediate sign of their wishes being fulfilled. Despite Mr. Hoover's alarms, Mr. Roosevelt is not the bearer of a new philosophy of American life into the White House. He is a party leader who has up till now devoted a great deal of attention to the primary problem of a party leader in America, the problem of holding together individuals and sections which should naturally fly apart. Whatever groups or individuals inherit the wreckage of the Republican party, will in all probability do everything in their power to avoid rationalizing that party and will attempt to assemble the fragments in the old pattern. They will try to bind together Iowa and Pennsylvania, trusting that the present breach is only a passing misunderstanding. Both parties will be strongly tempted to do everything in their power to admit impediment to that " marriage of true minds " which, to academic outsiders, seems so necessary—and so easy.

Unless all signs are deceptive, there will be no Republican reconstitution of the G.O.P. on a new basis, any more than there was in 1912. The old spells will be given another chance to show their power and if the recent débâcle will be held to have shown anything, it is the folly of letting an amateur take control. The rulers of the routed party are not, it is fairly certain, looking for a new policy, but for a new Harding or, at best, a new and more fortunate Hughes. " You can't teach an Old Guard new tricks " said, in 1919, that astute observer, Mr. Samuel Blythe. The disasters of 1932 have, indeed, removed from the scene such veterans of orthodoxy as Messrs. Moses, Smoot, and Watson, but the survival of the deluge by the faithful states of New England and the unshakable Pennsylvanian veterans is likely to be longer remembered than the triumph of such crypto-Democrats as Senator Norris. If there is a re-alignment, it will not come from

[1] Paul H. Douglas, *The Coming of a New Party* (New York, 1932), p. 195.

the Republicans, although a plausible imitation may be forced on them.   The G.O.P., like the Democrats of 1860, has become too hardened to change even when ordinary prudence demands it.

The initiative is in the hands of the Democrats.   The immense sweep of Mr. Roosevelt's victory conceals the difficulties of decision which are before him, but it will not do so for long. His nomination was a victory for the West and South ; a return to the Wilson alignment if not quite to that of Bryan's hey-day. Yet his victory was far more widely based than his nomination. He held a remarkably large proportion of the Smith gains and more than recovered the Smith losses and the temptation to cater to the East will be very great.   It is only too probable that the western states will fall away again as they have in the past, that the vast inherited assets of the Republican party will tell.   If prosperity, even comparative prosperity returns, the West is as likely to forget its grievances against the G.O.P. as it is to be grateful to the Democrats.   The weakness of the Democratic organization ; the comparative obscurity of its local personnel, the long tradition of tolerated dissent within the Republican party, these will handicap any effort to secure a basis for Democratic supremacy in the West.   If, indeed, a fusion could be managed, with the progressive Republicans playing the part of the Populists in 1896, if the assets of Senator Norris, of the La Follette machine, of the Farmer Labour party, of the Non-Partisan League, could be brought into the Democratic fold, then the future of the party in the West would be brighter, but such an amalgamation would encounter formidable obstacles in the vested interests of the existing Democratic party all over this area and it would mean the end of all hopes of repeating the Republican miracle, of uniting the West and the East.   The Democrats can only dig themselves in, west of the Mississippi, by a policy which will make for them very formidable enemies east of it, enemies such as no American politician will prudently make.   The past sixty years have shown that Wall Street pays its friends and punishes its enemies more efficiently than the farmers do.   The dazzling vision of winning over from the Republicans the allegiance of business is not one to be put lightly on one side, and the con-ditions of such an alliance are sufficiently well known.   To many Democratic leaders, especially to the leaders or allies of the great city machines, the temptations offered by the temporary demoralization of the Republicans are overwhelming.   Why should not the party pin all its hopes on securing the Republican strongholds of the North, passing through the breaches made in 1928 and 1932, keep the South in line and let the West do as she pleases ?   With Massachusetts, Rhode Island, Connecticut, New

York and New Jersey added to the South the game is as good as won. Then the old Eastern control of the party might be reasserted under happier omens. A Democratic party, so based, if it could secure its position, might be a far more formidable competitor of the Republicans, not merely in 1936 but for a generation, than any fragile alliance with those always suspicious and exigent western states who are so easily cajoled into the Republican fold. Such a plan of campaign involves a serious risk. The Democratic candidate who can hold the East must beware of catering to agrarian grievances as well as to agrarian morals. This means that the attack on the tariff and the trusts, which was a stand-by of Democratic orators in the past, will have to be abandoned. The great magnates of the financial world, the great rulers of industry, and the multitudes who still follow them, will have to be told that a Democrat will not do anything to upset the economic apple-cart, or will not allow anyone to put it on its wheels again—by unorthodox means. The Republicans, already shorn of their reputation as the party of the " full dinner pail ", must not be allowed to rally their shaken ranks by a return to the methods of 1896. With the prestige of power, a prestige to which business is always suscept- ible, it might be possible for a Democratic administration to make terms with business, to avoid all radicalism and put off the West with patent remedies of the standard Republican kind. Such a policy undoubtedly has friends among leading Democrats. On the other hand, there is the terrible example of Grover Cleveland to show that the fighting force of the Democracy is not to be won over to this policy and that there is a limit to the power of party discipline. There is always the possibility of a new Bryan. The risk might be run, if it were at all certain that the East could be won from its adherence to the Republicans. There is, as yet, no sign that the business world and all it still stands for has been convinced that it may have been mistaken, that Codlin's the friend, not Short.

Despite the size of his majorities in the industrial states, in New York, in Massachusetts, in Illinois, Mr. Roosevelt and his party have not bitten into the areas which control so much of the Republican machine in the East. To carry Allegheny County, which a few short years ago was the Mellon fief ; to run Mr. Hoover close in Philadelphia, to carry New Jersey, these triumphs may suggest an eastern conversion, but they are mis- leading. Mr. Roosevelt could not carry his own county (Dutchess) in up-state New York. In 1930 he carried the state outside the metropolis, but in this presidential year, although he had to face the weakest Republican candidate since Taft, he was badly beaten outside the city. In Massachusetts, neither he nor Governor Ely could raise the Democratic congressional strength to more than five against ten Republicans. So it was all over the East. The rural counties, stronghold of the Republican state machines, went down with their flags flying and nowhere east of the Alleghanies, perhaps east of the Mississippi, are the Democratic gains of the kind a prudent party-builder would use for a foundation. The East has not yet been won and its rulers will have to be shown that the new agency of their political needs is as reliable as the old firm that has never failed its owners.

Even if there were more substantial hopes of winning the East, the bias of the Roosevelt administration is to the West. It is probable, indeed, that the West is more open to conviction than the East, that the depression has finally disillusioned it and that what Lincoln called " the mystic chords of memory " are no longer as powerful in stimulating party loyalty as they used to be. Even in American politics, "there are no names with whatever emphasis of passionate love repeated of which the echo is not faint at last" and the spell cast by the Republican name may have been broken finally. The West may, then, be won, but that will not necessarily mean a new lease of life for the Democrats in 1936 if the new administration has given real hostages to the embattled farmers. It is not merely that Big Business will be alienated, for it has not been won, but the Democratic organization in the East will be hostile or lukewarm as it was in Bryan's time.

An organization of the farmers and workers on a class basis, instead of the existing sectional basis, is essential to any plans for putting the Democrats into the position of the Republicans as the regular majority party. Only by a return to the policy of Andrew Jackson will it be possible to undo the work of Lincoln and his heirs and assigns. Otherwise the Democrats will have to launch themselves on the perilous sea of choice between a western and eastern alignment, between allying the South with one of two untrustworthy sections. This is not an heroic policy, but it is a natural one, since it postpones the decision as long as possible.

Why should the Democrats hesitate to make themselves into a Farmer-Labour party on the lines laid down by Professor Douglas ? Because of the dangers inherent in such a step, for not only are the political obstacles great, but the existence of a practicable common programme doubtful. A thorough overhaul of the economic life of the country might provide a basis, but tinkering readjustments of the distribution of the dividend, which is the natural method of American politics, may well fail to find a common ground between the industrial worker and the farmer and so fail to prevent sectional splits, fostered by the vigilant powers of business controlling the Republican party. Old-fashioned politicians in both parties, but more especially in the Democratic party, for it has the choice, may well cling to their old-fashioned but workable fallacies, on the grounds attributed to the English Broad Churchmen by Mr. Birrell. " Why should they sell out of a still going and dividend-paying concern when they have not the faintest idea where to look for another investment for their money ? "

The choice, then, will in all probability be merely a sectional one between an eastern or a western bias and a western bias will come more easily to the Democrats than will an eastern which may not, in fact, be open to them. Short of making some such choice there will be nothing left to do but watch the attrition of the present majority and the recovery of its old authority by the Republican party. If the Democrats wish to dig themselves in, they will have to choose, even though the risks of choice will be great. " Under which king, Bezonian, speak or die." Yet it may be that the natural hopes formed by Democrats after the great triumphs of 1932 are not fallacious. It may be that there is no danger of Mr. Roosevelt being Cleveland over again, since Mr. Hoover may have proven the Cleveland or even the Buchanan of his party. Time alone can tell. It may also be true that all these party calculations are irrelevant, for if American society, and with it, the political system, are on the verge of fundamental change, the argument is raised to a higher plane where we cannot follow it, but short of such a revolution, the American people will have to put up with badly cemented and sectional parties. The weaknesses of the system and its lack of intellectual elegance will irritate or amuse the observer according to temperament, but in either case they will have to be borne, for men, as Bolingbroke pointed out two hundred years ago, " are to take their lot, perhaps in governments as in climates, to fence against the inconveniences of both, and to bear what they cannot alter ".

Chapter IV

PARTY SECTIONS AND THE DIRECT PRIMARY

A S has been shown, American parties are historical, sectional and non-doctrinal, and these truths must be borne in mind in any consideration of the future of the parties, for the service that the party performs in the political life of the nation is to arrange for the election of the public officials. A party which can elect its " ticket ", need not bother on what grounds it elects or for what general purpose ; to put its nominees in office is, for the American party, its final cause. In the Solid South, the Democratic nominees are always certain of victory [1] and over the rest of the Union, the Republicans can, in most areas, count their victory assured in normal times. It must not be assumed that this means that almost all American constituencies are " safe seats " of the type that we are accustomed to in England. There are, for example, " silk stocking " districts, which are as safely anchored to the party of respectability and prosperity, that is to the Republicans, as Bournemouth is to the Conservatives, and for the same reasons. In Britain an alteration in the social complexion of a constituency ; the degeneration of what was a suburb into a slum or an alteration in the electoral laws, may change the party strengths of a division without any conversion of voters. The Central division of Glasgow, for instance, was a safe Conservative seat as long as " plural voting " flourished and the electoral lists were barred to many a poor man. From the moment the Conservatives with a " business vote " were limited and the number of resident voters was increased, the division was no longer a forlorn hope for the Labour party. In America corresponding changes take place and a congressional district may change its social level very rapidly. Such a change has important political results, but only *within the party*. Except in cities where the Democrats represent a different social stratum from the Republicans, such changes have no effect on party strength. In Philadelphia, for instance, they might increase the strength

---

[1] The split in the South only affected the presidential election, though there have been occasional local victories in Virginia, Texas, and Tennessee.

of the machine, but the district would remain Republican all the same.

In the United States, party uniformity operates regardless of class or social views or prejudices, and, in most states, the party label covers the whole political gamut and the Democratic party in Georgia or the Republican party in Pennsylvania, is simply the whole body of the active citizens of the state. One consequence of this system is that the real election is that which gives the nomination, and the right to the party name to one out of the aspirants to the majority party's endorsement. That acquired, the election is over, except for the formalities. Knowing that over most of the Union, the electorate will vote for anybody who bears the locally dominant trademark, the real triumph is achieved when the nomination is gained, and the real contest is for the control of the nominating machinery.

Under the old system it was decided in the party Convention what persons should be the party candidates for office, what principles they should profess to hold, what measures they should promise to further. To the Convention, or the party meeting, were sent delegates chosen by the members of the party in elections called primary elections, and the choice made by these delegates was supposed to be binding in honour or morals on those who had taken part in the primary. The more complete the union of a state in its devotion to the fortunately vague principles of one party, the wider was the range of opinion represented by that party, and the more varied the sections striving for mastery in the Convention. There were certain doctrines that one could hardly profess in Pennsylvania and remain a Republican, the view that a tariff could not be too high was a shibboleth there, but as every voter in Pennsylvania, Democrat as well as Republican, was of this opinion, the issue did not debar one from active participation in the life of the dominant party. With that qualification, anybody could be a good Republican and in that great state the same party enfolds both the equivalent of Mr. Churchill and of Mr. David Kirkwood. In a state like North Carolina, it is merely necessary to believe in " white supremacy " and that shibboleth once convincingly bellowed, all liberty of political activity is permitted. It is true that within the dominant party some opinions are stronger than others, but circumstances alter cases, and if the Democratic party has held that a high tariff is robbery, it can change its mind and hold that a high tariff is excellent without ceasing to be the Democratic party. The erstwhile minority has become the majority, the former minority can continue to hold its old views and to vote for those who hold the opposite opinions.

From the often demonstrated fact that the great majority of Americans vote for a party name, has arisen the necessity and justification of the elaborate public regulation of all the inner life and organization of bodies, which, in other countries, are assumed to be essentially unofficial and controllable by their own members without any outside interference. However awkward in theory, the American custom is, in practice, just and necessary.

Some of the difficulties of American political life arise from the lack of the conspicuous leadership that is given to the controllers of political parties in parliamentary governments. The leader of a party in the House of Commons is marked out, by that alone, as the chief owner of the party's assets. No such automatic designation has been possible in American politics since the Jacksonian revolution. The Convention was, in theory, a parliament elected to choose the party leaders and draw up the party programme. But in normal times, few were interested in the choice of party nominees, except those who had their own ambitions to further, and still fewer had any interest in concocting the farrago of platitudes and reminiscences that was the official " platform ". Few troubled to vote in the election of delegates, and the smaller the number who troubled to vote, the more professional the voting class in the primary became. Moreover, while election frauds were far from uncommon in the formal elections, they were more flagrant and successful in the primaries, and thieves stick together better than honest men, so that the few disinterested or high-principled delegates were often unseated, if they had by any means managed to run the gauntlet so far. Once nominated, the candidates were entitled, by the political moral code of the times, to unquestioning support from the party members, and usually they could command it. Especially outrageous conduct, more intolerable nominations than usual, might provoke disgust strong enough to bring party members to the point of " bolting ", but, as has been explained, the hold of American party loyalties is very deep and revolts were rare and short-lived. Moreover, the remedy was often as bad as the disease, for the opposite party was only too likely to be run in the same way. As long as he kept control of the voting machinery in the party primary, a " boss " was secure. Bolts to the enemy, third parties, or independent candidates, troubled him little ; they were annoying but ephemeral. The threats of the rebels which were aimed only at his control of the state or city mattered little ; as long as he could keep the right of using the party name and of denying it to others, he could afford to wait and an American party leader, like Browning's cardinal, knew that his enthusiastic enemies could be crushed or bought. He, too, had known four-and-twenty leaders of revolt.

These truths were perceived by the reformers, and the modern primary system is an attempt to get round this obstacle to the free and uncorrupt expression of the popular will. Taking it for granted that the majority of the electorate would follow their party blindly, the reformers set about transferring the immensely valuable asset of the party trade-mark from the hands of a few into those of the rank and file of the party. They strove, originally, to purify the Convention system. The next step was to destroy, or control, the action of the Convention. A half-way house reform was the advisory primary in which delegates to the Convention were instructed by their electors what candidate they were expected to support. The direct primary was the next logical step and it has conquered almost all the states in the Union.

The direct primary in its pure form destroys the nominating power of the party Convention. Candidates for office no longer appeal to the delegates of the party, but to the enrolled membership of the party, and the candidate who tops the poll is thereby the official nominee of the party, and will appear as such on the ballot papers of the official election. It is obvious that this system creates a great many difficulties, and the variations of method in use in various states show that the sponsors of this system have recognized the existence of these difficulties. First of all, the direct primary accentuates the domination of states by one party. The minority party could, in the old days, keep alive by hoping for disagreement in the ranks of the dominant party. Under the direct primary the party vote of the majority party is, theoretically, at least, always concentrated on the successful candidate and no such excuse is given for bolting as was occasionally given in the old days. It is true that the sections within the majority party are not quite so easily destroyed, but they tend more and more to keep their quarrels within the party, and to devote their attention wholly to the primary. This practically stops recruiting for the minority party. Why join a party whose vote is, on all but the most unusual occasions, thrown away, when you can, by joining the majority party, have a voice in the election which really determines the policies and the offices ? As American parties are merely historical combinations, there is no doctrinal barrier to keep out recruits so minded and in a normal year in states like Wisconsin and Pennsylvania, the Democratic party almost disappeared. A few faithful devotees of various family idols or a few forlorn federal office seekers remain, but the real opposition to the dominant party is transferred to the direct primary. The second

official election is purely formal. From one point of view this
is a great gain. There have long ceased to be any real issues
dividing Republican from Democrat in most states, and the
direct primary has restored real political contests to many states
by excising the old sore of historical loyalties to dead and irrelevant causes, and like-minded men are no longer kept from
working effectively together because their grandfathers had
different views on the Kansas-Nebraska bill of 1854. Especially
valuable has been the effect of the direct primary in the South.
As the South was unbreakably solid, issues could only be
smothered or settled by various subterfuges, or produce great
upheavals such as accompanied the rise of the new Southern
demagogues of the type of Tillman and Watson. With the
coming of the direct primary, a regular political life was opened
to the people of the former Confederate states. All the white
population was Democratic, the terms Democrat and voter were,
for all practical purposes, interchangeable. It was a gain, then,
when this could be taken as read, when an ordinary election
could be held on local and, on the rare occasions when there
were any, on national issues, that the people could choose men,
or a policy, and the resulting man or policy, was the formal
choice of the Democratic party. To go through with the legal
forms, the final election must be attended by enough voters to
vote down the few white Republicans who dared to appear at
the polls, and with this harmless ceremony over, the will of the
people was done with as little intrusion of irrelevant issues as
possible.

But not all states are Georgias. There are states where the
margin of the majority party has been sufficiently narrow for
the direct primary to breed new difficulties for the reformer.
It is not unheard of for members of one party to enter the
primaries of the other, not as in Wisconsin, from despair of
having any political weight otherwise, but in order to impose
a particular candidate on the opposition. If his own party is
helpless a voter does as the Wisconsin Democrat normally does,
votes for that section of the dominant party which is closest to his
point of view. This is legitimate enough, as otherwise he would
have no voice in the government of his state or city at all.
Rather different is the case of the man who votes in the rival
party's primary to impose on that party a candidate with whom
he has no sympathy, but whose nomination he thinks will help
his own party's candidate in the final election. This game has
attractions for the less scrupulous partisan, but fortunately for
American politics, it is too dangerous to be played often, for
the electorate is like the peace of God, in that its ways pass all
understanding. Thus it is believed that some Democrats helped

to "wish" Mr. William Hale Thompson on the Republican party of Chicago, as an aid to the return of their own candidate, and learned to their horror, that in picking "Big Bill", they had all unwittingly picked a winner.

The last stage of this process is reached when one party so dominates the other that it nominates the candidates of both. Enough of the superfluous voters of the majority party are sent into the primaries of the minority party to swamp it. They nominate anyone they choose, either a farcical candidate or the same candidate as the majority has chosen, and the unfortunate victims are helpless. Sometimes this is done in mere boyish high spirits, but it has its practical advantages. It prevents any last-minute revolt of the discontented section of the majority party. They have no real opposition party to vote for, and the bonds of party discipline are thus strengthened. A last refinement of this method is reached when the majority party enrols in the minority party and not merely nominates, but elects the candidates of this party to office. These office-holders are at heart members of the opposition party, all power is kept in the hands of the rulers of the real majority, and the genuine party members are completely disfranchised. This refinement is rare as, in most cases, it is pointless. Why be elected as Republicans when you can win as Democrats? Yet there are local circumstances which may make this little comedy profitable and there are areas whose odd variations in local politics and equally permanent stability in state and national elections is attributed to an elegant mastery of the machinery of the primaries of both parties by one group.

To the old-fashioned party man, the primary has always been abhorrent. The thought of Democrats having a voice in the choice of the Republican candidates is blasphemous and the consequent decay in local elections, of the old historical party feeling, is to him an irreparable loss, for if that goes what is there to put in its place? Various devices have been adopted to prevent such contamination of the true text of party opinion, but none of them have worked very well. In Wisconsin, the primary is "open", that is to say, every voter is given the primary lists of every party, and decides which he will use. As a rule, almost everyone uses the Republican ballot and the last vestige of party regularity is gone. Most states, however, try to guard against this, by some form of "closed" primary. In this, an attempt is made to ensure that the voter is a member of the party in whose primary he has offered to vote. Sometimes he has to swear, if challenged, that he has supported the party in the past for a certain time, or will support it in the future at this election, or at several elections to come. There are two objections to this method. One is that the challenged voter may perjure himself, the other that it does not matter in many cases for whom he votes in the final election.

American ingenuity has not been baffled, however, and the last device of the " non-partisan primary " has been tried. In this, the candidates for all parties are chosen at the same primary, all voters are entitled to cast ballots in this election and the top candidates then fight it out among themselves, without any distinguishing party marks. This reform does away with the objections to the open and to the closed primary. Since there are now no party labels there is no temptation to hoist false colours. It had another consequence which might have been foreseen. The object of the primary was to deprive private persons of the right to issue to candidates the valuable certificate of party regularity. The direct primary did this by making all party lines meaningless and in many cases by reducing two parties to one. But the party label is, in itself, useful only if there is another less valuable party label to contrast it with. The Democratic label, as such, has next to no value in Pennsylvania. To be the Republican candidate for Governor of Pennsylvania is to be Governor-Elect of Pennsylvania. The Democratic candidate for Governor of Texas is Governor-Elect of Texas. But there are still parties and election machines, they can be called after men or they can take descriptive titles, but even in an enlightened state like Wisconsin, a candidate is often chosen, not on his own merits or on his own programme, but because he is part of a team and his orthodoxy is vouched for by a trusted individual or by a group or by an assembly of people who are believed to be the depositories of a special view or tradition of state policy. This tradition and its owners the rank and file take on trust, whether because they have decided to trust these men, or their fathers had decided to trust their fathers.

For a time it seemed that political tradition in Wisconsin was hardening round the memory of the late Senator La Follette ; that whichever candidate was the most plausible representative of his cause would win any election in that state ; that the opposition would be as feeble within the Republican party as the Democrats were outside it. The Democrats seemed to have withered away and the conservative Republicans to be imitating them. This would not, of course, abolish parties and divisions, it would merely transfer them into the La Follette-Progressive-Republican party of Wisconsin. The sudden revival of the Democratic party in the state, not to speak of the personal following developed by Governor Kohler, the leader of the conservative Republicans, has postponed such a development, but it has not made it impossible. It is necessary to postpone prophecy until the viability of the Democratic party in the state has been tested, but it is not inconceivable that the evolution of politics in Wisconsin and perhaps in other states is to reducing the first primary, as it has already often reduced the formal election, to a quaint and meaningless survival of once living forms, like the *congé d'élire* of an English cathedral chapter ! [1]

This peep into the future may be fanciful, but it is evident that the primary, especially the " non-partisan " brand, leave matters very much where they stood before there was any regulation of the primaries at all. If the primary is made really non-partisan, all the preliminary organization must be done in advance, if there is to be any party regularity at all, if there is not to be a mere agglomeration of groups. Thus the last state of the American electorate may be no better than the first, or even worse, for the whole business of putting forward a party list is now done without any public regulation. The more enthusiastic exponents of the primary thought they could have their cake and eat it, could maintain party loyalty and destroy party machinery. They have destroyed both, and are not always able to think of an answer to the attacks of the conservatives who assail the direct primary as the destroyer of party unity, the breeder of a group system and the weakener of personal and party responsibility.

With a prudent disregard of the original character of the primary, the American legislator in some states has adapted it to its new character. To get on the primary ballot may be as useful as was the straight party nomination in the old Convention days, and in some states the party holds a pre-primary Convention and decides what names shall go on the primary ballot. More names than one go on and usually a certain proportion of the vote at the Convention entitles the recipient to go on the ballot, so that the Convention nomination is no longer so exclusive as it was, but it is an odd turn of the wheel of fortune that the further the primary system goes, the nearer one gets to the old Convention system. In states where party lines are blurring it is an advantage to get on the party primary, comparable, if not yet quite equal, to the old party nomination, and it has been provided to remedy any abuse of this advantage, that a candidate defeated at a Convention may get on the primary list by petition and if defeated in the primary may run as an independent.   But

---

[1] In England, the right to elect bishops is nominally in the hands of the canons of the cathedral. When a vacancy occurs, the chapter receives a royal letter giving leave to elect (*congé d'élire*) and also the name of the man to be elected. The election of Senators by a state legislature, bound to follow the results of a primary election, before the adoption of the seventeenth amendment, was, of course, a perfect example of a *congé d'élire*.

as one could always run as an independent, wherein lies the advantage of the primary system except that it multiplies the number of possible elections ?   As far as the mechanics of voting go there is none, but, in fact, the increasing exclusion of national party issues and national party loyalties from local elections, is helped by the increasingly meaningless character given to the party label.   When one remembers the weight attached to irrelevant issues in the past this is a local gain, though it may be a national loss.

In the South, and in a few northern states, the primary being usually decisive, steps were taken to prevent a minority candidate securing the nomination.   Though Americans attach less importance to the absolute majority than do the French, they attach much more to it than we do.   They are always careful to distinguish between a majority, that is a majority of all the votes cast, and a plurality, which is merely the accumulation of more votes than any other candidate.   In Texas, for instance, it is provided that if no candidate has a majority in the election, there must be a " run-off " which enables the electors to decide between the two highest candidates.   This is in many cases a desirable proceeding as it prevents a closely organized minority from overriding a loosely knit majority.   Thus, in a state like Texas there may be three official elections, a primary, a " run-off ", and a formal election.   In a state like Wisconsin, it has been doubtful at times whether it would pay the dissident Republicans better to continue their struggle with the La Follette machine in the Republican primaries, or to run as independents in the final election.   It would obviously make the primary system healthier if the latter course were uniformly adopted, for it would then express the truth that the old parties had disappeared.

A purely party primary may impose a candidate who is, perhaps narrowly, the strongest within the party ranks, but who has little if any power to win necessary outside support.   The Republican party in Illinois and in New York City and the Democratic party in Chicago have, in recent times, had fundamentally weak candidates imposed on them by strong sections within the party working through the primary.   The same sad story can be told of other states and a "run-off" lessens this danger.

Under cover of the old parties, new sectional parties are forming, and the apparent anomalies of the system should not blind us to its real coherence.   In 1924, for example, the senior Republican Senator for Wisconsin, Robert La Follette, Sr., ran for President with the junior Democratic Senator for Montana, Burton M. Wheeler, as running mate.   All over the West the electors voted for or against the Republican régime and the dissidents who normally would protest against Wall Street by voting for a Bryanite Democrat, voted for the mixed Progressive team. Enough of the old party loyalties remained in national elections to defeat the movement in every state, except Wisconsin, but the normal western Domocratic vote was almost entirely cast for the Progressive, for the normal Democratic vote, as far as it represents a political policy, is, all through the West, a Bryanite vote. But the western radical feeling more and more abandons any trust in the traditional party lines in state, and even in national politics ; Senator Wheeler, in Montana, could not be driven out of the Democratic party because he had run against the official ticket in 1924. As for the Wisconsin " Progressive " Republicans, they have long seceded from any party but the La Follette family. In 1928, the successor of Senator La Follette in the leadership of the "progressive bloc" in the Senate, Senator George W. Norris, of Nebraska, displayed his sense of reality by coming out for Governor Smith against his party's nominee, Mr. Hoover. The Republican party displayed the same zeal to punish him as the Democrats did to punish Senator Simmons, but they could no longer count on the enrolled Republicans of Nebraska, so after an ingenious attempt to befog the issue, they incited their supporters to rally behind the Democrats. They failed, the state elected Senator Norris and a Democrat, Mr. Charles Bryan, as Governor. This was not an example of voters adhering to one party in state and to another in national politics, but of the same party, if by party we mean people of the same mind in politics, carrying both state and federal election. The same drift of voters in the West away from nominal party moorings has been illustrated in other states by the careers of less formidable " independents " than Senator Norris, in states where the nominal opposition, the Democrats, had not the nucleus of support they owe in Nebraska to the potent memory of the state's most famous "favourite son", William Jennings Bryan. The outlines of a sectional party, or of a real doctrinal cleavage within the parties in western states, are already drawn and every election, since the western revolt of 1924, has shown that the La Follette revolt, however ill-timed and however inept its party strategy, represented a political force that the old parties cannot neglect. In this movement of opinion, the orthodox Republicans are inevitably the sufferers, for they have the assets of tradition which attract covetous raiders and they cannot, without a fundamental breach with the owners of the party, really cater convincingly to western grievances. So it happens that their defeats are striking and their victories barren.

In the disastrous year of 1932, the hearts of the Republicans were cheered by the defeat in the Wisconsin primaries of the progressive candidates, Mr. Philip La Follette and Mr. John J. Blaine ; to the more superficial observers it seemed that Wisconsin had tired of her radicalism and was returning to its allegiance to the dominant section of the Republican party. Calmer observers noted, instead, the sudden revival of the Democrats in the state ; the very impressive total of votes cast in the primaries of that party, long deemed moribund in Wisconsin. A large number of voters had returned to their old party allegiance and, in the final election, which for once was no formality, the electors of Wisconsin demonstrated their permanent hostility to the national rulers of the Republican party by going Democratic by a sweeping majority.

Such results illustrate both the usefulness of the primary in separating national from state issues and its meaninglessness as a test of party affiliation. It is the last which rouses old-school politicians to fury. Obviously, the Blaine supporters who were beaten in the Republican senatorial primary in Wisconsin did not support the party nominee ; they voted for the Democrat in the final election. Yet in this demonstration of party disloyalty, they were following good conservative example. In 1924, Iowa, permanently with a grievance, elected Smith L. Brookhart to the Senate. The election was contested, and the Senate, which had a nominal Republican majority, seated the Democrat, Daniel Steck. 1924 was a presidential year when party loyalties are revived even in western breasts, but it is certain that there were many Republicans who felt that, by voting for Mr. Steck, they were annoying their chief, President Coolidge, a good deal less than they were by electing Senator Brookhart. On the other hand, many of the old Bryan Democrats, seeing no reason for following a nominal Democrat like Mr. Steck into what was, for all practical purposes, the " regular " Republican camp, supported Senator La Follette for President instead of Mr. Davis and, tacitly, Mr. Brookhart for the Senate.

The action of the Senate forced Mr. Brookhart to wait till 1926 to take his revenge on his enemies within his party by defeating the once radical, but now tamed, Senator Cummins in the Republican primary. At this point the conservative Republicans gave up the game and accepted the fact that, for the time being, the Republican party in Iowa was quite different from the Republican party in the East. The Democrats again attempted to win the conservative Republicans, but as this was not a presidential year they failed, and Brookhart was elected. In the meantime, the real meaning of Mr. Steck's election as a Democrat in a year of great Republican triumphs was underlined by his defeat in 1930 in a year of Democratic victories. Two years later, Senator Brookhart was beaten, like Senator

Blaine, in the Republican primaries, but ran as an Independent —and the Democratic candidate carried the final election !

Because of the primary, the economic discontent of the farming states has been enabled to have free political expression and all over the West the Republican party has gone radical. Both sets of Republicans have used the primary to their own ends ; neither when pressed sticks to its nominal party allegiance. Faced by this change, the controllers of the Republican party in the East have abandoned all pretence of party loyalty to their western colleagues who, in turn, have supported the national ticket very lukewarmly, if at all, and have at times had occasion to regret even their lip-service.

When it was discovered that an agent of the National Republican Committee had been attempting to defeat Senator George W. Norris in the Nebraska primary of 1930, there was much indignation at this treachery, but even if the methods employed were foolish there was something to be said for the zealous Mr. Lucas. If his diagnosis of the party situation in Nebraska was correct, if " more Republicans voted for Hitchcock than for Norris " and " practically all of the Democrats in the state voted for Norris ", and if a leading Republican Senator, like Mr. Norris, could with impunity support the Democratic candidate for President, was Mr. Lucas far wrong in asserting that this state of affairs was " bound to, in the end, tear down our two-party system " ? [1] If we think of American parties as we think of English parties, as based on common opinions, Mr. Lucas was, of course, right.

What is there to be said for a system that produces such complications ? Only this, that it is necessary and inevitable. Two-party systems are rare ; they require an artificial unity that clear-minded nations find it difficult to command. There are so few issues or groups of issues that hang together, round which parties can group themselves. This is true even of small and comparatively homogeneous countries. Much more is it true of a half-continent like the United States. By the working of the federal system a vast number of conveniently controversial issues are removed from national power, the residuum is usually made up of economic questions and economic questions of a kind that excite cupidity or alarm, rather than heart-warming or lung-filling sentiments. Moreover, the economic causes are necessarily sectional as they would be in Europe. In taxation, the interests of sections are, or are believed to be, different, there is normally no common ground of " principle " on which a party can fight. As Bryce pointed out, forty years ago, the issues that kept English

[1] *Nye Committee Hearings (Nebraska),* pp. 864–5.

politics alive and " political " were all over and done with in America by 1850. The Democrats all over the Union had abolished religious tests, disestablished state churches, equalized the franchise, redistributed the seats, made militia service optional, reformed the state constitutions in the direction of democracy, overthrown aristocracy of wealth, religion, birth, at any rate as far as any purely political measures could do it. Once this had been achieved, the party had no national issue to use, it became sectional and traditional and collapsed.

The Republican party has never been national, even in theory. It was in origin definitely sectional, its official programme was simply that of forcing one section, the slave states, to accept another and more powerful section's views on the use of the national domain. Since then, there had been only one chance of a national party, that is, the forming in 1892–6 of a party of the poor against the rich. If Bryan had managed to unite both the farmers and the town proletariat, if he had won his election, it is conceivable that we should have had two parties, but only if a true alliance of interests and hates had been formed between the less successful everywhere, that is, if it had been possible to revive the driving power of the Jacksonian Revolution in a new Bryan Democracy. The Republican, which professes to be a party of all classes, an honest broker between all Northern sections, cannot be a fighting party for that very reason, for a national party assumes that there is a common enemy and the Republican party, except for the brief period when it was forced by Bryan to show its colours, has had no convincing common enemy since Jefferson Davis. In this America is much less unlike other countries than we imagine. The English Liberal party has been in hot water ever since it accomplished its political objects. It was no accident that the " unauthorized programme " and Home Rule came when the Third Reform Act (1884) had exhausted the mandate of the old purely political party.

Why, then, should the United States not have, as we have, class parties ? There are answers to this question that are outside the scope of this book, but it has some which can be given without involving any profound analysis of American economic life. Why should it be much easier to build up a class party in America than it has been to build up effective international unions in Europe ? When Polish miners effectively unite with the British miners, when shipbuilders of Sampier d'Arena lament the cessation of work in Clydebank, it will be time enough to reproach Americans for not having effectively organized the soft coal and anthracite mining fields or the cotton workers of Massachusetts and North Carolina in one united band of brothers.

The difficulties in America are not so great in degree, but they are of the same kind.

Nor is it necessary to compare Europe with the United States. Has the British Labour party really got round the problem of winning over the agricultural labourer, much more the farmer? Is it certain that the growth of government interference with industry and the consequent sectional differentiation between the exporting and the home market areas may not do very serious damage to the present degree of party unity, and that, with all the pressure of the parliamentary system, the high degree of centralization of political leadership and the living tradition of real party unity pulling the other way, in vain?

In other countries the existence of the multi-party system shows that the difficulty has not been even nominally surmounted. What is the really uniform line-up of the French parties to-day, what stirs up the "stagnant pools" of the constituencies? A question which is at least as old as the Revolution, the Civil Constitution of the Clergy. What has the French Left done for an "issue" since the Laws of Separation and the dissolution of the religious orders? What did it do in 1924 when it tried to hold together after the great victory of the "Cartel des Gauches"? It revived the religious war or the memories of it. What does the French Right do, since it learned that the defence of the Church no longer pays? It revives the memories of the German war. As long as politics are just politics, it is the fear of Rome and the fear of Berlin that strive for the mastery in France.

It can be argued, indeed, that France has the direct primary for the same reasons that America has it. What is the first ballot in a French election but the primary which decides which of the Left candidates shall go forward to fight reaction? The same working of minds and methods was displayed in the German presidential election of 1924, when at the second election, the candidates were reduced to Chancellor Marx for the Left, Field-Marshal von Hindenburg for the Right. The first election was an open primary. It is also obvious that one of the motives behind the insistence of English Liberals on the alternative vote is the belief that the "progressive parties" have, over a great part of the country, a natural majority, hence the demand for the alternative vote which is a primary and final election in one.

The argument from Germany need hardly be pressed; what is the Centre party with its recruiting field ranging from quasi-Communists to "crypto-Nazis", with leaders whose background runs from Arembergs and Furstenbergs to Stegerwalds and Erzbergers? The Republican party is no more heterogeneous than that. All over Europe, we find the same difficulties of uniting parties merely on political or economic grounds even in small countries and more parties than would confess it, are as simply based as that candid Dutch agglomeration that calls itself " the Christian Historical Party ".

Nor are the dominions much better. Need we dwell on the racial basis of parties in South Africa, on the false bottom of the Canadian Liberal party, which has to unite Quebec and Saskatchewan in common loyalty to incompatible policies and ideals, or the Conservative party that must remember the Battle of the Boyne in Ontario, and try to make the electors forget conscription in Quebec ?

In Australia, we have class parties indeed, but should Australia's staple export industries fail to support the inflated industrial system, what would happen to party unity ? Western Australia suggests an answer that might have been given long ago, if the pastoralists had had political power comparable to their economic importance. It remains to be proved that democratic party organization is, in fact, capable of carrying through a fundamental political programme, whether the discipline of parties will stand that disregard of local loyalties and local interests that such a policy would involve. Till that question is settled, till we are sure that there is any room in a democratic state for a real class party, or for any party that does not depend on some convenient least common denominator of prejudice and passion, it will be too soon to attack the American party system for its remarkable artificiality. It must be artificial or cease to be national, and the political fiction of the existence of two " national " parties is the price that the American people has to pay for certain very real tangible benefits, notably for being the United States and not another South America. For the unity of the American republic has had to be purchased at a great price, both parties to the bargain have had to make compromises disastrous to intellectual integrity. States have had to pretend to unity in dead or irrelevant matters with states and sections from whom their immediate interests and passions would naturally divide them. The nation has to see its nominally united legislature act, not in the interests of the whole, but in those of dominant sections; and if that can be said of other countries as well, in America it has a deeper meaning, for the interests of the whole get hardly even lip service and there are times when only the minimum of party unity is observed. It is possible that if Congress *had* to provide a national Government it would do so, as the Canadian House of Commons does, but with the American constitution what it is, Congress cannot do this and has long ceased trying. The burden is thrown on the electorate which is in itself incapable of harmonizing the very different interests in reality, so the parties exist, as national bodies, to harmonize them by fiction. It is, if not a noble, a most important task, and the American people has never shown its power of working the unworkable to better advantage than it has in its devotion to its two artificial parties which provide the minimum basis of unity, and in the skill with which it has reduced those parties to nothing in many of the states, without seriously damaging their usefulness in the nation. That usefulness—and it is a sufficient ground for their existence—is that they make possible a fairly national election of the President of the United States.

PART THREE

ILLUSTRATIONS OF SECTIONALISM

For the ashes of his fathers
And the temples of his Gods.
MACAULAY.

Chapter I

ECONOMIC SECTIONALISM

THE United States stretch three thousand miles from
east to west and sixteen hundred miles from north
to south ; one part of the Union may have a tem-
perature of 60° while another is enduring zero weather—or
even weather far below zero. One half of the country has a
climate and agricultural resources like those of central Europe,
the other half has the climate of a more arid Spain—with winter
cold unknown even in Castile. Over an area as great as Europe
are scattered mineral resources whose presence and distribution
dominates the economic life of vast regions. It is, then, inevitable that there should be marked economic differences between
various parts of the Union and that such differences should have
great social and political consequences.

The area now comprised within the territory of the United
States has been ruled, in the past, by England, France, Spain,
Mexico, Russia, Holland, Sweden. Over a land destined by
nature to great economic diversity has poured a flood of men
and women of differing languages, religions, ideals. To expect
such a people to be united, in the sense that France or England
or even Germany is united, would be absurd. Hardly any
degree of diversity would be surprising ; what is astounding is
the degree of unity that has been attained. The Americans are
one people ; they are more like each other than they are like
any European people, but their surface uniformity conceals
internal fissures that do not, indeed, go as deep as might be
feared, but which do produce cracks in the social and political
structure, cracks whose political aspects will be sketched in these
chapters.

Part of the political sectionalism which is so marked in

93

America is due to immediate political causes such as the separation of powers and judicial review that are in their origin accidental, though they have now acquired some of the dignity of
natural phenomena. Part of the sectionalism is due to the
comparative absence of outside pressure ; it is a luxury that an
isolated people can permit itself ; part is due to the comparative youth of the nation, a youth that not only weakens the
prescriptive appeal of institutions but encourages, as a useful
virtue, an aggressive local loyalty that survives its practical
justification. To aid one's state or city to add a cubit to its
stature is an act of loyalty to one's neighbours who are committed to its fortunes. To this common end, all means are
legitimate, notably all political means, and the action or inaction
of the government is too obvious, too recent, and too potent a
force in economic and social progress, for Americans to adopt
easily the assumptions of European apostles of *laissez-faire* ; the
political foundations of economic life have not been buried in
America under a centuries-old superstructure.

The United States is a federation, and a federation of more
potent and real units than the states, although state patriotism
is far from being negligible. The prosperity of Minnesota has
little or no meaning for Mississippi ; the same season may ruin
one section and favour the other and until this difficulty can
be got round, the economic sectionalism of the United States
cannot be neglected in any consideration of American politics.
Even if we grant that a national economic policy can be usefully
planned for an ordinary country, with a unified government,
it cannot be usefully planned for a continent with a disjointed
government which is, in practice, responsive to local appeals, but
has few and imperfect organs of national will.

The economic sectionalism of American politics is most easily
illustrated by the tariff. It is unnecessary here to enter into the
abstract economic question of free trade ; only at rare moments
has any such study had relevance to the American situation.
The American politician and voter, whether he was in favour
of a high or a low tariff, agreed with Senator Foraker that,
" We are too old, have had too much experience . . . to waste
time listening to impracticable teachings about theoreticalisms." [1]
American tariff politics are, as far as possible, emptied of any
theory other than that the chief duty of a politician, on a tariff
bill, is to swap favours for votes, to look out for a chance to
benefit his own constituents, in bulk, or one by one, to disregard
any questions of general policy that interfere with a local interest
and to remember that the safe rule is to do as you would be
done by. A tariff bill then consists of two classes of bargains,

[1] J. B. Foraker, *Notes of a Busy Life*, vol. i, p. 249.

those between sections and those between individuals for individuals. It is the latter that attract most of the attention and criticism, the "jokers" which are smuggled into bills and are afterwards found to have benefited some friend of a Congressman or Senator, some lucky manufacturer of pliers or the solitary nickel mine owned by Mr. Joseph Wharton, to give instances. But these occasional abuses are less significant than the sectional bargaining that illustrates the formal character of American party lines. Traditionally, the Democratic party is the party of low tariff and of states' rights ; in fact, the Democrats are just as little interested in the one as in the other. When the sections strongest in the Democratic party had economic interests that were best suited by a régime of low tariff, the party was an effective low-tariff party, when the drift of industry and the adjustment of business to a high-tariff system was so marked as to have affected the Solid South, the fervour of Democratic devotion to a "tariff for revenue" began to cool off.

The strength of the American tariff system is not based on any theory of economics, though it has had distinguished theoretical defenders ; it is not to Carey and Simon Patten that the tariff should look for its most potent defenders, but to the widespread belief that it is the duty of a politician to protect his constituents against the foreigner, whether the foreigner is the dumper from England or Russia or the railroad-fed industry of a rival town or state. The emotional basis of the tariff is that attitude which makes it a duty to "support your naborhood store" ; to shop in your own town ; to ship through your own state port ; and to help to coerce, by law, the traitors who are not bound by any sense of such moral obligation. It is the business of the politician to administer his share of political power in the way most likely to give *obvious* benefit to the section he represents. The interest may not be that of the majority, but one definite, organized, and easily recognizable body of economic interests is worth, politically, any amount of unorganized or hidden interest. No delicacy of analysis can compete with the appeal of an obvious "infant industry", whatever its age.

It is true that one minor industry may find it difficult to get the community to tax itself for its exclusive benefit, but a real or apparent distribution of tariff benefits makes a combination that it is almost impossible to defeat. The main interests of a staple exporting state like Texas may be in free trade, but the mohair interests of Mr. Garner's district are politically worth conciliating, although the cotton-growers have nothing to get out of the bargain. The more elaborate and, from the point of view of rational protectionist economics, the more indefensible the tariff, the stronger it is politically. To secure Justin Morrill in his Vermont district, a preposterous duty on marble and maple sugar had to be inserted in a tariff. "Sockless Jerry " Simpson might be against a tariff, but if there was anything going he wanted his share for Kansas. Every schedule is the subject of a bargain ; the result is a tariff which, in details, is indefensible and undefended, but it is securely built up on innumerable sectional treaties, innumerable little concessions to minor businesses woven in with the great pattern of protection for the great industries.

In this nursing of the constituency, it is sometimes possible to make mistakes, as one Maryland Congressman discovered when he voted in all good faith for a high duty on binder twine to the annoyance of the wheat growers of his district. There are times when the consumer revolts, when the emotional dislike of some tariff measure overcomes the interested support of the local protected industries, but, in the main, it is hard to go wrong in asking as much as possible for any constituent or group of constituents. Here, as in the case of jobs and the pork barrel, too much zeal as a legislative agent is almost inconceivable.

More serious in their political effects are the grand tactics of sectional tariff-making. The object of an American tariff is to give real protection to some, and enough apparent protection to others, to build up a bloc of votes in both houses sufficient to carry the measure. The skill with which this has been done is worthy of all admiration. Until this generation, the manœuvre was one of great difficulty. The main agricultural industries were export industries, cotton and wheat had the world price fixed at Liverpool, and it was not easy to see why they should permit the artificial raising of the price level of manufactures when it was impossible to pretend, with any real plausibility, that protection could do anything for the farmers. Until the Civil War, this obstacle was too great even for so adroit a politician as Henry Clay, but the Republican party was able to combine an appeal to moral emotion, to economic interest, and to patriotism that worked the trick. Ever since the Civil War, Republican strategy has been directed to keeping the West quiet with nominal concessions, preventing an alliance with the cotton states, and steadily building up more and more vested interests in the tariff. The Democrats, based on the cotton states, had an obvious interest in a low tariff, but every cotton-mill in a southern state was a nail driven in the coffin of the official party dogma, " a tariff for revenue only ". The manufacturer was replacing the planter as the dominant force. All over the South, the old protectionism of Louisiana found more and more imitators and, while southern leaders were all as devoted verbal adherents to the low tariff creed as Calhoun or Henry Watterson, on any given tariff bill they behaved like all other politicians : they went out for what they could get.

If this was true of the South, it was still more true of the West. The Middle West grew more and more industrialized. Ohio had its great steel industry and its wool-growers ; Wisconsin had its dairy farmers afraid of Canadian competition ; the lessening importance of the agricultural exports in the national economy weakened the strength of the old low-tariff sentiment of the central states. Even the Far Western states were won over. The mountain states that had bolted the Republican party in 1896 in the cause of " free silver ", were won back by a high tariff on wool and a tariff on lead that helped, or appeared to help, the declining silver-mines. The net was spread wide, there was scarcely an area where there were not *some* beneficiaries of the tariff whose conviction that it was doing them good was much keener than the fears of others that tariff benefits were at their expense. What might have happened, had the Underwood tariff of 1913 been given a fair run, no one can say, but the war interrupted the experiment and in the wave of nationalism of which the great Republican victory of 1920 was a fruit, the tariff was at last canonized. The tariff of 1921 (the Fordney-McCumber tariff), the revision of 1929 (the Smoot-Hawley), marked the end of all real opposition to the doctrine that anything that can be grown, or made, in the United States, if it can command any political support worth conciliating, is entitled to a duty that will stop all competition. There may be practical, but there are no theoretical limits to the amount of protection an infant industry can claim or to the duration of infancy. The schedules are incapable of rational defence, they are not, as a whole, popular, but there is little or no chance of a remedy as long as politics are sectional, as long as there is no effective leadership from the White House, no way out of the endless permutations and combinations of sectional interest and political blackmail.

The recasting of the parties which is possible for other reasons may be, in the comparatively long run, aided by the mess into which tariff legislation has got. It is less and less certain that all the benefits of tariff legislation fall to the grasping East. The United States is now a great creditor nation and a great manufacturing and exporting nation. Another generation of old-fashioned tariff legislation may prove a serious burden to the manufacturers who have to compete in a world market, with costs enhanced by the tariff, and who have to sell their goods to customers whose buying capacity is lowered by the practical prohibition of entry into the American market. The automobile manufacturers might very willingly let English textiles and Canadian wheat, even, perhaps, let the Rolls-Royce and the Hispano-Suiza into the American market, if it were thereby possible to get Fords and Chevrolets into foreign markets. There has been a marked decline in the enthusiasm of really big business, which is more and more world business, for a system that prevents the free play of American capital. The great copper interests of Arizona may have a keener interest in being able to import from their Katanga mines than in the protection of their American holdings. At any rate, measured in cash and political pressure, the support of *big* business for a tariff with the sky as the limit, seems to be a thing of the past.

This is still more evident in the banking world. Wall Street is slowly acquiring an appreciation of the difficulties and responsibilities of an international money market. But not only is the recommendation of Wall Street a positive handicap for a policy, the political profits of the old attitude are still very considerable. It may be true that it is impossible to expect payment of the war debts except in goods, that the United States will have to choose between a lower tariff and a default, but no book-keeping, even if authenticated by an archangel, which showed that the loss by the whole American people on a foreign debt default would be greater than the individual losses of protected private interests, would move a prudent politician. A loss that is spread over the whole country will do him little harm and will enable him to acquire merit in speeches of sterling patriotic indignation, while a loss that fell on any important interest in his district might be fatal. It is true that the old pretence that the tariff benefits all sections has worn very thin and the naked truth appears ever more plainly below the threadbare rags of rhetorical patriotism with which the system is still decked. When the McNary-Haugen bill, which purported to " do for American agriculture what the tariff had done for industry ", was before Congress, the last appearances of party lines were abandoned.

" West of the Mississippi River the only votes against the bill in the House of Representatives were cast by congressmen from the cities. Among the representatives east of the Mississippi River and north of the Mason-Dixon line the only votes for the bill were by congressmen from the rural constituencies. This held true even of the delegation from as urban and industrial a state as Pennsylvania." [1]

If the " farm bloc " can keep its power, it is possible that at long last the farmer will benefit at the expense of the manu-

[1] *Recent Social Trends in the United States Report of the President's Research Committee on Social Trends*, vol. i, p. 547.

facturer. If all other means fail, grants out of the Treasury will be tried. It is in vain that Mr. James M. Beck protests against such interference of government in business. When the farm leaders have got their breath back after such a charge from a Pennsylvania Republican, they ask " What is the tariff ? " Is Pennsylvania ready to give up its share of the federal booty ?

That time is not yet. The average Republican politician is still convinced that the tariff is a remedy for most economic evils. It was the charm that was to exorcize the depression in 1930. Senator Watson assured the country that the depression would be gone thirty days after the passing of the Smoot-Hawley tariff, an opinion shared by Senator Smoot himself. The American public has always been a believer in *post hoc propter hoc* in politics and the failure of the tariff of 1930 to end the depression may prove to have been a serious blow to that belief in the magical powers of high protection that is part of the American credo. But the sad truth is that the Democrats are only against the tariff in bulk, in detail it is as much their handiwork as it is their rivals'. It took five Democratic votes to get the Smoot-Hawley tariff through the Senate in face of a revolt of the western Republicans. The objections of the Democrats to the tariff are of no more theoretical import than the objection of sound Protectionist Republicans from Pennsylvania to a duty that makes the cigar-makers of that state use Connecticut tobacco instead of the cheaper Sumatra.

There is no real sign that this system of mutual blackmail has outlived its political, as apart from its economic usefulness. In 1928, Governor Smith abandoned even nominal adherence to the old party cry of a low tariff, to the annoyance of the Republicans, and that year the Democrats carried Massachusetts, and made a good showing in Pennsylvania. The tariff issue, as a party test, was dead. The recent scandal of imposing fresh tariff burdens in the tax bill which was the Senate's most striking contribution to the budget debates of 1932, was largely the work of two eminent Democrats, Senator Thomas Walsh of Montana and Senator Alben W. Barkley of Kentucky. Yet Senator Walsh was the incarnation of Democratic orthodoxy and Senator Barkley was the official " keynoter " of the Chicago convention in 1932 !

If the Democrats have abandoned their old shibboleth, the Republicans have hardly kept their faith intact. The old arguments for a national policy, the old stirring pleas of patriotism, the old foreigner-baiting, are shown for what they are worth by the threatened abandonment of the Philippines, not in any spasm of good faith, but because Philippine goods and Filipinos attack the monopolized market of American producers and

American labour. What no amount of appeals to the sacred principles of the Declaration of Independence could do has been done by the spirit of protection and American imperialism has been wounded, perhaps mortally, by the fears of the Americans for their markets. Great empires and little minds go ill together and an American empire is too great a burden for the timid minds bred by the tariff. In vain may the New Englanders protest against the abandonment of the conquests of the heroes of '98 ; the security of Fall River, in these evil days, has to be paid for doubly, in the competition of the Carolinas and in the threatened abandonment of Manila !

But the incurable sectionalism of American politics has other causes and examples than the tariff. There has been no fusion of interests such as has been achieved in small and homogeneous countries like England and the tariff is only an aspect of a deep-rooted local patriotism which has many other symptoms. When northern agricultural states discriminate against cotton-seed oil by excise duties as a covert tariff in favour of the local hog lard ; when the whole rate structure of the railways is honey-combed with rates designed to help one port or area against another, when a bridge that makes it easy for border-dwellers to buy outside their own state is vigorously opposed on sound protectionist lines, it is idle to blame the tariff for breeding a disregard of national or international interest and for stimulating a blind sectionalism. It helps to increase it, but the evil, or weakness, is already there. The United States are at a lower level of national integration than England ; at a higher level than Europe ; they cannot be judged by any standard which disregards that truth.

Chapter II

COUNTRY VERSUS CITY

THE clash between the interests of agriculture and industry, exemplified in the struggle over the tariff is only one aspect of that cleavage between the man of the town and the man of the countryside that displays its power in a dozen aspects of the national life, and is an increasingly important factor in politics. In all countries there is a lag in development that makes the townsman and the countryman see things differently, that creates a conflict, for example, between the sentiments, as well as the interests, of rural Austria and Vienna, between Paris and the provinces. In America, such a conflict is old enough. The society bred by the frontier experience was suspicious of the social ideals as well as the economic dominance of the townsmen, a suspicion that manifested itself in many ways, notably in the deposition of the old cities from their political rôle and the creation of mere state capitals such as Albany for New York, Harrisburg for Pennsylvania, Columbia for South Carolina.[1]

Despite the urbanization of the United States, the supremacy of rural ideals is still part of the tradition of the nation : whatever the facts, the fiction of American politics is still that everything must be done to foster " a bold peasantry a country's pride ". To incline the balance in favour of the country and to look to the farmer for the American answer to social and political problems was the official creed. In the first report of the Interstate Commerce Commission (1888), the principle was laid down that

" in great cities great social and political evils always concentrate, grow and strengthen, and the larger the cities are the more difficult it is to bring these evils under legal or moral restraints ".[2]

[1] When Oklahoma was admitted to the Union in 1908, although none of its cities was more than twenty years old, the old rural suspicion of their bad influence on the legislator was revealed in a proposal to make a new capital to be called " New Jerusalem ".

[2] Quoted in Delos F. Wilcox, *The Study of City Government*, p. 5.

The doctrine of the innocence of the farmer and the almost axiomatic turpitude of the townsman has been preached so long that it has few sceptics in the country—and not as many as one might expect in the cities. When town and country differ on political questions the burden of proof is put on the townsman ; it is his patriotism and purity that are in question and his opinion that is taken as being *a priori* suspect. To this old clash, the growth of American cities and the stagnation of the country have added bitterness, for as the balance of population changed, as the virtuous farmers became less numerous than the town-dwellers, annoyance at seeing power slipping into unworthy hands grew in rural breasts.

Last aggravation of a bad business, the origin of the towns-men grew less and less acceptable to the countrymen. It was bad enough when the city dwellers were backsliding men of one's own kind, men who had known better things, had been " where bells have knolled to church " and knew, at any rate, by family tradition, the essential rightness of rural standards, " still, at least, our countrymen ", but in the last two generations, the fathers of the city-dwellers were less likely to be fugitives from the country than fugitives from Europe, immigrants who had never known the uniform discipline of the frontier, who congregated in masses compact enough to defy American opinion and who lived their lives in ways that the American tradition had definitely decided to be wrong. The life and liberty, and still more the manner of the pursuit of happiness of the American city-dweller of recent European origin was, in the eyes of rural America, a stumbling-block, and it was the custom of the rural American to make things unpleasant for all dissenters from the ancestral folk-ways—as it is the rural custom everywhere.

Rural America is Protestant America, and not only Protestant, but Puritan America.   For good and evil, the legacy of Puritanism has been attributed to the Pilgrim Fathers who are erroneously assumed to have founded Massachusetts, burned witches and been the spiritual ancestors of the Anti-Saloon League. In fact, if there had never been a Pilgrim Father, or a Massa-chusetts Puritan, there would still have been Puritan America, for John Wesley, not Increase Mather, is the father in God of the average rural American. It was the great revivals of the eighteenth century, the missionary work of the Baptists and Methodists that set the pace that the older, more intellectual, less flexible churches, Presbyterian and Congregational, had to try, with moderate success, to keep up with. All over rural America, the evangelists spread ; the powerful intoxicant of a highly emotional religion was swallowed by a starved popula-tion and all good things were connected with the God preached by Asbury and Embury and their successors.   Beside that power there was nothing to set.   In England the corresponding movement broke against the Church of England which, with all its faults, remained respectable.   In any case the complete identification of social worth with the evangelical churches was impossible in a country where, at the height of their power, the Evangelicals had to tolerate the irregularities of the gentry, however vigorously they suppressed the sinful animal spirits of the lower orders.   In America, there was no gentry over most of the country and in the South the old Deist followers of Jefferson found their own children converted under their eyes and their own states given over to clerical rule.   By the time of the Civil War, most politicians found it a help to have got religion, to be church members and to cater to the Church vote.   Moral legislation, especially one variety of it, came to be a bugbear of the politician and the legislative war to make America safe for modern rural Protestantism was on.

While the great evangelical revival was winning over the frontier and re-conquering the older states, its content was changing.   The Protestant churches began to shift the emphasis of their preaching from faith to works and to adopt a social mission.   Notably they adopted increasingly Manichæan views as to the sinfulness of alcohol and the duty of the Christian law-maker to put down the drink traffic as a social abuse—*and as a sin.*

The first wave of prohibition ebbed in the Civil War and the retreat was in part, at least, due to the resistance of political forces that were based on the support of the new immigrants, German and Irish.   It took German votes to elect Lincoln in 1860, and the Republican party had to conciliate this indispensable block of supporters by restraining the zeal of its Puritan element.   Liquor revenue became, in the pressure of war finance, indispensable to the Treasury and the brewers and distillers went into politics, as their English brethren did, to defend themselves against what they deemed excessive taxation.

Prohibition was never wholly wiped out ; in rural America it was the ideal to be aimed at and remained, in many areas, the system laid down by the law, if poorly observed in practice. The political rise of women, most notable in the western states, helped the good cause, saloons became definitely disreputable, like brothels ; they might exist by law or by custom, but they had few or no open defenders.   The drink interests were not seriously worried.   States neglected to revise their legislation, but there were not many teeth in the laws.   The godly state of Iowa refused to repeal its prohibition of the liquor traffic, but it granted permanent dispensation to saloon-keepers who paid a " mulcttax " ; the soul- and body-destroying trade was outlawed, but it was not abolished and the revenue was not sacrificed. Even more righteous Kansas got along with illegal toleration, till the lawless raids of Carrie Nation on the lawless saloons made it politically profitable to make the law more than a pious opinion.

There seemed little political profit in prohibition. A Prohibition party had been formed in 1869 to counter the reaction of the war period, but it never made much of a showing on its own account. The new party never polled more than a quarter of a million votes and usually polled a good deal less. It was a nuisance to the Republican party, for the dry voters were chiefly drawn from its ranks, but it was not a big enough nuisance to make it worth buying. Dry legislation was sometimes forced on the party in local elections, usually with painful results. Governor Foraker learned in Ohio that the German voters would bolt the G.O.P. in defence of beer and the dry sentiments of up-state New York were a joy to the Democrats of the Empire State who were suspected, on occasion, of stimulating dry revolts in the opposite ranks. But no very serious results could be credited to the Prohibition party except that of keeping the question alive.

> " The experience of the Prohibition Party demonstrated the fact that even friends of Prohibition and Christian voters who are favourable to Prohibition refuse nevertheless to leave the political party with which they are affiliated and vote for a new party, although that party may advocate the thing in which they believe." [1]

This was the lesson learned by the able men who, in 1893, founded the Anti-Saloon League.

The Anti-Saloon League was worked from the start on the lines laid down by such practical politicians as Jay Gould or the brewers. It left the parties alone ; it had no illusions about the character of these bodies ; it knew that they existed only as more or less honest brokers. The parties needed votes ; it was the strength of the League that in every district it had votes to deliver. These votes went without fail to the candidate who promised most for the cause. They were used in primaries to get good candidates ; they were used in elections to get good leg·slators and officials ; they were used, ruthlessly, to punish politicians who promised and did not perform. All over the West and South, where the rural population was Christian and dominant, it became less and less profitable to stand out against the new machine. The League did not ask much, only votes ;

[1] Ernest H. Cherrington, *The Evolution of Prohibition in the United States of America*, p. 168.

it was not interested in private conduct or in legislation other than dry legislation. A politician could make friends with any Mammon of Unrighteousness he chose except the liquor trade. No doubt the League preferred respectable candidates, but it could not afford to be too particular. It believed in measures, not men.

In their admiration for the political efficiency of the League, commentators rather tended to neglect the power behind its power. It was only powerful because it could induce a decisive number of men and women, over an increasingly large part of the Union, to vote, regardless of money or party ties, for a cause. It disciplined the American voter, not for an election or two, but for a generation. It was and is a great achievement. It needed a strong base and it had it. The Anti-Saloon League is the political counterpart of rural American religion as much as the Centre party in Germany is the political counterpart of the Catholic Church in that country. The voters who followed the orders of the League were convinced that they were doing God's work. All religious zealots are bound to be their brother's keeper, but Puritan zealots in America more than most, for they have a tradition of uniformity to enforce and the liquor traffic offended against all their standards. It was wasteful ; it produced only pleasure ; it hindered economic progress ; it was a stumbling-block and stone of offence to the faithful. It was never a help and often a hindrance to true religion, and it was usually in the hands of idolatrous Catholics or Laodicean Lutherans. It was sinful and it was foreign. The American conscience, incarnate in the descendants of the men who had hewn commonwealths out of the wilderness, was affronted by this defiance of its standards by new-comers who refused to conform.

Wherever prohibition went it found its course easiest where there were most Americans of the old stocks ; that is to say, Americans of the old American religion. Wherever Papists and recent immigrants were numerous, its task was harder ; wherever they were dominant, its task was hopeless. Attempts have been made at times to minimize this side of the movement. A Catholic archbishop was one of the founders of the Anti-Saloon League. Church councils deprecated the enthusiasm with which Catholics threw themselves into the saloon business, and no bias could blind the eyes of some of the Catholic clergy to the havoc wrought among their flocks by the Demon Rum. Nevertheless, Catholics as a body were strongly opposed to calling in the secular arm to put down a traffic which had no supernatural terrors for them. Germans were, whether Catholic or Protestant, strongly opposed to any interference with the beer supply. If their Anglo-Saxon neighbours could not drink civilized liquor in a civilized fashion, that was no reason for being dragged down to their level.

The great nationalist wave of the World War, following on a reform wave, gave the League its chance. The brewers were the forefront of the liquor trade and the brewers were Germans. Why fight the Kaiser and Hindenburg, when Pabst and Busch were allowed to divert the indispensable grain from the Allied cause to make their hell brews? The brewers were Germans; that is, very maladroit apologists, and the cause of legal drinking went down. There was war-time prohibition and then the eighteenth amendment and the Volstead Act. The social principles of the American countryside and of the American Protestant Churches were written into the constitution. That instrument does not contain God's name, but it now contains God's law, or what has been for a generation past taught as such in the churches of rural America.

If it was possible to doubt, ten years ago, that the eighteenth amendment was an expression of the social philosophy of the American countryside, it is hardly possible now. The burden of defence has fallen more and more on the churches and more and more on the rural population. Where the aliens are numerous, the amendment is opposed or ignored; where the population is churchless or Catholic, the economic and social arguments for prohibition fall on deaf ears. The drys and the wets alike know this. The defiance of the law by New York City has brought bitter abuse upon that alien island, full of Jews and Italians, ruled by the Irish for Wall Street. It is accused of having seceded from the Union; of being a modern Sodom, polluting the whole land.

The eighteenth amendment was, in fact, a hasty locking of the stable door and it was only one bolt among many. The new immigration laws that have barred the United States to Europe, are partly a form of protection for American labour, partly a recognition of the changed character of American social and economic life, but no one who has noted the transformation of the quota system to the present national origins system, can doubt that the object is to keep out non-assimilable races—and for non-assimilable races, read non-Protestant. The English Aliens Act was passed against Jews, but they were not mentioned. The American acts were passed to keep out Europeans who would reinforce the hordes already within the gates who were undermining American life and morality. This fear for the old ways, this conviction that the beliefs that made and saved the Republic are in deadly danger is not unjustified. If the American Republic can only keep afloat if buoyed up on the principles of nineteenth-century evangelical religion, it is in grave danger of sinking.

The political consequences of this rally of the American village have been immense. Prohibition, itself, has split parties and altered party lines to an extent unprecedented since the days of the slavery conflict, but prohibition is only one of the symptoms of this deep uneasiness. When the Democratic Convention of 1924 degenerated into a prolonged dog-fight over the question of the condemnation of the Ku Klux Klan, the nature of the conflict was revealed. The galleries packed with New Yorkers cheering on the Smith leaders and shouting down Bryan revealed that, far more than in 1896, the " Great Commoner " was in the enemy's country. Why should he and his friends be forced to condemn the Klan which was only doing, rather roughly, what the men whom Bryan and many of the McAdoo delegates represented, wanted done ? For them to condemn the Klan would have been political imprudence equal to a condemnation of the Orange order by an Ontario or Liverpool Conservative politician. Nor would there have been any use in it, for the delegates could not have delivered the goods. The Convention abandoned responsibility and the party went down to its most humiliating defeat in sixty years. Four years later, the conflict was kept out of the Houston Convention, and Governor Smith, nominated on the first ballot, was deserted by half the Solid South. The conflict forces itself into the Republican party, for that, too, has to choose between its city and its country clientèle. It has been ruined in New York by the dry control of the rural areas that are its backbone. It has suffered badly in Illinois and has not come unscathed out of the struggle, even in Pennsylvania. For the moment the Klan is ruined and the initiative is with the urban attack ; rural America is on the defensive, but the struggle is not over yet. Yet it can only end one way. On point after point the rural standards have been overthrown. The " monkey trial " at Dayton was a defeat, for it brought ridicule on the cause. In a nation increasingly devoted to bridge, how can the standards of the Methodist Book of Discipline be enforced by law or custom, even in the most respectable households ? Tobacco was banned by that great propagandist organization, the Woman's Christian Temperance Union, the W.C.T.U. of the politician's nightmare. Cigarettes ranked only after drink, dancing, and cards as doors to destruction, but despite the protests of Senator Smoot and the law in many states, the American girl smokes the deadly things and is represented as doing so in countless advertisements.[1]

---

[1] Senator Smoot denounced the advertising of cigarettes by companies " whose only God is profit, whose only Bible is the balance sheet, whose only principle is greed " (quoted in P. Odegard, *The American Public Mind*, p. 194). This outburst was explained by the cynical as not only embodying the protest

The Puritan Sunday is embalmed in laws that are never enforced effectively, and the drift of American city life is manifestly away from the faith of the countryside in particular as well as of all faiths in general.   The cities are growing, the countryside is at best stable ; the economic rewards of farming are less and less attractive to energetic spirits.   They flock to the towns, but there the *mores* of the countryside are not in control and on the children of the immigrants from the countryside, the acid of city life does its work.   The city churches of the Protestant denominations are recruited from the countryside ; they dry up in the atmosphere of the town or they lose their old standards and old beliefs.

As the rally against the imposition of rural morals on the cities gathers force, it is more and more evident that it is a fight between two populations with two different views of life.   In New York, it is the rural areas and Protestant areas that support prohibition.   Rural Pennsylvania, rural Illinois, have impeded the natural desire of the party leaders to conciliate the soaking wet and alien towns.   The most German of all the states, Wisconsin, has added beer to the other progressive slogans and the La Follettes and their allies have kept a united front against the dry, Klan-supported, " regulars ".   In New England it is the cities, full of Irish and Italians and French-Canadians, that have swamped the dry countryside.   In Missouri, it is the great brewing and German city of St. Louis that has protested against the moral zeal of the rural Democracy, and the Democrats of the other large town, Kansas City, have, and know they have, more in common with the Republicans of St. Louis than with their fellow-Democrats of the rural counties.   In Maryland, the old conflict between the eastern shore and Baltimore has been made more bitter by the unashamed wetness of the city and if the " Free State " has been the delight of the " wets ", it is not due to any special love of liberty in the rural Marylander.

The case of California is still more striking, for that state is oriented round its two great cities, San Francisco in the North and Los Angeles in the South.   The northern city is the less moral, less conformist, less dry and religious, not for any mere geographical reason, but because it is polyglot and what the Americans call " sophisticated ".   It has never lost something of the atmosphere of '49.   Los Angeles, far to the south, among its orange groves, with its oil magnates and its Hollywood stars, is, nevertheless, the most puritanical of great American cities.

of a Mormon Apostle against a habit condemned as sinful by the Latter Day Saints, but as being provoked by one advertisement in particular which advised Miss America to " reach for a Lucky instead of a sweet ".   The Mormon Church is one of the chief sugar producers of the Union.

In what other city of its rank would a Mayor dare to protest, in a rather unmannerly fashion, against wine-drinking in France ? Ridicule would have been plentiful and deadly, but in Los Angeles, the testimony given among the heathen was widely approved. In what other city would the Reverend " Bob " Shuler be such a political power with his denunciations of vice and crime in high places ? What are the thunders of Dr. Riley in Minneapolis, or even of Dr. Straton in New York, but blasts against the storm ? In Los Angeles the wind is with the preacher. The reason is not hard to find. Los Angeles, for all its world celebrity as a seat of sin, is the most rural of American cities. To it and to its neighbourhood flocked the farmers who had enough sense to retire with their war profits. It is made in their image. Here is a hundred per cent American city and, here, the fort is being held against tradition-dissolving novelties. In Californian politics, in addition to the inevitable jealousy of the two cities, is the jealousy of two attitudes to life. It is the North that is wet ; that wants racing and betting and that is poorly responsive to the religious stimulants that enliven life in the South ; it is Los Angeles, for all its sub-tropical climate, that enforces the morals of Iowa on the borders of Mexico, for this generation at least.

In this war of two traditions, the countryside has one advantage that it is reluctant to abandon. Its political power is far greater than its numerical strength justifies. Quarrels over the distribution of seats are old in America ; to secure for the frontier a political representation equivalent to its share of the population was one of the chief achievements of the Jacksonian revolution. In the federal constitution, from the start, and in state constitutions for the past century, the allotment of seats in at least one of the Houses, has been on a population basis. The usual provision has been for a redistribution every ten years, following on the results of the federal census. For the past thirty years there has been an increasingly marked reluctance to put these provisions into effect, since each redistribution would have increased the political power of the towns had it been made, and all over the Union the plain command of the constitutions has been ignored or ingeniously perverted. Congress blankly refused to allot more seats to the cities after the census of 1910, and it was only after the census of 1930 that the twenty-years-overdue increase was made. Any allotment of seats will hurt some states at the expense of others and that accounts for part of the reluctance, but it is also bound to hurt the rural areas at the expense of the cities all over the Union. Los Angeles, Detroit, Chicago, were all under-represented and there was in the making a fine rotten-borough system in the lower House to reinforce the excessive representation of the agricultural interest in the Senate.

Even the belated resolution of Congress to do its constitutional duty, and to apportion seats, in the lower House, on the population basis of the last census, although it ends twenty years' discrimination between states, does not remove the dangers of discriminations within states. The distribution of seats within a state is left to the State Legislatures and these Legislatures may, and almost certainly will, gerrymander the congressional seats as seems best to themselves. Already the good work has been taken in hand and very odd congressional election districts have been created. As most State Legislatures in the East and Middle West are packed in favour of the rural areas, there is a danger that rural dominance will return by the back door. Nothing but a healthy fear of public opinion backed up by such legal weapons as the urban areas have at their command, will keep the rural counties from digging themselves in again, and if they are allowed to get away with it, there will be adjustments of congressional districts which will earn the commendation even of experts from Northern Ireland.

In state government the problem is much older. With the rise of great cities like New York, Baltimore, Chicago, which, in themselves, were half or more of their states, the scales were deliberately tilted against the cities. A century ago, the rural areas were active for numerical representation: "King Numbers" triumphed over the fears of Chancellor Kent and Chief Justice Marshall, but to-day the rural areas think it the most natural thing in the world that the cities should be ruled by the country, regardless of the relative populations. In Georgia every one of the 161 counties has the same representation in the State Senate ; the average population of a county is 18,000, but Fulton county which contains Atlanta, has only one-third of a Senator, with 300,000 population.[1] In Rhode Island the most decayed rural town had the same representation as Providence. Connecticut, too, cultivated rotten boroughs as one of its steady habits. In Illinois all attempts to reform the state constitution failed because Chicago would not consent to make its present under-representation a matter of bargaining. It wanted its rights, not just as much of them as the legal majority of rural Illinois could be induced to let go. The same story is true of almost all states, the countryside is in power, even though, in population, it be a dwindling minority, and it shows no sign of letting go its hold on the political machinery, now almost its only ally in the war against the new America.

[1] In a southern state like Georgia, the situation is even worse than it seems, for the Democratic primary is the real election, and the scales are weighted even more shamelessly there against the city.

This old conflict, now more bitter than ever, is reflected in all manner of ways ; in the control of the police, in the character of state legislation, in the regulation of municipal autonomy, in the tax system.   As far as possible all power is kept in the hands of the state legislature against the municipalities on the one hand and the Governor, who represents the numerical majority, on the other.   City government is investigated, but rural government sheltered from the urban counter-attack.   To get justice or even tolerable municipal life from the state author- ities it is necessary to bribe or cajole.   It is not very surprising to learn that the city of Chicago paid retaining fees to the leaders of the legislature of Illinois to induce them to look after the city's interests at Springfield.   So did Indian princes or African kings bribe members of Parliament or senators in the great days of the British and Roman Empires.[1]

How is this blank defiance of democratic principle defended ? In part it is not defended.   The defiance of the constitutional provisions for re-apportionment is too brazen to be covered even by the most adroit political casuistry.   But there is a deeper conviction that occasionally comes to the surface ; the conviction that the citizens that are being deprived of their full political weight are not entitled to full political weight ; that they are, to borrow a term from M. Maurras, " métèques ".   The city- dwellers are new-comers or the children of new-comers.   They have so much to be grateful for that they should be content with a good deal less than their rights.   Where were they when the foundation of the Republic were laid ?   Why should they have a deciding voice in the conflict of traditions ?   Only " White, Gentile, Protestants ", to use the formula of the Ku Klux Klan, are entitled to a deciding voice in fundamentals.   There is a grave danger of the future of the nation being planned on lines not in conformity with the traditions of Protestant America. Newspapers owned or written by Jews cast ridicule on the traditions of the countryside ; it is an impertinence in the eyes

[1] Among the many obstacles to good government in Chicago, high rank must be given to the multiplication by the state of governmental authorities and the consequence on the Chicago front of the impossibility of unity of command—on the side of the law, at any rate. " There are no less than 415 local governing bodies in Chicago and Cook county, each with its own tax-levying and borrowing powers.   Within the city limits of Chicago there are 31 independent governments and six semi-independent tax-levying wards. . . .   Outside of Chicago, in Cook county there are 384 additional indepen- dent and semi-independent bodies, all empowered to levy taxes and to borrow funds.   Most sections in Chicago and Cook county are subject to at least seven independent governments, and within the whole county there are no less than 450 separate tax levies.   The citizens of North Village pay 37 different assessments " (W. W. Liggett, " The Plunder of Chicago ", in *The American Mercury*, March, 1932).

of the rural American ; as it was an impertinence, in the eyes
of many Frenchmen, for M. Léon Blum to be a leader in the
attack on the congregations and on the Alsatian concordat in
1924. That is why a Catholic " wet ", like Al Smith, is so
repellent to many Americans ; his origin puts him out of court ;
he cannot understand the deep and sacred feelings behind the
Puritan tradition. When there was talk of a redistribution and
vague threats of penalizing the South for its disfranchisement of
the Negroes, Senator Black of Alabama struck a popular note
in demanding that aliens be no longer counted in allotting seats,
and, in his heart, it is possible that the Senator sees little to choose
between a naturalized and an unnaturalized alien. You can
naturalize a Calabrian peasant or a fugitive from a Lithuanian
ghetto, but you cannot give him the traditions of the pioneer,
you cannot make him feel as they feel whose ancestors were slain
by the sword of the spirit in the great revivals and saved by
an American God.

For the amalgamation of the American people, the absorption
of such varied stocks is not yet complete. There are, in the eyes
of the average American of the countryside and the towns which
are rural in outlook, two classes of Americans, first- and second-
class Americans, and, with few exceptions, the first-class Americans are the Protestant Americans. It is not put so crudely as
that. There is talk of the " Anglo-Saxon " genius for self-govern-
ment that cannot be expected of the lesser breeds, and of recent
years there has been a good deal of pseudo-scientific propaganda
in favour of the inherent virtues and superiorities of the Nordic
Man. But these refinements have been too academic for the
average man ; they have been useful for more cultivated citizens
who wanted to rationalize their dislike of Catholics and Jews,
" Micks ", " Wops ", " Kikes ", as such, but as Dr. Denis
McCarthy has put it, " The Nordics were made by the Ph.D.'s,"
—and their popularity has been largely confined to academic
circles.

No dolichocephalic blond Piedmontese has ever got past Ellis
Island on the strength of his pigmentation and his cephalic index.
The high rank given to the Huguenots as an ancestral stock is
proof of how " unscientific " American racial prejudice is. These
" Celts " are eminently desirable citizens, although their Catholic
kinsmen from French Canada are suspect.[1] All Protestant Irish
are Scotch-Irish, even though they bear names that would brand
them, in any county in Ulster, as putative members of the
Ancient Order of Hibernians. The Jews, of course, suffer all the

---

[1] One of the oddest sidelights on the Huguenot's prestige is the assumption
that the bearers of the common Scottish names, Pettigrew, and Lamont, are
of Huguenot origin.

disabilities of the Catholics, and some of their own. Together they make up the block of " half-breeds " whose claims on the sufferance of their fellow-countrymen are claims of favour, not of right. In Louisiana and Maryland, however, Catholicism has a prestige it lacks even in states where it is really more powerful, as in Massachusetts and Rhode Island : and in California, the power may be to the Methodists, but the romance is in the Franciscan missions.[1] In the same way it is more respectable to be of Pennsylvania Dutch origin than to be of plain German stock arrived in the nineteenth century.[2]

It happens that the dividing-line of religion is also, very largely, the dividing line of " new " and old " stocks ". There were comparatively few Catholics in the United States before 1830 and few Jews before 1880. The immigrant has always provoked resistance to his economic competition and to his odd ways. The "Americans " of Gopher Prairie suspected the Scandinavians of the countryside of all kinds of open and concealed treason to American ideals, but a new generation easily amalgamates those who have values in common. But the problem presented by the Catholics and the Jew is a real one. They may think alike concerning the Republic, but they do not think alike concerning the next world, and everywhere that is a hate-breeding difference. American life has been based on the acceptance of the standards of Anglo-Saxon Puritanism. It is not the tongue of Shakespeare, but the tongue of the Bible and of Moody and Sankey that is the great bond between the English-speaking peoples.

[1] But even Californian respect for valuable tourist romance has its limits. Each state is allowed to put the statues of two figures from its history in the national capitol. When Wisconsin sent in a statue of Père Marquette there were loud protests, but when California decided that one of its two heroes should be Fray Junipero Serra, it was impossible to contest the claims of the great missionary and colonist, but a powerful agitation arose to force the state to make the Reverend Thomas Starr King the other great Californian to be commemorated at Washington. Few in California, and still fewer in the country at large, had any idea who the Reverend Mr. King was, but if there was to be a Catholic priest sent by California, there would have to be a Protestant minister as well.

[2] Pennsylvania Dutch are of German, not Dutch origin. " Funny ! Whole lot of people take Schmaltz for a German name, but of course, as a matter of fact, when you look into the matter, it isn't German at all but Pennsylvania Dutch, which is almost the same as saying New England Yankee." Thus Mr. Lowell Schmaltz, " The Man Who Knew Coolidge ". His friend, Dr. Lepewski, however, was anxious to explain that, " he was really of German extraction and not one of these Lithuanians or some foreign stock like that ". On the other hand, the acceptance of immigrants from the privileged stocks is very rapid. Both the candidates in the presidential election of 1916 were of as recent immigrant stock as Governor Smith, but neither Wilson nor Mr. Hughes suffered in their political eligibility for all that.

"The same basal religious feelings and theological conceptions are in Englishmen and Americans, and they would be at home with each other in discussing these questions as neither Englishmen nor Americans would be with French or German." [1]

The practical ending of immigration might have put an end to the old assaults on the new-comers that have come with each generation, but the immigrants of the last fifty years have not brought with them the equipment of moral ideas and standards that formerly made assimilation easy. The American Puritan has found his theoretical toleration put to a test that toleration seldom stands without a good deal of strain. It is not the habit of the zealot, in any country or time, to permit others to go to the Devil their own way. Modern Ireland has little to learn from modern America in this department of politics. A Protestant librarian in Mayo was opposed on principles that were very like those used to justify the proscription of Governor Smith by his more temperate opponents. Other issues, economic disaster for example, for a time may obscure the quarrel, but it will remain, for neither side will surrender willingly. The new-comers could not, if they would, re-make themselves in the model of the older stocks, for the rural-religious mould in which the older metal was cast is too obviously unfit for a new smelting. Nor will the older stocks, in the countryside, knowingly accept the new life of the cities ; their pride as well as their faith is too deeply involved.

Indeed, the long life of the Puritan old Adam has been sufficiently demonstrated in English politics in recent years : and the same disregard for the wishes of the people immediately concerned has been displayed on both sides of the Atlantic. When the House of Commons threw out the Prayer Book, it did so by a vote which went against the wishes of the English members, by the votes of Welsh, Irish and Scottish Protestants who were anxious to save the Protestant tradition of England, whatever the English themselves thought about it.

How is this quarrel which is continually interfering in politics and complicating issues and strategies, to be composed ? There is little indication that the rural American, no matter how disillusioned he may be as to the results of prohibition, will lightly let go his political power or abandon his watch over his erring city brother. Yet his game is lost, at least in its present form. Americans will stand a lot in the way of legal tyranny, but there is a limit. Chicago will not for ever be content to go on bribing the rural legislators to do its business, any more than industrial

[1] A. P. Brigham, *The United States of America*, p. 242.

England, a century ago, was content to put up with virtual representation. The census, the drift of economic power, is all one way. The ending of immigration is a futile gesture, for the damage is done. If it were merely a question of foreign ideas and foreign stocks being kept in their places, the politicians might rely on a long life of catering to American nationalism, but the real danger to old-fashioned Americanism is America. It was in vain to preach the old Roman virtues to a people conscious of its new empire and the American Catos are no more likely to be permanently successful than was their Roman exemplar. City life eats away the basis of the old folkways as of the old rural economy. Mr. Mencken has told us that, to the " peasants " of Tennessee, even Dayton is a metropolis of dangerous delights ; a sapper of the old customs and principles. That eminent rural statesman, " Alfalfa Bill " Murray, Governor of Oklahoma, proposed to keep his legislators away from the seductions of Oklahoma City by locking them up in dormitories staffed by women who, like the Cambridge college bedmakers, were to be old and ugly. A Governor of Ohio earned much popularity by announcing that he had never been in New York and never would be, but how many of his supporters would have refused a free trip to New York ? What town is there that does not see itself another New York, if it only had its rights ? It is not enough to stop the addition of inferior ingredients to the melting-pot, for the pot itself is melting. The defenders of the rural tradition have resorted to politics, not because of confidence, but because of fear. They see themselves at the breach defending the good old ways, on which depends the safety and prosperity of the nation :

Moribus antiquis res stat Romana virisque.

But behind them the wall is crumbling and their army is deserting, and the politicians are beginning to find it out. Once the tide is obviously on the turn, the politicians will turn on their recent allies with ferocity. The traditionalists are fighting, at best, a doubtful battle and they are shaken by the present crisis as never before. The years of prosperity, if they ate into the ascetic theory of the Puritans, at least provided a talking point for prohibition. But the depression hit the rural areas hard ; it created powerful economic discontents that destroyed the hold of the existing political personnel on the voters and the existing political personnel was " dry " in the main. The disasters that have befallen the " Hoovercrats " checked the political power of the churches in the South and even a sound " dry " who had the prudence to keep regular in party politics, finds his position less and less secure, if we may judge by the eclipse of Senator Cameron Morrison in North Carolina.

Over the rest of the land the " drys " are on the run.   As far
as politicians were concerned, they were held to the cause by
fear, not by conviction, and now the " wets " have proved that
there is more to be feared from them than from the Anti-Saloon
League.   Through the breach thus made in the defences of old
America, more things than beer will pass.   Yet the fight in its
fundamental aspects is not over, although prohibition is doomed.
It will, indeed, be a long time before the evangelical lobby in
Washington recovers even part of the prestige which it had in
the great days of Wayne B. Wheeler and Senator Wesley Jones.
But the countryside has not been remade for all that, and when
the present pressure of economic questions is a little abated, the
rural Americans will again hear " ancestral voices prophesying
war ".   The older Americans have not yet despaired of the
puritan Republic.

In this moment of their defeat, it is all the more necessary
to point out that the would-be defenders of Americanism, for all
their absurdities and meannesses, for all the premiums they put
on hypocrisy and all the evils that flowed from their greatest
triumph, raised a real issue and one that will have to be faced.
The American people will have to take stock of its ideals, and
come to some agreement, for

" in a hearty and sound democracy all questions at issue must
be minor matters ; fundamentals must have been silently
agreed upon and taken for granted when the democracy
arose ".[1]

America must get new folkways for her new life.

[1] George Santayana, *Character and Opinion in the United States*, p. 206.

PART FOUR

THE PRESIDENT

And choice being mutual act of all our souls,
Makes merit her election, and doth boil,
As 'twere from forth us all, a man distill'd
Out of our virtues.

Troilus and Cressida, Act I, Scene iii.

Chapter I

THE GROWTH OF THE PRESIDENCY

THE growth in power and prestige of the presidency of the United States is an example of the unforeseen possibilities of a written constitution, for, in normal times, the President's powers, as set out in the Constitution, would not account for his immense prestige, and for his great potency for good and evil. The executive power in the United States is legally hampered by all sorts of restrictions, some of his most important powers he has to share with the Senate, others are only made available by the financial grace of Congress, and he has no legal means of coercing either house or both together, and only slight facilities for persuading them. The customary comparison with the Prime Minister of Great Britain is hackneyed but useful. The accretion of power to the office of Prime Minister has gone on as fast as it has to the office of President, but in a more rational and predictable way. In the contemporary British Constitution, the Prime Minister is master of the Cabinet and of the House of Commons, for party discipline, at ordinary times, is based on adherence to the policy of the Prime Minister. The members of the party in power have all the reason in the world to support their chief, for they can only overthrow him at the cost of ceasing to be the party in power ; he can go out of office or he can do worse : he can dissolve Parliament and that is, in itself, a most effective means of party discipline. The theory by which the Cabinet holds its power at the beck and call of the House of Commons, loses all reality when a government has a clear majority, for that majority has been returned to support a policy and party, and both are

usually assumed to be incarnate in a man or, at most, in one or
two men. What House of Commons of the usual type ever
defeats its own government voluntarily, if it is made aware that
a defeat will be taken as a vote of no confidence and result in a
dissolution ? Short of a complete collapse of the internal unity
of a party, when does this demand for practically unquestioning
support, this perpetual confidence trick fail to come off ? Only
in a House of Commons in which there is no stable parliamentary
party majority and, despite the two Labour governments, that
type of House of Commons is still rare and an anomaly. The
picture of a House of Commons, vigilantly watching its delegates,
is a fiction that has had little truth in it for sixty years.[1]

A Prime Minister, with a party majority in the House of
Commons, commands all the executive and legislative power in
a fashion that the most potent American President has not done,
save for very brief periods. Not only is the Prime Minister the
political centre in a way unknown to American life, he is the
head of the party organization in a way that few American
Presidents have been. He cannot, of course, wholly disregard
the opinion of the rank-and-file members, not because it is
important in itself, not because he fears the action of the individual
member, but because their discontent may be a reflection and
a cause of party discontent in the constituencies, and may have
fruit, not in a party revolt, not in his deposition, but in a defeat
at a general election. A mere revolt of the politicians has few
terrors for an English Prime Minister if it be not reflected, fairly
soon, in the constituencies. Even if the official party organization
falls into critical hands or into hands other than his own, a Prime
Minister has large reserves of strength, as was shown in the last
years of the doomed Balfour ministry. Mr. Chamberlain could
win over the organization, stir up the enthusiasm, inspire the
fighting hopes of the party, but he was not Prime Minister, and
he could not unhorse the parliamentary leader of the party, and
knew this too well to try ; that was left to the opposition and
it took five years for the party to get rid of Mr. Balfour, even when
he had lost two general elections, and was merely leader of an
especially disgruntled opposition.

Nor is this due to a profound difference in the method of
election to the two offices ; an English general election has as
decidedly a plebiscitary character as an American presidential
election. In each case the country votes for or against a man,
usually not mainly on his personal merits, but on those of his
party. But Mr. Gladstone was the issue in 1880, as emphatically

_____

[1] It had some reality in the period Bagehot describes, of slack party
discipline between the fall of Peel and the rise of Gladstone, but there is
very seldom a place for Adullamites nowadays.

as Woodrow Wilson was the issue in 1916. It is too early to be dogmatic about the weight of Mr. MacDonald's name in 1931, but it was undoubtedly great ; he could only receive a personal mandate by the returning of a majority to the House of Commons, but some part of every constituency voted for Mr. MacDonald as Prime Minister and not merely, or mainly, for the individual member returned, or the National Government, or its policy. It is not the fundamental character of the mandate, but the office to which he is elected, that makes the difference and accounts for the fact that an American President is always more or less than an English Prime Minister, and usually less.

The President combines in his person the two offices of King and Prime Minister. In the English system the duties are divided between what Bagehot called the " dignified " and the " efficient " functions. The public liturgies are performed by an hereditary official, but the actual executive government is carried on by an elected one. In America the offices are united and the least-disputed function of the President is his activity at such affairs as the first baseball game of the season and the laying of foundation-stones. In a country where political office is not accorded the traditional respect it usually commands in Europe, it is something that the head of the political system is admittedly at the head of the national life and not merely a party chief as in England, or a none-too-impressive figure-head like the French President. He has had no king to compete with, there are no memories or pretenders to shadow the republican dignity of the chief magistrate, and though there are many Americans to whom a throne, especially the throne of the King of England, is sacred beyond any mere President's chair, for the vast majority, the majesty of the people incarnate in the President is as respectable as any government needs to be. This dignity has not always been appreciated, and after the pseudo-royalty of the Washington and Adams régimes, the Jefferson administration went to great lengths to make it clear that no divinity hedged a President. Nevertheless, the attribution to the President of the formal representation of the people has been useful as a cement of national feeling, and has also added to the authority of the chief executive, even with Senators. Criticism of the President in public has to keep within limits that would not be observed in the case of a minor official, though it is possible that this code is less binding in the case of a Democratic President than in that of a Republican. There are moments when one feels that a good Republican regards a Democratic President as a French legitimist regarded Louis Philippe, as a King *de facto* but not *de jure*, and so not entitled to the forbearance due to a real President. The same was true of Republican Presidents in the early days, when the party was still radical and disreputable, but even the most embittered Republican will pay formal respect to the presidential dignity and, since Harvard gave Andrew Jackson an honorary degree, the office is assumed, on formal occasions, to cover the man and the politician with the mantle of national majesty.

It is to Jackson's time, and to Jackson himself, that we owe another characteristic of the presidency, the assumption, that, in some special way, the presidency represents the people, and as he and some of his successors have asserted it, the presidency has a distinct flavour of the plebiscitary monarchy of the Bonapartes and the presidential authority has been presumed to embody " We the People of the United States " in a way impossible to Congress.   There is no foundation for this assumption in the Constitution.   The President is, in law, not a direct result of popular choice, but of an indirect election.   In theory, his contact with the people is less direct than that of the House of Representatives and no nearer than that of the Senate,[1] indeed, since the adoption by the seventeenth amendment, of the direct election of Senators, it is less direct.

Yet the Jacksonian assumption was accepted by the nation. The great President defied Congress and, especially, the Senate ; he used his veto power in a way unheard of before, not merely to protect his authority in its own sphere, but to hold up the action of Congress in the legislative field.   Since Jackson's time the President has been a third house, he has become entitled in custom, as he always was in law, to set his opinion against that of the legislature, even in fields in which the legislature is theoretically competent and even though the majority is fresh from the country and the President's mandate, as a European would regard the matter, is exhausted.   Negatively the presidential power overshadows that of Congress.   The great Whig parliamentarians, Clay and Webster, might thunder, but they were beaten and although fighting a desultory rearguard action, they, and the country, settled down to acceptance of the inevitable growth of presidential power.   The possibility of a veto has always to be borne in mind by Congress and some Presidents let it be known, in advance, that certain legislation will be vetoed.   The separation of powers that is so odd an aspect of American government, and has such unusual political effects, is defied by the veto, and politicians must take note of this anomaly that is, in fact, one of the chief links between two theoretically separate parts of government.

[1] As Senators serve for six years, a third of the Senate may be more remote in time from the people than the President who serves four years, but a third may be nearer.

The President's veto can be overridden by a two-thirds majority in each house and it has sometimes been suggested as a rough indication of a President's strength that one should count successful vetoes to the credit side and vetoes which have been overridden to the debit side. But a strong President has usually no need to veto, his relations with Congress make it easy for him to stop legislation earlier, unless, of course, he is completely at odds with both houses of the legislature. Congress often finds the presidential veto a convenience. It enables the harassed politician to acquire merit by supporting ridiculous legislation, confident that the President will see that it is brought to naught. In such cases the Congressman or Senator thinks he has done his duty and a two-thirds majority is not available. At other times, however, the forces behind a measure are too much for the politician to resist and are too zealous to be content with the formal homage of a bill. Then the presidential veto is overridden. Wilson failed to stop the Volstead Act and Mr. Coolidge the " soldier's bonus ". To veto a great party measure is a bold stroke for a President and rarely attempted. Whatever Mr. Hoover thought of the Smoot-Hawley tariff, he dared not veto it. Even so strong an executive as Grover Cleveland let the Wilson tariff of 1894 become law, although he refused to sign it.[1]

In normal times, however, the President is in a position to make his wishes known and felt. Congress may, as the Democrats did under Hayes, " tack " legislation to supply bills, but public opinion is definitely against this method of undermining presidential authority. Obviously were such a practice to be tolerated, real power would soon be transferred from the White House to the Capitol. Only in the quasi-revolutionary times of Andrew Johnson has it been possible to work up public opinion outside Congress to support the members of that body in the usurpations necessary to reduce the President to a figurehead. The country may be of the same mind as the majority in Congress, but it respects the right of the President to differ.

The modern presidency owes more than the free use of the veto power to Andrew Jackson. It owes to him a definite ending of any parliamentary character in the office. Jackson had been elected over the opposition of what we should call " the front bench ", he had ruled in defiance of all that parliamentary votes and talents could do and the Senate, in which he had

[1] If the President does not sign a bill within ten days of its being sent to him, it becomes law without his signature. On the other hand, a bill sent to the President within the last ten days of a session may be subjected to what is called a " pocket veto ". In this case the President does nothing with the bill, is saved the trouble of sending a veto message which involves giving reasons, and as the ten days' grace allowed him have not elapsed before Congress ends, the bill dies.

been as ill at ease as Cromwell in the House of Commons or Bonaparte before the Five Hundred, had resisted him in vain. Leaving the presidency to his nominee, Van Buren, he retired, having shown, once for all, that in resolute hands there was no danger of a President of the United States undergoing the fate feared for the British King by Shelburne, of sinking into a Peshwa of the Mahrattas, or, in the indignant words of Caleb Cushing, letting the United States suffer " a parliamentary despotism like that of Venice or Great Britain, with a nominal executive chief or president utterly powerless ".[1]

It is evident, then, that if American parties exist to carry out policies, they must make sure, for positive action, of the presidency. No congressional victories, no pressure of public opinion, will suffice to drive an obstinate President out of his constitutional fortress. Two cases sufficiently illustrate this truth. Whatever justification there may have been for Jackson's assertion of a special authority that derived from the deliberate choice of the people, this democratic anointing scarcely sanctifies the Vice-President, who, by the death of a President, enters upon his duties.[2] Candidates for the vice-presidency are never chosen because they are presumed to be fit to be President, should they be called upon, but usually for reasons that have nothing to do with their merit as presidential timber. As Walter Hines Page put it, the office is now a shelf, not a perch. Yet should accident promote the holder of this vague and ornamental office to the presidency, all the legal and all the conventional power of the office is his ; he is no mere *locum tenens*, bridging the gap till the next election. When Tyler succeeded Harrison in 1841, he not only assumed the title, but the position of the dead chief magistrate. The fact that he had been elected on the Whig ticket, did **not** prevent his putting obstacles in the way of the Whig programme, and defying the leader of the party that had, a few months before, swept the country. For nearly four years he ruled, to the horror of the blaspheming Whigs, in accordance with his own un-Whiggish views, and not only prevented their carrying through the restoration of a central Bank, but made possible the annexation of Texas and set on foot some of the measures that led to the Mexican War with its vast political consequences.

The case of Andrew Johnson is an even stronger example. Put on the " Union " ticket with Lincoln in 1864, in an attempt to gain support for the doubting Republicans at the blackest period of the war, Lincoln's murder made him President. In that office

---

[1] Fairlie, *National Administration of the United States*, p. 19.

[2] The custom whereby he also assumes the title of the President is a convention of the Constitution, not a provision of that instrument.

he showed himself a good States' Rights Democrat and opposed, and partly thwarted, the policy of the overwhelming majority of Congress, and of the party that had chosen him. Bills were passed over his veto, his action circumscribed by statutes, notably by the *Tenure of Office Act* which destroyed his power of removal and the last argument of impeachment was attempted, and failed. Few Presidents have had less personal power and prestige, the times were times of revolution under legal or quasi-legal forms, the Supreme Court had been intimidated and hamstrung, yet Johnson got as much of his own way as consisted in preventing his enemies from getting theirs. Overwhelming majorities in both houses, backed by a public opinion inflamed by the passions of a civil war and the desperate necessities of party politics, failed to overthrow the active identification of the legal powers of the presidency with the incumbent, no matter what were his relations with public opinion or with the dominant sections in Congress. Had the impeachment succeeded, had Congress tasted blood by putting one of its own, Ben Wade, into the White House, who can say what would have happened to the presidential office ? What remained of the theoretical powers of the French President after the expulsion of MacMahon from the Elysée ? What chance is there of a revival of the nominal powers of the office since the underlining of that lesson by the horrible example of Millerand ? It can be said, of course, that the failure of the Republicans to carry the impeachment shows that they had no chance of recasting the form of government in a mould closer to a Congressman's desire, but that does not affect the force of the lesson. The American President is one of the last monarchs ruling, for his term, by an authority with prerogatives of its own which cannot be diminished but may be increased. As the direct representative of the people, even after the people have discarded his party, he has " the right divine to govern wrong ".

It is from this basis of irremovability that the President operates and for two years, at least, he can afford to take a longer view than Congress. Sometimes his long view turns out to be based on a blurred vision. Wilson thought he could defy Congress in 1919, because the election of 1920 would decide between him and his enemies—as it did by ruining his party and policy. Until November, 1932, Mr. Hoover could still hope that a new House of Representatives would undo any partisan manœuvres of a hostile Congress ; for every President who has been rebuked in mid-term by the election of a hostile House or Senate, or both, must needs dream of the appeal from Uncle Sam drunk to Uncle Sam sober, though precedent suggests that the drunkenness is more likely to increase than to diminish.

Subject to even less limitation by Congress, is the administrative power of the President.   It is probable that, in the early days of the Constitution, it was not foreseen that the power of the President over the administration would exclude that of Congress almost completely.   Yet since the President appoints his Secretaries and removes them, it has been inevitable that the legal position should become that stated by Caleb Cushing in 1855 :

" I hold that no head of a department can lawfully perform an official act against the will of the president, and that will is by the constitution to govern the performance of all such acts." [1]

Thus armed, the President is able to divert and direct policy in many matters which Congress is anxious to deal with and, at times, he can defy Congress altogether.   As soon as he was able to get a sufficiently resolute agent in Roger Taney, Jackson was able to assail the stronghold of his congressional enemies by removing the deposits of the public funds from the Bank of the United States ; it was as if M. Poincaré had been able to carry out his financial policy of 1926 against the will of the Chamber, or as if Mr. MacDonald had successfully defied a hostile House of Commons and carried out his gold-standard policy by mere administrative act.   The Senate might, and did, condemn the presidential act as usurpation, but it was powerless to prevent it or to undo it.

[1] Fairlie, *op. cit.*, p. 19.

Chapter II

THE PRESIDENT'S CABINET

IT has already been pointed out that the President is ruler of the heads of departments, of his eight Secretaries, of the Attorney-General and of the Postmaster-General. Yet, as the Constitution in so many ways has thwarted the wishes of its framers, it might have happened that the Cabinet, in itself a body of which the Constitution has no knowledge, would have grown into powers that legally were concentrated in one man. The American Cabinet is composed of ten heads of departments under whose control, some, but by no means all, the administrative machinery is placed.[1] These officers are bound to give the President advice should he ask for it, but have no authority to tender it. They meet regularly and are known as the President's Cabinet, but they are not merely liable to dismissal individually, or in bulk, they have no corporate rights which are uniformly recognized by custom. There are two anecdotes which illustrate the difference between the English Cabinet and the very different American meeting that goes by the same name, that of Melbourne shutting the door and demanding a vote on the Corn Laws, " It doesn't matter what we say, but we must all say the same thing ", and that of Lincoln putting a question to the vote in his Cabinet and announcing, " Noes, seven, ayes one, the ayes have it ".

The President is no mere *primus inter pares* and no matter how great the authority of an English Prime Minister is, he is not yet the complete master of the situation as is the President in what is justly called " the President's family ". The Prime Minister, as Mr. MacDonald does, may talk of " my government ", it is still far in fact, however near in fancy, from the force of " my administration " on the lips of even the mildest occupant of the White House.

The political side of the President's power over his official advisers is best seen in his manner of choosing them. In fact, of course, he is limited by party necessities and by certain, not

---

[1] There are bureaux, and other governmental agencies, not under any department; such are the Library of Congress, the Printing Office and the great judicial commissions.

very stringent rules, but he is free to choose, in a way the English Prime Minister, harassed by the co-existence of too much new wine and too few old bottles, must envy. The degree of independence depends, of course, on the strength of the President and on his relations with the party, but the weakest President is still strong. The workings of the electoral system often, one almost writes always, pass by the man who in England would be the obvious Prime Minister; the cause of the long list from Gallatin through Webster and Clay, to Seward, Blaine and Bryan, naming only the dead, who were of the first rank and had to be content with the second place, is discussed elsewhere. What is here to the point, is the relations of the second-rate President with the first-rate party leader. All the leaders mentioned were invited into Cabinets or otherwise employed by their less eminent chiefs, and three of them, at least, have been cast by their friends and by uninformed public opinion, as " Prime Ministers ". Seward, who was Lincoln's chief rival for the Republican nomination, and who towered far above his chief in public fame at the beginning of the administration, took his appointment as Secretary of State as being equivalent to being Prime Minister and was foolish enough to say so. Lincoln cared nothing for what he said, but when Seward began to act on this theory, he was quickly and kindly reminded that Lincoln was President. The contemporary history of England shows the difference, for Lord John Russell could not dominate Lord Palmerston, nor could Palmerston have disregarded Russell in forming or conducting an administration. Woodrow Wilson had been only two years before the public, when a chapter of accidents, from the English point of view, made him President. He was compelled, by prudence, to make Mr. Bryan Secretary of State, for Mr. Bryan was the incarnation of that western radicalism which had made a Democratic victory possible—if only by splitting the Republican party. Bryan's influence with the more determined holders to the Gospel of 1896, it was thought, would be useful, and, in fact, it was invaluable in giving a certificate of orthodoxy to such measures as the Federal Reserve bill. His presence in the administration was, on the one hand, an assurance to the old school that the party had not sold out to Wall Street, and was, at the same time, a hostage to conservatism. That is, Wilson was forced to take Bryan into his Cabinet for much the same reasons that Mr. Gladstone had to take in Mr. Chamberlain in 1880, that led Lord Palmerston to offer a place to Mr. Cobden, that has led various " reactionary " French Prime Ministers to put up with M. Briand at the Quai d'Orsay, and, perhaps, induced Mr. MacDonald to take Mr. Wheatley into his government in 1924. But once the ship was well launched, Mr. Wilson was able to drop his pilot with no trouble at all. The case is strengthened when we consider not Lincolns and Wilsons, but the weaker Presidents, the equivalents of our Liverpools and Goderichs. President Arthur succeeded to the presidency by the death of Garfield. The nomination of Garfield had marked the dominance in the party of the " Half Breeds ", and the nomination of Arthur had been an unavailing attempt to solace the " Stalwarts " for the failure to put Grant forward for a third term. Few Presidents have been in an intrinsically weaker position and yet Arthur, in the most natural way in the world, got rid of Mr. Blaine, the most popular Republican and the greatest force in the party, as easily as their sovereigns got rid of Wolsey, Choiseul and Bismarck. One last example will close this demonstration. Roosevelt chose as his successor, his Secretary of War, William Howard Taft, passing over his Secretary of State, Elihu Root, who was as suspect to the country as Sir William Harcourt was, in 1894, to the Court. But if Taft was the Rosebery of this situation, he was, if not a stronger man, in a superior position, for he dropped his rival from his Cabinet and with him all his colleagues save two, and those not the most weighty. In the American system, the Cabinet is only what the President wants it to be, it is his tool and as for its members, " a breath unmakes them as a breath has made ".

In forming a Cabinet, however, the President is limited by negative, if not by positive, custom. He must distribute the offices through various sections of the country and usually must give an appearance of allotting them among various sections of the party. Cabinet offices are one of the greatest gifts in the power of the President, and they must not be squandered. It is not prudent to give a first-class embassy and a post in the Cabinet to the same state, save in the case of New York, Pennsylvania or Massachusetts, commonwealths rich in first-class ambassadorial material and usually also containing political figures which would adorn a Cabinet. While in normal times party orthodoxy is essential, it is on occasion advisable to cater to useful allies who are not of unimpeachable party regularity. McKinley recognized the services of the " Gold Democrats " who had helped him in 1896, by the nomination of Lyman Gage as his Secretary of the Treasury. Hayes attempted to placate the outraged South by nominating an ex-Confederate to the Cabinet and even thought of giving the War Department to Joe Johnson, the most eminent surviving Confederate soldier. Former Democrats have adorned several Republican Cabinets and there were two in Mr. Hoover's. In his ability to choose his associates almost without hindrance, the President is in a much stronger position than the Prime Minister, as is easily seen when we remember how party feeling was powerful enough to prevent Mr. Baldwin making Mr. Reginald McKenna his Chancellor of the Exchequer, and made Mr. Churchill's entrance to that office less warmly welcomed than might have been desired, while Mr. Cleveland was able to make Mr. Gresham Secretary of State in 1893, though Mr. Gresham had been, as recently as 1888, one of the leading aspirants for the Republican nomination.[1]

Not merely can the President disregard party lines, he can call into office men little associated with politics, personal friends or men eminent in a dozen other ways, without having to find them seats or keep them in them. The importations from the business and academic world made during the late war were quite out of place in the English system, but not at all odd in the American. The long official career of Mr. Mellon at the Treasury is an example of an appointment that an English Prime Minister could not have made and the return of an Adams to high office has been made possible by an exercise of the presidential prerogative.[2]

It cannot be said that the President has often taken advantage of his opportunity to surround himself with a Cabinet of men of first-class talent, who were not politicians of the first rank. As a rule, the importance of a Cabinet officer has been in rough proportion to his political eminence. The great Secretaries of State, John Quincy Adams, Seward, Hamilton Fish, John Hay, were all politicians, though none of them, except Seward and Adams, was of the first class. Yet the President can call in friends as Mr. Cleveland did when he brought his private secretary, Mr. Daniel Lamont, into his second Cabinet or, like Woodrow Wilson, appoint men quite unknown to the public and party and very slightly known to the President himself. Wilson had never seen two members of his Cabinet before he appointed them and he filled what was to turn out a very important post indeed, that of Secretary of War, with an eminent New Jersey lawyer, Mr. Lindley Garrison, with insufficient sounding of the nominee's willingness to take orders from his masterful chief. But this free hand given the President in the choice of his Cabinet is a result of the comparative unimportance of that body in the American political, as apart from the administrative, system. A

[1] The " regular " Democrats were very annoyed, but helpless.

[2] Mr. Hoover's Secretary of the Navy, Mr. Charles Francis Adams, 3rd, is the head of the greatest of American families, but has had no political career and was generally thought to be a Democrat, to which party most of his family had adhered since it ceased to be powerful in Massachusetts. The Republicanism of Mr. Adams is another sign of the political change in the Bay State which is now Democratic.

Cabinet crisis of the English kind is unknown in America.[1] Even in England a dissenting minister may resign without any startling result, but if Lord Randolph Churchill had reason to regret forgetting Goschen, an American President, in the place of Lord Salisbury, would have had no need to look for a Goschen at all. He could have done what Harrison did in 1892, and Wilson in 1915, replaced the most prominent member of the party in power by a permanent official, and thus demonstrate how completely the American Cabinet is the shadow of its chief.

In a paragraph of negatives, the limited political importance of the Cabinet may be demonstrated. It has no independent powers or prestige. It need not be, or pretend to be, unanimous, for its will is the will of one man and his is the power and the glory—and the responsibility. Thus if not in strict morals, in good constitutional theory, Mr. Coolidge, Mr. Mellon, and Mr. Hoover, could disclaim all responsibility for the disgraceful plundering of the Treasury by two members of the Harding Cabinet, for there is no Cabinet responsibility.

The members of the Cabinet are not necessarily chosen from the front-rank politicians of the country, or even of the party in power, and they do not become front-rank politicians by becoming Cabinet members. Even a transient member of an English Cabinet carries with him, with his " right honourable " title, an aura of past and possibly of future greatness. In France, the slightest member of a two-day Cabinet is M. le ministre to his dying day, but if there is a more shadowy figure in the American political landscape than an ex-Vice-President who is that and nothing more, it is a former Cabinet officer who is that and nothing more. To be a Cabinet officer in one of the more prominent offices may be a pleasant or even profitable episode in the career of an American politician of the first rank, but rare indeed are the cases in which that rank owes much or anything to the service in the Cabinet. Mr. Hoover, however, made a great part of his legendary reputation for efficiency by his eight years' tenure of the Department of Commerce. Like Mr. Joseph Chamberlain at the Colonial Office, he raised a minor department to the front rank. Various members of the Wilson Cabinet have tried to capitalize the eminence they had attained for later political use, most of them in vain. John Sherman, serving under a President who was not a candidate for re-election, tried to exploit for himself the possibilities of convention patronage

---

[1] The only plausible imitation of the break-up of an English Cabinet, was the struggle that went on in the winter of 1860–1 for the control of the executive between the northern and southern sections of Mr. Buchanan's Cabinet. That was possible because the first act of a revolution coincided with the rule of one of the feeblest of Presidents.

when he set out to win the presidential nomination in 1880, but his strength was insufficient and he failed. Indeed, the true rank of the Cabinet is displayed in the practical wisdom displayed by two master politicians of the hey-day of the Republican party. Oliver Morton of Indiana refused to relinquish his power as a leading member of the senatorial oligarchy, for a post from which a man could dismiss him, and Mark Hanna, when he decided to come out of the obscurity which had enveloped the earlier part of his career as president-maker, exerted his power to force the decrepit Sherman *into* McKinley's Cabinet as Secretary of State, in order to leave the way clear for his own entry into the Senate in Sherman's place !

If we wish to see the real masters of national politics, the equals of our front-bench men, we shall look for them, not in the Cabinet room, but in the Senate, a body which attracts the really vigorous and powerful figures in national politics and one whose present standards of eminence are so high, that only three former Cabinet officers have managed to pass the gate.

In general, the political Cabinets have been at least as impressive, and respectable, as those in which the personal taste of the President has been given fairly free play. The Cabinets of General Grant were composed on no known political principle and they represent the lowest point in American executive government—and the runner-up, the Harding administration, owes its bad eminence to the presidential choice of an Ohio manager and of a senatorial associate for key-places. Another Cabinet generally deemed weak, Woodrow Wilson's, was not, indeed, picked on mainly personal grounds, but it was a collection of mediocrities, or of men of talent who had little weight with the country, or with their chief. Roosevelt had some exceedingly good servants in his quickly changing roster of Cabinet members, but he was, like Wilson, on top of the machine all the time, and he was able to make an important Cabinet officer out of Mr. Charles Bonaparte, a Baltimore lawyer whose appointment seemed, to the country at large, a little too romantic.[1]

---

[1] Mr. Bonaparte was remarkably like his most famous kinsman ; the face and the name are supposed, by the uncharitable, to have influenced Roosevelt's choice.

Chapter III

THE PRESIDENT AND LEGISLATION

SOME, if not all, Presidents have more objects in view than thwarting Congress or carrying on the routine of administration ; how does a President get something done that needs positive action by Congress or by the Senate ? He has no such resource as parliamentary government gives a party leader, he cannot challenge votes of confidence or rather cannot do so with any real results ; a failure to support the executive has no immediate terrors for legislators, even of the President's party, and there is no very effective means of transmuting a promise of support into action with the certainty of disciplined voting that the party in power can rely on in the House of Commons. The President can communicate at any time with Congress and send or read a " speech from the throne ", but he has no other direct part in carrying his recommendations into effect.[1] That must be the work of the party leaders in the two houses. Over these party leaders, the President has officially no authority, and often his real power is no greater in fact than in theory. He cannot appoint them to office without making them incligible to sit in Congress, he cannot punish them by a dissolution and his powers of appeal to party discipline are often limited. In dealing with a Senator, the President has to remember that he may be out of office before the rebel has to face his constituents. Senator Jim Reed of Missouri was able to postpone his reckoning with the outraged supporters of President Wilson in Missouri till 1922 when the President was out of office and deprived of power to reward the faithful or punish the disobedient, and when events had shown that the Senator, not the President, had seen which way the cat of popular opinion was going to jump. Mr. Cole Blease found presidential hostility a handicap which, when added to other weaknesses, cost him his Senate seat in 1918, at the height of Wilsonian dominance of his party, but Wilson did not stay in office for ever and the old Tillman party returned to its natural leader and Mr. Blease to the Senate.

[1] From Jefferson's time, all messages were read to Congress, till Wilson in 1913 revived with considerable dramatic and political effect, the older custom of appearing before the Congress in person.

The peak of a President's authority is reached, normally speaking, in his first term, although even then he may not be able to display, too openly, his discontent with powerful, if ill-disciplined members of his party whose support may be indispensable to re-election, and at the end of his second term, the certainty that he is soon to pass into the Nirvana of ex-presidential obscurity, emboldens the timidest member of Congress to play to his local gallery, regardless of the wrath that his action may breed in the White House. The moment it was known that Roosevelt was not to run in 1908, his control over Congress weakened noticeably and if President Coolidge's ambiguous announcement of his intentions in the summer of 1927 had no other advantage, it kept the politicians guessing long enough to prevent any immediate desertion of the ship that was not to put to sea again.

A President's power is at its highest at the beginning of his term, because he has then most prestige, he has not worn out his welcome in the country and, most important of all, he has still time to excite that gratitude that is a lively sense of favours to come. With the horrid example of England before them, the " Fathers of the Constitution " were resolved that there should be no flying squadron of President's friends in Congress to build up an extra-constitutional power and corrupt the virtue of the representatives of the people. They underrated the power of friendship, for if it is not possible in the American system to win a member by giving him an office, it is possible to bind him by appointing one of his friends to the public service, or as it is usually, and coarsely put, by giving him a place at the public trough. The " spoils system " is too vast a subject to be dealt with in passing, but its relations to the presidential power can be disposed of briefly.

If American party lines were closely drawn, if party policies were uniform all over the country, and if the President were, like an English Prime Minister, the custodian of party orthodoxy, he could excommunicate party rebels and leave the electors to execute the sentence. For reasons given above, this method often fails to work, but in the offices the President has a weapon which, if he can bring himself to use it, is usually decisive. The party limitations that hamper other means of discipline, help the President in his use of this one. If there is no party policy enough worth bothering about to justify electors in discarding their member, there is usually no party issue making their adherence to him a matter of principle. When, therefore, a Congressman quarrels with the President, and in consequence is deprived of his share of the patronage, his starved constituency has no strong moral motive to back him up at the cost of going without the loaves and fishes.   To refuse the federal patronage is often enough to turn the scale in an inter-party contest, and the mere chance of a new share out will, in itself, breed a contest.   If a Senator is deeply rooted in his state, he may resist, but he does not like it nor do his supporters and when they do fight, warriors like Cole Blease in Wilson's time are made more savage than ever by a diversion, in whole or in part, of the refreshing showers from their own backyards.   To use the popular metaphor, political fences are best repaired with federal posts.

The most striking example of the use of the patronage to over-come congressional opposition is the forcing through of the repeal of the Silver Purchase Act in 1893.   President Cleveland had just come into office for the second time, with a Democratic majority in both houses pledged to reform the tariff and to remedy the wrongs of the suffering poor, when a financial panic broke.   The President summoned Congress, in special session, not to apply any of the party programme, but to undo one of the few acts of the previous Congress which the country had not decisively repudiated.   President Cleveland's position was very like that of Mr. MacDonald in 1931 and the majority of the Democratic party clung to silver as determinedly as the Labour party clung to the rights of the unemployed to an uncut " dole ".   Yet the President forced through a measure nauseous to the sections of the country and of society that had elected him, and the club he employed to re-enforce his argument was the threat to withdraw the federal patronage from the recalcitrant Senators.   It is said that one Senator told the President that he and his friends would resist the bill till Hell froze over, and was informed that Hell would freeze over at 4 p.m. prompt.   The repeal went through.[1]

Such measures are rare and it takes a President more than usually indifferent to senatorial hostility to carry through such a

[1] The awkward position in which the denial of patronage put politicians is illustrated by the sad case of Senator Voorhees of Indiana, " The tall Sycamore of the Wabash ", who had been a radical silver man but who was forced by Cleveland to vote for the repeal of the Sherman Act.   " Voorhees declared over and over again that he never did change his views on the coinage question, but that he faced this situation : ' In Indiana were thousands of faithful Democrats who had followed him loyally and unfalteringly through three decades.   If he aligned himself with the President he could reward at least some of them.   If he did not, all of his friends would be cut off from any hope of preferment, and that out of love for these veterans who had borne the heat and burden of the day in so many hot conflicts—and political conflicts were nowhere on earth hotter than in Indiana—he supported the presidential policy ! ' . . .   No doubt other Senators and Representatives were actuated by motives similar to those of Voorhees " (Champ Clark, *My Quarter Century of American Politics*, vol. i, p. 322).   Conflict between the party, that is to say, the professional Democrats, and the policy of the Democrats, is a permanent danger of American politics.

coup d'état ; a *coup d'état* which resembles such episodes in French parliamentary history as the administrative pressure used, fruitlessly, by the ministry of the " Seize mai " more than anything in modern English history.   This, perhaps, is less owing to inherent virtue than to the fundamental difference that English constituencies can be relied on to decide between the parties to a dispute of this kind, and the existence of the power of dissolution makes it possible to consult them.

If, at times, a President can use the patronage, as a substitute for the parliamentary pressure at the disposal of the English Prime Minister, he has normally to leave most of the local patronage in the hands of Senators and representatives.   To do otherwise would not only cause political, but administrative, chaos.   Given the lack of a regular civil service hierarchy in America, the immense presidential patronage would swamp the executive should he attempt to administer it himself, as even Woodrow Wilson learned in office.[1]   But the dangers of presidential patronage are almost as great as the advantages ; if a higher standard of party discipline could be enforced, if the political rewards of " standing by the president " were more useful, and more certain, than they now are, the weapon of the patronage could be abandoned in America as it has been abandoned in England, with a strengthening, not a weakening, of the executive power.

A reform, which has much to commend it on other grounds, would work to increase the presidential power in the same fashion, for if withdrawal of the patronage punishes and thus incites to mutiny all the professional politicians of a state or district, a veto of a " pork-barrel " item involving the constituency, would punish all the voters.   The President can only veto a whole " River and Harbors " bill in bulk ; had he the power to veto items, as have some state executives, he could punish mutineers

[1] When Woodrow Wilson took office in 1913, he was full of reforming plans and his Postmaster-General, A. S. Burleson, had to show him the dangers of his illusions.   Wilson told Burleson : " ' My administration is going to be a progressive administration.   I am not going to advise with reactionary or standpat senators or representatives in making my appointments.' . . . ' When I heard that,' remarked Burleson, ' it paralysed me. . . . I knew it meant ruination for him.' . . . ' Mr. President,' I said, ' if you pursue this policy, it means that your administration is going to be a failure.   It means the defeat of the measures of reform that you have next your heart. These little offices don't amount to anything.   They are inconsequential. It doesn't amount to a damn who is postmaster at Paducah, Kentucky, but these little offices mean a good deal to the senators and representatives in Congress. . . .   If you pursue the right policy, you can make the Democratic party progressive, as Cleveland made it conservative, and you can avoid the kind of rows that Cleveland had in Congress ' " (Ray Stannard Baker, *Woodrow Wilson, Life and Letters*, vol. iv, p. 45).

very effectually. At present he can only rain upon the just and unjust alike, with unfortunate consequences to the Treasury and the presidential authority.

It is evident that the presidential control over legislation, his capacity for carrying out a policy involving congressional co-operation, is very limited and that until some more effective link between the executive and legislative departments is found, the position of President may be more splendid than powerful, involve responsibilities without sufficient powers to meet them, and be an obstacle to that nationalizing of politics which is so imperative a need of the American system.

Since Jackson's times, in short, the presidency has been a monarchy with all the caprice and inequality that a monarchical system necessitates. Some Presidents are like Louis XIV, some like Louis XIII ; but none can divest his office of its residual powers, or, by abstaining from action, give to the United States a parliamentary government. The President is always a driver or a brake, he is never a spare wheel. If the presidency is on the crest of the wave, the United States for good or ill is governed ; if it is in the trough, the government is confined to mechanical administration and to sectional bargaining. If his own weakness, or the jealousy of Congress, prevents a President from doing his job, there is no one else to do it and it is to the White House that the people looks for aid, not only when the President is a great personality or popular leader, but when he is a nullity, for in that office, if anywhere, is represented the national life of the American system.

PART FIVE

CONGRESS

"You can't use tact with a Congressman ! A Congressman
is a hog ! You must take a stick and hit him on the snout ! "
Adams knew far too little, compared with the Secretary, to
contradict him, . . . but he knew a shorter way of silencing
criticism. He had but to ask : " If a Congressman is a hog,
what is a Senator ? "

The Education of Henry Adams.

Chapter I

THE HOUSE OF REPRESENTATIVES

DESCRIPTION and criticism of the American national
legislature has usually been summed up in regrets
that it is not the House of Commons, and in suggestions that it had better be made as like that body as possible.
Professors point out to the American young, that no country
making a new constitution, in an age of the making of new
constitutions and the collapse of old ones, has thought fit to
imitate the American system, and that the oldest written constitution in the world has received only the faint flattery of
verbal imitation in the less orderly republics of Latin America.
The causes of this regrettable difference from the accepted model
of legislatures are obvious, and, in the main, unalterable. The
geographical and historical factors that make for the unusual
character of American party politics are no less patent in the
working of the two houses of Congress ; absence of real party
unity, the existence of faintly concealed " blocs ", the absence
of issues capable of easy dramatization, all would go to make
the American legislature, whatever constitutional frame it had
to inform, something very different from the mother of Parliaments.

Yet the American system is as much the work of man's hands
as it is of great and uncontrollable forces ; though it must be
admitted that the dead hand of the " founding fathers " has
become as potent a force of nature as the size of the country
or the diversity of its interests and sentiments. Parliament, that
is, the House of Commons, exists to support a government or

to destroy one ; that government is chosen from among the members of the legislature and the new government will, in the main, be recruited from the same body. The great test of party fidelity, the object for which each individual has been returned to Parliament, is to support or oppose a certain group of men in whose hands lies, while in office, all the executive and, in practice, all the legislative powers of the constitution. These facts are conclusive in determining what kind of man attempts and succeeds in becoming a member of Parliament, what kind of talents and service reward efficiency in meeting the demands of the system, and colour all the activities of the members as a body, and as individuals.

The American Congress is the legislative aspect of a government which has its powers severely limited by a written constitution which leaves many of the questions which a democratic system handles with the greatest political success, to other legislatures. Much of the most conveniently heart-stirring material is pre-empted by the states and, in the main, it is the less easily digestible raw material of political programmes and excitement that is left to the federal government. Not for Congress the long and stimulating debates on education and its effects on tender consciences : not for Congress the simpler forms of labour legislation : not for Congress the possibility of long and varied programmes, meeting all the immediate demands of the party in the country, for if the party in the country is in the happy position of having a common programme, it has normally to convert two different kinds of legislatures. This is a drawback of any federal system, but it is very marked in the United States, because the United States is a very federal federation, as compared with Canada or Germany.

Congress is not only shut off from many fields of action, but the powers that are left can only be exercised, in many cases, under a constitution that leaves the last word to the Supreme Court, and so the legislators have not only to think what their constituents want, or will stand, but whether what Congress does decide will seem to five elderly lawyers the sort of thing the framers of the constitution would have approved of, if they could have foreseen what, in fact, they by no possibility could have foreseen. When all legislation has to run this kind of gauntlet, the results are apt to depress the legislator and his supporters, to blunt the edge of zeal and hope and to turn the minds of both parties to more practicable and tangible achievements, favours and jobs.

Lastly, the American legislature is shut out of a great deal even of the federal field, by its constitutional inability to find out what the executive is doing and, consequently, shut out from the chance of hindering or helping in the doing of it. Even if it is assumed that the House of Commons has abandoned, save in the rarest cases, the pretension to control the executive, the executive has to command the House of Commons ; even if the relation is that of officer and soldier, it is a constant relation, and the soldier knows that promotions are always made from the ranks. But a congressional career must be an end in itself, it leads to nothing else and the rewards it offers are the rewards of a game whose essential dullness requires, like American football, the cover of an elaborate apparatus of rules and stratagems that are difficult without being subtle. It offers some local fame, but seldom combines fame and power, and suffers the last indignity, that the few great prizes offered to the American politician are open to permanent competition from outsiders on terms that would make our politicians dumbfounded at such a disregard of their vested interest.

At the foundation of the position of Congress and its members, is the working of the " locality rule ". The constitution commands that the Senators and Representatives shall be residents of the states that they represent and convention insists that Representatives shall, in addition, be residents of the congressional district that they wish to represent. Though this refinement on the constitutional requirement has no legally binding force, it is very rarely disregarded.[1] The consequences of this rule are far-reaching in all departments of public life, but are most manifest in the composition and powers of Congress. The working of the rule is, in itself, enough to encourage and justify the practice of going outside Congress for presidential candidates and for Cabinet members. It is useless to look for the natural leaders of a party in a body in which many of them will never, be they ever so willing, be able to find a seat. An executive recruited from Congress would, under the present rule, exclude from a political career all Democrats over a great part of the North and all Republicans over a great part of the South. The tendency for the minority party to shrivel would be accentuated, for if there is little enough at present to attract an ambitious man to be a Democrat in Pennsylvania or a Republican in Alabama, there would be nothing at all, if the summit of a political career were necessarily dependent on entering Congress, for the minorities have no chance of being elected in their own states and no right to try elsewhere. A parallel from an anomaly of the British Constitution will show the position as it is in America. A Scottish peer who is not also a peer of Great Britain, or of England, cannot serve in the House of Lords except as one of

[1] Occasionally, residence in a neighbouring district is sufficient, but even such meagre dispensations are rare.

the sixteen Scottish representative peers and he cannot be elected
to the House of Commons. A Liberal, who is a Scottish peer,
is as effectively debarred from parliamentary life as a Republican
in Mississippi, or a Democrat in Vermont, but what is, in our
system, an anomaly affecting a handful of persons, affects the
hundreds of thousands who are inhabitants of the pocket boroughs
of the dominant parties in their localities. No ability, no brilliance of party service, no popularity in the country at large,
can enable a politician so situated to enter Congress, and if it
were necessary to enter Congress to get into the front rank of
American politics, the locality rule would debar millions from
the chance, as effectively as Liberal Scottish peers are debarred
with us.

Since, however, the prizes that are open to non-congressional
competition are usually monopolized by politicians who have
won their spurs in state politics, where the same rule obtains,
the only first-class prize really open to all is the presidency of
the United States and such offices as are in its gift.

If we think of the illustrious " carpet-baggers " who have
adorned the British political scene in the past, and those who
adorn it at present, we can imagine something of the change
that would result from such a rule being applied here. The
long procession of constituencies that marked Gladstone's political
progress from Newark to Midlothian, the varied electoral history
of Mr. MacDonald and of Mr. Churchill, the search for safe
seats and the readjustments that follow a general election and
result in the providing of new mounts for champions unhorsed
in the fray, are all impossible in the American system. We find
it hard to follow a system that lets the careers of the leading
members of a party depend on the accidents of local politics,
that would, in 1906, have compelled Mr. Balfour to wait till
the next general election to return to Parliament with the risk
of finding that Manchester had not repented, yet the leader of
the Republican party in Ohio, the sponsor of the McKinley
tariff which had been the issue of the election of 1890, was
defeated and left out of the Congress in which his policy was
one of the chief issues. The Republicans fought the congressional
election of 1890 on the slogan " Bill McKinley and the McKinley
Bill ", but though they had to stick by the bill, they had no
means of sticking to its author and he was defeated by a local
opponent. More startling still is the premium put on " gerry-
mandering ". By altering the boundaries of his district, the
Democratic legislature of Ohio was able to make it pretty certain
that McKinley would be defeated. What possibilities would
open out if a Labour majority on Durham County Council could
arrange the boundaries of the Seaham division so that Mr.

MacDonald would be defeated—and could not be elected elsewhere or if it were possible to exclude Mr. Lloyd George from Parliament by submerging the Caernarvon Boroughs in the county ! As the case of Northern Ireland shows, the temptation is not always resisted by those who have grown up under the parliamentary system, still less is it resisted in America. In a European country, ingenious electoral laws may help a party or harass its opponents, but they cannot destroy the opposition. The electoral system in 1924 helped the French Left, but M. Tardieu was able to return to the Chamber by the Belfort by-election ; M. Léon Daudet, defeated in Paris, could try his luck in the senatorial election for La Vendée, unsuccessfully indeed, but, at least, he could try ; M. Léon Blum could move into Toulouse with general approval. Would Mr. Churchill's career have been possible if every change in party had had to undergo the scrutiny of the same constituency ? It is a help to have a perfectly safe seat, never to know the uncertainty and humiliation that comes of a narrow electoral margin, but it is a luxury, not a necessity, for a politician under the parliamentary system. Happy are M. Herriot in Lyons ; M. Poincaré in the Meuse ; M. Clémentel in the Puy de Dôme ; happy Mr. Baldwin in Bewdley ; the Chamberlains in Birmingham ; Mr. Lloyd George in his Celtic fringe of North Wales ; but their rivals are not permanently handicapped by the fickleness of their constituencies. Unless their party collapses, as has happened to the Liberals, or they are completely out of touch with it, as happens to various independently-minded members, other seats will be found. On this possibility depends a good deal of parliamentary discipline. As a rule, a constituency will punish defection from party orthodoxy, but it sometimes happens that a member has to choose between displeasing his supporters and obeying the party whips. If he supports the party he can face the music, knowing that his fidelity, if he is at all prominent, will be rewarded, even if his constituency revolts. An American Senator or Congressman, no matter what his eminence, who obeys the party call against the wishes of his state or district, knows that if he is defeated, the President or the party can do nothing for him, cannot procure for him a seat outside his own bailiwick, can only solace him with a job—and cannot always do that. Can we wonder that, in fact, the politician keeps his ear to the ground, that the whims of any important section of his home-folks are more to him than the most weighty representations of national or international figures, since with them lies all his political power and his future ?

Rare, indeed, in English politics are such catastrophes as those which cut short the careers, to name only two recent instances, of Senator Wadsworth in New York,[1] and Senator Pomerene in Ohio. The case of Mr. C. F. G. Masterman whose Cabinet career was stopped by his failure to find a seat in Parliament is so rare as to be noteworthy ; in America, numerous corresponding failures to keep a seat have led, as in the case of Mr. Kellogg, to an embassy and the State Department, but more often to permanent obscurity. The working of the locality rule is, then, in itself, enough to explain the parochialism of Congress, even if there were not so many other good reasons for it.

Congress is organized in two houses : the lower of these, the House of Representatives, was to be the popular branch of the Legislature and it was assumed, on the precedent of the House of Commons, that it would consequently be the more powerful. The House of Representatives was designed to exercise all the powers of the Commons that were not incompatible with the federal system and the independence of the executive. It is probable that the framers of the constitution did not foresee what a far-reaching difference the latter was, that in itself the exclusion of the members from any direct share in the executive power was a change of such moment, that had the House of Representatives been, in every other respect, a replica of the Commons, that difference alone would have deeply marked off one from the other. Not only is the absence of direct relations between the executive and the legislative fundamental to the position of the American lower house, it accounts, in part, for its failure to dominate the Senate, for in any parliamentary government, the decisive factor is not legal power, but the responsibility of the ministry to one house and not to the other. Where the executive is not a creature or master of either house, this easy means of determining where the real power lies, as between the two houses, is absent. The responsibility of the Ministry to the lower house in Australia is, in itself, enough to account for the failure of the Commonwealth Senate to acquire the power and prestige that have accrued to the American Senate which, in other ways, it resembles. Yet the House of Representatives, despite this difficulty, exerted at the beginning of the federal government a decided predominance over the Senate. In the lower house was concentrated most of the parliamentary talent, Madison, Fisher Ames, Gallatin. In the lower house, the war was carried on between the parties, and the aggressions made on the executive. Time was to show that the

[1] Mr. Wadsworth has recognized the inevitable in the present disposition of party strength in the state of New York and has entered the lower house from his own loyal section of the state. Had he been a resident of New York City that resource would not have been open to him.

weakness of the infant Senate, its excessively small numbers (twenty-six), and the existence of a semi-parliamentary form of government, were only temporary, and when the Jacksonian revolution showed the real character of the American Government, the Senate stepped into the first place and has retained it ever since. An examination of the constitution of the House and of its methods of working will demonstrate the inevitability of senatorial dominance.

The House was directly representative of the people, the President and the Senate were each, in theory, the result of indirect election. The sudden nullification of the indirect election of the President provided the House with a rival in the chief of the executive, a rival with all the advantage of unity, and all the prestige of being the choice of all the people, not of any sectional constituency. Since Jackson asserted the doctrine that the President is peculiarly the representative of the people, the House has fallen into the background as an embodiment of popular sovereignty. The members have been felt to be, and have acted as if they felt themselves to be, not the corporate representatives of the American people, but an agglomeration of local delegates. It is easy to see why, in effect, the presidential claim has so easily vanquished that of the House, but how did the Senate, until recently elected by the state legislatures, and still fantastically defiant, in the distribution of its representation, of all democratic theory, successfully defy the representatives of the people? One reason which is almost enough to account for the senatorial success, is the remarkable time arrangements of the constitution. Every even-numbered year, the whole House of Representatives and one-third of the Senate is elected. Thus, at any one time two-thirds of the Senate has been less recently commissioned by the electorate than has the whole of the House. Yet this advantage was lost by the way in which the House used to meet. Elected in November of 1930, the Seventy-Second Congress met in December 1931, thirteen months after its election. Unless summoned by the President in special session, Congress had no power to meet sooner and when a midterm election resulted, as in 1930, in a defeat for the presidential policy or party, the President had usually no mind to add to his troubles by summoning Congress. Thus an administration which had been rebuked at the polls at the congressional election, could ignore Congress altogether till more than a year later, when it was hoped things would have changed for the better, and it was probable that Congressmen would have tired of "nursing their wrath to keep it warm". This system was odd enough. It allowed a Congress which had, in theory, been chosen to carry out a programme, to put off doing this until it was quite possible it could no longer be done usefully, or at all.   When it did meet, any extreme claim to act as a popular mandatory was weakened by the fact that the will of the people had had plenty of time to change, and if the President, or Senate, or both, were inclined to slight the claims of the House, it was impossible to be at all sure that they were displeasing the public by doing so.   It will be remembered that Mr. Baldwin was beaten in the general election of 1923 in November, but did not resign till the new parliament met the following January.   In the United States, he could have waited till the December of 1924 before meeting the hostile legislature, but we had actually three governments and two general elections in the time it took for an American " general election " in an " off year " to produce even the preliminaries of legislative effect. Nor was this all or worst.   The Congress that at last met thirteen months after it was elected had to face another election eleven months ahead, and members had no time to think of what they had promised, since all their thoughts were concentrated on what they would have to promise in November.   If the election year was a presidential year, the whole attention of Congress, and especially of the lower house, was devoted to election politics, and in the few months of its first session that elapsed between December and June,[1] every law, every vote, every speech, was the result of election strategy.   Lastly, when the election had come and gone, Congress met for its last session, and regardless of the fact that many of its members, perhaps a majority of them, had been rejected at the polls, it exercised its legal prerogative in an orgy of jobbery that gave a bad repute to what were happily called the " lame duck sessions ". The unfortunate members who failed of re-election had often to look forward to a meagre and unattractive life in a small town where, it was probable, their financial situation was not easy—or they would not have gone to Congress.   Few businesses improve by neglect and these Congressmen were in a position which made them welcome any financial aid.   If they were of the same party as the President, they had a claim on his patronage.   They were stuffed into all vacant nooks and crannies of the federal patronage, unless, as sometimes happened, the slaughter had been so great that nothing worth the attention even of a defeated Congressman was available.   Such was the sad case of Abraham Lincoln when he came to the end of his one term in Congress and there was, oddly enough, a Whig President in the offing.   It was in the " lame duck " session that the worst jobs were put through.   The memory of the last session of

[1] When normally it adjourns to leave the field clear for the presidential Conventions. In 1932 Congress remained in session during the Conventions.

the Republican Congress which met after the great Democratic triumph of 1874, was far from fragrant, and though there has been no equally scandalous performance since, the record of the short sessions is not impressive. The President was in such a strong position to win the approval of the rejected, that their votes, however unjustly, were suspect in the public eye. Even had there been no " lame duck " session, fellow-feeling, at any rate in the Senate, is strong enough to provide for at least as many of the brethren who have fallen by the wayside, as is good for the moral health of the upper house and the touchiness of the Senate, as revealed in the indignation over the publication of the vote on the confirmation of that distinguished " lame duck ", Senator Lenroot, of Wisconsin, is proof of the uneasiness of senatorial consciences.[1]

The anomaly of the " lame duck " session had some justification when the constitution was drafted, and when the road to the capital from Georgia or Maine was both long and uncertain. It has no justification now and has long been under attack. The Senate repeatedly passed the " Norris amendment "[2] which would make the inauguration of the President and the new Congress fall in January instead of March. Repeatedly smothered in the lower house, this amendment has at last been passed and ratified by the necessary number of states, ending one of the least defensible features of the Constitution. Even if there were no personal abuses connected with the " lame duck " sessions, their existence was an outrage against democratic theory, and the long resistance of the House to so obvious a reform a commentary on its character.[3]

Can we wonder that an assembly so elected is incapable of real resistance to its rival, the Senate, a rival which never dissolves, two-thirds of whose members are free, for the moment, from electoral cares, and which may reasonably laugh at any special claim for popular authority coming from such a body as the House of Representatives ? For these reasons it has been impossible for the House to seize any powers (other than those

[1] The confirmation of the appointment of this martyr to Republican orthodoxy was voted on in executive session, that is, privately, but some journalist published the vote, to the indignation of the majority, who preferred to do good by stealth and raged to find it fame.

[2] So called after its sponsor, Senator Norris of Nebraska.

[3] It should be noted, however, that the adoption of the Norris amendment will still leave in both houses of Congress, real, if not technical, " lame ducks ". The primary system in fact, involves the election of many Senators and Representatives long before the formal election of November. It has happened, and will happen, that members of both houses, defeated in the primary, in the spring of one year and so really rejected by the electorate, continue to legislate until next year.

bestowed by the Constitution), and to make of them a ruling convention ; so that the only chance for the House to make its weight felt, is to exploit to the full its legal powers and these are not enough to make the House an equal partner with either the Senate or President.

Chapter II

THE HOUSE AT WORK

THERE have been in the United States, leaders of public opinion, great figures in the history of the nation, who owed their power and fame to their membership of the House of Representatives. There have been far fewer of them than of the great House of Commons men, but there have been some. Yet in reading of their achievements, it is odd how much stress is laid on their parliamentary talents and, by parliamentary talents, is meant something much more technical than any customary English use of the word. The efforts that are remembered, or, at any rate, recalled, are often displays of presence of mind in application of the rules, traps laid for unwitting rivals or enemies, skilful obstruction or resolute disregard of it. Such abilities have their place in every assembly. Yet although Gladstone, after nearly sixty years in the House of Commons, declared that he was an old parliamentary hand, and won the House by doing so, his parliamentary greatness meant much more than that he was a master of the rules, or that he could outmanœuvre Stafford Northcote or W. H. Smith in the disposal of parliamentary time, or the artful use of the closure. Yet the fame of a leading member of the House of Representatives is, if one may judge by what their admirers say, the fame of a master of guerrilla warfare. If an impossible parallel be again permitted, Biggar, or Healy, or Randolph Churchill, would fill a place in parliamentary annals equal to that of Disraeli or Gladstone. There were, of course, other claims to greatness, and such men as Blaine would have come to the front in any assembly, but the House of Representatives has, since the Civil War at any rate, rewarded the talents of a criminal lawyer, quick to drive a coach through a badly drafted bill, better than it has those of a statesman or a jurist.

That this should be so is not surprising. In an assembly like the House of Representatives, where party lines are eminently artificial, where irresponsible action has no immediate unpleasant consequences, as it may have in a parliamentary system, discipline is extraordinarily hard to maintain. Just as it was the Irish party, quite without compunction for the fate of the Government, or of its programme, and quite outside the ordinary discipline of public opinion, or party responsibility, that made it necessary to tighten up the rules of the House of Commons, so it was the existence of a whole house of nascent Irish parties, that made it necessary to tie up the House of Representatives, till it is a caricature not merely of a ruling assembly, like the Commons or the French Chamber, but even of a deliberative assembly like the old Reichstag or the modern Italian Senate. The body which it most resembles is the Corps Législatif of the First Empire, a Corps Législatif without the Tribunate.[1]

With no ministerial body to defend or attack, with no direction from without, the House can only do two things, abandon itself to its powers, luxuriate in pointless debate and let the President and the Senate do as they will, or secure power for some of its members, at the cost of the liberty of all the rest. The latter course is usually adopted. Normally, all power in the House of Representatives is concentrated in the rulers of the majority party. At one time the business of the House, with its short life, its short sessions, its absence of the previous veto of the Cabinet system, was put into the hands of an individual, the Speaker. By reducing the open business to a form, by making all legislation pass through committees nominated by the Speaker, the minority party and—equally important— the dissidents among the majority, were rendered helpless. All real business was done in the committees, there the minority members could do what they might, they were always in a minority and it was made, in all but the rarest cases, impossible to get a bill out of committee without the consent of the leader of the majority party. This system was inevitable, if the House was to be an efficient agent of a party programme; it had its begetters among Democratic as well as Republican Speakers, but its greatest master was " Czar " Reed, who destroyed the last effective resistance by his counting of present, but unanswering, Democrats, to make the quorum ; by rigidly disciplining the Republican majority ; and by assuming all the powers of the House to himself and the little group of committee heads which he had appointed. It was the " Lords of the Articles " of the Scottish Parliament brought up to date. In one of the most striking instances of his power, Reed and his " Cabinet " arranged the Dingley tariff before Congress met, and it was " steam-rollered " through in record time. Reed retired, but his system was carried on by Henderson and " Uncle Joe " Cannon, and no English leader of the House, commanding a

---

[1] The Corps Législatif of the Second Empire was a very different body. If Morny had had the powers of the rulers of the House of Representatives, the " Cinq " would not have given much trouble.

large and docile majority, ever had a firmer hand on his flock than had the Speaker. With a similar, though less secure control of the Senate under Aldrich, the Republicans would have had no reason to complain of the difficulties of the separation of powers, if fate had not given them Roosevelt in the White House. What the Speaker let through, went through, and what he vetoed was decently buried in the committees, and the growing resentment of the minority had no legitimate vent. The Democrats were used to this, but the " insurgent " Republicans from the West were goaded into revolt. In a similar situation, a " ginger group ", on the right of a Conservative ministry, the I.L.P. on the left of a Labour Government, could at least ask questions, make speeches—even scenes, give some publicity to their grievances and force the Government to give excuses, if not reasons, for its acts. Put on useless committees, denied the floor and with no ministry to harass, the position of the minority was far inferior to that of a private member, in even the most docile of British Parliaments, or in any other Parliament. The situation had only one weakness, it required real unity in the majority. The fission between the eastern and western Republicans brought about the revolution against the autocratic Speaker—and the final proof as will be shown that the House of Representatives is doomed to futility or silence.

There are Congresses which, from natural incoherence or special circumstances, choose liberty at the price of anarchy. It is not very unusual in the American system for one house to be controlled by a party other than that in control of the other and the presidency. Between 1874 and 1896, the three parts of the government were nominally united for only four years, 1889–91, 1893–95, and in the latter Congress, Democratic control of the Senate was formal only. In such situations little can be done, and there is a temptation for Congress to " play politics " at the expense of legislative efficiency. Without any real chance of putting through a programme, it is difficult to enforce discipline on irresponsible Congressmen. When it is a matter of passing bills designed to make things awkward for the President, the party in control of the lower house may preserve an appearance of unity, though even this requires such skilful handling as Champ Clark displayed in the last Congress of the Taft administration. But more positive action needs a firmer lead than even the ablest Speaker can give. In the long period of Democratic dominance of the lower house between 1874 and the election of a Democratic President in 1884, the difficulties of a party in control of the House, but not of the presidency, were made sufficiently manifest. It was easy enough to unite Democrats in denunciation of the " theft of '76 ", but impossible to unite them on a more positive programme. Samuel Randall, a Pennsylvania Democrat—that is to say, a Democrat who differed from a Republican by the thinnest of hairbreadths, could be a leader of the embattled Democracy as long as the party was in opposition. He, and his kin, could sabotage all low-tariff measures without incurring any effective discipline. When, however, there was a Democratic President, support of whom was a rough test of party orthodoxy, the old freebooting days were over and Randall was no longer a power.

It is impossible, as a rule, to reduce to one common denominator the mass of sectional discontents and grievances that lie behind a transference of authority in Congress.

" Patronage and pork amalgamate and stabilize thousands of special opinions, local discontents, private ambitions." [1]

A Congress which is not in political sympathy with the President, which does not share even the scanty responsibility of the American party system, has no patronage and so is extremely hard to stabilize, as Speaker Mr. John Garner found out in 1931. In such circumstances, the separation of powers is fatal to positive action, only a common fear or some extraordinary pressure can drive the three horses together.

"Les trois pouvoirs sont séparés. Ainsi, sauf l'illumination d'un bref délire, ils ont plein pouvoir pour s'empêcher d'agir." [2]

In such collapses of collaboration, it is easy and usually not unjust, to blame the House. The action of the President, or of the Senate has an appearance, at any rate, of unity and purpose which is usually lacking in the obviously fissiparous character of an ill-disciplined House of Representatives. It is this sad truth which always restores the iron rule of the committee chiefs in the House. Either there arises from the tumult a new synthesis of sections, a new party control, or the revolt spends its energies in its negative triumphs and the old gang, or something very like it, returns to power.

This was demonstrated by the fate of the revolt against " Cannonism " which was undertaken in the 61st Congress and was designed to restore the liberty of the House. The legal powers of the autocratic Speaker were curtailed, but Cannon showed his sense of the realities by forcing his Republican enemies either to abandon their party orthodoxy by voting for a Democratic Speaker or to stultify themselves by re-electing him. He was re-elected and, characteristically, reserved his full scorn for the faint-hearted rebels who had come so easily to heel. The

[1] W. Lippmann, *Public Opinion*, pp. 219–2.
[2] B. Faÿ, in *Figaro*, July 6, 1931.

revolt had merely nominal results. The next Congress was Democratic and though the new Speaker, Champ Clark, was not as autocratic as Reed or Cannon, there was no real independence for the private member. The powers of the Speaker were limited in the nomination of committees, the dictatorial power was put into commission, but the new directory was the old monarchy writ large. The attempt to restore the " private member's " rights failed. In the first six years of Wilson's administration, the docile Democratic majority was led by delegates of the President ; in the last two years the assault on the President was dominated by the great struggle in the Senate and the House failed to impress either itself, or the outside world, with any conviction of its own importance. Since then, the control of the House was, until 1931, with the Republicans and, with some difficulties arising from outbreaks of " insurgency ", the legislative and debating powers of the assembly were concentrated in the hands of the Speaker and of the handful of party leaders at the head of the great committees. With such minor concessions as were necessary to secure the co-operation of the minority leaders, it was possible to make of the House a law machine of great efficiency, turning out such legislation as the party chiefs wanted and stifling not only inconvenient bills, but inconvenient discussion. When the Democrats got control of the House in 1931, for the first time since 1919, they resumed the task of " liberalizing the rules ". The amendments were not very important, but they did make it possible to " discharge " a committee more easily and the collapse of the leaders, Speaker Garner and Mr. Crisp, during the budget revolts of 1931, may have been due, in part, to the increased facility the new rules give to the leaders of sectional " caves ". It may also have been due to mere parliamentary incompetence and to a real cleavage between the opinions of the old-school southern Democrats, elevated into the seats of the mighty by the seniority rule, and the majority of the House which had been elected in a revulsion against " a business man's government ". In any case, the overwhelming Democratic majority of the new House will have to decide whether it will be led from the chair or from the White House, or whether it will let its history be a series of wrangles and raids. The choice is again imposed, freedom or power. It is probable—and desirable—that the House will choose power and that we shall see a return to the old system of rigorous control by the leaders and the limiting, or stifling, of debate.

This is the necessary condition of legislative efficiency and we may assume that it will be accepted. What little remains of the forum will be confined to the open hearings of the committees and there it may be that the educative work and the effective propaganda will be done, not by the members, but by the witnesses who represent the interests involved in the measure under discussion.

The House provides one kind of satisfaction abundantly, real power which falls to the handful of senior members, but they have power without fame, they must be like Holstein or Père Joseph ; the limelight shone on them by obedient press correspondents, or press-agents, cannot make good drama out of their dull but important task, although the absence of a Treasury bench permits the leaders of the House (and of the Senate) to attach their names to legislation.   The " Adamson Act ", the " Esch-Cummins Act ", the " Smoot-Hawley Tariff ", are examples of a type of legislative immortality rare in English political life, where Lord Hardwicke's Act, Fox's Libel Act and the Plimsoll Line stand out from among the vast bulk of anonymous legislation.   There are in every Congress a few men, not rulers of the regular hierarchy, who are, none the less, well-known public figures.   Messrs. Tinkham and La Guardia, for example, men whose identification with some well-known cause, above all, with the attack on prohibition, makes them good copy, and whose independence of party ties makes them defiers of committee tyranny.   But how limited are the opportunities open to such men, when compared with those available to such very different types of private member as Lord Hugh Cecil and Mr. Maxton, and if we reflect, how faint becomes the memory of even a prominent English private member compared with that of a Cabinet minister of equal talent !   If we compare Dilke with Chamberlain, Labouchere with Morley, if we try to remember who were the members of the " Fourth Party " besides Lord Randolph Churchill and Lord Balfour, we have some idea of how little the House of Representatives can offer to a type which still seeks fame in the House of Commons.

The average member can neither achieve fame nor, perhaps, is he really anxious to do so.   He nurses his constituency by jobs and by the easy propaganda of speeches, printed in the *Congressional Record*, but fortunately undelivered.   These harmless closet orations serve the purpose of the questions with which the British private member proves to his constituents that he has not been idle, or the " *ceci est grave* " with which the Prince des Laumes interrupted Ministers and showed the voters of Méséglise that he was not neglecting his political duties.

To emerge from the ruck, it is even more advisable in Congress than in most parliaments to ride a hobby of some publicity value.   Congressman Butler of Iowa acquired the distinguishing name of " Pansy " Butler because of his long campaign to make the pansy the national flower.   Other members may propose to prevent dramatic critics ruining such an important New York industry as the stage, by their highbrow criticisms, especially criticism of plays by Congressmen. There are always facilities for the Congressman of the type described by Speaker Reed, as " never opening their mouths without subtracting from the sum of human knowledge ", but the necessity of competing with such variety artists does not attract the serious-minded.

The dull lot, and meagre opportunities for fame, that the House of Representatives offers to what we should call the young private member, are accentuated by the co-existence of the locality rule and the committee system, for a necessary consequence is the highly gerontocratic character of both Houses, but especially of the lower House.

An over-emphasis on age, and on the claims of long party service, is common to all modern democratic governments which have not had their normal life cut in two by revolution. A war and a world upheaval are not enough to upset the regular roster of promotion in a party, provided the party does not die. How comparatively few are the new-comers in French or English politics and how enduring were the laurels won in the religious controversies of France, or the fiscal combats of an earlier age in Britain. And, when the disintegration of Italian parliamentarianism had begun and the aged Giolitti was recalled from Dronero to office, the hierarchical nature of the political party was neatly displayed.

From one aspect, the American system is less subject to mere party seniority than the typical parliamentary government of Western Europe. The executive power in nation and state may fall into the hands of a man young in years, or in political service, or in both, but a Governor and still more a President, is not the typical American politician in office. In the House and in the Senate, power goes with years, for, to an extent unparalleled elsewhere, seniority dictates promotion. In a parliamentary body seniority is a great asset, but it is only one of several qualifications. The mere " Father of the House " in England may be a leading politician, as the present bearer of that empty title is (Mr. Lloyd George), but long service is, in itself, quite helpless to place a member in the front rank. Every House of Commons has its quota of venerable Conservatives, and of senior miners' representatives who have no claims to, or hopes of, office. The same is true of the French Chamber. In Congress, the locality rule works to put age in power for its own sake, since a member who loses his seat is out till the same district re-elects him. It is impossible for a promising young man to be brought in, or kept in, by the leaders to strengthen the debating strength of the party. What they cannot have they do not prize, and the ordinary parliamentary talents that are prized—adroitness in handling the very complicated rules and the necessary astuteness in keeping all quiet on the home front—are the one learned, and the other displayed, in long service. If a Congressman is, first of all, an effective master of a complicated and technical system of local and private claims, it is reasonable to put the older members at the top, for there is a probability that the fact that they are old members means that they have acquired this technique. Mistakes are made, but no more commonly than in a parliamentary system, in which facility in debate is presumed to include administrative and political ability before it has been disproved—and sometimes after. Consequently, in the lower House, the ranking positions in the powerful committees go to the older members ; the burden of proof is removed from the aged to their rivals. To disregard seniority in committee assignments is at least as grave an affront as the omission of a member of a former administration from a new Cabinet is in the English system. It is true that mere seniority in the key positions is not quite enough. The office of Speaker is too difficult to be given to the oldest inhabitant as such, and the headships of the chief committees represent long service and the absence of proved incapacity and uncontrollable distaste for the subjects dealt with. And an occasional fighting orator, like Joe Bailey of Texas, may force his way to the front in a few terms, but in no national assembly does mere seniority in membership pay such regular wages as in Congress. This is true both of Senate and House, but the effects in each are very different.

The locality rule and the insistence on long service have a result which Republicans have long deplored when the Democrats control either, or both, Houses. It puts " the South in the saddle ". In the low-water marks of Democratic representation, only the " Solid South ", and a few oases like the Tammany districts in New York, can be relied on to send Democrats to Congress.[1] When the Democrats do get control of the House, all the merit has been acquired by the southern members who step into authority, even though the movement that resulted in a Democratic victory is antipathetic to all or most of their views. Thus the capture by the Democrats of the control of the House of Representatives in 1931 made sixteen of the twenty-two chief committees spoil of war for southern veterans. In the Seventy-Third Congress, the triumph of 1932 introduces a new possibility, for the first time since the Civil War, the Democrats have a majority in the House independent of the block of southern members, but the vested interests of the South in committee assignments remain to be dealt with, and, there may be a real

[1] After the landslide of 1920, of 131 Democrats in the House, 120 were from the " Solid South ".

cleavage in the majority which will shake the system of committee seniority to its foundations.

The results of a Republican triumph are not so paradoxical, for the distribution of safe seats and, consequently, of committee power, is less sectional. Pennsylvania, Illinois, California, Iowa, have all their secure bailiwicks and the Republican party in the House is not likely to be so misrepresented by its venerable leaders as the Democratic party may be. Yet even the more widely-spread Republicans sometimes find themselves unduly under the control of one section.

> " Thus in the Sixty-Eighth Congress, [1923–5], the Speaker of the House, Mr. Gillett, the Chairman of the Committee on Interstate and Foreign Commerce, Mr. Winslow, the Republican leader in the Senate, Mr. Lodge, President Coolidge and the Chairman of the Republican National Committee, Mr. Butler, were all Massachusetts men." [1]

If the House of Representatives had no other than parliamentary attractions, service in it would be for the rank and file almost without compensation and we might have to attach a new name to the term " conscript fathers ". But there *are* other attractions. There is the salary, at the moment $9,000 a year, with some not inconsiderable perquisites. Though the salary counts for less in America than it would be here, and though Washington is an expensive city, it is more than a good many Congressmen could earn at their own profession, which is usually that of a minor country lawyer. To many a party hack, devoted to the petty services of the cause, working his way from sheriff or state legislator to mayor or lieutenant-governor, a seat in Congress is very desirable and the due reward of good and faithful service.[2] Until this generation, in the West, it was regarded as a part of the party patronage and sent round, and many a loyal party man took, like Lincoln, his one term in Congress and gave up his place to the next on the roster, without too much grumbling. Nowadays, a Congressman is to blame if he loses his seat ; normally party changes are few and a member is entitled and expected to dig himself in by strict attention to his duties as a broker of jobs and favours. With his share of the federal patronage, if his party is in power, with fragments from the pork barrel, whatever his party, the representative must be constantly vigilant in defence of his electors ; no failure in this will be pardoned and no failure in other duties

[1] P. D. Hasbrouck, *Party Government in the House of Representatives*, p. 186.
[2] Economical Congressmen have been able by rigid economy and ingenious handling of the allowance made for secretarial work, to save a good deal of their salaries, enough to set them up in a modest way. There is a story of a Congressman who saved enough in one term to start a bank.

will cause much trouble, if the home fences have been well looked after. Gifts of seeds, of farm literature, of speeches which are printed though not delivered ; the reading into the *Congressional Record* of the poems of his constituents ; the presentation of whatever fancy laws a powerful section wants, in the well-founded hope that they will be smothered in committee or that, if the same pressure has been applied generally, the results and the responsibility will be shared ; the personal visits to the departments to secure jobs or concessions ; above all, the diversion to his district of some of the federal manna and quails, are the essential duties of a representative. As in most cases his party is anchored in the constituency, he has not to fear the competition of a rival body of principles, a few rotundities on the immortal principles of Jefferson or of Lincoln will do to maintain his orthodoxy, combined with a ready compliance with party leadership in unessentials, that is in matters which do not affect his district or stir up any emotions in it. On all general issues, on foreign politics, on financial policy, on general legislation, the wise member will support his leaders, he has little chance to do anything else if he wishes to move upwards in the committee hierarchy. The politics that pay are local politics ; a Congressman who allows his mind's eye to wander from the parish pump to Geneva or Tokyo or, for that matter, to Washington, runs a serious risk of ceasing to be a Congressman. His district expects the whole time of its attorney, with a minimum of decent respect for the opinions of mankind. He may have his hobbies or principles, but his first task is to be a legislative and administrative agent for the district which has conferred on him its most valuable piece of patronage. He should never forget that he is primarily the Consul for Buncombe at Washington. In this, he is not necessarily different from the run of private members in other countries ; notably, he is not different from the French Deputy.[1] In France a Deputy will be forgiven a good deal of doctrinal irregularity, if he is able to nurse his constituency at the public expense, or if he brings it honour and profit by becoming a Minister. His outraged party colleagues may denounce him as a " Saxon ", but, after all, Saxons have no bad name in Saxony.

Even in the British Parliament, the wise member will look after his constituency, will fight to have a liner built at Clydebank, or an aeroplane at Southampton, with a generous disregard of

---

[1] This consular character is most evident in the strange institution of the territorial delegate, that is, the representative of a territory not yet admitted as a state. This officer sits in the House but cannot vote, though he may speak if he gets a chance, combining the office of Agent-General with that of privileged lobbyist for his territory.

financial difficulties he could not command if his own constituency were not in question. The sugar-beet subsidy looks very
different to a born economist who sits for an urban constituency,
from the more smiling countenance it wears when he is member
for an area which is being refreshed by the public funds, and,
as the British Government does more and more in this way,
we may expect members, more and more, to devote themselves
to local interests. But Members of Parliament work under
great difficulties. They can do nothing directly, since the
Government alone can secure a vote of money, and party discipline is still so strong that no amount of local service will, as a
rule, justify voting against the party. Thus a Government,
or an opposition has, as yet, little temptation to bribe *one* constituency out of the public funds ; most activity of this kind must
be spread over the whole country, or over a sufficiently large area
to acquire the dignity of a policy. In Congress, things are very
different ; the local interest of each is the general interest of all
and, in combination, the members have managed to bring to
a high state of perfection that institution known as the " pork
barrel ". The pork barrel is, in general, all legislation designed
to put public money at the disposal of local authorities for
private interests. Lobbying for this end may include anything
from the grants to publish Force's *American Archives* to deepening
Goose creek so that Napoleon may set up as a river port. The
" Rivers and Harbors Bill " has been, in the past, the great
storehouse of " pork ", but with the growth of the activities of the
federal government, the raw material for legislative pork has
become even more abundant. The money to build a harbour
at Napoleon will be voted as part of a bargain to build an air
port at Zenith City, or to locate a hospital for inebriated veterans
at Spoon River. Generous aid to uneconomic irrigation projects
in the West, may bear fruit in votes for new federal buildings in
cities of New England ; the preservation of a useless navy yard
in Maine may have beneficial effects on the digging of a still
more useless canal in Tennessee. It is not wise to be dogmatic
and to assert that *all* improvements are more expensive than
they need be, if they need be at all, but it is fairly certain that
even public undertakings for which there is much to be said,
such as Boulder Dam or the adoption, by the federal government,
of such waifs of private or state enterprise as the Cape Cod Canal
or the New York Barge Canal, have their counterpart in public
works that no prudent government would undertake ; in the
spending of money on Post Office buildings that had better
have been spent on the mail service ; in maintaining useless army
posts and ill-placed navy yards ; in irrigation works that make
the desert to blossom like the rose, at a cost that would pay for

the free distribution of roses to the whole population; and in the digging of navigable channels in a fashion that reminds one of Lincoln's praise of the Navy in the Civil War, they went everywhere the ground was a little damp. There have been members whose constituents were sated, or who were by temperament or political position able to assume the rôle, who became known as " watch-dogs of the Treasury ", but no pack of Cerberuses can suffice, if the robbers are able to make the rules under which the guards must work.[1] Indeed, the expenditure on public works, on " internal improvements " has been on a scale that recalls the more profligate Oriental monarchs of the type of Ismail Pasha, with the important qualification that the American system re-distributes the wealth of the country, but so far has not usually involved the mortgaging of the national credit abroad.

The pork barrel, for all its possibilities of abuse, is not to be condemned off-hand. In a young and growing country, there are many desirable things which have to be done by the government or not done at all. It is a task of great difficulty to allot the shares of the national resources and the American system, for all its prodigality, is probably less harmful to local political loyalties than the system bred in parliamentary countries of the same economic type. In Canada, the control of public funds by the Cabinet prevents some abuses, but it produces others. The Conservatives of an Ontario port, which was eager for federal aid during a Liberal administration, refused to contest a by-election for fear of alienating the powers at Ottawa and candidates have openly promised certain public works if they were returned.[2] In the United States, party lines are not so rigidly drawn, and a Democrat can look after his district or state about as effectively as a Republican.

The resulting expenditure is seldom what an all-wise dictator would have approved, but the system of policy which is at the heart of American political institutions in, at any rate, their modern form,

" identified the public interest with the encouragement of every phase of private productive enterprise. It had deliber-

[1] The watch-dogs occasionally forgot themselves and when Speaker Reed caught one stealing some " pork " for his own district, he quoted Don Juan :
" 'Tis sweet to hear the watch-dog's honest bark
Bay deep-mouth'd welcome as we draw near home."
[2] A Canadian friend told me of an election in which the Liberal candidate promised to resign should he be elected and a Conservative government be returned. In such circumstances, he would give way to his Conservative rival who would be able to do the " riding " more good. Just before the War, a Liberal candidate for a Scottish constituency made lavish promises of governmental gratitude to be expressed in harbour works should he be elected. He was returned, but there was a good deal of outcry.

ately sought to bestow upon the farmers, the manufacturers, the miners, the cattlemen, the timbermen, the railroads and corporations of all kinds direct or indirect subsidies. Such had been the national economic policy since the Civil War." [1]

Beside the immense extravagance of such a policy, the most spendthrift pork barrel was hardly worth mentioning ; the grease from the pork is the necessary oil of the legislative machine.

However natural it may be, the pork barrel is, nevertheless, a powerful factor in the demoralization of Congress, and a result—and a secondary cause—of the endemic sectionalism of American politics. The notion of a share-out is so deep-rooted that hospitals for tuberculous soldiers cannot be planted where hygiene demands, for that would not be politics. The expert may say Arizona or New Mexico, Congress must say Winnemac. A scheme of federal aid to the unemployed will have to meet not only open opposition, but the claims of Senators who wish for a mere share-out and can see no reason why Tennessee should not have its numerical share regardless of its quota of unemployed. It is easier to see the fault than to suggest the remedy. The mere adoption of the Cabinet system would not, as the history of Canada shows, undo this evil. The adoption of a more self-denying attitude by the Congressmen and Senators is hard to conceive and the precedent of the Confederate Constitution is not so hopeful as is sometimes suggested. The Confederate Constitution was a temporary embodiment of the current grievances of the South ; its limitation of the spending power of Congress was a reflection of the southern dislike for the whole system of internal improvements and in any case, as Professor H. J. Ford pointed out, was no very serious barrier to extravagance.

Since 1921, the " budget " has introduced a little more order into the anarchy of congressional finance, but the reform is more superficial than real. The President is now obliged to do what he could have done before, that is to say put before Congress a statement of the current financial position and of the proposed expenditure and revenue of the next year. In so far as this remedies the old muddle whereby the committees spending money were ignorant of what the committees raising money might do, it is a marked improvement, but real budgetary control, as understood in parliamentary countries, consists in more than in letting the right hand know what the left hand is doing. The division between the executive and the legislature is too deep and broad a gulf to be bridged by such devices. Nor has even the minimum regularity of the American budget system been observed. That Congress should upset presiden-

---

[1] H. W. Croly, *Marcus Alonzo Hanna*, p. 353.

tial plans on both the expenditure and revenue side is in the nature of things, but the old bad days of multiplied agencies with no real co-ordination are not yet over.

Given the organization of Congress, the existence of " lobbies " is inevitable. The " lobbyist " is one of the most familiar figures in Washington, if not under that name, and lobbying is one of the leading local industries. Bodies for the improvement of the world and especially the United States, according to Methodist, Catholic, and other plans ; lobbies to look after labour, or out for capital ; all are permanently on the spot, often very handsomely housed in buildings in convenient reach of the Capitol— convenient, that is, for the lobbyists. Then there are the temporary lobbies which descend on Washington when some special issue is being debated, sometimes to reinforce the permanent staff, sometimes to bring a new point of view. At the public hearings before congressional committees, these deputations sometimes act Congressmen, or even Senators, off the stage, especially if they are women. It is no wonder that the average politician shudders when faced by such an ordeal. At times there are explosions ; after Wilson's denunciation of the sugar lobby during the discussion of the Underwood tariff of 1913, there was a hurried rush for cover and an ostentatious if temporary drawing away of congressional skirts, but the lobby is a necessity, if a painful necessity, of the American system. The same forces that occasionally organize pressure on M.P.'s in England have to do it constantly in the United States, where the Congressman or Senator has seldom the firm lead that the Cabinet imposes on the English politician.

The lobbyist may be an expert manipulator of political machinery like the great boss of the Anti-Saloon League, the late Wayne B. Wheeler : he may be an " up and coming " young journalist, or former secretary, like the hero of *Capitol Hill* ;[1] or a lame duck who has not been put into a safe job. He may also be that more doubtful figure, the serving Congressman or Senator who is on the permanent, or occasional, pay-list of a propagandist organization. Such was Congressman Richard Hobson, a former Spanish war hero who was a very highly-paid " dry " ; such was Congressman " Willy " Upshaw. Both these dry orators may be defended, for their remuneration, if not trumpeted abroad, was not secret, and they were entitled to make as much as they could out of their belief in the dry cause. Less easy to defend is the acceptance of remuneration or loans or gifts from powerful bodies which had axes to grind. The relations of Senator Foraker to the Standard Oil Company gave scandal to the suspicious in Roosevelt's time ; there may be

[1] Mr. Harvey Fergusson's novel.

suspicions, but there is no proof, that the devotion of some members of Congress to certain interests is due to direct financial inducement. However dangerous the lobby may be, whatever suspicion it may breed, its existence is an inevitable result of the emptiness of party programmes, the consequent looseness of discipline and the dispersal of responsibility. The lobby is as natural a result of the congressional system as it is, in another form, of the French system. The Panama scandal[1] was a result of the necessity of " sweetening " a great many deputies ; if no lobby has spread its net so wide in American history (and the Crédit Mobilier was a good runner-up) it is perhaps as much due to the superior honesty of the Congressman as to the merits of the American system. In a parliamentary system of the English type, lobbying is unnecessary. If you can " influence " the Cabinet, or its leading member or members, you need not waste any time on mere legislators, and the occasional scandals that arise in the British Dominions are not marked by lobbying in the American sense. The Canadian Pacific Railway could go straight to headquarters and get what it wanted. The lobby in state or nation is bred by the dispersal of power over ill-disciplined and irresponsible bodies. At best it is likely to be misleading as a source of information as to the merits of a measure or the drift of public opinion : in a government which is continually doing economic favours on a large scale for individuals, it may often be worse than misleading.

It is evident, then, that there cannot be in the House of Representatives a homogeneous body of front-bench politicians who can rely on the support of the country at large and who can, on occasion, defy the local opinion of their constituents. Fortunately, there is no absolute need for such a body, for the House does not exist to carry on the government but to unite the claims, public and private, of various areas in a body of delegates who have powers which they can use to further general interests, or particular jobs, according to taste.

The House exists alongside the executive ; it has certain things to do in collaboration with the executive, but the government of the country is, as a rule, not one of them. In quiet times the business of government is carried on from the White House, and the House can devote itself to the task for which it is best designed and which it likes best to undertake—the securing of favours and privileges for sections and individuals. It is thus

[1] The French Panama Company, possibly misled by the title of his office, offered a very handsome retaining fee to the Secretary of the Interior in the Hayes administration, but the President vetoed the arrangement. A connoisseur in corruption might regret the loss of material for a comparative study of the effects of the same poison on two different bodies politic.

that the House can be of one party, while the President is of the other, and that party discipline can be so slack, that a nominal identity of party affiliations between the House and President need have only formal results. The House can harass and irritate, it cannot make and destroy.

In petty local business the average Congressman is at home, and he cares little that the effect is to reduce the House, in Burke's phrase, " ' to a confused and scuffling bustle of local agency ' ".[1] There is no place here for those high views of a representative's duties which Burke preached to the electors of Bristol, and were a Congressman rash enough to preach or practise such doctrine, his district would soon reject him as, for that matter, Bristol did Burke ! It is not hard, then, to see why the office of " Representative in Congress " fails to attract the best political material or, at any rate, the recruits which we are accustomed to think make the best parliamentary material, and the final condemnation of the House of Representatives is that it has purchased legislative efficiency at the cost of all the dramatic and educative values which believers in parliaments are accustomed to prize so highly. It was said in explanation of the low estate of the Reichstag under the imperial régime, that it was only a debating society ; the House of Representatives is not even that. The politician who seeks the first rank of fame or of usefulness will stay in the House no longer than he can, even though he be Speaker, he will seek that haven for which all politicians who do not belong to it yearn, the Senate.

[1] Lindsay Rogers, *The American Senate*, p. 102.

Chapter III

THE SENATE

THE Senate of the United States has long excited the admiration and the wonder of the foreign observer. He sees in it the only second chamber in the world that has held its own, and more than held its own, with the popular house ; what conservatives in other lands have dreamed of is here achieved, a body not representing the people in any crude numerical fashion, exempt by the terms of its election from the ordeal of facing, as a body, popular approval or disapproval, the only branch of the American Government which never dies. Presidents come and go, every two years a House of Representatives vanishes into the dark backward and abysm of time, but the Senate remains. Nor is this body unconscious of its importance and fame. It is touchy of its dignity and not to be put upon by any power in the land or in the world, and a long career of successful usurpation has bred in its members a confidence of ultimate triumph that in itself is no mean aid to victory. " *Qui mange du sénat en meurt.*" Of course, there have been senatorial defeats, the Jacksonian triumph is too famous to be forgotten, but many a President has set out to bully the Senate, to defy it, and has been openly beaten or forced to climb down, with as much dignity as he could command. American political history, indeed, falls into epochs in which the Senate is on top and others in which the President has, for a moment, forced his dangerous associates to some degree of quiet. From 1913 to 1919, Woodrow Wilson ruled with the acquiescence of the Senate, but, in the great conflict of that year, the Senate conquered a more hated enemy than the League of Nations and since then it has been the terror of three Presidents. Harding, newly promoted from their body, and still conscious of the humble place he had occupied in it, hardly dared to resist the oligarchy that had defeated Wilson, and had imposed him upon the country. Mr. Coolidge, despite a few bold words, was forced to submit to pressure that was in the letter of the law unconstitutional, forced to dismiss two members of his Cabinet and forced to undergo the humiliation of seeing his nomination for the post of Attorney-General rejected, an exercise of senatorial prerogative unknown since the revolutionary days of the Johnson administration. There seems no reason to think that Mr. Hoover has been much more fortunate in his relations with the upper house, and until a President comes in with more force of character and more fortune than the last three incumbents, the Senate will continue to dominate the scene.

Tocqueville attributed the great difference he noted in the two houses of Congress, to the indirect election of Senators, and since the adoption of direct election (by the seventeenth amendment, 1913), prophets of evil have been numerous. By the original arrangement, Senators were elected by the state legislators, a proceeding that gave colour to the belief that Senators were state ambassadors, representing the steady interests of the States, not mere delegates of popular emotion like the representatives. The indirect election made it possible, in theory, for a state to choose from among its most distinguished citizens, men who would do honour both to the State and to the Senate. Freed from the necessity of a direct appeal, they could concentrate on the great issues of the day, avoid demagogy and take the long view, giving their judgments and not merely their voices to the State and the Nation. In practice, there was something in this theory ; some states did so look on the senatorial office, notably South Carolina. Even in more recent times, Ohio treated John Sherman as her predestined ambassador in Washington, before and after his service in the Cabinet. Senators were usually, except in the case of a party turnover, sent back term after term as long as they chose to stand, thus creating a body of elder statesmen like Hoar of Massachusetts, Allison of Iowa, Platt of Connecticut, Aldrich of Rhode Island on the Republican, and Williams of Mississippi or Gorman of Maryland, on the Democratic side. It was argued, that direct election would replace these men by mere demagogues, that the turnover would be rapid, that the Senate would sink to the level of the House. Yet the movement for the direct election of Senators went on increasing in force. It had the same basis as the movement for the direct primary. A State Legislature, in a year which was to see the filling of a senate vacancy, was chosen, not on local issues, but on strict party lines. There was, too often, a submerging of all issues in one, and the necessity of saving a seat for the party was often the excuse for all sorts of less desirable triumphs in state affairs. To remove the senatorial election from local politics was a move towards that loosening of party lines in the states which was essential to any reform. Moreover, State Legislatures or the legislative caucuses of the victorious party were, like Conventions, suspected of listening to voices other than that of the people, to the bosses or to the great vested interests. It was alleged, for example, that the Democratic party of Ohio wanted to send to the Senate, George Pendleton, in 1883, but the Democratic legislators chose to send there the candidate of the Standard Oil Company, Henry B. Payne. Occasional outbursts of flagrant corruption like the buying of the Montana legislature in 1901 by the great copper magnate, William F. Clark, and the graft associated with the Lorimer case in Illinois in 1909, seemed to show that the election of a Senator was too valuable a perquisite to be left in the hands of the kind of statesman who was sent to the average Legislature. The Senate that resulted from this system acquired more and more of a timocratic character, became known as the " millionaires' club " and acted up to its title.[1] The first steps to reform came when state laws began to provide that candidates for the Legislatures should be bound to vote for the winner of the open primary. In 1908, a Republican legislature in Oregon was thus forced to elect a Democratic Senator and a way was open to evade the provision of the federal constitution. With the position thus turned, it was hardly worth defending and, in 1913, direct election of Senators was written into the constitution.

The results have neither justified the hopes nor the fears with which this great innovation was greeted. It has been discovered that not only the servants of the people, but the people itself is corruptible. A series of scandals made it evident that the problem of the money power in politics was not abolished by the seventeenth amendment, and that there was some danger that the entrance fee to the Senate would be so high that it would become the multi-millionaire's club. The Newberry case, when Mr. Henry Ford was defeated by the lavish expenditures of his Republican opponent in 1918, was followed, in 1926, by the great scandals of the primary elections in Pennsylvania and in Illinois, which made disgusted conservatives sigh loudly for the comparative purity and cheapness of the Aldrich régime. It was shown that to be elected in Pennsylvania or in Illinois,

---

[1] Many Legislators took it for granted that their votes had a high market value when a Senator was to be elected. "When Stephen M. White was Democratic candidate before the California legislature in 1892, his financial tightness was not agreeable to a body used to millionaire candidates. ' White is simply rigging a plan ', said the future lawmaker, ' to get elected to the United States Senate without its costing him a cent, but we legislators as is to be are going to stop that little game ' " (Edith Dobie, *The Political Career of Stephen Mallory White*, p. 140).

The Californian legislators were as startled at the suggestion of a free election as was Mark Twain's " Mr. Bigler " in *The Gilded Age*. " ' I tell you what it is, gentlemen, I shall go in for reform. Things have got pretty mixed when a legislature will give away a United States senatorship.' "

it was necessary to spend at least hundreds of thousands of dollars, that, consequently, the candidate had to be a millionaire or a nominee of millionaires, and it was inferred that the last state of the Republic was worse than the first. It is true that the contests that cost the money are senatorial primaries, not the formal election, but always in Pennsylvania, and usually in Illinois, the primary is what counts.

One part of the charge may be admitted at once, if an election is going to be corrupt, it will cost more under the new than under the old system. Then it was necessary to buy only a few legislators at what might turn out to be a very high figure a head, but it was cheaper than distributing bribes over the whole voting population. A competent boss of the old school, a Cameron, a Quay, a Penrose, could certainly send himself to the Senate free, and could, if he chose, give the other seat away or quote a very reasonable figure, c.i.f. Harrisburg. But was the poor man any better off, since the rich man could outbid him, if he had no more chance of raising a hundred thousand dollars under the old system, than a million under the new? Yes, it was asserted, for the boss could pick a worthy man whom his henchmen in the legislature would vote for, and send him to Washington without any cost, at any rate to his pocket. The same man, nowadays, had to appeal, not to the occasional benevolence of the single ruler, but to the venality of the rascal multitude. This argument is, of course, familiar ; it is the defence of the rotten boroughs of Old England. Did not Pitt enter the Commons for Old Sarum and his son for Keswick, and Gladstone for Newark and Macaulay for Calne and Burke for Wendover? The list is long. Could or would these young men have entered Parliament so early, if at all, had there been no patronage and had they had to face the expense and turbulence of Eatanswill or to encounter the influence of the Duke of Omnium? Was the effect of the reform not simply to extend the area of corruption, to make the formerly reasonably cheap " close boroughs " and " rotten boroughs ", as expensive to contest as Yorkshire had been? Despite the fears of the English croakers, the corruption of elections steadily diminished as the franchise was extended. The long-lived abuses of English elections grew less and less, they put up a stubborn fight, but they died. Nor is the American case very different. There are cases of ornaments to the Senate being defeated in popular elections who might have won had the old system survived, but the argument is an argument for oligarchy and the raw materials for oligarchy in America are not very attractive. No state is more venal now than in the good old days, many are less venal. Montana is surely more to be congratulated on the system that returns the two present Senators than on that which enabled Clark to debauch the state?[1] The reform has made the tenure of one type of Senator less secure, and it is from that type, and the interests which he represents, that most of the complaints come. It is no longer as easy as it was in the old days to remain in the Senate by buying or stuffing a legislature which, as in the case of Rhode Island, might be a caricature of a representative assembly. Does the Senate suffer if the breed of the Gormans and Platts is rarer or, if Pennsylvania is as corrupt as ever, because its corrupters have to spread their filthy lucre more widely? Either the direct primary and the direct election of Senators have weakened the power of the boss, or they have not. If they have not, is it any grievance that a boss has to compliment the electors by allowing them to ratify his choice and is it probable that, with this possible check existent, he is less likely than of yore to pick a good man? If Pennsylvania politics are in an undisciplined state, it is too bad, but under the old order the Senate seats would have been at the disposal of the victorious faction just as they are at present, and if Mr. Mellon wanted to pit his wealth against Mr. Vare's votes, he was no better off, if no worse. He had, it is true, to spend a good deal more than would have been necessary in the old days, but it was thought he could afford it.

In so far as the politics of a state are corrupt, the direct primary and direct election can do little to improve things. It transfers the bribery from the Legislature to the Forum; it spreads it wider and makes it more easily identifiable, but it does not damage a really healthy state. Can we doubt that, if money could have unseated Senator Norris, it would have been found? Had there been any real horror of corruption in Illinois, the electors could have elected Mr. Magill instead of Mr. Smith. Not all of the assailants of the reform are fools, but some of them are disingenuous, and some have a talent for willing their judgments that is valuable in the politics of a state like Pennsylvania. The real case for Pennsylvanian independence was put candidly by a witness, Mr. R. W. Childs, who told the Senate committee investigating the Pennsylvania primary of 1930:

" I would prefer to maintain what sovereign rights the State of Pennsylvania and other states have now, even if we do not have as clean elections as we might have."[2]

The direct primary has not purified the politics of the Keystone state, but it has certainly not corrupted them to any serious extent. After all, there is a saturation point.

[1] Written before the death of Senator Walsh.
[2] *Nye Committee Hearings (Pennsylvania)*, p. 176.

Chapter IV

THE SENATE AT WORK

THE activities of the Senate, some of which at least could not be openly denounced, are not always such as to commend them to Presidents or to orthodox party men, and one result of the agricultural domination of the Senate has been to provoke an attack on its most characteristic feature. If the House of Representatives is the most shackled deliberative body in the world, the Senate is the freest, and in the complete absence of any effective control over senatorial eloquence or obstinacy lies the secret of senatorial power, for the rules of the Senate can be summed up by a quotation from Lewis Carroll, " a controversy may be raised about any question, and at any distance from that question ". Again and again, the anarchy of senatorial debate has been attacked as an insult to the popular will, to the decorum of Congress, to the prestige and authority of the Senate itself, yet though—like the weather—a great deal is said about it, nothing is ever done about it. Nothing is a slight exaggeration. Two-thirds of the Senate can, since 1917, impose the closure. In the heat of patriotic indignation at the obstinacy of the " wilful men " who opposed Woodrow Wilson's war programme, this very mild restriction on the unlimited freedom of a Senator to speak as long as his wind lasted was adopted and it is as far as the Senate has been willing to go in theory, and a good deal further than it has been normally willing to go in practice. The Senate has, in fact, too acute a sense of what makes for its own power, or for the power of its members, to consent to any restrictions, however plausibly defended, which would make it a mere legislative sausage machine like the House. It prefers to be a talking shop.[1]

It is the laxity of Senate rules that makes possible that much attacked and occasionally abused institution, the senatorial " filibuster ". This is obstruction carried to the point of veto.

[1] I have heard a distinguished Senator defend, in private, the comparative inefficiency of the Senate as a law machine. " All these proposed alterations in the rules are designed to cut down talking. What happens in a factory when you put up a notice, ' No talking-' ? The output goes up. The output of the Senate is laws. Does the country need any more laws ? "

Since a Senator can speak as long as he likes, he can threaten to block all legislation till he has his way. His power of effective veto is limited by his physical endurance, but if one or two senatorial brethren make themselves a band, their powers of obstruction are very formidable indeed. They were multiplied a hundred-fold by the " lame duck " session. Since, in every odd year, Congress died on the third of March, the leaders of a filibuster had a chance of preventing, absolutely, any legislation, including the voting of money, and thus of exacting their price. Such vetoes were rare, but there have been some that have been very famous or notorious. A filibuster killed the Lodge " Force " bill of 1890, a proposal to use the federal army to help to return some Republicans from the Solid South. In defence of their treasured right to local freedom [1] the southern Senators filibustered to such good effect that the Republicans abandoned their bill. A similar filibuster killed the Dyer Anti-Lynching bill of 1921,[2] the Ship Subsidy bill of 1923 and other legislative proposals which have never been revived. As can easily be shown, a filibuster has seldom killed a bill which popular feeling really wanted to live. Senators, that is, have used their power as a prudent House of Lords was advised by Bagehot to use its vetoes, with an eye to the state of the public mind, and we can conclude that this power has been used by Senate minorities with more discretion than has been the habit of the House of Lords. And, although from time to time Senators assume a " holier than thou " attitude, all types of Senators have used the filibuster to secure their ends. Southern Senators use it to defend White supremacy, western Senators against eastern dominance, and even eastern Senators, like Mr. Dave Reed, have been known to filibuster in defence of the right of Pennsylvania to manage her own elections, without having her political private life pried into by Senators from indigent western states. The senatorial veto requires the tacit support of at least a third of the Senate which can prevent a closure and so it cannot be merely frivolous or personal, and lastly, the most abusive kind of filibuster, the hold-up of all business on the last two days of the short session, will disappear with the adoption of the Norris Amendment, along with a good many other abuses.

It is not, however, merely by permitting occasional vetoes

[1] In this case, a technical term meaning their right to intimidate Negroes into refraining from exercising their legal right to vote.

[2] It must not be thought that all the southern Senators who killed this bill approved of lynching ; many deprecated it and some actually opposed it, but they regarded the bill, with some justification, as the thin end of a wedge that might deprive them of their right to handle the Negro in the way which experience has convinced the southern White makes for greatest social progress and general good feeling.

by minorities that the Senate rules add to the power of individual Senators or groups of Senators. The Senate is, next to the Presidency, the most effective platform in the United States. What the President says is always news, but while not every Senator can " break into the front page " merely by speech in or out of the Senate, some Senators can. The ability to express a point of view, to expose a scandal, or to seek for information on some current mystery of high politics, is a great advantage to the Senate and, in the long run, to the country. An ably planned assault in the Senate, a curiosity-stirring demand for information, or even a bold assertion of facts yet to be proved, has often had remarkable results in quickening the consciences of Cabinet officers and even of Presidents.

In their finest form, these activities of the Senate are seen in the investigating committees. These prying and intrusive bodies have not always had a good press. Full of admiration for the English system, the young Woodrow Wilson poured scorn on the feeble attempt to do by " smelling committees " what the House of Commons did, he thought, by its control over the executive. There is, inevitably, something of the drawback inherent in all stable-locking in the working of a Senate committee, but, for better or worse, the controlling, the censorial, power of the American system is in the investigative power of Congress, or—to be exact—in the investigative power of the Senate. The reasons why it is in the Senate and not in the House illustrate both the strength and weakness of the system. The legal powers of the two bodies are the same, but the real powers are very different. One difference inheres in the short term of the House. A House investigation in the second session has very little time to get under way, and even an investigation running from the first session of the House to the last has only, in normal cases, fifteen months to live. The Senate never dies and its committees do not die, either ; they have to be killed. A more fundamental difficulty is that the House is a useless body for any more serious purpose than saying " Yes " quickly or " No " at length. If it agrees with the administration, it agrees pretty completely ; if it disagrees, it disagrees beforehand with a steadiness which detracts from the moral authority of the verdict. In short, the House is partisan either way. The Senate is, or may be, independent. Two-thirds of its members are always free from the immediate terrors of an appeal to the electorate and so less subject to executive or party pressure. Party lines are very vague and party discipline binds only those who are already of that way of thinking. Equally important is the power given by the rules to air any grievance, any rumour, any suspicion free from obligation to verify or to prove. A *prima facie* case is all that is needed to set the public by the ears and to make the setting up of a committee apparently desirable.

The result has been a series of investigations that have washed a great deal of dirty linen in public. It may be desirable that dirty linen should not be washed in public, even if that means that it will not be washed at all. The revelations of turpitude in high places have increased the cynicism of American youth without raising the indignation of their elders, but, at any rate, the leaders in the carnival of corruption that marked the return of the Republican party to power in 1921, were seriously discommoded by the activities of the Senate and their profits eaten into to a degree that made the game hardly worth the candle. These investigations, the exposure of the " Teapot Dome " by Senator Walsh, of the Department of Justice by Senator Wheeler, were the fruits of senatorial independence. There is no reason to believe that either the President, or the House, or the Courts would, by themselves, have succeeded in exposing the scandals. The credit for the house-cleaning that followed the exposure of 1924 must go to the Senators who, for whatever partisan or personal motive, had defied the opinion of the " best people " and had probed into the abscess that lay beneath the façade of prosperity. In 1926 the Reed Committee, whose investigations were prompted by rumours and statements that would not have stood a court trial, was able to throw much light on the mechanism of popular government, for the benefit of the student, and to reveal a standard of political morals among the politicians of Illinois and Pennsylvania which disgusted everybody but the people of Illinois and Pennsylvania.

What are the differences between the American and the parliamentary system of control ? The senatorial investigation is usually too late to do more than denounce and deplore, the sovereign Parliament can arrest the executive in the act, can compel it to defend its action, and defeat it, should the defence seem unsatisfactory. The theory is not quite like the practice. A parliamentary majority has, as a rule, an interest in keeping a government in office and little interest in exposing it. We do not expect a party to foul its own nest. Among the many superiorities of Canadian to American government, moral control by Parliament is not to be counted. A Conservative ministry may rejoice that the Beauharnois case is capable of useful exploitation against its rival, but it has more power to see that an inquiry does not get out of hand than has an American administration or, for that matter, an American Senate, once the committee is appointed. Party feeling is not confined to any country, and we can guess what would have been the character of a mere party investigation of the Harding scandals by remembering the stolid refusal to defend or deny which the Republican party in the country so resolutely adopted. It is, then, far more easy to pack a select committee, or a royal commission, than a senatorial committee, since the Senate is an assembly of ninety-six individuals, rather than a body of two parties. The process of " whitewashing " is infinitely harder when it is probable that the majority of a committee has no motive for concealing the sins of a rival part of the Government, and where the anarchy of the rules makes it difficult to stifle the opinion of the minority. The force of an investigation may depend on the ability and resolution of the Committee ; the Senate has not always such talented investigators at its disposal as Messrs. Thomas Walsh and Jim Reed, but the very unpopularity which the Senate has incurred among the devotees of party fidelity is a testimonial to the skill with which the probe has been inserted. It is a coarse remedy and it is deplorable that it should be necessary to apply it, but since there are many countries like the United States, where financial disinterestedness among politicians is not to be taken for granted, it is by no means certain that a parliamentary system is, for such unpleasant jobs, as effective as the more independent action of the Senate. It is its " nature's to plague, to spy into abuses, and oft its jealousy shapes faults that are not ", but, though honest men have been harassed and spite vented, the Senate has kept adroit hands from picking and stealing too often for its worth to be questioned by anyone who still thinks that corruption should be kept down to a bare minimum.

Nor is the importance of the Committees to be estimated solely by the evil they have uncovered, or even prevented. They are one of the most important modifications of the separation of powers and consequently one of the indispensable driving belts of the American system.

" The investigation committee has become more than a particular form of parliamentary procedure. Together with the standing committee system, it is ' the buckle that binds, the hyphen that joins ' the legislature to the executive, it has taken the place of the Cabinet in the English constitutional system, has provided an effective means of control, has informed public opinion, and has considerably augmented the power of Congress ".[1]

A survival of the Privy Council character of the Senate is to be found in the necessity of ratification of all treaties by two-thirds of that body. It was originally intended that the Senate

[1] G. B. Galloway, " Investigative Functions of Congress ", *Pol. Sci. Rev.*, XXI, No. 3 (Aug., 1927).

should be, or could be, consulted before a treaty was made, but Washington soon found that this would not work—or that he could not work it and since then the Senate has dealt only with treaties in their final form.[1] The use made by the Senate of the powers thus conferred on it has not been widely admired by foreigners, or by "forward-looking" Americans. There is a long record of treaties killed or mutilated, despite the pleas of Presidents and Secretaries of State, and the annoyance or indignation of foreign powers. John Hay, embittered by experience, complained that to send a treaty to the Senate was like sending a bull into the arena. It was impossible to say when and how it would be killed, but killed it would be, for "'there will always be 34 per cent of the Senate on the blackguard side of every question'".[2]

He was compelled to withdraw the first Hay-Pauncefote treaty, whose negotiation he and his friends thought a masterpiece of diplomacy, and to set about making another. Roosevelt found the American almost as much a nuisance as the Colombian Senate and dodged the difficulty by negotiating "agreements" rather than treaties. The fate of the Treaty of Versailles and of the League of Nations drew the attention of the world to the difficulties, not to say dangers, of negotiating with the United States, and, on the Atlantic seaboard, at least, the obstinacy of the Senate has been violently criticized and the fitness of the average Senator for the powers entrusted to him by the constitution has been questioned.

It is easy to see what can be said against the present American law and practice. In a country full of racial groups, arriving with difficulty at a national synthesis of interests and sentiments, the Senate has abundant opportunity to serve as a sounding-board to demagogues or cranks. Free from all responsibility, Senators may alienate foreign governments, do great damage to world, and even American interests, all under cover of a sensitive patriotism and to the electoral profit of the least responsible of the Senators. Foreign politics are dragged into local politics and stand or fall with a tangled mass of local interests. But this would be true even if the Senate had no special power, for it is the essence of American parties that the same "ticket" should send a Senator to Washington and put a new dog-catcher in office in Sauk Center. The history of American demagogy in foreign affairs is not confined to the Senate and not necessarily

---

[1] President Polk, faced with the difficulty of fulfilling the Democratic party promise of "fifty-four forty or fight", laid the compromise on the Oregon question, which he proposed to make with the British Government, before the Senate, justifying his request for advice by the Washington precedent.

[2] W. R. Thayer, *Life and Letters of John Hay*, vol. ii, p. 254.

connected with the treaty power. " Big Bill " Thompsons need no constitutional powers to play up to popular passions and there have been times when the Senate was looked on as a useful brake on impetuous Presidents. The Ostend manifesto, the San Domingo policy of President Grant, the varied activities of Secretary Blaine and the Venezuela Message of President Cleveland were examples of what happens when diplomats and their executive rulers do as they please.[1] The seizure of Panama, and the various occupations and peaceful wars in Central America, were adventures undertaken without senatorial authority. It may also be asserted that the Senate, however wrong from the point of view of good citizens of the world, has been eminently representative in its actions. Despite John Hay, the second treaty that the Senate forced him to make was, from the American point of view, a much better one than the first. Whatever disasters have befallen the world from the failure of the United States to enter the League of Nations, the Senate interpreted, or created American public opinion in 1919 and ever since. In either case it was justified from the point of view of democracy. It, not the President, read the popular will or informed it ; an absolute monarch might have been wiser and a Peace Congress of absolute monarchs in 1919 might have done a good deal better than the leaders of the democratic victors did, but the United States, like the other associated powers, had deprived itself of the resource of despotic or oligarchic wisdom.

It may be regrettable, but it is also certain, that the Senate in its most recalcitrant moods, in its most violent attacks of xenophobia, has seldom misrepresented public opinion. The American public has no trust in the impartiality of its diplomats, in the prudence of its official leaders, or in the ability of its representatives to hold their own in a diplomatic duel with any crafty European. Politically, the Senate veto has been justified ; action has been delayed until the popular sentiment was decided and, as a rule, the Senate has been upheld. For a century, the United States neither had nor needed a foreign policy ; when in doubt, do nothing, was the true wisdom of a growing people, and when times had changed, it was possible to argue that the United States was now above a foreign policy as she had been, in her earlier days, below one. It is also true, that, in these circumstances, the United States cannot give the world a lead or save it, it is even possible that the United States can no longer save herself by such a negative policy, but in the past the attribution to a third of the Senate of a veto on irreparable

[1] Visiting America in 1896, when British public opinion was still smarting from the humiliation of the Venezuela Message, G. W. Steevens saw, in the foreign affairs committee of the Senate, a useful body of elder statesmen.

commitments to foreign powers has had, at least, the justification of being as close to the will of the people as was the foreign policy of Britain or France before the War. Such democratic vetoes may be luxuries beyond the means of the European peoples, but it is hard to see that the United States has suffered much in the past and easy to see what dangers she has avoided. The very extent and irresponsibility of the Senate vote has, by preventing a policy, even reduced the intrusions of domestic politics into the dealings of the Republic with foreign peoples, a small but real mercy.

" We have in this country millions of people of foreign birth and parentage. . . . We cannot Americanize them if we are continually thrusting them back into the quarrels and difficulties of the countries from which they come. . . . We shall have a large proportion of our people voting not on American questions and not on what concerns the United States, but dividing on issues which concern foreign countries alone." [1]

The lesson that the last word lies with the Senate has been painfully learned by Europe and the White House and there is no sign that the Senate will relax a jot of its prerogatives or show any sign of receding from the advanced position occupied in the days of the war against " Wilsonism." Until there is a President who can fight back with some hope of success, the foreign policy of the United States must remain timorous and negative—which is probably what the American people want it to be.

In the Senate, the influence of seniority is less important than in the House. Mere survival has less importance or is proof of greater capacity, since election to the Senate is, in most cases, an indication of more serious political ability or importance than is election to the House. A Senate seat is a prize so esteemed that the competition makes it certain that the winner will either be a man of weight, or represent some weighty interest or cause. The Senator may be a crank, the interest may be corrupt, the cause absurd, but they are all certain to be of a larger growth than the accumulation of parish-pump politics and personalities which accounts for the presence in Washington of so many members of the House.

The rules and temper of the Senate work to deprive the seniority principle of much of its danger. A Senate committee is much less important, in itself, than a House committee. The small numbers of the Senate, the generosity of the debating rules,

[1] H. Cabot Lodge, Speech in the Senate, August 12, 1919, quoted in *The Senate and the League of Nations*, pp. 406–7.

the prohibition of Senators monopolizing chairmanships, all combine to diminish the difference between the rank and file of the Senate and its leaders. This has been demonstrated again and again. The exiling of dissident Senators to unimportant committees is humiliating and inconvenient, but it is not nearly so effective a punishment as corresponding action in the House. What serious harm was done to Senator La Follette by the persecution he suffered and lamented in his early days in the Senate? What could the Republican majority do that would seriously incommode the action of Senator Norris to-day? The most brilliant part of Senator Jim Reed's career began when he was a minority of a minority, a dissident Democrat in a Republican Senate, disowned by his own party and disliked by the leaders of the majority. It is probable that the importance of Lodge's chairmanship of the Foreign Relations Committee in the League of Nations fight, and that the importance of Senator Borah's succession to the chair were both exaggerated. The humiliations that have befallen the nominal leaders of the Senate in the last ten years show that the Senate resembles the Polish Diet more than any other modern assembly, and as long as the rules make possible a *liberum veto*, the terrors of committee rule will fail to daunt any reflecting Senator. A good position on a good committee is an asset. It provides literally and metaphorically a forum ; [1] it adds a little to the weight of words not intrinsically important, but the great Senators of the past, and of the present, have based their importance as leaders of the Senate and of the nation on other grounds than on their titular leadership of committees. Stephen Douglas lost no real strength when he was deposed from the committee on territories and Sumner's unimportance in his party was emphasized rather than revealed when Grant forced him out of the Foreign Relations chairmanship. President Buchanan discarded from weakness and President Grant from strength, but the two Senators were as strong and as weak as before.

On the other hand, Senators have to consider the country and one development of recent years has been to turn the publicity assets of the Senate over to the dissidents from party orthodoxy. It was pointed out that, in the House, service was fairly widely distributed among the senior Republicans, but this is not true of the Senate. In the main, long service and prominence in the Senate have become a monopoly of the western Senators. The direct primary and the accident of death have prevented such sure Republican states as Pennsylvania building up senatorial vested interests by long service. A change of

[1] The excellence of the committee rooms is in rough proportion to the importance of the committee.

party affiliation has worked to the same effect in New York and Massachusetts, and when Republicans are in nominal control of the Senate, the most famous and powerful Senators are party heretics. It is impossible to do anything about this, for it has become harder and harder to hold on to a Senate seat in the more populous states. The direct election and the direct primary have imposed on the Senator the same problems of keeping his fences in repair that worry the Congressman. How to act as legislative agent for ten million people in Pennsylvania or twelve million in New York is enough in itself to keep a Senator's attention away from higher things, and when this is combined with a rapid turn-over, the lot of a western Senator becomes one to be envied. Senator Borah, with his constituents a tenth as numerous and ten times as far away, can devote time to great public questions while his eastern colleagues have to concentrate on less general topics. Senator Thomas Walsh, of Montana, was much more happily placed than his fellow-Democrat, Senator David Walsh of Massachusetts. It is easy to see that it is pleasanter being Senator from Idaho or Montana, than being Senator from New York or Illinois, but why should it be easier to stay Senator ? Since the duties are less arduous, they can be more easily done to general satisfaction, but there are many aspiring legislators in both states who would do the " chores " of the office as well as, or better than, Messrs. Borah or Walsh. The strength of these gentlemen, and of their brethren, is that they are believed by their constituents to be great men worthy of their jobs. It is impossible in these critical days for anyone to bring glory to Pennsylvania or Massachusetts, the senior Senator from either of these states is that and nothing more ; the office is greater than the man. But there are at least as many Americans who have heard of Senator Borah as have heard of Idaho. He reflects glory on his remote and sparsely populated commonwealth and the inhabitants know it. He is not merely the senior Senator from Idaho, he is Senator Borah. The state can devote him to the nation, and his colleague to the chores. Some states go further and, like Montana, send two well-known figures to the Senate in the persons of Messrs. Walsh and Wheeler. A last reason for the loyalty with which western states cling to their leaders, is their realization that western sectionalism is intrinsically weak. Idaho cannot afford to send nonentities to represent her, for if she did she would not be heard ; a Senator from Pennsylvania has always the weight of his office, but a Senator from the western states must throw his own weight into the scales.

As late as 1910, the Senate could seem to Bryce still the chief conservative body of the American system for the presidency and the House were no longer as safe and sound as they had been in the happy days of McKinley, Hanna, Aldrich and Henderson, when all things worked together for good and the Senate was the driving wheel. But with the direct primary and the direct election of Senators, the old dominance of the Senate by the conservatives ended and to-day the Senate is assailed as a disturber of the peace, as a libeller of office-holders, as the sore spot on the body politic. The presidency and the House, in the main, made their peace with Wall Street, but the Senate is the home of the " Wild Asses " who investigate, filibuster and blackmail the other sections of the government and their allies, the great business interests. Confronted with this painful development, the conservative forces have begun to grumble at the over-representation of the " acreage states " of the West. For reasons that have been explained, the most experienced and formidable Senators among the Republicans come from the permanently disgruntled agricultural states. In the old days the Senate had to put up with an occasional demagogue like " Pitchfork Ben " Tillman of South Carolina among the Democrats, or a populist like W. V. Allen from a normally Republican state like Kansas. Since there seems to be little hope of replacing the present insurgents by men like Allison of Iowa, Ingalls of Kansas or even such time-tamed Radicals as Messrs. Cummins and Lenroot, the assault has been directed against the equality of states in the Senate. The possibility that a majority of the Senate may represent a fifth of the population is only the extreme form of a rotten-borough system of representation that makes a farce of democracy, if democracy is a mere counting of heads. The fundamental compromise of the constitution was the equal senatorial weight of all states ; it is so fundamental that it is the only part of the constitution exempt from the ordinary (and sufficiently difficult) process of amendment. In consequence, a majority in the Senate may be a very small minority in the country. The least populous state, Nevada, has 90,000 inhabitants, New York has 12,500,000, but both have the same number of Senators. Indeed, the population of New York equals that of eighteen states. Pennsylvania has 9,500,000 inhabitants, but its tiny neighbour, Delaware, whose independent existence is an historical accident, has only 250,000. Leaving aside the legal impossibility of getting round this system by amendment, why has American public opinion not worked to reduce nominal senatorial prerogatives to a fiction ? If the American people really felt that the Senate was blocking the way, with no regard to the real weight of opinion in the country, a combination of the President and the House might have forced a conventional decorum on the Senate.

Even in the United States, respect for the written constitution has its limits and the Senate, had it disregarded them, might have been taught, as the Supreme Court has been taught at times, that whatever its nominal powers, it is wise to follow the election returns. That no such agitation has ever acquired force, that complaints of minority rule in the Senate have been occasional and partisan, shows that the grievance, if there be one, works out fairly evenly all round ; it certainly does not remain a grievance long enough to breed a settled resentment. In fact, the Senate is not so unrepresentative as it is declared to be. The argument has been too simplified. It is assumed that the western Senator who opposes Pennsylvania is opposing the half-million people of whom he is the delegate, to the ten million of Pennsylvania, but the western Senator may be disregarding the wishes of a large minority in his state and representing the feelings of a larger minority in Pennsylvania. Senator Norris represents less than all the population of Nebraska, but then all the inhabitants of Pennsylvania are not partisans of the infallibility of Senator Reed. The arbitrary party lines, the existence of solid blocks of one-party areas, the working of the locality rule, all make it possible, and even probable, that important sections of opinion or interest must look for their representation outside their own states, or not be represented at all. Up to the present, the Senate has seldom been long aligned by small states against large, or a minority section against a majority section. That is not to say that interests and sentiments strong in rural America are not over-represented in the Senate, and—for that matter—in the House, or that it is impossible that the rapid change in the distribution of party weight and sectional interest may not produce a " line-up " of urban versus rural interests and ideals, in which the Senate might again become what it was in the days of slavery, the last stronghold of a minority section. When that time comes, the fictitious equality in the Senate will serve the threatened states or sections as little as it served the South. At a crisis, the equality of states in the Senate cannot withstand the drive of passion and power, but in normal times what passes for party policy in America has behind it neither passion enough, nor power enough, to break through the constitutional barrier of state equality.

It is impossible to take seriously the contemporary attacks on the Senate as an unrepresentative body ; they were not heard from the same sources when the solid block of the New England states with their twelve votes served as barrier to western radicalism. There are always sections that rely from time to time on the Senate ; there are few, if any, sections that are secure enough to dispense with the protection given to temporary

minorities by the composition and rules of the Senate. A
permanent minority, blocking the way of a permanent majority,
would be quite another matter, but the modern Senate has
never divided long on purely sectional lines ; it has never set
itself against a powerful current of opinion without, in the long
run, giving way. It is because it has given way that it is now
so different a body from what it was twenty years ago, and
that its new enemies are its old friends.[1] That the Senate of
Aldrich and Hanna has become the Senate of Borah and
Norris is a proof of necessary flexibility and only when the
Senate loses all power of adjustment to new situations will its
assailants have behind them that long-lived resentment that
is needed for constitutional reforms in America.

Nor is there much more in the complaint that the quality
of the membership has declined. It may not be as high as it
was in the days of Clay, Webster and Calhoun, or of Douglas
and Seward, but it has certainly not declined below the general
level of American politics. The effects of direct election have
been marked, but that they have produced an obvious and
incontestable degeneration can only be asserted by those who
forget what the Senate was like before the adoption of the
seventeenth amendment. Twenty-five years ago, when the
Senate was most conservative, most representative of the better
elements, it was described by a far from radical observer in
very unflattering terms.

> " The traditional and honourable title of Senator now
> covers the mountebank, the unscrupulous lumber or mining
> king, or the successful manipulator of State legislators through
> the use of corporation interests within the States." [2]

Such was the Senate in the great days of conservative dominance, with masters of the arts of political manipulation like
Aldrich in control, ably backed up by open grafters like Matt
Quay of Pennsylvania and with such odd parodies of popular
representation, as Clark of Montana and Lorimer of Illinois,
coming in at times to add a note of farcical contempt of the
democratic process to the more sober evasion of its consequences
by the elder statesmen. When a member of this oligarchical body
absent-mindedly answered " Not Guilty " on a roll-call, the

---

[1] One of the latest attacks on the western Senators and on their domination of the Senate comes from Mr. Harry Daugherty who feels, very truly,
that if Ohio and Pennsylvania and their like had been in control, there would
have been less mud thrown at the reputations of the late President Harding
and his friends, including Mr. Daugherty.

[2] J. L. Laughlin, *Industrial America*, p. 54.

country laughed ; popular contempt of the " millionaires' club "
was too deep for tears.

Thus it is that the Senate reverses many of the rules and
practices of the House, puts a premium on personality, on power
of dramatization, on defiance of party loyalty, on candour and
plain speaking. Its powers, its methods of election, the disregard of population in the allotment of seats, its irresponsibility
for its actions, all combine to make it a legislative body unlike
any other in the world. It is not a popular body ; it can and
sometimes does defy popular opinion and, at other times, it
plays on the least creditable passions. The Senator is credited
with something of the *prima donna's* temperament and scenes
confined in England to the comparative security of Cabinet
meetings are often played out in America before the public.
The roll of Senators has included fools and knaves ; it omits
some of the most celebrated leaders of the people, but on the
whole, the highest type of American politician has sooner or
later got to the Senate. In a different system, its existence would
be intolerable, but in the American system it has been invaluable.
The choice has lain between presidential autocracy and senatorial
aggression and though the alternatives are unfortunate, if there
may be the danger of one, there must be the chance of the other.
Short of a complete reform of the American system, few will
tinker with the Senate to advantage. It has its faults, but among
the numerous bodies that bear the title, the American Senate is
the only one whose powers, traditions and conduct do not make
the august Roman name ludicrous.

PART SIX

THE SPOILS SYSTEM

Thou shalt not muzzle the ox when he treadeth out the corn.
Deuteronomy xxv. 4.

Chapter I

THE RISE AND DECLINE OF THE SYSTEM

AMONG American political institutions, the spoils system is, to the ordinary observer, the least defensible. To the Briton, accustomed to a civil service that is accused of many faults but never of corruption, and to politicians whose rewards must, in general, be sought elsewhere than on the national pay-roll, the American system is a blot evident even against a sufficiently dingy background.

"To the victors belong the spoils." In the too famous phrase of Senator William Marcy of New York, horrified enemies of Jacksonian Democracy saw summed up the greed, brazen effrontery and contempt for right and efficiency that characterized, in their eyes, the dominant party. It is largely because of the phrase, that it is part of the American credo that to President Andrew Jackson belongs the infamy of introducing the spoils system. It is charged that Jackson removed from office all the supporters of the fallen President and that he replaced them with partisans chosen only for party services, regardless of competence. The clean sweep at the beginning of a new administration and the filling of office for reasons irrelevant to the efficiency of the departments thus staffed, are the essential character of the American spoils system and it is, with serious qualifications, true that Jackson was the innovator.

There is, however, some defence to be made of his action. His removals were not nearly so numerous as tradition alleges, and the charge of " cruel removals of faithful officers " had been made against Jefferson. In his great onslaught on the united powers of business and finance, Jackson found it hard enough to get loyal support in his Cabinet without having to tolerate lukewarm subordinates. Even in those days, great popular movements were not kept going without money and his enemies were much better supplied with that arm than was the President, and Jackson, who held in all simplicity that he was the guardian of the rights of the Republic and of the poor against the money power, would have been astounded at any suggestion that he should not use the people's money to reward the people's defenders and still more, should leave that arm in the hands of public servants appointed under the old order and so, *a priori*, suspect of *incivisme*. Jackson was typically a man of the frontier and his own career an example of frontier versatility. He had, with no formal education, been a successful planter, soldier, lawyer, judge, " everything by turns and nothing long ". All of these rôles he had filled to his own and his countrymen's satisfaction, and arguments based on the necessity of special competence got little attention at the White House and arguments based on the hardship of turning out officials who had calculated on a life tenure were annoying, at the least, to the frontiersman who held that offices, like all good things, should go round. Any sound Democrat was capable of filling any, or almost any, office ; there were more deserving Democrats than there were jobs, so there should be rotation in office and as long as one Democrat had to go short, it would be insufferable to allow opponents to enjoy the spoils of political battle.

The long quasi-hereditary rule of the Virginian dynasty had masked, in this as in many other things, the real character of American political life and, once the dykes of precedent were down, the flood of office-seekers poured in. The Whigs, the party of the old order, had to follow suit, nor was there much reluctance. The first Whig President, Harrison, was killed by office-seekers, six weeks of fending off the hungry faithful were too much for the feeble old man. From the lowest and most worthless office to the great prizes of the game, all politicians were united by a common concern for offices, for themselves, their friends, or negatively, in the exclusion of their enemies.

There were not, in those days, many very technical offices that suffered from ignorant administration. The average intelligent man could learn the ropes very quickly. With a very uncertain tenure and with no professional *esprit de corps*, the temptation to plunder while the chance was open was too much for weaker brethren, and the great default of the Jacksonian Collector of New York was an early commentary on the possibilities of the system. Nevertheless, the evils were in the main political, not administrative. On the political side, however, the evils were great, for the system corrupted politics from top to bottom.

The first stage of the spoils system was completed by 1841, both the great parties had adopted it and it had won as complete a victory in state as in federal politics. A new refinement appeared when the sectional fights in the dominant Democratic party became acute. President Franklin Pierce in succeeding the Whig, President Filmore, in 1853, had of course swept out the offices very thoroughly. For various reasons, President Pierce failed to secure renomination and President Buchanan, the successful Democratic candidate, cleared out the existing Democratic incumbents who had worked, as was their simple duty, in the interests of President Pierce. This was going very far and was too much even for Senator Marcy, who called it pillaging one's own camp. This was bad enough, but when President Buchanan split with the most prominent Democrat in the country, Senator Stephen A. Douglas of Illinois, he dismissed from office all Douglas partisans and in the famous senatorial election of 1858, Douglas was assailed by Lincoln and by the Republicans in front and by the whole weight of the federal office-holders' machine in the rear.

The Civil War displayed the full possibilities of the spoils system. Like every incoming President, Lincoln was assailed by office-seekers and they were especially ferocious and unmanageable. The Republican party was taking office for the first time, both sections of the party, the former Whigs and the former Democrats, had to be sated or put off. All the time that politics were being pursued in Washington, the great crisis of the history of the Republic was increasing in intensity. Of course Lincoln was conscious of the incongruity of his political and official tasks and he once compared himself to " a man so busy in letting rooms in one end of his house that he cannot put out the fire that is burning the other ". Yet, it should be remembered that Lincoln had some national, as well as great personal interest, in managing his own party, and as a master politician, he often used the patronage to further public ends, as when he won over Congressmen by judicious use of the jobs to consent to the admission of Nevada as a state in 1864, an admission which was considered necessary to secure his own election and that election, he felt with absolute justice, was essential to the safety of the Union.

The Civil War increased the possibilities of patronage a hundredfold. The army was in itself the means of building up half a dozen political machines per state by the immense increase in offices it entailed ; the navy was a good deal less useful as far as commands at sea were concerned, but there were administrative jobs on board ship that served to initiate at least one future statesman, and there were the Navy Yards. The necessities of the financing of the war bred a new swarm of treasury officials and the Secretary was accused of using this new patronage to build up his own machine in aid of his insatiable presidential ambition. Chase was above the more vulgar methods of some of his associates, but the Treasury was, and remained, one of the great fields for office-holding and for corruption. The Republican party began its long tenure of office with a meal of offices that tested even the American capacity for digestion, but numerous as the offices were,[1] they were not enough to go round.

Lincoln was the first President to succeed himself since Jackson, and at the end of his first term it was strongly urged on him that he should clear out all the existing incumbents and give the rest of the party stalwarts a place at the public trough. Fortunately, Lincoln was both strong enough and bored enough to disregard the pressure brought to bear on him. He had no mind to wear himself out again in attempting to satisfy the insatiable and he had nothing further to fear personally from the enmity of disgruntled supporters—or so it might seem. This marked the turning of the tide ; for the first time the principle of the rotation of offices had been resisted. The next check on wholesale removals came from the tragedy of Lincoln's death. His successor was a very new convert to Republicanism, he had been given the nomination to win over the Union Democrats and the Republicans, like the Whigs in 1841, found themselves in the horrid position of having given custody of the loaves and fishes to a mere catechumen. It was soon evident that President Johnson was not destined to a peaceful administration. He quarrelled with his party and had his only support from the Democrats. The quarrel was over great matters of policy, but in that quarrel, the President was forced to use what weapons he had and chief of these was the patronage. He did his best, but Congress, at the height of its ambition, attacked the very centre of presidential power by passing the *Tenure of Office Act* which forbade removals without the consent of the Senate. That stern embodiment of the New England conscience, Senator Sumner, attempted to extend senatorial control of removals to all offices, but his colleagues were more moderate and only presidential offices were covered, that is, those which had hitherto required the consent of two-thirds of the Senate to appoint, now needed a two-thirds vote to remove. Even when party harmony was restored by the election of Grant, the Senate refused to let go of its prey, and though the Cabinet was left to the President, the legal rights of the Senate were jealously guarded under four Republican Presidents.

[1] The offices rose from under fifty thousand in Buchanan's time to one hundred thousand under Grant, a permanent doubling of the federal political army.

Much more important than the legal control was the stiffening into a constitutional convention of " senatorial courtesy ". By this convention the major federal patronage of a State, represented in the Senate by one or both Senators of the party in power, was the perquisite of the Senators and should a President attempt to appoint against the wishes of the Senator or Senators concerned, the courtesy of the Senate enjoined on all other Senators the duty of refusing to sanction the appointment. If there were no Senators of the administration party, the patronage fell to the Representatives ; if the State was without any administration representation, to the local party constituency.

The grounds on which senatorial courtesy could be claimed varied a good deal. There were occasions in which extreme exercises of this prerogative were too much for the Senate, but, as a rule, the Senate was very loyal to its rights or claims. David Hill was able to defeat two of President Cleveland's nominations to the Supreme Court. Both the nominees were from his own state, New York, and belonged to that faction of the Democracy of New York which was more loyal to Cleveland than to the party at large and Messrs. Peckham and Hornblower had to pay for their opposition to the Hill-Maynard machine. In 1916, Senator Gallinger, of New Hampshire, was able to prevent the nomination of a member of the Federal Trade Commission who was " personally obnoxious " to him ! In another category, however, must be put the opposition to presidential nominations based on sectional or national policy, the opposition that defeated Mr. Warren and Judge Parker.

The control by Senators of patronage in their states is not, of course, always complete. President Cleveland, who was notoriously given to " smoothing out party differences with a brick ", frequently annoyed Senators by disregarding their claims. Vance of North Carolina, Tillman of South Carolina, White of California, all suffered in this way. One Republican and two Democratic Vice-Presidents since the Civil War, Fairbanks, Hendricks and Marshall, strove to have a share in the patronage of their highly political stage, Indiana. There are also difficulties between Senators. When the great " national boss ", Mark Hanna, entered the Senate, the senior Senator from Ohio, Joseph Foraker, felt that President McKinley paid more attention to his friend's recommendations than was good for party discipline, and when McKinley was succeeded by Roosevelt, Foraker tried to secure the nomination to the postmastership of Napoleon as a sign of equality with Hanna. Platt, in New York, was in control of the federal patronage during Republican administrations, but, although he got his way, he thought it beneath his dignity to have to ask through Senator

Hiscock and so entered the Senate himself. One solution of this difficulty is to divide the offices between the Senators. Thus, it is asserted, that Senators Watson and New of Indiana agreed to distribute patronage, Mr. Watson taking internal revenue and the United States Marshal, Mr. New, the District Attorney, Collectors of Ports and Prohibition Director. Another solution is to have the Senators of opposite parties, for although an opposition Senator is not quite helpless in the matter of patronage, his claims are of favour and not of right. Minor patronage falls to the Congressman of the district concerned, or, failing a Congressman, to the local party machine, an organization which has, in many districts, no other *raison d'être*. Of course a congressional leader, notably a Speaker, has a voice in more than local patronage. The little state of Maine had to provide for the patronage needs not merely of two Senators, but of two great party figures, Mr. Blaine and Speaker Reed. Even an opposition Congressman of the first rank, like Samuel Randall or Champ Clark, has some patronage to dispose of, since the committee system puts power into the hands of minority leaders.

The local political machine, at any rate the Republican machine, is kept alive even in the most hopeless areas by the spoils. Nevertheless, some politicians find the spoils, even in their modern attenuated form, more of a nuisance than a help. Quarrels over patronage have wrecked a party in a state before now. Whether a particular job should fall to a Senator, to a Congressman, to a Governor, to a party leader, may cause a President very serious anxiety, and the same difficulties are repeated all down the line. A Senator may find himself beset by the applicants for the fourth-class post office of New Jerusalem, Cal., at a time when he should have his hands free for serious matters of state or national interest. On the old proportion of ten enemies to one ingrate for every job given, the game is hardly worth the candle. Some politicians, secure in their own position, throw the burden on other shoulders by taking the opinion of the local party faithful, a method that diminishes the number of friends as well as of enemies.

Nevertheless, whatever irritation might be caused within the party that was in control of the patronage, it was nothing to the rage caused in the opposition party by practically complete exclusion from the fruits of office. The Democrats were slow to abandon the Jacksonian dogma of " to the victors belong the spoils ", but after twenty years in the wilderness, they began to realize that their chance of being victors was slight, as long as there were spoils to solidify the Republicans in power. The party interests of the Democrats combined with a widespread public opinion to weaken the spoils system. In the orgy of corruption that followed the Civil War, the weaknesses of a politically appointed civil service were made painfully obvious. The system of appointing, with a complete disregard of fitness for, and with an almost complete disregard of conduct in, office, showed its fruits in scandal after scandal. The government was robbed in all directions by its servants and with the connivance of its servants and so generally was peculation taken for granted, that the federal Marshal of New York, General Barlow, in the days of President Grant, was assessed for party funds, not merely on his salary but on his assumed pickings. There was a feeble attempt at reform under Grant, but the politicians agreed with Senator Morton of Indiana that the civil service of the United States was " the best upon the planet " and heartily applauded the assaults of Roscoe Conkling on reform and reformers :

> " ' Their real object is office and power. When Doctor Johnson defined patriotism as the last refuge of a scoundrel, he was unconscious of the then undeveloped capabilities of the word reform.' "

Yet it was Conkling himself who gave a death-blow to the old unadulterated spoils system. Spoils were often as much the insignia as the actual prize of victory. It was with a true sense of the game that " Jethro Bass " staked his prestige and crushed a rebellion in his satrapy of New Hampshire, by getting for his nominee the post office that the rebels had already earmarked for their own.[1] Conkling had been shut out of the federal patronage in New York by President Hayes and had been defeated in the Convention of 1880 when Garfield was nominated by the " Half-Breeds " over the candidate of the " Stalwarts ", Grant. President Garfield chose to rub salt into Conkling's wounds by nominating one of the Senator's dearest enemies to the great post of Collector of the Port of New York. Conkling fought the nomination to the death, but " senatorial courtesy " proved to have its limits and the Senate refused to back Conkling and his obedient junior Senator, then known facetiously as " Me Too " Platt. Conkling was unpopular, his brethren may not have been unwilling to express their opinion of his " turkey gobbler strut ", and his bid for the complete control of the most important piece of patronage in the United States was decided in favour of the President. Garfield paid for his victory with his life, for it was an enraged office-seeker of the " Stalwart " faction that shot the " half-breed " President and made Conkling's right-hand man, Chester A. Arthur, President of the United States.

It was ironical that under the President whose chief claim to fame had been acquired as spoilsman Collector of New York and

[1] See Winston Churchill, *Coniston*.

henchman of Roscoe Conkling, the first effective blow at the spoils system was delivered. The act passed under Grant had been ineffective because Congress had carefully neglected to renew the grant for the expenses of the Civil Service Commission but, by 1883, what had been the hobby of Anglophile cranks, was regarded by a large and important section of both parties as the only hope of moderately efficient government. A public opinion had been created, at least in the East, that made it possible to pass the *Pendleton Act* and to begin the long haul of the offices out of politics. The *Pendleton Act* was a mild enough measure, it provided for examinations in such branches of the public service as the President should classify and, at first, only covered thirteen thousand offices and these the minor ones. Even this act and its successors showed how deeply the " share out " idea was rooted, and how averse opinion was to building up a professional caste, by providing that offices in Washington should be apportioned among the states and territories according to population. The importance of the *Pendleton Act* was that it showed that it was possible to recruit officials without creating a mandarin caste and without ruining party government. It was made more and more evident, that no one suffered from civil service, and no one benefited from the spoils system, except the professional politicians. The burden of proof was shifted from the reformers to the spoilers and every President was conscious that he was putting himself in an awkward light, if he did not add to the number of " classified offices " and that, in the still open service, his appointments and removals would be scrutinized in a spirit very different from that of the old days.

Almost at once, the new reform was put to a test which might have been fatal. After twenty-four years in the wilderness, the Democrats elected a President and the veterans who could remember the days when there were office-holding Democrats in Washington and the young men who had long dreamed dreams, descended on the new President with a zest that recalled Lincoln's troubles in 1861. Unfortunately, Grover Cleveland had made an appeal to the reformers and owed his election, it was thought, to the support of the " Mugwumps ", the Republican purists who could not stomach James G. Blaine. An ingenious journalist had put into the mouth of the new President a very effective slogan, " Public office is a public trust ", and Cleveland was honestly anxious to live up to the spirit of his speeches. His first term was a constant fight between the old order and the new. To make no removals would leave the public service entirely Republican in personnel and expose his supporters to the deadly taunt, " You could get your President, you could not get your Postmaster." The President wavered from one side to the other but, on the whole, he carried out the Civil Service reform in the spirit and the letter. Indeed, he went further than most Presidents would go to-day in leaving public offices of great tactical importance and large emoluments in the hands of efficient " hold-overs " of the old régime and he annoyed party zealots like Vice-President Hendricks more than he outraged the feelings of the "Mugwumps". Cleveland acted on a rough local option system, putting in or maintaining efficient officials in the East where reform sentiment was strong, and gratifying party feeling in the West where reform had few real friends. Even with these limitations, it was possible to make a pretty thorough clearance. After three years, there were only a hundred Republicans in presidential offices in the state of New York out of over two thousand—and these were almost all in minor posts, but that there were any Republicans left in jobs at all was an outrage in the eyes of the old Democrats. To conservative thinkers of both parties, the defeat of Cleveland in 1888 seemed a sufficient lesson on the futility of reform and President Harrison was no enthusiast for the reformers. He courted the old soldier vote by sweeping away examination requirements for veterans, and many departments of the government were run on strict party lines, notably the Post Office, under the control of the great Christian business-man, John Wanamaker. Yet the tide of reform did not really ebb. Young Theodore Roosevelt was made a Civil Service Commissioner, and he was determined to put teeth into the law ; the Commission was made effective and the classified lists increased. The second Cleveland administration, in some respects, fell below the standard of the first. There were no "Mugwumps" to conciliate now, for they had usually become Democrats or had lapsed into Republicanism and the patronage was a weapon which a President at loggerheads with a large and growing section of his own party could not neglect.

McKinley did what no President since Arthur had dared to do, he de-classified part of the service, but he had an especially hungry mob to deal with. Under Roosevelt, and all subsequent Presidents, the classification has proceeded rapidly, till to-day over four hundred thousand federal officials are protected against arbitrary removal and are appointed by examination. Thus, in numbers at least, the greater part of the federal bureaucracy has been removed from the clutch of the spoilers. On the other hand, the offices still filled by uncontrolled patronage are the best paid, nothing has induced Congress to let go its hold on the really lucrative jobs and the Post Office is still the centre of federal patronage and the great prize of victory.

An indictment of the spoils system can easily be drawn up. Abroad its workings have caused the United States to be represented by many incompetent and some disgraceful amateur diplomats. A nation that makes a fetish of efficiency has tolerated such important aids to business success as the Post Office and the Consular Service being only as efficient as the necessities of patronage permitted. The mind of the President has often been distracted by quarrels over patronage at moments when all his energies were needed for decisions important to the United States. Two Presidents, William Henry Harrison and Garfield, have paid for the system with their lives. It has helped to professionalize politics, to discourage disinterested service and has bred, indirectly, scandals that took root through the ramifications of the spoils system, in the Treasury at the time of the " Whisky Ring ", in the Post Office during the " Star Route " scandals and, to take a more recent instance, the great Sugar Trust debauching of the New York Customs House.

If patronage has been an effective means of enforcing party unity, it has as often bred or embittered party quarrels. The " Barnburners " of New York, through whose revolt, in 1848, the Whigs carried the presidential election, were animated, in part at least, by patronage grievances. The use by President Buchanan of the federal patronage to punish the Douglas Democrats in 1858 helped to divide even more deeply the Democratic party and to make impossible a compromise in 1860 when a compromise might have postponed or even avoided the split which ruined the party for a generation and was the immediate occasion of the Civil War. The disgruntled " Stalwarts " of New York, in 1884, helped to elect Grover Cleveland to the presidency, as the disgruntled " Half Breeds " had helped, two years before, to elect him to the governorship.

The sectional character of parties has been accentuated by the spoils system. Whatever chance there is of building up a " Lily White " Republican party in the South is destroyed by the existence of the black office-holding machine, whose votes in the National Convention of the Republican party no President or presidential candidate can afford to disregard, and whose character makes it impossible for a self-respecting southern white to join the Republican party.

From one point of view the movement for the reform of the Civil Service has been an astonishing success, from another it has stopped short of its goal. To the zealots of the reforming sect,

> " ' our matter is the greatest of all matters ; that if we are to preserve our form of government intact . . . it is to be done . . . by giving the government the kind of service which the experience of mankind has shown to be the best." [1]

[1] Rollo Ogden, *Life and Letters of E. L. Godkin*, II, p. 185.

The Civil Service which Godkin and the reformers had in mind was, undoubtedly, the Indian and British Civil Service as reformed by Macaulay and Trevelyan. It was not a means of getting non-political postmen which Godkin aimed at, but the creation of a body of higher civil servants owing no political allegiance and recruited among the highly educated classes, and the present American system leaves untouched most of the offices which the reformers had in their eye.

The apostles of civil service reform often did their cause harm by a childish belief in the magic powers of written competitive examination. Chiefly of the " Brahmin caste ", they were unconscious of the existence of the problems which arose when posts requiring the qualities of a Sikh, rather than those of a Bengali, were entrusted to the Brahmin, learned in books. Theodore Roosevelt, who prided himself, with some reason, on combining the qualities of both castes, objected to appointing carpenters, detectives, and inspectors of cattle along the Rio Grande, on the same basis as clerks in Washington departments and Senator Ollie James of Kentucky protested, only a few years ago, against proposals to make prohibition agents subject to civil service examinations. He observed, that in his part of the country what was needed was not college graduates, but graduates of a shooting gallery and when the reputation of Kentucky as the American Corsica is remembered, he had right on his side. In that well-armed and quick-shooting state, mere reforming consistency might have been sacrificed, on the principle of *inter arma silent leges*.[1]

A doubtful blessing which has followed the adoption of recruitment by examination has been the extension of the system from being a test for admission to the service, to being a test of fitness for promotion. The existence of free choice in promotion is, of course, a chance for political pressure. The heads of departments in Washington have their hands full in keeping members of Congress, especially Senators, out of their offices and thus preventing the ruin of the morale of their subordinates by politically inspired promotion. Nevertheless, it is hard to resist the plea of a prominent politician for the irregular promotion of a clerk who has earned senatorial gratitude in the past, or, more potent motive, is believed to be in a position to earn it at an approaching election. The head of the department has to choose between demoralizing his staff and earning the enmity of a politician who is in a position to hurt the department very

[1] Representative Boylan in 1932 objected in Congress to the requirement that prohibition officers should be teetotallers at the time of appointment. He asked, reasonably enough, how men ignorant of the very smell and taste of alcoholic liquors could be efficient prohibition agents?

seriously when there is occasion to appeal to Congress for legislation or funds. Yet the risk of petrification from mechanical standards of promotion is very great, not only in the federal service, but in that of such states and cities as have, in theory, at least, adopted the reform. The testimony of an expert witness like Miss Jane Addams as to its effect on the teachers of Chicago; of others to its effects on the Cleveland police; of Professor Dawson to its effects in Canada, reinforce the necessity for a more fundamental reform than mere rules can provide. Promotion and transference are ways in which an adroit politician in the United States, Canada, or France, can drive his coach and six through regulations, but no official class can give spontaneous service if most of the regulations are devoted to " keeping the rascals out " and few, or none, to making the best of the raw material that gets through the preliminary tests.

It must not be concluded that the reform failed. The capture from the spoilsmen of the vast reservoir of power contained in the lower ranks of the federal and, to a less extent, the state and city services, was an achievement which should have disconcerted the excessively cynical. The vested interests of the professional politicians were all one way, as were the forces of tradition, of party loyalty, of the democratic dogma. The advocates of the reform were not always unworthy of the scorn of the "Stalwart"; they were naïve in their faith and often annoyingly and unjustifiably self-righteous. Yet their propaganda told ; the conscience of the country, or of large and influential sections of it was aroused and lip-service had to be paid to the reform—and, as often happens—deeds became words.

Why was it that the reform, having got so far, has got no further ? Mainly because the reformers had a less good case than they thought, that their motives and their understanding of other people's motives were less perfect than they imagined, and that not all that was said in defence of the old system was insincere or unworthy of consideration.

The spoils system met a need of democratic government as old as Periclean Athens. It provided party funds. The exploitation of the public service was not a good method, but are its substitutes much better ? Was it an improvement to substitute for Roscoe Conkling assessing the office-holders, John Wanamaker or Mark Hanna " frying the fat " out of manufacturers who wanted a high tariff or bankers who feared free silver ? Had not the old American method at least the merit of frankness compared with the secret party funds of England or the encouragement of wealthy candidates in France ? No democracy has solved, to any reasonable man's satisfaction, the problem of the cost of political organization. The American system which regarded office as a prize to be fought for, and to be enjoyed, was at least candid and the reformers never did, one may say never dared, to attempt to answer the question, who shall pay the costs of political war ? For there must always be spoils—or indemnities. But there was more to be said for the spoils system, than that it provided the sinews of war. It really was a demo-cratic solution of the problem of government patronage. It is true that there is no necessary connection between *political* democracy and the spoils system, but there is and was a marked social equalization in throwing office open to contestants on a basis of equality. It was the English theory, as set forth by Macaulay, that competitive examination introduced equality into government patronage in place of favour, since all could compete and official careers were thrown open to the talents. It did not matter, said Macaulay, what was the character of the intellectual test imposed, it happened to be a knowledge of Greek and Latin, it might be Cherokee, but if Cherokee became the subject of higher education, the result would be the same, the recruitment of the government service by the ablest men of the day. All this was true as far as it went, and the truth was firmly held by the American Reformers, a civil service recruited on the English model would in fact be a civil service whose higher ranks would be filled by the sons of the readers of the *Nation*. What Macaulay did not notice, or preferred to ignore, was that the facilities for learning Greek and Latin in the England of that time, and the facilities for learning Cherokee, were about the same as far as the poor Englishman was concerned. The Civil Service was open equally to rich and poor, like the Ritz Hotel. The reform in England made it harder for the Duke of Omnium to plant out his dependants in the public offices, it made it harder for young men like Trollope to slip in, but it made it even more certain that the better-paid posts would be the mon-opoly of Trollope's class. It was, from a democratic point of view, useless to open the Civil Service and keep Harrow closed. England was not then a democratic state, though the Civil Service was made safe for the middle class at the time the fran-chise was being given to the town workers. The rules of the game were altered just in time. The United States *was* a democ-racy and the English system, with its perpetuation of class dis-tinctions in the public service, was quite impossible in America.[1]

[1] While the growth of popular education in England has made the class character of the Civil Service less apparent, there is still a bias in the examina-tion in favour of the classics, that is, in favour of the upper middle classes. The limiting of class privilege in this matter which has resulted from the spread of secondary education in England is recognized for what it is by that zealous defender of class interest, Dean Inge. To tamper with the basis

In consequence, the American Civil Service has not been able to attract to itself the intellectual élite of youthful America or to compete with business or the professions as a career for the energetic and enterprising. The English system, in broad outline, consists of two classes recruited from two different levels of education and, usually, of society. The upper of these classes starts off as officers and from the beginning the opportunity for interesting work and good prospects of authority, prestige and reasonably high remuneration are held out. The rest of the bureaucracy consists of " N.C.O.s and other ranks ". Promotion from the rank and file is not unknown, but it is rare. In America, the Civil Service is recruited by a large number of special examinations destined to sift out a technically competent rank and file. There is no preliminary selection of an officer class and the prospects offered to the recruits are far inferior to those offered to the administrative class in the English system. Consequently, the American bureaucracy has had to recruit itself at a lower intellectual level than the English Civil Service does. The result has been to encourage mediocrity, for the more brilliant men whom this service does attract, it fails to keep. Under the unmitigated spoils system, the political appointees might include, and did include, men of first-rate talents and abilities, even if their tenure was short and their attention divided. Nowadays, the Civil Service has become a jumping-off ground for the brilliant and a refuge for the unenterprising. The brilliant, indeed, get their chance of coming to the top more rapidly than they do in the English system and comparatively young men, even in recent times, have wielded great power in important departments in Washington as long as they consented to stay, which was usually not very long. The migration of important English or Indian Civil servants into business is still comparatively rare, but in America, the business world is always on the look out for able young men who have shown their ability and learned their business under the government. Especially

of this profitable monopoly *is*, in fact, to deprive the upper middle classes of a valuable asset and what seems to the innovators belated justice, seems to the Dean, robbery. He feels about it as a minor French noble of the eighteenth century felt about giving army commissions to roturiers.

The Headmaster of Sherborne School (Mr. C. L. F. Boughey) has recently expressed the same point of view. " He did not think in these days the country should or could afford to subsidize secondary education. It was hardly British justice that those who paid fees for the further education of their sons should have to pay taxes to subsidize other people to be rival and competitors for the limited number of jobs available" (*The Times* June 27, 1932). In fact, the English civil service system is "congenial to the aristocratic character of the social system of England. Primarily it adoption was due to this fact " (W. W. Willoughby, *Principles of Public Administration*, p. 217).

is this true of the officials of the Treasury department and eminent Treasury-trained bankers like Mr. Milton Ailes and Mr. Frank Vanderlip have had their imitators since.[1]

Bureaucracy has increased till a professional reformer, like Mr. Frederick Howe, speaking out of his own experience, sighs for the days of the spoils system where one had to do with men and not mere safety-seeking clerks. The most eminent authority on the history of the American Civil Service, Professor C. R. Fish, tells us that in the old days

"Government service was speculative, and because of the opportunities it afforded attracted clever, sometimes brilliant men. Now it offers, in the main, the advantages of steady, light employment at a moderate remuneration and attracts the steady-going and unimaginative." [2]

It is obvious that such a bureaucracy, however honest it may be, cannot hope to acquire the power or prestige of the English Civil Service or to be an instrument of the highest efficiency. It is for this reason that one regrets most the inevitable weakness of the American governmental machine. However natural in the circumstances, the spoils system bred an attitude to governmental action that still hampers efficiency. At one critical moment in American history, a great problem was unsolved and, indeed, made insoluble, because the United States had nothing like a competent civil service. The problem of reconstruction after the Civil War was, possibly, so involved in politics in their ugliest form, that nothing could have been done about it, but whatever could have been done, would have required a capable and disinterested civil service to do it. The South had undergone a social revolution more complete than any in modern history outside Russia, it required skilled and trustworthy guidance ; what it got was a parody of it. The Freedmen's Bureau and the "carpet-bag governments" were a stopgap attempt at a solution of a real problem. The absence of a competent civil service has accounted, in part, for some of the blackest aspects of American conduct towards the Negroes and the Indians, but the suspicion inbred in the American public limits the usefulness of the thousands of zealous and competent men and women who, for inadequate reward, serve the Republic

[1] Some other recruits to business are liable to have their actions misconstrued. "A solicitor of internal revenue who retired to practise law secured the United States Steel Corporation as a client and got it a tax refund of thirty-five million dollars from the Department in which he had formerly worked. In an action at law it was revealed in 1930 that he claimed a fee of five million dollars for his 'services'" (C. A. and William Beard, *American Leviathan*, p. 330).

[2] C. R. Fish, *The Civil Service and the Patronage*, p. 233.

in Washington and all over the Union. Low salaries and irregular promotion dishearten the office-holders and discourage possible recruits, and leave the public interest helpless in face of the rapacious Congressman and Senator.   It is frequently complained in England, to-day, that the bureaucrats are the masters of the situation, that the politicians are figureheads.   In the American system the politicians are still powerful, not very often for good, and though their power has many roots, one of the most nourishing is the effect of the spoils system which, though but a shadow of its former self, has left a tradition of which the American public mind is not yet free.

It may be asked why in the modern American world it is not possible to introduce the English system, since with the universal opportunity of popular education to the highest levels, there could be no democratic objection to the English method. The answer seems to be that this is true, but true too late ; the American system is too firmly rooted.   To an American it seems obvious that civil service recruits should be tested for special aptitude, that, consequently, there should be large numbers of special examinations, and that the new-comers to the service should all, in theory, start even. The English theory assumes a general capacity for executive functions to be tested by a general academic examination. The successful, it is believed, will prove to be persons of great capacity who can be trained to become anything from Treasury experts to palæographers. There are obvious historical reasons why Americans should believe one thing, and Englishmen another. A *summa cum laude* in America, or membership of Phi Beta Kappa, has not the general prestige of a " first " in England because the career specifically open to the scholar in America is scholarship, while in England it includes many other possibilities, some of them, such as governing an Indian province or ruling the Treasury, highly attractive to men whom an academic chair would fail to stimulate to exertion. What the giving of bishoprics to editors of Greek plays was supposed to do in the eighteenth century, was done in the nineteenth by the varied rewards in cash and prestige of high academic honours. Academic brilliance has become a presumption of general ability because it has been made attractive to men of general ability. In America there has been no such presumption. The point can be illustrated by another comparison. Academic brilliance in legal studies in England has only academic rewards, if any. In America it leads to eminence and wealth, so that American law schools produce in abundance young men who regard their studies as do the more ambitious scholars of Balliol and, for the same reason, an American teacher of law is something very much higher in general estimation than an English teacher of law can be. It will be as easy to make English law teaching as important a job as American, as to make American civil servants as professionally respected and satisfied a body as their English brethren. Till that is done, it is useless to expect politicians in America to abdicate the power and satisfaction the remnants of the spoils system leave them, or to set up in the popular mind a rival authority to politicians, public relations counsel and all the other charlatans who flourish so abundantly in fields left here to the trusted, if not too popular expert.

Chapter II

THE WORKING OF THE SYSTEM

THOUGH the Reformers have greatly diminished, if they have not wholly destroyed the spoils system in the lower ranks, and though they fight, with some success, against the interference of politicians in the normal routine of promotion, the federal office-holding machine still plays a part in American politics, both national and local. There are still many offices susceptible of political manipulation, and office-holders can be used by a competent tactician to win, at any rate, local battles. Federal patronage plays an important part in state party battles, in Illinois it has been one of the fortresses on which armies have pivoted in the interminable political wars of the local Republicans. It gives authority and some real ammunition to the faction backed from Washington, but, all in all, it is a mere relic of the great days of the past, when Conkling overthrew Fenton and was himself overthrown by aid of the dispensers of good things from Washington, when the New Orleans Custom House gang altered the history of Louisiana and, all unconscious, made possible the " stealing " of the presidential election of 1876 from the Democrats, when Ben Butler defied the " better elements " of both parties in Massachusetts when he had the Boston jobholders under his hand, and Platt could call on the thousands of federal officials in New York who owed him suit and service to defy alike Democrats and reforming Republicans.

Yet the spoils system plays an important part in the psychology of the American politician and he regards Presidents too often as mere controllers of the public trough. The ideal President, from the party point of view, should be a Calonne, as was Harding, not a Turgot, as, in some indignant political minds, some Presidents have seemed to be, but with all the will in the world, a President to-day has meagre resources of patronage compared with the good old days. For one thing, the expansion of the federal service has been often in technical fields where spoilsmen work at a special disadvantage. Then, the reservation of many of the most important departments of government to the states seriously diminishes the field open to federal patronage. The Post Office alone has expanded enough to satisfy the practical

200

politician—and even the Post Office has to endure civil service rules protecting all its employees except the best paid. Yet the Post Office is the typical spoils department, the American equivalent of the Ministry of the Interior in France. The Postmaster General is, *ex officio*, the political chief-of-staff to the ruling President, for under him are the captains of tens and hundreds all over the Union, the Postmasters. Whether he presides over the office of a great city or of a village, the American Postmaster is the regular federal representative in local party councils, the *jefe politico*, the *préfet*, of the party in power.

The only possible rival of the Post Office is the Treasury, which, however, has not the same wide range. In the ports, indeed, the Collectors rival and perhaps surpass the Postmasters in political importance, and the creation of an income tax has made many new political as well as administrative jobs. But the Secretary of the Treasury is primarily a statesman. He may, like Mr. MacAdoo and Mr. Mellon, be an eminent political manager in his own state, but his first business is with high policy.

To turn from these departments to the rest of the federal administration is to come down to the dregs, for the rest of the patronage is very small beer indeed.

The State Department, it is true, has a good deal to give away. Many a faithful worker has been rewarded by a consulate, and some of these are financially very great prizes indeed. They have the disadvantage, however, of being of little use for political manœuvring at home, and their incumbents may be regarded as temporarily at least on the retired list of the political army.[1] The higher ranks in diplomacy have been, and are likely to remain, very useful for rewarding service and adjusting rival claims. An embassy or legation has more than once been a means of kicking a Senator or Cabinet officer upstairs. Thus Simon Cameron was edged out of the War Department during the Civil War, when Lincoln finally decided that the South was unlikely to be conquered by Pennsylvania machine politics. Cleveland similarly consoled Secretary Bayard when he passed him over in his second administration, and there have been examples since. Party squabbles that seemed likely to be dangerous have been composed by the removal of one of the contestants to a foreign land. Thus an editor whose absence from Pittsburgh was not unwelcome to a powerful member of the Coolidge Cabinet was sent to Madrid. Foreign missions have

[1] The appointment of Mark Hanna's medical attendant to a consulship conveniently near Aix-les-Bains where the great man took his cure under the care of the Consul may be counted, it is to be presumed, active political service, but such cases are rare.

also served to reward services rendered by journalists like
Whitelaw Reid and George Harvey, men of letters like Washington Irving and George Bancroft and, of course, a large number
of contributors to the party funds, for such contributions are
not only meritorious in themselves, but evidence of the possession
of means sufficient to make the financial burden of representing
the United States abroad not too onerous.

The results of dispatching active politicians to foreign parts
have not always been satisfactory. Cassius Clay, General Schenck,
Patrick Egan and, in more recent times, some of Mr. Bryan's
" deserving Democrats " have in various ways proved liabilities
rather than assets. Mark Twain was not an unprejudiced witness,
but his picture of Vienna might have been extended to other
places.

> " The new minister is a good man, but out of place. The
> Secretary of Legation is a good man, but out of place. The
> Attaché is a good man, but out of place. Our government
> for displacement beats the new White Star ship." [1]

No doubt, for a country with a serious foreign policy an
amateur diplomatic service of this kind can be more of a handicap
than even a professional service of the European type, but the
American people, regarding foreign policy as a game in which
its representatives are sure to be swindled anyway, cares little
whether the victims of European guile are professionals recruited
under the Rogers Act, or amateurs taken from the intricacies
of machine politics. In either case, the American lambs, it is
firmly believed, will be shorn.

Although the other departments have little that can be seized
on even by the most rapacious expert from Pennsylvania or Texas,
what little there is is strongly fought for. Navy Yards (*anglice*
dockyards) used to provide a powerful fighting force, for they
employed large numbers of labourers—numbers which could be
handily increased at election times. Brooklyn Navy Yard ranked
along with New York Post Office and Custom House as a federal
fortress, and in a small and poor state like Maine, Kittery Navy
Yard was perhaps the citadel of party power. With the increased
importance of the Navy and the resolution of the American
people to make it both powerful and efficient, the atmosphere in
which the technical and administrative methods of the Grant
era were tolerable passed away. They did not pass away,
however, without a fight, for during the Spanish War, the
Secretary of the Navy had to devote a great deal of his time to
placating Boies Penrose, who, perhaps rightly, thought the needs

[1] *Letters of Mark Twain* (English Edition), pp. 354–5.

of the Philadelphia machine a good deal more important than the campaign against " the hated Casteel ". Even Mark Hanna, more of a statesman than a boss, worried in what now seems a ridiculous way about the danger of leaving a minor Democratic official in a Navy Yard in an election year. The War Department had even less to offer. The nominations to West Point (like those to the Naval Academy at Annapolis) were, and are, a useful piece of congressional patronage, especially for those unfortunates, the " Congressmen at large," who have little else to dispose of.[1] Indian agencies used to be prizes whose pickings were worth having and the War Department, as the Belknap scandal showed, had its finger in that pie. Indeed, the Indian service was the nearest approach to such a Golconda of patronage as Dundas found in India. The results might be unfortunate for the Indians and for their white neighbours when the savages were swindled into revolt and massacre, the cost might justify the jest of the *New York Times* that the cheapest way to provide for the Indians would be to board them at the Fifth Avenue Hotel, but some very handsome competences were acquired by deserving politicians. It was one of the redeeming features of Senator Quay that he exempted his red kinsmen from his ravages, constituting himself their guardian and making up for it by plundering the territory of Alaska. To-day, Indian administration is nothing to be proud of, but its weaknesses are not solely or mainly due to the survival of the spoils system.

The courts, of course, are full of political judges, district-attorneys, referees and receivers, but in this the United States does not differ much from Britain. These are all parts of normal legal patronage and call for no special comment, although attention may be drawn to such self-denying conduct as that of Mr. Taft and of Mr. Hoover, each of whom, following a precedent first set by Benjamin Harrison, has disregarded mere party affiliations in nominations to the Supreme Court. The rest of the departments are hardly worth mentioning. Every ten years the census puts some patronage of a casual kind in the hands of the Secretary of the Interior and every office has something to give the politician, but not even the most enthusiastic professional expects much from the Departments of Agriculture or of Labor. Indeed, the whole spoils system is to-day but a shadow of a great name and the Civil Service of the United States is in the main like the Civil Service of most countries and,

[1] A Congressman at large represents the whole of his state, not a district. He exists, as a rule, because the State Legislature has not been willing to allot the extra Congressman given it in a new apportionment of seats. In patronage matters he, or she, is squeezed out between the Senators who take the general state patronage and the representatives who take the local spoils.

since a tenth of all federal employees are voteless inhabitants of the District of Columbia, possibly less of a force in politics than the bureaucracies of many other lands.   Three-quarters of the six hundred thousand federal employees are under civil service rules, and most of the remaining quarter are ill-paid labourers, hardly worth bothering about.   At the top, it is true, are the politicians attached to offices from which they serve their political masters.   As a means of administering government departments, the system is even further from the ideal than the English academically recruited bureaucracy, but to an increasing degree the standards of efficiency have risen and the political importance of the spoils system has diminished.   However desirable from the point of view of efficient government a further reform of the spoils system might be, it may be doubted if the complete adoption of all the dreams of Curtis and Godkin would seriously alter— or reform—the present working system of American politics.

PART SEVEN

THE PENSION SYSTEM

A pox of this gout ! or a gout of this pox ! for the one or
the other plays the rogue with my great toe. 'Tis no matter if I
do halt ; I have the wars for my colour, and my pension shall
seem the more reasonable. A good wit will make use of anything ; I will turn diseases to commodity.
The Second Part of King Henry the Fourth, Act I, Scene ii.

Chapter I

THE G.A.R. AND THE G.O.P.

WHEN President Grant retired from the presidency he
made a tour round the world and, while in London,
was a guest at Apsley House. He is said to have
gazed long at the portrait of the first Duke of Wellington and
to have complained, audibly, " I commanded more divisions
than that man did regiments—and look at what they did for
him ". Indeed, from Grant's point of view, the Republic must
have seemed only too traditional in its ingratitude, for he received
no Strathfieldsaye, no gifts of money. When he became President
he had to give up his army pay and his rank and its emoluments
were only restored to him on his death-bed. But if the Commander-in-Chief was, by British standards, badly treated, the
rank and file more than made up for him and the essentially
democratic character of America is excellently illustrated by
the growth of the military pension system.

Military pensions played an important part in American life
from the start, for the Republic was generous to its soldiers, in a
way unknown in Europe. The main lines of American pension
legislation and administration were, according to the greatest
authority on the subject, already laid down in the pension system
which dealt with the soldiers of the Revolution.

" Conditions of Treasury surplus encouraged the enactment of expensive service-pension provisions, thereby making
precedents immensely costly when applied to later wars. . . .
As in later days, it was felt that the pensioners and their friends
were a political force to be reckoned with. Loose and extrav-

agant legislation brought frauds, public indignation, and attempts at reform. . . . In many cases pension frauds were discovered which involved criminal acts of a grave character on the part of persons who had been respected and trusted." [1]

What was of minor importance in the days of little wars became of great political and considerable economic importance after the Civil War.

The earlier wars had involved few men, no long-lived party passions and widely diffused interests. The Civil War was something very different. Three million men passed through the ranks of the Union army and they were a block of voters with common interests to defend and common claims to advance which no politician dared disregard. Moreover, the character of the war gave a special importance to the soldier vote. Most of the Union soldiers were Republicans, it had been largely a Republican war so the rewards of valour had a good chance of going to men whom it was natural and desirable to encourage in loyalty to the party that had served the nation. When reconstruction had run its course and the Democrats had secured control of the " Solid South ", it was some consolation to think that very little of the money spent by a grateful country on her crippled heroes would go to the states which were the backbone of the opposition party. Thus it was to the interest of the Republican party to cultivate the soldier vote and, as in every crisis when the Democrats seemed on the point of seizing power it was customary to " wave the bloody shirt " and appeal to the fading emotions of war-time, so it was still more useful to buy up the goodwill of the old soldiers. The further away the war, the less effective the appeal to mere emotion, the more necessary it was to forge links of gold, and from this simple political necessity arose those features of the American pension system which baffled a generation of actuaries.

Normally speaking, it is possible to calculate when the peak of war pensions should be passed, and by the rules of the actuaries, the burden of pensions should have begun to diminish about 1875. It was at this time that the Democrats first got a majority in a presidential election—and that the great raids on the Treasury began to turn back the tide. The soldiers were organized in the famous G.A.R. (the Grand Army of the Republic) and at the annual encampment of this organization, the voice of the political veteran began to be heard more and more easily by the average politician of both parties—in the North. The politicians acquired merit by two methods. They passed, decade after decade, acts liberalizing the conditions on which

[1] William H. Glasson, *Federal Military Pensions in the United States*, p. 96.

pensions could be claimed, diminishing the burden of proof to vanishing-point, widening the grounds of eligibility till only modesty, truth, or a complete lack of the acquisitive instinct debarred a veteran from a pension—and service of three months made à veteran.

The procuring of pensions was put on a business basis and weekly newspapers were established appealing to the cupidity of old soldiers, of their kin, and of common rogues. The most famous of these was *The National Tribune,* and its great circulation was a hardly concealed asset of the Republican party. It was impossible for the Democrats to compete effectively, for they were suspect of lukewarmness in the cause, many of their leaders had been either open or concealed rebels, and the most vocal leaders of the veterans were Republicans. In the Pension Bureau was a political asset which was not neglected by the managers of the party in power and when an election was imminent, decisions on doubtful cases were rushed through, especially if the applicants possessed the asset of residence in a state which was both " doubtful " and had enough soldier votes to tip the balance. In addition, the bureau had a large staff which was thrown into the field at election times and, in 1884, the resources of the pension machine were lavished on the attempt to keep the Republic safe for Republicans.

As it turned out, the country went Democratic and the Pensions Machine passed into the hands of the enemy. The attitude of Grover Cleveland to the pensions question was a subject of angry debate all through his first term. Neither he nor the Vice-President, Hendricks, had served in the army during the war and during the campaign both had been assailed for this dereliction of duty. When it was discovered that Cleveland was vetoing pension bills, and accompanying his vetoes with rude exposures of the methods of the pension agents, the rage of the G.A.R. was boundless. All decorum was cast aside and the President of the United States was forced to postpone his visit to one of the great cities of the nation because the annual encampment of the G.A.R. was being held there. Yet Cleveland was far from any desire to offend the veterans. He knew the political value of the Pensions Bureau and if the chief he appointed, General Black, was more rigorous or business-like than his Republican predecessors, he was as sound a politician and fought his office as a ship of the line in the great presidential battle of 1888. It was all in vain. The Democrats were written down as the enemies of the soldiers and what else could be expected of a party which relied on former rebels for its chief support ? Yet President Cleveland had earned, if not gained, the gratitude of all who cared for public probity by his pension vetoes, for if the general pension acts were bad, the private acts were worse. Cases that no general statute would ever dare to include, cases that not even the most " broad and flexible outlook " on the part of the pension officials could bring within the regulations, were considered fit subjects for private bills. Congressmen made hardly a pretence of examining the cases which were considered fit for special legislation. Mutual tolerance made possible the grossest abuses. Pension bills were proposed to compensate heroes who had acquired their alleged infirmities in military prisons where they had been confined for desertion, for wounds self-inflicted to escape service, for sorrowing widows whose husbands were drowned fifteen years after the war—because their war-won rheumatism prevented their swimming ashore, and mothers sorrowing for sons lost on the battlefields who were still alive by the unanimous testimony of the neighbours. When the facts on which the President based his vetoes could not be disputed, the tone was objected to and soldier enemies of the administration were advised to bide their time.

It is probable that discontent with Cleveland's pension policy lost him the election of 1888, for he failed to carry Indiana, despite the zeal with which that former " copper-head ", Senator Voorhees, worked to get pensions for the heroes of a war which he had not supported with any enthusiasm, and New York also went back on her favourite son, though the treachery of Tammany and David Hill was alleged to be more potent here than any pension vetoes. At any rate, Harrison got the votes and his party had promised an end to the pettifogging Cleveland policies and nobly did they keep faith. It is not to be supposed that honourable men like General Harrison had anything like sympathy with the more voracious pension agents, whose stock-in-trade ranged from useful connections with Congressmen, to ability to remove desertion marks from the official records of hitherto diffident applicants. There was, however, an overwhelming political justification for generous pension legislation. The official issue of the election of 1888 had been the tariff, and one of the main Democratic " talking points " had been the surplus that the tariff piled up in the Treasury. The Democrats proposed to abolish the surplus by lowering the tariff, the Republicans to prevent its accumulation. No more respectable way of doing this could easily be found than a generous expenditure on pensions, and no expenditure promised more direct political returns and threatened less danger of the money getting into wrong, that is, Democratic, hands.

The charge of the Pension Bureau was given to a famous G.A.R. orator, " Corporal " Tanner, and he is reported to have taken office with the prayer, " God help the surplus ", and the

declaration of faith, " I am for the old flag and an appropriation
for every old comrade who needs it." Tanner's administrative
methods were too much even for his own party—he shovelled
out money as fast as he could, but red tape got in his way and
his gallant efforts to cut it brought him into conflict with his
nominal chief, the Secretary of the Interior. The pilot was
dropped, but not before he had helped to run the surplus on the
rocks. The real work was done, not by administrative action,
but by the Pension Act of 1890. This act extended widows'
claims, cut down the necessary length of service and, by its
disability tests, made it possible, in the words of the G.A.R., to
put on the pension rolls, " all of the survivors of the war whose
conditions of health are not practically perfect ". Long before
this, travellers had noticed a national talent for hypochondria.
In 1907, it is estimated, this act had cost £200,000,000 !

Nobly had the government responded to the appeal of that
noted soldier statesman, Julius Caesar Burrows :

" Take money enough out of the overflowing Treasury of
the United States and go to every poorhouse and plant down
every dollar, and take these comrades by the hand and support
them in their own homes." [1]

Pleas such as this were, in normal circumstances, almost
infallible means of supporting the speechmakers in the way of
life to which they had become accustomed, and the generosity
with which the Harrison administration and Congress treated
the soldiers deserved a better reward. No gratitude could induce
the country to stomach the McKinley tariff and there was a
lull in soldier buying till 1897 when McKinley replaced Cleveland
in the White House. McKinley was an old soldier himself and
the claims of the veterans had now become oddly like those of
a Roman Prætorian Guard, a donative was demanded from each
new President. McKinley's chief of the Pension Bureau, however,
failed to come up to the increasingly exacting standards of the
G.A.R., his pedantic adherence to form won for him the denunciation of the veterans who suspected, justly, that he was tainted
with the heresy of economy. General Sickles put it in a masterly
fashion :

" that policy is born and reared in the Pension Bureau, it is
conceived in a desire to turn money back into the Treasury
that belongs to you and me, my comrades, a policy born of a
cringing desire to serve taxpayers and earn newspaper applause
by reducing expenditures, a mean, stingy, grinding policy,

[1] W. D. Orcutt, *Burrows of Michigan*, vol. ii, p. 9.

unworthy of a great and generous government and a noble
and grateful people." [1]

General Sickles was right, the people, or at any rate the
politicians, had no desire to stint the largesse. As late as 1896
G. W. Steevens had tried to make English flesh creep with the
tale of the vast sums available for naval building as the pension
lists shrank year by year, but Congress discovered a method of
countering the work of nature. President Roosevelt found it
advisable to remove the economical Commissioner Evans to the
remunerative post of Consul-General in London and gratified
the G.A.R. by " Order 78 " issued in the election year of 1904.
Democrats foolishly attempted to make a campaign issue out of
the bold exercise of executive power, but generosity triumphed.
The order was given statutory force in 1907 and pension expenditure rose from $74,000,000 in 1906 to $105,000,000 in 1909.
The Democrats had learned their lesson, and it was a Democratic
Congress that passed the Sherwood Act in 1911. The southern
Democrats who, save for some Mexican War veterans, had to
see all this plunder going past their section, opposed in vain.
By 1912, over eight hundred thousand pensioners had cause to
thank their country and its rulers for a generosity unparalleled
in history. The private pension bill was still needed, and
President Taft signed almost sixteen thousand, the total output
of this brand of legislation being almost seventy thousand acts.[2]

[1] Glasson, *op. cit.*, p. 245.
[2] The possible lack of sympathy with pension claims debarred a Southerner,
Walter Hines Page, from the Department of the Interior in the Wilson
Cabinet of 1913.

Chapter II

THE VETERAN PROBLEM TO-DAY

THE Great War had its own special problems. The Wilson administration very prudently tried to stave off the inevitable assault on the Treasury that had followed every previous campaign, with an ingenious war insurance scheme, but nothing could really hope to serve as an effective barrier to a well-organized attack. " The American Legion " cast itself as the new G.A.R., and if it has not yet got all it wants, it is still young.

It can hardly hope to rival its predecessor for various technical reasons. The looseness of procedure and the inadequacy of records that made possible so many of the old private bills was lacking in a war so well run, from the bureaucratic point of view, as the last was. As far as disability pensions went, the World War victims were taken in hand at once and the actuarial oddities of the Civil War avoided.[1] Probably of greater importance, in the long run, than any administrative differences, is the absence of long-lived passions bred by war which it paid one political party to cultivate at the expense of the other. One party had as much or as little interest as the other in the war with Germany and consequent claims were spread over the whole country. On the other hand, the years 1917-18 saw many rash promises made and wild language about " equality of sacrifice " uttered, which made it harder to resist the veterans when they returned.

> " The world, and the sun and the moon were promised them. Soon they learned that while they had served and suffered at a dollar for a twenty-four-hour day, those who had not endured these hardships and dangers, but had remained safely at home, had received fabulous salaries." [2]

[1] In 1921 "We were . . . paying over twice as much for Civil War pensions as for death and disability compensation for the World War. In 1926 we were still paying more in pensions for a war ended sixty-one years before, than for the World War, only eight years in the past " (J. M. Clark, *The Cost of the World War to the American People*, p. 196).

[2] Major-General Smedley D. Butler, " The Soldier Asks for Pay ", *The New Outlook*, November, 1932.

The veterans of the Civil War had got a good deal less than a dollar a day, but they had bounties for joining and a dollar went further then, and it was harder to make war service *as such* a claim for cash rewards after the Civil War than it has proved to be since 1918. The old claims had to be based on injuries, real and imaginary, not on mere service for which no compensation, other than pay, had to be given. When the armies disbanded in 1919, the soldiers felt, with some reason, that they should get some of the loot that they believed had been so abundant in the lush war years. The sight of the fortunate munition workers with their mythically high wages, of the opulent bricklayers, even of the selfless " dollar a year men " in Washington, roused envious feelings which took shape in the demand for a " War Bonus " and for " adjusted compensation ". The injured were well looked after, so were their dependants, so what the soldier politicians have had left, apart from raids on radicalism and licensed orgies at their annual meetings, has had the coarse flavour of a hold-up compared with the old pension ramp. Nevertheless, Congress has come to heel ; the spoils which Mr. Coolidge and Mr. Mellon had earmarked for the relief of the rich were wrested from them, in part, by legislation passed over the veto. At a time when reverence for the financial policy of Mr. Mellon had not yet lost all its force, and when suggestions of unemployment insurance were still treated as Bolshevistic, it was possible for very subversive utterances to be made as long as it was a question of asserting the rights of the veterans. A Congressman told an assembly of disabled soldiers :

> " ' *Ill fares the land to hastening ills a prey*
> *Where wealth accumulates and men decay.*' "

After this ominous opening, he went on to suggest a means for putting an end, at any rate, to the wealth accumulation.

> " I am for taxing the profits of the last war in order to take care of the deficit, care for our disabled veterans, redistribute the wealth of the Nation, and lift the burden of taxation from those least able to bear it. I am told that Andrew W. Mellon himself has an income of $30,000,000 a year. If I had my way we would put a wound stripe on his purse big enough to be seen from Pittsburgh to Philadelphia [Applause]." [1]

[1] Congressman Rankin, who was the author of this inflammatory discourse, is a Democrat and so a party enemy of Mr. Mellon, nevertheless, it is very, very doubtful if he would have dared to utter such levelling doctrines if he had not been covered by the mantle of the veterans, a garment which was ample enough to make it possible to distribute this speech—and others of the same kind—as public documents.—*Proceedings of 11th National Convention of Disabled American Veterans of the World War* (*House Doc. 50, 72nd Congress, 1st Sess.*, p. 16).

The demand for immediate cash instead of certificates maturing in 1945 has become louder and the appeals of the classes which have an obvious interest in national economy—in this direction—fall on deaf ears. The veterans assert that to demand an immediate cash bonus is not to sell patriotism and, even if it were, it is not the first stock of patriotism that has been put on the market.

"Millions of dollars' worth of patriotism was bought during the war, not from the soldiers, but from huge industrial corporations on a ten per cent plus cost basis—corporations, the representatives of which now raise the cries of 'treasury raiders' and 'Don't buy patriotism'." [1]

Thus that eminent marine, General Butler ; when such is his language, one can imagine the words and the thoughts of the hungry veteran who regards the advances to banks and railroads as part of the normal political "hand out" and demands his modest share to revive him—and the national purchasing power—again.

The events of the summer of 1932 and the expulsion of the "Bonus Army" from Washington, *manu militari*, was one of the many disasters which befell the Hoover administration and threw the veteran vote, in all probability, to Mr. Roosevelt. It was in vain that the "Republican Service League" did its best for the party's candidate and that Colonel Hanford MacNider attempted to renew the old bond between the Republican party and the soldier vote. Mr. Hoover had to come out openly against immediate payment of the bonus, thus putting himself in what was a very awkward position for a Republican President. Mr. Roosevelt, however, was happily able to avoid the necessity of saying "yes" or "no" and contented himself with pointing out that there was no money in the Treasury to pay the bonus, leaving open the question of what he would do if there were.

How long the veterans can be staved off remains to be seen, that they will return to the assault is as certain as such things can be, but it may happen that they will meet a less warm response. When it is remembered how few, comparatively speaking, served and for what short times, it must be admitted that the veterans [2] have done very well. By the end of 1930 World War Veteran Relief had cost $5,450,000,000 and "loans on insurance" $1,187,000,000. Yet it may be doubted whether the World War veterans will do as well out of their service as the Civil War veterans did out of theirs. On the one hand, the South now gets its share and its representatives are spared the

[1] Major-General Smedley D. Butler, *op. cit.*, p. 24.
[2] "Veteran" in America is a technical term meaning merely ex-soldier, not, as with us, old soldier.

humiliation of seeing money poured out on Union heroes while Confederate ex-soldiers had to be content with free pedlars' licences, and meagre state pensions. On the other hand, the veterans are no longer, for that very reason, in an important strategical position in doubtful states. Moreover, they are less numerous, as well as more evenly distributed than were their predecessors. Finally, it may turn out to be important that the war with Germany has left a far shallower impression on the mind of America than did the Civil War. All the efforts of Hollywood to the contrary, the war in France was a mere episode in the national story and its heroes make a far less potent appeal to the emotions of their fellows than did the Civil War veterans. The same forces that helped to render the army of 1917–18 of slight importance in a political career, may hinder the designs of the professional veteran on the Treasury.

Nevertheless, the whole pension story is full of enlightenment for the student of American politics. It illustrates, in the crudest form, that aspect of American politics that Mr. Smellie has summed up as " the allocation of an economic surplus ". The American soldier, having been told that he had saved his country, wanted a share of what he had saved. In a political system based on the satisfaction of potent blocks of opinion and power, he was easily organized into a body that had to be listened to, and in a system that divorces the issues of politics almost entirely from the language of politics, his claims were of a kind that it was particularly gratifying to meet. What the flag-waving about the tariff did with occasional success, the eloquence of the soldier orators did with always increasing success and that success had its uses not only for the soldiers, for their leaders, and for the pension agents and their congressional tools, but for the dominant party and for the interests that party existed to serve.

But there is another lesson to be drawn from this tale. However legitimate the grievance of General Grant and however legitimate the corresponding grievance of Marshal Foch, the expression of them was based on a misunderstanding. In an aristocratic society there was every reason to shower wealth on Wellington from which he could, when he chose, spare a guinea for his old soldiers. Wellington had to be absorbed into the highest ranks of English aristocracy and the highest ranks of the aristocracy were, then as now, the richest ranks. It was natural at the end of the late war to give large grants to successful soldiers like Haig and to sailors like Beatty ; they were made earls and an earldom without money is not an honour but an insult.[1] Foch

---

[1] It may be remarked that the sums given to the military and naval leaders in the late war did not compare favourably, relatively or absolutely, with those given to the leaders of the much smaller wars of the past. Lord

was forced to refuse the £100,000 offered him by the British Government and had to be content with being an honorary Field-Marshal. As Montesquieu remarked, virtue is the essential character of a republic. General Pershing got his pay, Lord Haig got his grant, the American soldiers got their war bonus, the British, that much more modest affair, a gratuity.

It was a mark of the old British aristocratic conception of the state that one of the most sincere opponents of the old age pension of 5s. a week, offered to the poor by a prodigal Liberal government, was himself a recipient of a political pension from the Treasury to enable him to live in the style he had been accustomed to—before he had gambled away most of his fortune. It took a long time to persuade a duke's son that the handsome dole he drew was meant to be accompanied by a " Means Test ". If the British proletariat has developed an appetite for public money it has had aristocratic exemplars, for, as Professor Namier shows us, there is little to choose between a modern proletarian burden on the public purse and a French or English eighteenth-century aristocrat striving for something *de par le roi*. It is the mark of the American pension system that it is democratic and not equal-itarian. It is a lottery in which the entry is free to all who can, singly or in groups, force their way in, barred to those who have only the common bond of misery, barred, that is, till the majority of Americans realize that the days of endless opportunity are over. In the meantime, Representative Patman is in the best tradition when he asks why should money be poured into Wall Street by the government to help the banks and be denied to the veterans, although, he asserts, the immediate cashing of their insurance would spread money and prosperity farther and faster than any further donations to the rich. In this simple programme is summed up the American political version of the national dividend.

Haig had to buy Bemersyde out of the proceeds of a public subscription, a poor recompense compared with Blenheim or even Strathfieldsaye. On the other hand, the rank and file did a good deal better than their predecessors. Democracy was telling.

PART EIGHT

THE MACHINE

Nothing appears more surprising to those who consider human affairs with a philosophical eye, than the easiness with which the many are governed by the few, and the implicit submission with which men resign their own sentiments and passions to those of their rulers.

HUME.

Chapter I

HOW THE CITY MACHINE MAKES ITS FRIENDS

SINCE the Civil War, there has been one part of American politics that has had few defenders, and even patriots who were ready to explain or defend other aspects of the national life hung their heads in shame when they contemplated, or saw their foreign friends contemplating, the spectacle of city government. There corruption and waste ruled almost without interruption, there the forms of democracy were parodied by " machines " which were in the hands of mercenary politicians, ready to buy and sell and free from any political principles or scruples.

The existence of these machines and their deep roots in city life were an affront to the American temperament, so intolerant of evil, so confident in the power of good to conquer its enemies—if the issue were once presented frankly to the great heart of the American people. It was a first, and easy, explanation of the machine's existence to point out that it was strongest in the cities where foreigners congregated, where the spirit of American institutions had not had time or opportunity to reach and reform the ignorant new-comers, that education and example would teach the lesson that civic honesty was the best policy, and that then the boss and the machine would disappear.

These comforting illusions have died, and in every American city to-day, the machine and the boss, or bosses, is a present reality or a constant danger. Both seem as deeply rooted in the foundations of American politics as ever, and few and timid are

217

the faithful reformers who still believe that there is some panacea to be found for this disease of the American city. If city governments are designed to give a rational and efficient service, to be ruled by the free choice of the citizens by officials who are anxious to serve the city and not merely themselves, then the average American city is governed by a system which is condemned by all canons of political right doing.

What is the hold of the machine and of the boss, why have both lasted out so many storms? The machine and the boss are brokers, they have at their disposal large blocks of votes which are in the market and, with them, they can usually guarantee that the rulers of the city will be the creatures of the machine, will do its bidding and will deliver what political goods are for sale, to such customers as meet the machine's price. The base of the machine's power is its ability to command voters, or, at any rate, votes. Leaving aside, for a moment, all question of election trickery, how does the machine win the solid core of faithful voters on whose fidelity its power and prosperity depend?

The machine meets demands made by a large section of the city in a way that no other public or private organization does; it may do badly what, were the coast clear, other organizations would do well; but it is important to remember that every machine has its nucleus of support because it has earned it. Whether it has earned it for its ill or good deeds matters little on election day.

All American cities contain immigrants and all immigrants find the American world strange to them; always strange and often inimical. The agents of the machine see to it that the immigrant is helped to settle down, that his first legal difficulties are got round, that he acquires the habit of coming to the local officer of the machine when in a difficulty—and that he is put in the way of becoming a qualified voter or, at any rate, a voter. There can be little doubt as to whom he will then go for directions how to vote. But the city boss serves more needs than those of the immigrant, still terrified by his experience of Castle Garden, or, in modern times, by the moderately ingratiating hospitality of Ellis Island. The immigrant is usually poor and he comes into a community where he rubs shoulders with the poor, and in that community many of the difficulties which accompany poverty in all countries, are alleviated by the machine. Should a man want to enter a trade, there is often a difficulty about a licence.[1] The machine arranges things. A head of a family or an anxious father may want a job for himself or a son or a friend; there are many businesses, notably businesses like contracting and street transport which employ a vast amount

[1] New York licenses 169 occupations.

of unskilled labour and which have reason to wish to serve the machine ; the recommendation of the boss often works wonders. Some idea of the hold a machine can gain in this way is given by authoritative evidence from Chicago :

" We soon discovered that approximately one out of every five voters in the ward at that time held a job dependent on the good will of the alderman. There were no civil service rules to interfere and the unskilled voter swept the street and dug the sewer as secure in his position as the more sophisticated voter tended a bridge or occupied an office chair in the city hall. The alderman was even more fortunate in finding places with the franchise-seeking corporations ; it took us some time to understand why so large a proportion of our neighbors were street car employees and why we had such a large club composed solely of telephone girls. . . . Added to these were hundreds of constituents indebted to him for personal kindness from the pedlar who received a free licence to the business man who had a railroad pass to New York." [1]

Then there are difficulties with the police whom the poor in all countries, except, we are often told, Britain, regard as doubtful friends—to put it conservatively. There are many petty offences that can be committed, especially by boys and girls, many encounters with the law which may be taken seriously or not—as the court decides and the court has a way of listening to the machine. All the harshness of bureaucracy, and all the rigidity of law, is tempered by the machine, and the shorn lambs are grateful. What follows is a picture of his own machine drawn by a famous boss of modern times, but it does not differ much, in all probability, from the picture drawn by his clients and followers :

" MR. VARE. ' Taking a city like Philadelphia as an illustration, let me explain that part about the Philadelphia organization . . . it is an extremely highly efficient party organization, as I have told you, gentlemen, based on direct service to the people. You say, " What do I mean by ' service ' ? I mean anticipating the needs of a growing community and assisting and co-operating with public developments, the building of schools, the building of children's playgrounds, assisting in hospital work, and all things that go to make up a happy community.'

THE CHAIRMAN. ' And occasionally getting somebody out of jail ? '

[1] Jane Addams, *Twenty Years at Hull House*, pp. 316–17.

MR. VARE. 'We always feel—I say "we". I mean to say that I believe and many of my friends believe in tempering justice with mercy.' " [1]

Such are the serious claims of an efficient machine on its followers' loyalty, but they are not the only ones. There is charity. What is done by philanthropists, with distressing ideas of good conduct, or still worse, by inhuman public charity, is done with good fellowship by the machine. Coal is sent round, rents are paid, shoes are distributed ; the machine is a human and kindly instrument, for its agents are picked for their ability to give " service with a smile "—and they have the satisfaction of knowing that they are casting their bread upon waters that will return the offering on election day. Mr. Vare was a witness to the general policy of a great machine—as it wanted that policy to appear. Mr. Morris Eller is boss of the Twentieth Ward in Chicago, which, through his dominance of it, became known as Morrisellia. His testimony as to the methods that carry wards, that provide regiments of voters in the great army of the machine, was given to the Reed Committee :

" MR. ELLER. ' If you wish, I will explain how our organization works, Senator. I have lived in that neighbourhood forty-three years, and have been in politics there thirty-five years right in that immediate neighbourhood. The ward is cosmopolitan ; what they call the melting-pot. We have various nationalities—Jews, Russians, Croatians, Lithuanians, Germans, Irish, and coloured. They are not a very prosperous people and need our help a little. If it is not one thing it is another. . . . All my committeemen mingle with them every day, and so do their assistants ; and once a year they respond to our request when we request them to vote that ticket.' " [2]

Men and machines do not live by bread alone and the skilful leader appeals to the love of good, clean fun that is ineradicable, even in the poor. Mr. Ollie King of Chicago runs an annual picnic that pays so handsomely, that from its profits the machine charities of the ward can be provided for, but were there no profits, the picnic would pay politically, would be, as William Hale Thompson (Big Bill), called it, " corking good politics ".[3]

The competent politician in New York runs " clambakes and chowder parties ", the women and children can amuse themselves, the men can run obstacle races, all can appreciate the admirably cordial manner with which the local leader dispenses hospitality and the generosity with which he asks, in return, nothing but

[1] *Reed Committee Hearings*, pp. 497 and 504.   [2] *Ibid.*, p. 1882.
[3] *Ibid.*, p. 1788.

votes. It was one master of all the arts that win and keep the poor, " Big Tim " Sullivan of the Bowery, who won an informative tribute from his people : " such a model statesman, philanthropist and ideal citizen . . . deserves the reverence of posterity, his fame the praise of ages, and his illustrious deeds the perpetual homage of countless years." [1]

When told that all this costs money, and asked to consider whose money it is, the populace turns in disgust to the boss who rebukes such ill-intentioned curiosity in terms like those used by Martin Lomasney of Boston :

> " ' I don't care anything for this cheap loaf of economy. I never saw a man in my life who made economy his watchword who was not always defeated before the people. . . . I would sooner vote any day to increase a salary than to cut it down. . . . The men who live are those who look out for the people, and when the people receive the benefits, they never grumble about taxes.' " [2]

The building up of a faithful following by generous hospitality was illustrated by the case of Thomas M. Farley, Sheriff of New York County, who was removed from office in 1932 by Governor Franklin Roosevelt of New York, because he had failed to disclose the sources of the $400,000 saved in seven years on a salary of $15,000. With such revenues, it was possible for Mr. Farley to consolidate his position in his district, the Fourteenth, known, because of its polyglot population, as the " League of Nations ". An annual picnic for the children of the voters, three thousand Christmas dinners, an annual ball of the " Thomas M. Farley Association ", kept his people faithful to the Tammany statesman and his acquittal, on a charge of grand larceny, ended the risk of a conviction which the average " East Side " New Yorker would have thought a gross miscarriage of substantial justice.

A great ward leader, master of his own independent machine, justified his profession to a critic.

> " ' I think ', said Martin Lomasney, (' Czar ' of Boston's Eighth Ward), ' that there's got to be in every ward somebody that any block can come to—no matter what he's done—and get help. Help, you understand ; none of your law and justice, but help.' " [3]

Yet, when all has been said that shows how natural the machine is, what real political services it performs, there remains the ugly

---

[1] H. Zink, *City Bosses in the United States*, p. 95.
In fact, Big Tim lay unidentified in the morgue for thirteen days after his body was found.
[2] *Ibid.*, p. 271.   [3] *Autobiography of Lincoln Steffens*, p. 618.

fact that the American city machine, at the best, is a clumsy and expensive way of performing some necessary functions—and that the price it exacts is too often far in excess of any services it renders.

" They (the bosses) do give them (the poor) coal and help them in their private troubles, but as they grow rich and powerful, the kindness goes out of the charity and they not only collect at their saloons or in rents—cash for their ' goodness ' ; they not only ruin fathers and sons and cause the troubles they relieve ; they sacrifice the children in the schools ; let the Health Department neglect the tenements, and, worst of all, plant vice in the neighbourhood and in the homes of the poor." [1]

The indictment is thirty years old ; its details would have to be amended a little now, but in the main it is still a true bill.

[1] Lincoln Steffens, *The Shame of the Cities*, p. 302.

Chapter II

THE RURAL MACHINE

MOST of the limelight of American reform has been concentrated on the cities. They had more newspapers ; they had, in their large foreign populations, obvious sources of civic corruption whose existence supplied comforting " causes " such as illiteracy, lack of American traditions, lack of sound religion, presence of false religion, all convenient surrogates of real and painful thought about the nature of politics. In assuming that the city was the breeder of the machine politician, the early students of American practical politics undeservedly slighted a body of practitioners who were at least as competent in their own field as any city boss in his. Under the shadow of the state boss, and side by side with the more violently coloured city boss, the county boss was a modest violet. For one thing, his friends, victims or accomplices seldom complained ; there were, and are, few reform movements in the rural counties. For another, the rewards of the machine in rural America could not compare in splendour or notoriety with those of the great cities ; they were meagre, although they were regular. Lastly, the political master of a county, or a small country town, was not the obvious villain of the writer or cartoonist, no bloated, illiterate, coarse parasite on the body politic. He was usually not a professional politician in the sense that he lived obviously and directly by politics. His political power, as a rule, was, or seemed to be, a function of his economic position.

In a county, the leading banker, or lawyer, or the agent of the railroad, could and usually did turn his economic and social assets to political advantage—and his business, as a rule, did not suffer. He might hope, in normal circumstances, to hold his power as long as he liked. Rural areas were, and are, far more constant to one party, to the mere label, than the towns ; the regulation of party activities has meant far less in the country than in the cities and there were fewer motives for and means of overthrowing the rural boss than his more vulnerable—and possibly more guilty—city brother. In the jungle of the city it is easy for a boss to slip, to notice treason or placate revolt too late ; he is very much in the hands of his subordinates and may be much weaker than his friends or enemies suppose—as was shown in the case of Croker of New York and Cox of Cincinnati, two of the masters of modern times.

Little is known, though much is guessed, concerning the ways of the rural boss. He may re-enforce his power by holding mortgages as a banker, or by ingenious handling of the tax-system or by equally ingenious handling of the prosecutor's office. He may be in a strong economic position whether as a landholder or as owner of the chief local industry, whether it be a factory or, as in one Illinois town, an inebriates' home. In any event, he has something to give away and if he starts with his own property, he soon has the property of the county or town to play with. And in these activities he is much less hampered than the city boss. Rural organization in America has hardly altered in a hundred years, and endless possibilities of jobbery and worse are concealed in the archaic organization which still serves for rural local government in America. Lastly, owing to the preposterous over-representation of rural areas in all, or almost all, American states, the county boss is in the happy position of having public funds to give away that neither come from his pocket, nor from those of his constituents. As long as he can deliver his county or town in the state to the party that has the distribution of the state revenue, he can cultivate his garden at very little cost to anyone except the unfortunate city taxpayer who has no friends or rights. It is as county, chairman, or in some other capacity as representative of the dominant party in the state, that the county boss is really formidable and he will remain so as long as state politics are what they are.

> " The chairman of the county committee is ' likely to be an important figure in local affairs, and may wield great influence in party councils ' ; he is the executive head of the party within the county and is held responsible for the success or failure of his party at the polls. Through his power of public patronage he is often able to build up a powerful party organization in his county ; in such cases he is able to wield the authority of a ' benevolent despot '." [1]

The sympathy of the local Press, or its useful silence, can be relied on as a rule ; the editor can be intimidated or bribed. Platt expressed his indifference to anything that the city Press could say against him, but the attitude of the local papers was another matter and he was adept in handling them. In this he was of the opinion of the Irish M.P. who refused to waste

[1] J. A. Fairlie and C. M. Kneier, *County Government and Administration*, p. 182.

time on what *The Times* had said of him, what he wanted to
know was what the *Skibbereen Eagle* would say of him. There
may be occasional rebels, like the irrepressible editor of the
Democratic weekly in " Middletown ", but even if not all states
are Indianas with judges who keep such objectionable persons
in their places, the average rural journalist is decidedly a " booster " not a " knocker ". Because there are few open scandals in
American rural government, it would be rash to conclude that
county government, and the government of such a town as
Muncie, Indiana,[1] is much, if at all, purer than that of the
great cities.

The differences and the similarities between the American
county boss and the English leader of the type of Spence Watson,
are brought out by Mr. J. A. Spender's account of the English
local leaders :

> " This [class] consisted of men who stood outside Parliament
> but who were the political leaders of their localities and had
> the purely disinterested object of keeping their fellow-citizens
> in the right path. Most of them were business or professional
> men to whom politics were necessarily a side-issue, but they
> were the mainstay of the local clubs and Associations . . .
> it was everywhere recognized that they had to be consulted
> before a candidate was ' sent down ' [that is, by the party
> headquarters]. . . . The dissent of any one of them was
> recognized as a matter of grave import which might entail
> the loss of a seat or indeed of several seats." [2]

In America such leadership is available in the counties.
It is to be feared that the result of keeping the government
in the hands of the best, that is, of the richest elements in
these areas, has been disappointing—or that the actual survivor
of the better-class contestants for local supremacy is corrupted
in the contest, for the county is the least reformed · and the
least reformable part of American government. When for
political or administrative reasons it is found necessary to investigate the affairs of the counties, the results are astounding
to spectators who are used to the more decorous graft of the
modern city machine. Even the hypocrisy of orderly, if
deceptive book-keeping, is often disdained and the electors
care little what is done as long as the " share-out " is fairly justly
administered. The crude bribery of the old-school city politician
is still used in rural areas and the moral purity that one expects
of the virtuous peasant is confined to legislation for the wicked

---

[1] I am using town in its English sense to describe what would be called
a small city in America. Muncie, Indiana, is " Middletown ".
[2] J. A. Spender, *Sir Robert Hudson*, pp. 65–6.

cities. If one has to hope for the salvation of the Republic for the spread of such political methods as supported the power of Len Small, " the Kankakee Farmer ", in Illinois, or of the rural faithful who help Mr. Roraback to keep Connecticut safe for the power trust, the reform game must be up.

There are attempts to introduce reforms in such states as North Carolina, occasional assertions of state authority by energetic and city-supported governors such as Al Smith. The flooding of the counties near New York City by suburban residents may breed revolt such as the attempt to unseat " Boss " Ward in Westchester County, or the defeat of the Republican machine in Rockland County may upset the old system, temporarily, at least, but in the real rural counties of the eastern and middle western industrial states, endemic corruption is one of the permanent features of rural life—and one of the most flourishing forms of farm relief. It seems evident that American farmers either, as in the west, vote for class interests, regardless of party lines, or, in the east, rejoice that they have a country to sell. Reform will come, if at all, from a falling off in the demand ; the average farmer in the older states is too poor to keep a conscience.

Chapter III

THE MACHINE AND THE ELECTIONS

WHEN a war over voting rights was threatened in South Africa, Mr. Dooley gave President Kruger some advice that would have been superfluous if directed to any competent American boss ; he told Kruger to give the Uitlanders all the votes they wanted, but to count them himself. In the happy pre-reform days, elections in an American city were real contests. To vote at all was an effort of civic courage in face of the toughs who infested the very primitive polling booths and who had no hesitation in assaulting anyone who seemed likely to be voting wrong. It was still more courageous, when it is remembered that there was no certainty that the vote, if cast, would be counted, and if counted would have any weight against the floods of ballots cast by " repeaters ", " colonizers ", " mattress voters ", or plain " ballot stuffers ",[1] and, lastly, it was humiliating to learn, as not infrequently happened, that one's vote had been cast, hours before, by some active agent of the machine. After the Civil War, especially, election frauds on a great scale were frequent and bold. It is probable that the Tammany Democrats " stole " New York for Horatio Seymour in 1868 ; there was reason for the scepticism with which returns were awaited all over the Union, and for the advice of the expert, who said the safe rule was to " claim everything till the last returns were in and then shout fraud ".

Electoral laws were much improved, especially after the adoption of the " Australian ballot ", that is, an official ballot which replaced the ballots hitherto issued by the parties. The old private ballots, printed by the machine and handed to the voters as they entered the polling booth, made the delivery of the machine vote easier and more certain, but even with these disloyalty was possible. The great Bowery boss, " Big Tim "

[1] The terms are probably self-explanatory, but repeaters are citizens who vote too often ; colonizers and mattress voters, non-qualified voters imported into the constituency for the occasion. The useful class of repeaters have their martyr in the person of " Bat " Shea of Troy, N.Y., who " went to the chair " for killing an inquisitive Republican worker.

Sullivan, was said on one occasion to have had the ballots which his faithful were ordered to use to the exclusion of all others, perfumed, but not all machines could think of, or achieve such masterpieces of organization.

One resource of the machine still lies in padding the electoral lists. Since the days of Sir Robert Peel the importance of " registration " has been appreciated by all practical politicians in Britain, but in America " registration " has not meant merely the securing of votes for friends and the denying them to enemies. It has not been a mastery of election law that has marked the American expert, as much as a mastery of all possible illegalities. To flood the electoral rolls with mythical voters whose ballots can be cast by skilled personators and repeaters has often been the primary activity of a machine. The creation of " dummy " votes requires tact. It was giving in to a mistaken sense of humour that led a politician in Terre Haute, Indiana, to register his dog.[1] A well-planned reform attack on a machine in Philadelphia, Chicago, or Atlanta, begins with an attempt to remove from the voting lists the men in buckram who have been put there by prudent professional politicians. Sometimes, the reformers get their way ; but the purging of election lists requires, like their padding, that day-to-day attention to the job, at which the machine is so much better than any body of men animated merely by public spirit. Yet electoral frauds are hard to check if the official guardians of the purity of the polls are less than whole-hearted, and competent witnesses suspect that the most rigid election laws, and the most foolproof voting machines, cannot keep really competent hands from helping on a good cause. Violence, intimidation, illiteracy's artful aid, misuse of absent-voting privileges, are all charged against various machines. In Cicero, the protectorate of Mr. " Al " Capone, it was alleged by serious witnesses, that gunmen carried off two zealous workers of the opposite side in 1924, and from the pleased surprise which greets a peaceful election in Cook County [Chicago], it is probable that completely free voting is a luxury in parts of Illinois. Mr. Norman Thomas has made very serious charges against Tammany conduct of the election of the borough president of Manhattan in 1931, and the astonishing uniformity of mind displayed by the voters of Philadelphia has aroused suspicion, if it has not produced proof of wrong-doing.

Fraudulent dealings with the votes cast are hard to prove, but American politicians are ready with stories of " steals " that are, at least, ingenious. According to Judge Jarecki, for ways

[1] The same Caligulan sense of humour has been displayed by a French artist in politics.

that are dark and tricks that are vain, Chicago election officials are peculiar, but that is only local " boosting ".[1]

It is a dull election in Pennsylvania that does not produce its stories of election trickery ; of fraudulent registration and " phantom ballots ", that is, sets of voting papers which appear to have been marked by the same hand or which, having been left incomplete by careless voters, have been finished by industrious election officers. If one can believe half of the charges made, one is entitled to speak of these experts as men " who have been accustomed to stealing elections for years, and they are artists at it. Give them one night complete and they will change any election if it requires only the changing of 15,000 votes." [2] In the South the necessity for securing the power of the dominant race has sanctified many odd electoral practices. Mr. Cole Blease of South Carolina gratified his constituents and did not really surprise or shock his colleagues when he told the Senate that " ' Mr. Coolidge received 1,100 votes in my State. I do not know where he got them. I was astonished to know they were cast and shocked to know they were counted.' " [3] Even the theoretically fraud-proof voting machines which are made to facilitate speed in counting and to avoid the possibilities of trickery inherent in the old ballot sometimes fail to come up to specification, and a large number of New Yorkers who wanted to express their contempt for the Tammany nominee for Mayor in the election of 1932 found the voting machines strangely reluctant to permit this scratching of the ticket. Nevertheless, election " steals " of the old and bold style are undoubtedly rarer and a moderately reassuring verdict has been given by a competent

[1] A fraud described by Judge Jarecki is interesting : " Another thing that is very difficult to disclose is the vote that is changed by what we call a short-pencil artist. When the votes are being counted in the boardrooms of the various local boards some man will come in there with a short pencil concealed in the palm of his hand and make a lot of crosses on the ballots. That fraud will never be disclosed. It never can be found excepting in one or two cases that I have run across where the ballot happened to be marked in ink, and those artists you know, not realizing the fact that the ballots were marked in ink, marked them again in lead-pencil " (Reed Committee Hearings, p. 1849).

A variant on this trick was described to me by a Hoosier friend as common in the great days of the Ku Klux Klan, in Indianopolis. For the clumsy short pencil of the Chicago version was substituted a piece of lead and a long thumbnail. This was easier and more elegant, but the political arts of Indiana are to those of the rest of the United States, as the election devices of Marseilles, and the Midi in general, are to those of the slower-witted north of France.

[2] Mr. C. C. McGovern's testimony. Nye Committee Hearings (Pennsylvania, p. 174).

[3] Paul Lewinson, Race, Class and Party, A History of Negro Suffrage and White Politics in the South, p. 109.

authority : " Honest elections already prevail in many of our states, including some of our largest cities." [1]

One useful ally of the machine has been the " long ballot ". In their hostility to aristocracy and centralized authority, the constitution-makers of the Jacksonian era inflicted on the states the direct election of a great number of officers who had hitherto been appointed by the executive. Not merely the Governor, but many subordinate officials, the Attorney-General, the State Treasurer, the Judges, and local state officials, were made to undergo the ordeal of direct election. Then it was customary to hold all elections on the same day and in the same place, so that one ballot paper might contain the names of candidates for President of the United States ; [2] candidates for the House of Representatives and, in two biennial elections out of three, candidates for the United States Senate ; candidates for state offices ; for both houses of the state legislature ; for the judicial vacancies ; for mayor and a number of other local officials ; for the city council or councils. Of course, this long list of candidates contained obscure names that no human being could be expected to distinguish one from another, and minor offices that few could care who filled. " Within the city of Chicago each voter is expected in a brief series of years to vote for at least 178 different officials, and in Cook County, outside of Chicago there are nearly as many officers to be elected." [3] In addition to the long lists of candidates, there are complicated constitutional amendments to be voted on in many cases. The objection to the long ballot was put by Horace Greeley in 1867 in the Convention to reform the constitution of New York : " ' When-the-people-take-up-their-ballots-they-want-to-see-who-is-to-be-governor : that's-all-they-care-about. They-don't-want-to-read-a-whole - chapter - of- the - Bible-on-their-ballots ! ' " [4] Nevertheless, democratic theory was called in to enforce the resistance of the practical politician. The Socialist objected in the name of popular control, and also because his chance of success as candidate for the leading offices being small, the absorption of them in the greater offices, would destroy whatever faint hope of office, or even of a good showing, he might have had. Bosses had objections to this reform whose chief value lay in concentrating authority and responsibility at the head of the ticket, and depriving the machine of a useful mechanism for creating that public bewilderment on which machines flourish. In the interminable lists of candidates

[1] *National Municipal Review* (Election supplement), September, 1930,
[2] Strictly, until recent times in all states, and still, in most states, the list of presidential electors of the parties.
[3] W. F. Dodd, *Government in Illinois*, pp. 69–70.
[4] A. D. White, *Autobiography*, II, p. 145.

for office, the people very easily lose their way. Expert practitioners are not slow to take advantage of the ignorance of the
electorate. Humorists have induced cities to elect mythical
persons to office and identity, or similarity, of names has given a
chance for odd mistakes.

" In a recent primary in an Eastern state a man by the
name of Burrell sought the nomination for State Treasurer,
the office then being held by one Burrill. The former was
patently lacking in certain fundamental qualifications for that
office, but adroitly adopted the campaign slogan, ' Experience
Counts '—and won the election." [1]

A similar confusion of names almost gave Ohio a blacksmith
Chief Justice, and though it failed to come off, the public utilities
corporations and the central Republican machine attempted to
prevent the re-election of Senator George W. Norris, by entering
a young man called George W. Norris, in the Nebraska Republican primary of 1930, in the hope that enough confusion would
result to defeat the veteran " insurgent ". Though the execution
was faulty, and the subsequent lying incompetent, the idea was
ingenious enough to deserve more skilful application. Even
small rural areas have far too many elective offices and too complicated elections.

Here, the reformers hit at a real evil. It was impossible to
expect intelligent choice in such circumstances and the temptation, not to say the necessity, to vote the " straight party ticket "
was overwhelming. Various reforms have been adopted. The
number of elective offices has been a little diminished by state
reorganization and the lumping of all elections together, at one
time, has been successfully attacked in some areas. The regular
mayoral elections in New York are held in odd-numbered years,
thus cutting them off from the national and state elections, which
are held in even-numbered years. An attempt has been made to
lengthen the term of the Governor from two to four years, thus
reducing the elections to that extent, but party interests have
come into conflict with an obvious reform. Both parties are in
favour of the reform, but it is to the interest of the Republicans,
in New York, and in other doubtful states, to have the national
elections and the state elections at the same time, as the Republican vote is more easily got out for the national than for the
state party. The interest of the Democrats is, of course, quite
the opposite. The only time they have failed to elect the
Governor of New York since 1918, was in 1920, when the Harding
wave carried in Nathan Miller against Al Smith and, in

[1] H. R. Bruce, *American Parties and Politics*, p. 226.

1924, Theodore Roosevelt, Jr., made a much better showing on Coolidge strength than was made on his own, two years later, by the intrinsically stronger Ogden Mills. The interests and assets of local and national parties are so artfully entwined in the American system, that a complete separation of elections, on the English model, would have unforeseeable effects. It would probably so increase the notorious contradictions between the national and local strength, that is, increase Democratic strength in Republican states, that further advance on these lines will await a real party transformation.

But the real strength of the machine is in its agents, not in defective election laws or fraudulent elections. Their business is to get out the vote, and to that they devote remarkable pains and skill. They are, as has been explained, on the job all the year round, storing up gratitude and drawing on it at election times. The odds are always on the machine candidate ; he seldom needs to resort to election trickery.

It is not, however, the final election that the machine fears. As a rule the final election is, in boxing language, a " set-up ". Chicago is, perhaps, the only big city where the parties are on sufficiently even terms, and sufficiently ill-disciplined internally, to make the final election always doubtful. In other cities, it is the seizure of the party label of the dominant party that counts. Had the Boston Democrats composed their differences in 1925, there would have been no chance for the Republican candidate. It was the defeat of Mayor Hylan in the New York Democratic primaries in 1925, that made " Jimmy " Walker Mayor of New York. The subsequent massacre of the unfortunate Mr. Waterman was a legal formality. It is for control of the primaries that professional politicians, of all ranks, strive. For the earnest party worker, anxious to rise in his profession, there is no nightmare so dreadful as a primary defeat :

> " He can afford to lose the precinct in the general election. That will not hurt him much. It may not be his fault. He may be a Democrat in a Republican stronghold, and the most he is expected to do is to make a good showing. But there is no excuse for him to lose in the primaries. He must deliver the goods there." [1]

Now, strong as the machine is in acquired voting assets and whole-time service in the final elections, it is twice as strong in the primaries, for they are persistently neglected by the large class of citizens who know and care nothing for the organization of the parties to which they belong ; even if they, as good citizens

---

[1] Frank R. Kent, *The Great Game of Politics*, p. 3.

should, roll up in November to ratify the *fait accompli* by casting their superfluous votes. Roughly speaking, half as many people vote in primaries as in general elections.[1] The proportion of machine votes, in that half, is exceptionally high.

" The machine vote always registers and always votes, and even in the wards exclusively populated by the rich there are always votes the machine can get in a primary—chauffeurs, maids, watchmen and workmen who belong to the ward clubs and follow the executives." [2]

When we reflect on the power of party labels, the indifference bred, in most countries, by mere municipal politics ; the strong hold the machine has secured on the electoral machinery in most cities ; and all the temptations to acquiescence held out to the citizen ; the deliverance of the city from the bosses, by mere voting, seems a forlorn hope indeed.

[1] This is not true of states where the primary is manifestly the chief and, often, the only election.
[2] *Ibid.*, p. 37.

Chapter IV

SPOILS AND REWARDS

IT was one of the beliefs of the reformers of the eighties, full of the reverence for English methods that they learned from their Irish mentors, E. L. Godkin and James Bryce, that the spoils system was at the root of the city machine and that the introduction of the " merit system " into the local Civil Service, would work the miracle it was expected to work in the national sphere.

The machine has of course to pay or reward its adherents, the officers as well as the rank and file. Though civil service is theoretically in force in most of the big cities, its execution leaves a good deal to be desired and there is a widespread belief that it is desirable to have a friend at court, as well as a high rank in the examination. Rightly or wrongly, politicians are able to give the impression that they can find a way into jobs for their friends and a way of punishing their enemies, that makes for good party discipline. In Chicago, though the city has civil service rules, Cook County has not, and the machine can usually get its way in one or other of the numerous nests for politicians provided by the Chicago governmental system. In any case, as in the federal system, the best jobs are in the uncontrolled patronage of the machine in power. Out of 121,000 city employees in New York 3,000 are exempt from all civil service control and these 3,000 include most of the district leaders, who usually have jobs paying $5,000 a year in salary apart from pickings. In Pittsburgh and Allegheny County, 689 districts have their leaders on the public pay-roll, either of the city or county. It is the district and ward leaders and the assistants in the precincts who do the real work, both in the primaries and at election times. As Mr. Mackey put it to the Reed Committee :

"The Republican organization of Philadelphia can live without a Senator, because we have had that experience a good many years, but it cannot live without committee men ; and we have almost 3,000 ward committee men to elect, and that is of the first and vital importance to that organization." [1]

[1] *Reed Committee Hearings*, p. 575.

The Deneen faction in Chicago has been able to keep a nucleus of its fighting force together, because it has always had *some* hold on patronage, through the federal government when the leader was a Senator, through local legal officials, with useful resources, when all else failed. The spoils of war not only quarter party mercenaries on the public, but they can be made profitable to party headquarters. "The old-fashioned assessment of public employees, pruned a bit and equipped with a modern system of underground irrigation, still flourishes."[1] The relation of offices to politics is still taken for granted over a great part of the United States.

In this respect, there is little to pick and choose between the state and city machine. Even the small rural patronage is party ammunition. It was on his county patronage that Platt relied in New York when David Hill, the Democratic state boss, had everything else. It provided the Republican machine with just enough nourishment to keep it alive. In more recent times, Governor "Len" Small has shown what can be done with state patronage and the squeezing of his campaign funds out of the state employees in Illinois was worthy of the best models. Indeed, with the growth of state activities, there is a good deal more to be raised from state employees than used to be the case, whether the state is nominally under civil service or, like Connecticut, has abandoned tiresome pretence and hoisted the Jolly Roger of uncontrolled spoils. In the main, offices, though in the cities they are well paid, are not in themselves first-class prizes. A man can live off his salary as alderman or borough president or mayor, but he will not make a fortune that way, hardly even a competence. The Sheriff of New York, in the old days of fees, did pretty well and the nomination was something the machine did not throw away lightly. In one case, it was suspected that Sheriff Hugh Grant drew, but did not keep, all the revenues of the office ; he was believed to have Croker for a silent partner, he was a "tulchan" sheriff.[2] It was after profitless years as an Assemblyman that Al Smith had his family needs and his honesty recognized by nomination as Sheriff of New York County.

There remain, however, a distressingly large number of voters who cannot be won with jobs, because there are not enough satisfactory jobs to go round. This produces plain

[1] "The New Tammany", by Joseph McGoldrick, in *American Mercury*, September, 1928.

[2] The Regent Morton, in Scotland, thought of an ingenious way of getting hold of the Church revenues after the Reformation. He made dummy bishops who drew the revenues of the sees, but turned the greater part of them over to the leaders of the machine, of that time and place. The irreverent populace christened these prelates, "tulchan bishops", a tulchan being a straw calf, put beside a bereaved cow to make it give milk.

bribery and fancy variants. It is not necessary to bribe a majority to get a majority. A machine may have almost enough regular voters to carry the election, and it is the business of the officers to know where the necessary additional voters are to be got. Some can be got for nothing, by speeches, letters, personal influence, by appeal to party, or racial, or religious prejudices, or affiliations, some have even views on public matters, yet when all this has been allowed for, there remain the venal—who may be decisive.

As has been suggested, it was a comforting illusion of the early reformers that corruption was a city disease, that in the sturdy American farmers was represented the hope of public purity. Few share this illusion now. It is generally believed that rural voters are, indeed, less subject to machine pressure than are city voters ; either the rural machine works less effectively or the farmer is less constant and less grateful. It is, at any rate, fairly certain that when a farmer is open to bribery, he requires a greater temptation than the less thoroughly Americanized voter of the towns. He is better able to judge of the market, he can make a better bargain and he usually does.[1]

The sad cases of Vermilion County, Indiana, and of Adams County, Ohio, are in the text-books as examples of rural degradation, but they are far from being unique. The rural machine can do less for the average voter and so has often to pay cash— and seldom cash raised on the spot. Indiana had long a reputation for venality and, as it was a doubtful state, money was poured into it at emergencies. Democrats have usually less money than Republicans so it was their party which always felt that the Republicans were "stealing" a naturally Democratic state, full of partisans of the type that told an anxious inquirer, "Of course we'll win—if the other side doesn't bribe us." The crudities of Indiana practice have been given refinement in the great state of Pennsylvania where the legal expenditures are so generously planned that it would be churlish to go outside the law. The multiplicity of elections puts such a burden on the private citizen that he is permitted by the state to draw a modest compensation for acting in an administrative capacity at the election. Pennsylvania electors require a lot of watching and they get it from the numerous watchers hired by the candidates. The price varies according to the wealth of the candidates and the business acuteness of the elector. Not everybody is a good watcher, a family man is preferred, he may be able to interest

[1] Mr. Frank R. Kent tells a story of a politician from rural Maryland, who was in Baltimore on an election day and was so surprised at the cheapness of metropolitan votes that he could not resist the temptation to buy some— though he had no interest in the election that was being held.

others in the cause, and if you enrol every fourth or fifth voter as a watcher you manage to win a great majority of the electors—and to spend a lot of money.

When machines fall out, as the Mellon machine fell out with the Vare machine in Pennsylvania in 1926, money flows in a way that would have astounded even the Yorkshire electors of a century ago, but if all is working well, the overhead takes care of most liabilities. There are always emergencies when cash has to be had suddenly and in large quantities, but it is abnormal that the machine should need constant flooding with oil. There were pessimists who thought civil service would kill free machine service, that everything would have to be paid for in spot cash. Elder statesmen like " Plunkitt of Tammany Hall " thought that patriotic service—unrewarded by jobs—was sure to die. As the old song puts it, " senza speme di diletto vano affetto è sospirare." Their fears were unnecessary : the machine has always been able to reward the faithful ; political victory, now as always, means spoils, not, perhaps, of the old simple kind, but highly marketable spoils, nevertheless. Even if jobs and bribery were done away with, the fruits of political victory would remain, power, and power has always its attractions and, if it is for sale, its buyers. There is the permanent strength of the American machine, in the city, in the county, in the state.

Chapter V

SOME OF THE MACHINE'S CUSTOMERS

WHAT have the machines to sell that so many want to buy? There are, to begin with, the fruits of the ill-considered industry of the state legislatures.

"Americans, with a singular faith in legislation have crowded the statute-book with pains and penalties. Every penal enactment, whether it is sound or fantastic—whether it prescribes a minimum weight for a dozen hen's eggs or sheets of a certain size for hotel beds, whether it forbids the carrying of concealed weapons or the use of a foreign language on the menu cards of restaurants—affords opportunity for favouritism in the enforcement." [1]

These laws may be farcical, or occasions for petty blackmail, or desirable, but inconvenient to obey. From all the consequences of such legislation, machines, at times, perhaps usually, sell protection, that is, keep off police action or guarantee the buyers of protection immunity from private police extortion, should the police have trespassing habits.

Into another category fall those laws which a famous District Attorney of New York called " administrative lies ". Designed to curb or eradicate some evil, they only force it into allotropic forms, or even make an open defiance of the law possible, and profitable. All countries have their administrative lies, laws that express some hotly held opinion, but have survived the emotion which gave them birth, or laws never enforced, or which have proved not to be worth enforcing. France has or had some fine samples, the now dead laws against café-betting and the laws against the religious orders. Bookmakers and Jesuits both survived the official disapproval of the law ; it became an administrative lie. But it is in the " Anglo-Saxon " countries that the administrative lie flourishes most, because insistence on the difference between the real and the ideal, the desirable and the possible, the good and the prudent course, is not encouraged : no politician has ever suffered from lying on such

[1] E. M. Sait, *American Parties and Elections*, p. 363.

topics half as much as others have suffered for telling the truth. Yet if all English-speaking countries have suffered from the administrative lie, the United States has been the peculiar home of the moral legislator who will do good though evil may, and almost certainly will, come of it. It is in " moral " questions that the administrative lie is most powerful, that is, in legislation designed to reduce the opportunities for man to sin against certain selected commandments. These moral questions are especially the prey of zealous clergymen, and women, who press their views on legislators who have rather a more extended view of the world and of the possibilities of law than their mentors, but who neither like nor dare to appear indifferent to the great moral questions involved. In consequence, the statute-book is filled with laws that are not enforced, or are not enforceable. Not only do they do no good, but they do harm, since they prevent the enactment of more practical, if less ambitious, statutes. The law against street-betting is, perhaps, the best English example ; no one with eyes in his head can believe it is enforced, or that the whole machinery of illegal betting has no toleration from the police, or that the toleration is free, but experience shows that legis- lation on betting which promises to produce some remedy or revenue, will be opposed by the moralists and sabotaged by the bookmakers. The law on prostitution is in the same state and, despite occasional scandals, will continue in that state as long as laws are made with good intentions instead of prudent fore- sight.

But our unenforced statutes, and their resultant corruption and weakening of the force of law, are as nothing to the tangle of moral legislation that has been such a consolation to the good and such a blessing to the wicked in the United States, for

> " The passion of the simpler-minded Americans for aggressive legislation controlling private morality, has made the control of the police a main source of party revenue, and dragged the saloon and brothel, essentially retiring though these institutions are, into politics." [1]

Laws that are not enforceable, or are only enforceable at a cost the community will not stand, are one of the most notorious assets of a corrupt American machine. Prohibition, over a great part of the United States, is an administrative lie of the first magnitude, but it is not the only one or the first one. Long before the days of national prohibition, Sunday closing of the saloons was a stumbling-block to the reformer. The law was explicit, but the law was extremely unpopular in the cities where

[1] H. G. Wells, *The Future in America*, p. 176.

it had to be applied. Should a reform administration defy the opinion of the city, enforce the law and thus bring about a revulsion in favour of the defeated " machine ", or wink at the breach of the law and thus keep on the side of reform many good citizens who would be irritated beyond endurance by having the religious taboos of rural puritanism enforced on them ? The same story occurs, again and again, in American city history. Laws that expressed the moral sentiment of the community, but which no one was willing to have thoroughly enforced, laws that expressed the moral sentiments of the politically dominant countryside, but which had few friends in the cities for which they were designed, have been made a touchstone, and the citizens have resolved to have cakes and ale from the machine, rather than honesty and rural morals from the reformers. If it was said that it was disgraceful that men should sacrifice the public good to their appetites, it could be replied that the moral appetites of the legislators were no more sacred than the fleshly appetites of the citizens. One or other had to be sacrificed, or both had to be served at the cost of law and honesty. Faced with the dilemma, the great heart of the American people has seldom faltered, the law has expressed the highest aspirations of the body politic and the consequences have been denied or discounted.

At times, bold spirits have refused to be bullied. Governor Marshall abandoned the farcical attempt to enforce Sunday closing in the cities of Indiana ; Carter Harrison I in Chicago, and Tom Johnson in Cleveland, annoyed the righteous by their refusal to sacrifice great public interests to the shadow-boxing with vice demanded of them by the public opinion of the churches and of the women's clubs ; *de minimis non curat praetor*, but they sacrificed thereby a good deal of support they might otherwise have expected to gain. On the other hand, one of the three reform police commissioners under Mayor Strong, Theodore Roosevelt annoyed many of his supporters by closing the saloons on Sunday and thus breeding friends for Tammany and lessening his chance to keep on with the good work of purifying the police.

As a rule, however, the legislation that looks so well on paper, looks even better in practice to the men who have to work the machine, for at some period in the history of every machine, the most obvious, though not necessarily the most profitable sources of graft, have been the three Bs, booze, betting, brothels.

The saloon has always been a great force in American politics, as its sisters have been in Europe. From a saloon, or through the saloon, many a boss rose to the top and the regulations that the trade in alcohol seems to necessitate in all countries, make the publican or saloon-keeper particularly at the mercy of the police, particularly in need of political favour or power.[1] In the United States, the power of making life easy for a saloon-keeper or of making it very difficult for him, has been a weapon of every machine. If the saloon licence is in itself of value, the granting of it, in all countries, is a favour, either to a powerful industry like the brewing " trade " in England ; or to a grateful individual, as in Scotland, where the houses are not so regularly or openly " tied " to the brewers. In America, the favour is granted by a political machine which has to be paid in cash and service. A saloon is a natural centre of political influence, and so is a speak-easy. How much better it is if you can guarantee that all that influence will be thrown one way, as was done in Pittsburgh, when the local bosses were doing their best to carry out Mr. Mellon's wishes in the 1926 primary ! Mr. Dooley's opinions had more weight in the Archey Road, delivered from behind a bar, than they would have had at a street corner, and the saloon was one of the chief weapons of the famous " Hinky Dink " Kenna in the First Ward of Chicago at the time when Mr. Dooley was in his prime.

In a rural area, the local bootlegger was not an unknown figure, even before national prohibition, but the farmers did not allow saloon-keepers the high social position he had in the cities. Platt, in his earlier days, used a drug store as his city colleague would have used a saloon, a difference at least of name.

But it is not only the quasi-legitimate use of the saloon, as a source of revenue, or as a forum, that the machine exploits. When a saloon-keeper threw his key into the Hudson, this high-spirited defiance of the law was only possible, thanks to a com-plaisant police, and the police were only complaisant to those of whom the politicians approved. The stricter the regulation of the liquor traffic, the better it paid to disregard it, and the more had to be paid for the privilege. The inevitable relation between the saloon and the machine was used to discredit both institu-tions ; the saloon was abused as an ally of political corruption, and the machine as a friend of publicans and sinners ; but the hostility did not do the machine much harm, whatever damage was suffered, in the long run, by saloon-keepers who were, legally, abolished.

In close connection with the drink traffic went prostitution. The connection was an old one, the frequent association of Venus and Bacchus was noticed in Roman times, but the Americans went " all out " to make the connection inevitable, instead of

[1] The ward politician was normally a saloon-keeper. There is a story that a Tammany meeting was emptied by a wag who shouted through the door, " Alderman, your saloon's on fire." In a minute the future lawyer-boss, George Olvany, stood alone in the hall whence all but he had fled.

merely common. By the social taboo on the saloon, it was barred to women of respectability and so it became purely masculine—or impurely mixed. In the regulation of prostitution, that is, the control of it to produce a revenue, the saloon was a great help. It canalized the trade and joined up two of the activities of the machine. Not all saloon-keepers catered to all appetites, but the reformers often made it hard for them not to. The story of the Raines Law in New York ought to have been a lesson to reformers. In order to cut down mere drinking, a well-known " up-state " politician induced the legislature of New York to pass the law that bore his name. It forced saloon-keepers to turn their saloons into " hotels ", by providing bedrooms. There were far more saloons in New York than any possible demand for hotel accommodation could fill, so the saloon-keeper had to choose between leaving the bedrooms empty —or using them in another profitable business. Soon a " Raines Law Hotel " was a synonym for brothel, or house of assignation, a result that no doubt shocked the righteous, but did not breed in them a sufficient scepticism of the wisdom of legislating for a great city according to the ideas of moderately upright rural politicians.[1]

Apart from the association of the saloon with prostitution, the machine has to face a serious problem in its dealings with the latter traffic. There is no shortage of laws, but there is a marked shortage of people to enforce them without fear or favour. There have been candid leaders, on both the machine and reform sides, who have admitted their inability to deal with the problem and have been content to let it alone, if it was kept within tolerable limits, both geographically and psychologically. Tolerated areas, " red-light " districts, were permitted and a crude system of licensing was put into effect. Some honest and independent mayors forbade any charge for the privilege of operating, but, in general, the liberty of the profession had its price ; the only question was whether all the money should go into the pockets of the local representatives of the law, or whether the machine, as a whole, or powerful individuals in it, should have a share. A really good going machine, in New York for instance, would, perhaps, have liked to do without the " dirty " graft of prostitution. The supporters of the machine might not have the high civic sense of their betters, but they were in general good family

---

[1] The Raines Law had, of course, other attractions for its sponsors than those of moral endeavour. Its excise provisions added considerably to the patronage at the disposal of the state boss, Mr. Platt, and the necessary bonding operations helped the business of such organizations as " Fidelity Companies "—in one of which, the son of " Uncle John " Raines was interested.

men and women, who objected to a brothel in the neighbourhoods where they had to bring up their families. When the traffic became too open, when it became too public a nuisance, there was grave danger of a revolt. Many of the Irish bosses had special scruples about this side of their business and preferred to leave this asset of the machine to minor operators. This sentiment found its voice in the great revolt against Tammany that followed the revelations of the Lexow Committee and resulted in the election of Mayor Strong in 1894. A few years later, the veteran boss of Brooklyn, Hugh McLaughlin, fighting the Tammany-provoked revolt in his own territory, and defending the autonomy of his machine against the encroaching Tiger, appealed to the good people of Brooklyn to keep Tammany and its brothels at the other end of the bridge.

In other cities, the problem arose in very odd ways. The Ames régime in Minneapolis, in its endeavours to make the city an Alsatia for the crooks of the Middle West, exploited all the resources of the traffic in the city. The Mayor himself was the chief agent in farming out the revenue from this, as from many other illicit sources.[1]

The voting strength of the profession was not contemptible, for the " runners ", and the " cadets " could and did vote, not merely solidly, but often, for their protectors. One writer goes as far as to assert that the brothel interests in Philadelphia were worth 85,000 votes—which, with all allowances made for the city of homes, suggests a good deal of repeating and colonizing, for which arts the houses were admirably adapted. In Denver the women, thanks to the early feminism of the state of Colorado, could themselves be polled, and their votes were among the most valued assets of whatever faction controlled the city police.

In recent years, the high tide of moral legislation and feeling has cramped the style of the profession and of its political protectors. It has not abolished the traffic, but it has spread it all over the cities and has given it protective colouring that makes open political protection less possible and less necessary. Of course, the financial possibilities of the profession have not been neglected. The recent scandals of New York show how much a humble policeman could do in the way of taxing and of blackmail, thanks to the co-operation of a woman magistrate who did not ask too many questions. There may be cases of the old type in the chartered anarchy of Cook County (Chicago), but the revenues have to be collected over a wide area by minor agents whose honesty is hard to guarantee.

The third element of a " wide-open " town, the toleration of

---

[1] One refinement of extortion practised under Ames in Minneapolis was the forcing of the women to buy illustrated biographies of the city officials.

gambling, takes more varied forms in America than in Britain. There is much more legal gambling on the stock market than among the English poor ; the American working man is free to hazard his savings in Wall Street, while his English brother has to be content with betting on horses or football matches. " Playing the ponies " is a much less important feature of the American world than of ours, but there is a good deal of racing gambling and the pool rooms (billiard rooms), there, as here, are often centres for bookmakers and their clients. They pay for protection to the police, and to the masters of the police, but they are not so important as the clubs and gambling houses which provide for games of chance, cards, roulette and the like. These may be private enterprises, paying handsomely for their existence, or they may, like some clubs run by Tammany district leaders, be active units in the political machine, entitled to free immunity—as one rash police commissioner of New York is suspected of having discovered recently. Gambling, however, has so many legitimate outlets in America, that it plays only a minor part in the public support given or refused the machine.

It can hardly be denied, by the most optimistic Briton, that these evils are not exclusively confined to the United States : but if Britain has her share of administrative lies, the profits of them are not often paid into the war chest of any party or political organization.

It will be observed that the revenues of the machine from these illicit sources involves co-operation with the police, and in the control of the police lies the seat of power for many an American machine. In the jungle of administrative and taxing authorities that buries the unfortunate city of Chicago, the one asset of city control that is really different in kind from the assets of the Parks Boards, the Sanitary District, etc., is the control of the police. Some bosses have concentrated on the police to the comparative neglect of other sources of revenue and power, such was " Doc " Ames of Minneapolis. Others, like Butler of St. Louis, have reckoned that the control of the police was all that was needed to hold their own against a hostile city administration. In the power of the police often lies the secret of Empire.

It is easy to see how this is so in dealing with the illicit activities of the underworld. Not only have the pimps and bootleggers money to contribute, they have numerous counted votes. The great days of election slugging are over, but intimidation at the polls is by no means a thing of the past, and not only can the police fail to repress this abuse, but they can conveniently provide sluggers when needed. All the powers of evil can be mobilized by a police that knows its business in favour of common friends. The immense importance of control of the police has not escaped the eyes of the American politician and over this arm of political war, factions and parties have fought. One of the liveliest episodes in the history of New York was the attempt to preserve the municipal police force, after the state had established its own police. In the cause of municipal autonomy, Fernando Wood gave battle to the intruding mercenaries, in a serio-comic war. New York state soon got tired of policing New York City, or the politicians did, but similar enterprises have been tried in other cities.

One powerful motive, in all these assumptions of authority by the state, has been the necessity of taking the enforcement of moral legislation into more friendly hands than those of the average city administration. It was to enforce the liquor laws that the General Court (legislature) of Massachusetts attacked the police autonomy of Boston, and though repelled by the vigorous war governor, John A. Andrew, the necessity of abandoning the licence policy of the state, or taking over its enforcement finally forced, or excused, the destruction of the city's control of its police. Though the experiment has been made in many other states, it has seldom lasted and all the great American cities, except Boston, Baltimore, St. Louis and Kansas City, have control of their police, though, of recent years, the states have begun to build up state police forces in rural areas. The experience of Boston may seem to show that state control is a boon, but if the Boston police system is administratively a success, it is an exception that proves the rule. An impartial, objective control of the police, by some body outside local politics, might be the solution of the American police question, if the impartial authority could be found, but the average American state government is not such a body. The greatest authority on the American police has given an unmistakable verdict :

" There is scarcely a city in the United States in which the police department has not been used as the ladder by which political organizations have crawled to power. Obstacles in the way of complete dominance by party machines have been overcome by the easy processes of law, and police departments have been revamped and reshaped, not in the interests of public service, but to facilitate the operation of the spoils system or strengthen the grip of some political machine." [1]

Few, indeed, are the cases when police efficiency had anything to do with the reform ; it might be the ostensible reason, but plain party politics were usually at the bottom of the reorganization. Politicians in the state capitals could not endure

[1] R. B. Fosdick, *American Police Systems*, pp. 115–16.

to see all the power and patronage a police system gives, in the hands of a rival machine. The police changes have usually represented the attempt of one party, or faction, to steal the assets of police control from rivals, who were stronger in the city than in the state. Ohio police history has been full of interest for the critic. Both Cleveland and Cincinnati have had their police autonomy taken away from them, at different times, to make things pleasanter for the party in control of the state government in Columbus ; the efficiency of the police force was a minor, if any, consideration. When the police of Denver were put under the control of the state government of Colorado, the Populist Governor removed the Commissioner " ' because the good of the Populist party in Colorado demanded it '." [1] He was merely more candid than most of his brethren. The rural and moral Anglo-Saxon Democrats of Missouri refused, in 1914, to admit the right of St. Louis to police " home rule ". Ex-Governor Folk, backed up by the " better elements " of the city, declared the object of the movement was not home rule, but brewery rule, and he and they were unwilling to allow the city to decide for itself whether it really objected to brewery rule. " Boss " Platt was anxious to seize the control of the New York City Police, but Governor Odell, perhaps with history in his mind, refused to carry out this highly dangerous policy ; profitable, no doubt, if it came off, but dangerous all the same. Tammany would fight to the death for freedom, and few in the city would hesitate to fall in to defend the inherent right of New York to have its own type of bad police, rather than the type favoured by the rural moralists and grafters.

The battle does not end with the legislative assertion of state supremacy, for, to be effective, the police must be paid for out of city funds. With the good will of most of the citizens, the local machine can at times sabotage the police administration, as the Democratic administration has recently done in Kansas City, and thus force a retreat on the state, or compel a further invasion of civic autonomy which endears the city politicians even more to the insulted citizens.

In the control of the police lies one of the chief marks and causes of machine success. The moment " Big Bill " Thompson took over in Chicago from Mayor Dever, the Chief of Police walked the plank, and there could have been no more open sign of the zeal of the Pittsburgh machine for the Mellon ticket, than the adoption of the Pepper-Fisher badges by the police of the city in 1926. The bear and ragged staff were no more evidence of livery and maintenance in medieval England than this ! Since there have been regular police forces in America, they

[1] R. B. Fosdick, *American Police Systems*, p. 101.

have been political forces of the first order. If the police be with me, what care I who is against me ? So might a boss say and he would be right, half the time, at any rate.

American police forces, if not " the finest in the world ", are more like other police than Europeans like to admit, and are a good deal better than they are sometimes painted. They are the victims of a bad system and in contemplating past and present scandals, it is as well to remember, that even at the worst, as Mr. Don Marquis has pointed out, " the police departments of our great cities are honeycombed with honesty ".

It is not sufficient to control the police, there are other important public officials to be squared or silenced. The office of district, or state's attorney in America has an importance that we can hardly appreciate. The discretion of the Attorney-General in England, who can refrain from prosecuting a Sir Edward Carson or a Campbell, can make an example of a Lord Kylsant or of a Communist agitator, is, of course, an important part of our political system and has its difficulties but, in America, the power is less centralized, less public and less responsible. The recent assailants of Tammany judged rightly when they struck at Mr. Crain, the District Attorney ; if the machine is vulnerable, it is there. In Chicago, the State's Attorney's office was the support of the authority of Mr. R. E. Crowe and has had its martyrs to duty in the gang wars. What duties Mr. McSwiggin was performing when he was " bumped off ", it is hard to discover, but the ability to prosecute and not to prosecute, to call a friendly instead of an inquisitive Grand Jury, is a great power, and is worth fighting and killing for. A District Attorney who forgets his makers, may do serious damage to a machine, as was shown by Folk in St. Louis, or to individuals as Whitman and Jerome showed in New York, damage ranging from convictions and executions like that of Lieutenant Becker, to comic episodes like the arrest of a leading politician, Maurice Holohan, in a gambling " joint ".[1]

The power of a District Attorney, for good and evil, is so far reaching that he is worth placating by all ranks in society— and so are his masters.

> " Basically there is no ethical distinction between the prosecutor's entering of a nolle [prosequi] in a case against a friend of a political ' boss ' in order that he might gain or retain the favour of that ' boss ', and the refusal of the counsel of a leading bank to attack that prosecutor's entering of that

[1] Jerome caught this eminent politician and was told that he had gone to the place to rescue a " wayward son ". The " wayward son " came back at his father with great vigour and the whole episode bred unhealthy levity at the expense of Tammany Hall.

nolle for fear that such an attack may enable that ' boss '
directly or indirectly to harm that bank." [1]

It was as District Attorney, that Oakey Hall made himself
a popular figure in New York, and, when he was Tweed's Mayor,
he remarked, "'Few persons have so many *tried* friends as I have,
and tried friends are always magnanimous.'" [2]

In a good-going machine, the judges are part of the system.
Nominated by the bosses, they are expected to know their master's
voices. Sometimes it is merely a matter of patronage. In
New York, the Surrogate, with his great resources in the way of
referees and administrators, is a central figure in the patronage
system. The nominee of Tammany is expected to take heed
to the advice given him as to the disposition of the political
assets, and should he, like one impetuous Irish incumbent of
modern times, forget the implied conditions of his " election ",
he will be defeated when he appeals for the suffrages of his
indifferent fellow-citizens. Other judges have pickings to give
away to the promising young lawyers whose professional careers
Tammany takes in hand. Substantial justice may be done, but
Tammany men get " all the breaks ". In minor cases, at least,
a good boss looks after his own. The magistrate, the prosecutor,
get the tip to go slow and a mild reproof may replace a sentence,
if the local agent of the machine thinks fit. The quality of mercy
blesses him that gives and him that takes in the American
system. Suspicions of class bias in the English local courts have
not yet died down so that too many stones cannot be thrown at
a system which systematizes the adjustment of the law to the
individual, but it may, of course, go further than tempering
justice with mercy and the judicial systems of all the great cities
have been suspect, from time to time, of very unjudicial conduct.
The machine nominates judges ; the election is usually a formality ; it punishes them ; and, in New York, at least, it takes
money for selling places on the bench. We have the French
precedent to show that a venal magistracy may yet have a high
standard of conduct, but not all American judges are worthy
specimens of the *noblesse de la robe*. They undoubtedly listen
with special attention to lawyers who are part of the machine ;
they thus add to its revenue, for service of the machine has its
legal reward and the endorsement of a lawyer, or of a judge
by the machine, has a serious cash value and is only given for
money or money's worth. The survey of *Criminal Justice in
Cleveland* revealed a state of affairs in which it was the height of
imprudence to appear before certain judges against or without
machine lawyers ; a good witness tells us that practice in the

[1] *Criminal Justice in Cleveland*, p. 220.   [2] M. R. Werner, *Tammany Hall*, p. 118.

lower courts of New York is a racket ; and the whole system is elegantly symbolized in the ceremony whereby a new magistrate in New York is invested with his gavel by his (Tammany) district leader.

Administrative discretion, whether it is applied to carrying a gun, or to the issuing of boxing licences,[1] is a rich seam for the administrators and it is prudent to pay twice for services that are really necessary. The docks of New York yield a substantial revenue to more than the city, and from time to time the investigations reveal that the tribute is being paid. It used to be the French Line, now it is the Norddeutscher Lloyd, but it seems probable that the other lines which have not testified to this kind of extortion have not, therefore, been immune. It helps, in most dealings with a machine, to pay for service, or to have a season ticket, or to get a pass from someone in power, and when the habit is really ingrained everything from the issue of marriage licences to the sale of judgeships is in danger of being overcharged for and so involving disagreeable publicity when at last the victims " squeal ".

The great discovery of the machine, made in comparatively modern times, is the infinite possibilities of " honest graft ". There were, of course, pioneers of earlier days who had stumbled, almost by accident, on the secret, but the turn-over of the officers of the great machines to legal larceny has only become general in the present century. " Plunkitt of Tammany Hall " expressed his political philosophy in the dictum : " I seen my opportunities and I took 'em." It is the mark of the " New Tammany " to make the opportunities. The Duke of Wellington congratulated himself on his ability to guess what was on the other side of a hill ; the well-commanded machine makes the hill and uses the advance information it thus obtains. Honest graft is " essentially gambling for a rise in the market, with the advantage of inside information ".[2] The condemnation of property to make a park, to build a school, to make way for a new road, all such legitimate enterprises pay anybody handsomely for skilful guessing—and still better do they pay the well-informed politician who can bet on a sure thing. Yet how is such investment in

[1] The handsome returns from heavy-weight boxing which attracted attention a few years ago opened new vistas of graft to politicians. As New York was, by far, the best market for this entertainment, the State Boxing Commission which acted as a legal " N.S.C." in the matter was believed to be open to persuasion in the exercise of its administrative discretion. Mr. Tunney was induced to sign away 25 per cent of his share in the first Dempsey fight to an agent, Timothy J. Mara, to secure a New York venue for the fight. Mara failed to do so and Mr. Tunney refused to pay. It came out in testimony that Harry Wills, in whom a few enthusiasts saw another Jack Johnson, had signed away 95 per cent of his future takings to get a chance at the title !

[2] *New Republic*, October 1, 1930.

inside information to be prevented or even deprecated, since in such ways are legitimate businesses run and respectable fortunes made ? It takes remarkable fortitude to refuse to speculate, in a speculative society, on inside information, whether that information refers to new improvements, profitable contracts that are about to be made with a government or city department, or other activities, in which time is of the essence of the profit. Only exceptionally sensitive spectators can expect the average politician to display the virtue necessary to resist such temptation —the more that the public, far from admiring his virtue, is likely to write him down as a fool for his pains.

The difficulty is that such " honest graft " slides, imperceptibly, into less defensible practices. From buying property that is to be condemned by the city, at a handsome price, to buying property in order that the city may condemn it, is a narrow and a frequent step. From that, the descent to all kinds of jugglery with the city's interests is easier still. What has begun as ordinary business practice ends, quickly, as one more " racket ". The fruits of informed foresight soon become a " rake-off ". The advantages of knowing the specifications of a city contract in advance, and of knowing the bids, are manifest, and still more manifest is the advantage of drawing up your own specifications. It was the prescription of a special type of drain-pipe, which only one firm made, that brought about, a few years ago, the downfall of one New York politician and was one of the first swallows of the present summer of Tammany scandals. Yet it is a type of abuse very hard to root out. Something so like it that only a patriot can see the difference, has happened recently in at least one British city, and more flagrantly in an Australian city. There are dark rumours of " rings " in government contracting circles even in Britain, and the sad story of bribery in private contracts need hardly be dwelt on. What does, in the main, mark off the American system, is the systematization of it and its direct political causes and consequences.

Another source of power and profit has been the archaic and absurd taxing system of the American states and local authorities. The personal property tax is not merely a general invitation to bold and safe perjury, it is a means of using and selling influence. So it is with other taxes. Joseph Pulitzer believed that Croker punished him for his anti-Tammany attacks in the *World* by ridiculously high tax assessments, and similar stories have spread in Chicago in more recent years.

The growth of a long and complicated building code has been a godsend to the machine. In the jungle of regulations and possible inspections lies the possibility of levying endless blackmail on the owners of real estate, and of selling protection

handsomely. Can we wonder, then, that to the old and traditional connection between contracting and Tammany Hall, there
has come to be added a new " racket " and that the ex-leader,
George W. Olvany, in his practice before the all-powerful
" Board of Standards and Appeals ", has acquired a practice,
and an income, that put him in the running with the ablest
advisers of law-hampered corporations ? The roof has recently
been removed from this section of Tammany Hall, but it is
highly probable that, undisturbed by any Seabury, machines
in other cities are working the same seam.

The drawback is, of course, the same as in police graft : the
rank and file are not content with their pay ; they insist on
pickings. From the ransom paid to the men at the top of the
tree, down to the petty pilferers at the roots, the business of the
country pays an endless ransom to the machine,[1] that threatens
to kill the ultimate source of revenue. Minor graft of this kind
in not unknown in British cities ; not all inspectors of food are
above turning a profitable blind eye to substitutions of materials
on which the law frowns, any more than all policemen are above
taking a tip from an erring publican, but as yet, we have no
unifying system, no public stealers' union such as the American
machine so easily becomes.

There *are* abuses that arouse public indignation : immunity
from fire regulations that has lined the pockets of officials at the
subsequent cost of lives ; extortions in connection with food for
the poor, such as the " Ice Trust " in the days of Croker and
Van Wyck ; interference with business which alarms the whole
community, such as was thought to account in part, probably
falsely, for the retrogression of Cincinnati. A combination of all
possible kinds of scandals such as has afflicted Chicago ; a tax
system whose corruption has finally stopped the taxing machine,
and made the city bankrupt ; an alliance of politics and crime
that threatens to stop the growth of the city's industry and
commerce ; an endless chain of political and criminal " rackets "
that destroys the normal rights of government as a force for
public order and drives despairing citizens into " commending "
themselves to great criminals as poor men in the early days of
feudalism, despairing of the vanishing authority of the king,
commended themselves to the Capones of the time ; such a
chain of object-lessons may breed a temporary revulsion against
the price of politics—or it may breed what Israel Durham,
Boss of Philadelphia, thought the greatest asset of a machine,
public despair. It shows no signs of breeding the spirit which
alone can promise much hope of a permanent reform.

[1] On a nominal salary of $7,500 a year, the Under-Sheriff of New York
County saved, as far as is known, in five years $600,000.

Chapter VI

TAMMANY HALL

A DISTINGUISHED Pennsylvanian expert, Mr. W. H. Kemble, described the political system of that state as "addition, division and silence". It has been the misfortune of the most famous of American machines, that it has only mastered the first two of these arts ; silence has, to its regret, been beyond it. There are two reasons for this defect. Tammany has always been a poor man's organization ; that is, its rulers have been poor men, at the beginning of their careers, and its appeal has always been to the lower orders. It has done its best to make the best of both worlds, but it has never forgotten that its strength came from below ; whatever its practice, its theory has been democratic ; it has clung to the less respectable of the two great parties and has, consequently, had a bad Press. Its friends have had at least to pretend to be ashamed of it ; its enemies have been able to regard themselves as *ipso facto* good citizens. Its depredations and its crimes have had to be committed in a good deal of unwelcome limelight and the slightest murmur of discontent has been magnified into a roar of revolt.

The second cause of Tammany's permanent notoriety has been its rashness in taking a local habitation and a name. The other machines have borne the names of individuals, such as the " Cox machine ", the " Vare machine ", or of special forms of graft, like the " Gas House Ring ", or have been named merely after the party they supported or belonged to, but Tammany from the start had its own name ; it has had, in the various buildings that have served as " the Wigwam ", a notorious physical headquarters ; the citizen of New York has always had a very tangible object and group on which to vent his grievances and the critics have never had to hunt for their target.

The Patriotic Columbian Order of St. Tammany was born within a few weeks of Washington's inauguration in Wall Street and the machine and the government have, on the whole, got on very well together since they started life, in little old New York, in the momentous year, 1789. Tammany was, from the start, a democratic society, hostile to the better elements, radical in politics and levelling in social principles. Though it has had dreams of spreading over the whole country, it has wisely concentrated on the city of its birth, and since it first tasted the sweets of office in 1800, has seldom been forced to live on its own fat. Already the Americans had developed a passion for " orders " and " rituals " and Tammany catered to this taste with its Sachems, its Sagamores and its Wiskinskies, but it has more serious objects than glutting the romantic tastes of its members. In Aaron Burr, it had the first great American master of democratic politics ; of the arts of winning voters ; of casting and of counting votes. When the organized proletariat of the city defeated the plans of Alexander Hamilton in 1800, the long career of the society as a political power began. New York was growing enormously ; into it poured the immigrant tide and the immigrants were seized by Tammany and converted into some of the finest brute votes in the United States. Despite schisms, revolts and periods of disrupted chieftainship, the men who held the Wigwam were sure, in the not very long run, to hold the city ; to them gravitated the mass of voters and their chiefs ; adherence to Tammany was the sign of Democratic orthodoxy and in the Sachems of the Hall were vested the increasingly valuable assets of the political control of the city. There were moments when the Hall seemed threatened by dangerous popular movements, when its clientèle was seduced away by demagogues with principles, by working-men's parties and the like, but the Hall was always able to preserve its hold on the affections of the poor ; it was able to cut itself off ostentatiously from too open collusion with the wealthy, or with the middle classes ; it was never long in heresy or in popular disfavour ; *ubi Tammany ibi potestas*. By the time of the Civil War, the lesson had been learned and for the buyers and sellers of political goods, all roads led to the Wigwam. There were occasional revolts and schisms, bred by personal ambitions ; there were anti-popes who set up rival Avignons ; but they surrendered, or disappeared, or were received back into the fold. So it was with " Mozart Hall ", started by Fernando Wood ; so it was with John O'Brien's " Apollo Hall " :

> " In diesen heilgen Hallen,
> Kennt man die Rache nicht,
> Und ist ein Mensch gefallen,
> Führt Liebe ihn zur Pflicht."

By the outbreak of the Civil War, the Hall was, in all essentials, much the same as it is to-day. It could, in any normal time, deliver the vote of the populace of Manhattan, to any candidate it chose, and though nominally Democratic, was a mercenary auxiliary that was more feared than loved by the rest of the party. Its leaders were, in the eyes of many, disgraced by their disloyal attitude during the war, a feeling strengthened by the great riots against the draft in July, 1863, but the Hall cared little for the opinion of anybody living north of the Harlem River. Secure on its right little, tight little island, Tammany set out to get its share of the abundant loot that the war and its aftermath revealed. Under Boss Tweed, the Hall, for the first time, gained rank as a national institution. The city machine and the boss were typified in Tammany and Tweed and it acquired, in addition to a name, an emblem, " the Tammany Tiger ".[1]

The story of the Tweed ring needs no re-telling. Its methods were crude, and later masters regard them as examples of Tammany's early bad manner. The false bids ; the grafting in contracts and supplies ; the adroit placating of business men of high reputation, considerable acquisitiveness and little curiosity ; these are permanent methods of the system, but were crudely practised. It is doubtful if they will even stand comparison with the quieter achievements of the contemporary Gas House Ring in Philadelphia. As for the bolder Tweed measures, the cooking of accounts and the mere stealing of public funds without due process of politics, Tammany would be rightly ashamed of such methods to-day. Practitioners of such crudity are fit only for the Sanitary Board of Cook County, Illinois—or the penitentiary. The last, indeed, was Tweed's fate, and the lesson has not been lost on Tammany. Minor leaders have gone up the river to Sing Sing, but the Hall itself cleansed its hands, if not its conscience, of the perilous stuff. Henceforward the Wigwam was in principle for " Honest graft ".

Tweed and Tammany were overthrown, and New York got a reform administration that kept down local taxes, was not to be seduced into such dangerous measures as relief for the unemployed, and in a short time was swept away by the " New Tammany ", reorganized and reformed by " Honest John " Kelly. " Honest John " deserved his title, he did not steal himself—or was not caught, he was a man of great respectability, as befitted the nephew of a cardinal, and he was a master politician. He was, indeed, unpopular in the country at large, for he repeatedly sacrificed the interests of the Democratic party in the state and in the country, to those of Tammany in the city.

---

[1] The Tiger had adorned one of Tweed's fire engines. It was made the emblem of the machine by the great cartoonist, Thomas Nast, who also invented the Republican elephant and the Democratic donkey. After the great triumph of 1932, Mr. Josephus Daniels suggested the adoption of a rooster (*Anglicé* cock) as the Democratic emblem.

But his tact and devotion to business, his resolute leadership of the legions of the city, mark him as the refounder of Tammany. New York was as certain to have a machine as any other great city, but the long continuance of power in the hands of one group of leaders, the substitution of a legitimate oligarchical succession, for the tyrannies and revolutions which have marked machine history in other cities, is due to Kelly who salvaged Tammany at a time when it might have become a total wreck. On the whole, not only Tammany, but New York have cause to be grateful to him.

Though Tammany has its hierarchy, and its discipline, even Tammany cannot make a boss. The leader of a great American machine must impose himself on his rivals and the interregnum may be long. So when Kelly was dead, out of the ruck of district leaders, rose Richard Croker, another decisive figure in the history of Tammany. It was Croker who exploited to the full the possibilities of honest graft ; it was Croker who taught the leaders of other Democratic factions in New York that there was no hope for them outside Tammany ; it was Croker who survived disasters that threatened him with the fate of Tweed, and it was Croker who would have taught reformers the hopelessness of their merely moral assaults, if they could have learned that, or anything else. Finally, it was under Croker that Tammany was enabled to advance from its narrow island and unite in one hand the rule of the five boroughs that made up Greater New York. If the Boss retired in defeat, he had given his supporters reasons to hope for better days and new worlds to conquer.[1]

Croker had his weaknesses, just as Tweed had. He learned that there were abuses that not even the Tammany voters would stand ; that theft in legal form was one thing, but that the too overt association with the brothel was a danger ; that the police could be a handicap as well as an asset and that lesson was also learned by his successor, Charles Murphy. Decorum must be

---

[1] New York is divided into five boroughs : Manhattan, the old city on Manhattan Island ; Brooklyn and Queens, the two great cities on Long Island ; Richmond, on Staten Island ; and the Bronx, on the mainland, across the Harlem River from Manhattan. Of these five boroughs, only Manhattan and the Bronx are directly under Tammany control, though there are Tammany members everywhere. The population of Manhattan Island has begun to fall behind that of Brooklyn, but nevertheless, with great tact, Tammany has kept its primacy in New York. The Wigwam had to allow a Brooklyn candidate, Hylan, to rule as Mayor for eight years, with consequent growth in prestige for the Brooklyn boss, McCooey, but even then Tammany was in control. By beating Hylan in the primaries and electing " Jimmy " Walker, Governor Smith and Judge Olvany, in 1925, restored the complete authority to the Wigwam which would have been badly shaken had Hylan succeeded in defying the Society.

observed. Just as the Tammany leaders were less " tough ", were less uniformly saloon-keepers and could now wear dress clothes without looking like amateur waiters, so the whole appearance of the Hall was altered. There was again a " New Tammany " and, in the history of the machine, Commissioner Murphy plays the part of a second Kelly. He preserved, and improved, the system laid down by Croker, but he learned, as the great trust magnates learned, the importance of politeness, of the soft answer, of the services that a public relations counsel can render.

At the moment, Tammany is as strong as ever ; its hold on the votes and, perhaps, on the voters, is unshaken. A storm of scandal is beating round the police and the judiciary ; the profits of politics are being revealed in an atmosphere less tolerant than it would have been in the prosperous years, but if the paint has been scraped off a little, if the Tiger's stripes are showing through the lambskin, there seems no immediate danger of a revolt of the faithful against the great machine.

The size of the vote given to the Socialist candidate at the special election of 1932, the painfully large number of citizens who insisted on voting for Acting-Mayor McKee, although that obedient statesman was not a candidate, reflect the discontent bred by the revelations of the Hofstadter committee and the ignominious collapse of Mayor Walker and the rebuke administered to " Boss " Curry by Messrs. Roosevelt and Smith at the State convention. Nevertheless, Tammany has elected its nominee as Mayor, although it is safe to say that not one New Yorker in a hundred thousand would have thought of Mr. O'Brien for that office, if Tammany had not put him forward. The deplorable financial situation of the city may be largely due to Tammany inefficiency and corruption. The only way of restoring the city's credit and enabling it to meet the crisis, and care for the poor it professes to cherish, may be a rigorous pruning of the city's budget. That pruning, however, would involve losses which would fall heavily on the rulers of Tammany and the average New Yorker does not expect such abnegation from " the braves."

The mechanism of Tammany does not differ markedly from that of any other machine and its methods hardly at all. The leader of the organization, the boss, may hold no important office, but his authority is immense. To him are referred all the final decisions, to him come all the problems of discipline, of promotion, of policy. Once thoroughly in the saddle, he is hard to dislodge, for all the key positions are filled with his men and, though treason is not unknown, it is not, as a rule, profitable. But this office of boss is too important and requires too great

talents and accomplishments to be disposed of lightly. When
death or retiral makes a vacancy in the chieftainship, the war of
the succession is apt to be prolonged. Mere election is not
enough, as the cases of Louis Nixon and George Olvany show.
Nixon was incapable of filling the place left vacant by Croker,
and after five years' rule, Judge Olvany retired to be succeeded
by a leader of a more robust school, the present ruler of the Hall,
John T. Curry. Round him are his Cabinet, the district leaders,
who have their own authority, and their own independent
position in the organization, their own blocks of support. The
wants and feelings of the subordinate organizations in Brooklyn,
Queens and Richmond have to be considered, and there are
times when. public figures, like Mr. Al Smith, have to be
listened to. Yet Tammany and all good machines are one-man
shows. The experience of committee control, thirty years ago,
out of which Charles Murphy emerged to individual leadership,
was decisive. There must be unity of command if New York
politics are not to degenerate like those of Chicago into a war
of factions. The district leaders are the corps commanders.[1]
They are usually high up in the Tammany Society, the driving
force of the machine and, from their ranks, as a rule, comes
the boss, as Mr. Curry rose from the leadership of the fifth district
to the leadership of " the Democracy of New York ",[2] that is,
to be what is usually called the boss of Tammany Hall.

In reality, the district leader runs all the local machine ;
if he delivers the goods, that is, wins the primaries and elections,
and obeys the boss in big matters, he is left to his own devices.
He usually has a good city job, he has many means of raising
funds and, for party purposes, has to " find himself ". Deduct-
ing what he needs for local purposes, he pays a surplus over
to the headquarters which has farmed out the district to him.
Leaders differ one from another in power and personality.
The Sullivans, in the Bowery, were more than mere viceroys
for Croker ; they were more like tributary kings, but the risks
of rebellion are too great to be lightly run, each satrap knows
that he has a self-designated successor ready to assail him at
the slightest encouragement from above.

The Tammany officer is chosen, by the ruthless test of success,
from the ruck. He must be a leader ; at every stage in his
career he must have a following. With the first group collected,

[1] In most cities, the ward is the unit, but in New York it is the assembly
district, that is, the constituency that sends an assemblyman to the state
legislature at Albany.
[2] I have not gone into the social side of Tammany and have called by
the old name the organization of the Democratic party in New York County
and the Bronx.

in an athletic club, in a dramatic club, as a gang leader or popular orator, the first handful of private voters to dispose of, the politician is able to begin, possibly as a supporter of a rebel faction, as Al Smith did, but there is no substitute for the power to win affection, trust, fear, one at least of the emotions that bind leaders to followers. The little group will grow, be absorbed into the general Tammany following, courted and won by the methods common to all machines.

They may vary slightly, from place to place ; there seems to be more political club life in New York than in Philadelphia, but the real strength of the district leader is in the tireless work of his precinct captains, of all the ambitious young men who try to deliver the goods, and in his own ceaseless toil. Like David Hill, " up state ", the leader must make himself agreeable at fairs and funerals, must cultivate all races and sections, must never neglect detail or get above himself. " God and the people ", said " Big Tim " Sullivan, " hate a chesty man." What can be more comforting to a poor man than to know that his petty grievance may be carried to the highest quarters ? What does it matter to him that for one trifling favour done the poor, a hundred great ones are done the rich ? The Boss, Commissioner Murphy, standing under a lamp-post listening to all comers, was, as a politician if not as a man, near to St. Louis doing justice under a tree at Vincennes. That it was favour, not justice that was done, was all the better for Tammany, for all of us love favour and few of us are content with, or are grateful for, our deserts.

Tammany has always known how to win gratitude. Few can pretend that, in the abstract, it has given New York a good government. It has delivered over the city to vice and given legal protection to all manner of extortion. But the question is not a simple one. Has Tammany given New York a worse government than she has a right to expect ? Tammany has given a better government than most other machines have given their cities, a better government than, perhaps, was absolutely necessary for political success. In any event, Tammany is the normal government of the city ; they have both grown up together and this old and famous corporation is more conscious of its duty to its own reputation and to the city than are the anonymous and fly-by-night machines of lesser places. Many New Yorkers loathe Tammany and, in the country at large, enmity to the Tiger has been a popular " talking point " for two generations past. But the people of New York do not echo the famous denunciations of General Bragg or of " Alfalfa Bill " Murray. It is their machine and they are confident no other city has as gaudy a one. Not for Gotham the drab corruption of Philadelphia, or the indiscipline of Boston, or the anarchy

of Chicago. Tammany always puts on a good show and occasionally rules the city quite decently. If it goes too far, a few
years' reform will tame the " braves " and make them behave
themselves, for a time. Many New Yorkers really think they
dislike the machine and would destroy it if they could, but most
New Yorkers, if they have to have a machine, are glad they
have the biggest and best, and so far from being ashamed of it,
are proud of it. When one looks at other cities it is hard not
to feel that they are right.   ·

But it is only by comparison with its own past and with
the present condition of some rival machines, that Tammany
shines. The " New Tammany " soon lost its gilt. At the
present moment when well-grounded fears of Tammany honesty
and efficiency hamper the task of meeting the unemployment
crisis in the city, when the price of improvident financing has to
be paid by the poor, it is less easy to look tolerantly on Tammany
or to be sure that the semi-toleration which the machine has
won is not a sign of a fundamental breakdown in democratic
government in New York, as well as in the other great machine-
ruled American cities.

Chapter VII

WHAT SOME REFORMERS LEARNED

SIXTY years ago one of the most famous machine Mayors of New York, Fernando Wood, gave it as his considered judgment, based on having tried both ways, that it was wise, at times, " to pander a little to the moral sense of the community ", and neglect of this precaution has brought down many a machine in temporary ruin. A wise boss will attempt to avoid " police graft " or " dirty graft ", but it is very hard to prevent it. The average machine administration would no doubt like an honest police administration that would only disregard the laws of the land, or of common decency, when ordered to do so from above but, as yet is often found in other businesses, it is hard to get honest service in a dishonest undertaking. The time comes when the minor agents of a machine go too far, take to plundering on their own account and finally squeeze the last ounce of profit out of the system and produce a reaction. It was the pushing of legal blackmail beyond what the traffic would bear, the disregarding of that decent respect for the opinions of mankind which is the mark of the statesman, that brought about the great Tammany defeats. Even the most faithful adherents of Tammany were shocked when the enormous toll on brothels and prostitutes was dragged into the light of day, and the voter who was compelled to bring up his family in a Tammany-protected district and whose protests against the corruption of his children were insolently disregarded, was ready to listen to the reformers who were leading the assault on the machine. He was willing to teach the machine a lesson, if not to desert it permanently. The same was true of such outrageous pillaging of the public treasury as marked the Tweed régime in New York ; the " Gas House Ring " in Philadelphia ; the State House robbery in Pennsylvania ; the culminating " steals " of the Butler machine in St. Louis ; the complete candour of the Ames administration in Minneapolis ; and the final orgy of the last Thompson administration in Chicago. Public patience has a limit and a machine must not drive its supporters too far. Yet these revulsions were temporary and sooner or later the devils returned to the swept and garnished city, their appetites

whetted by abstinence and their tactics improved by defeat. It
was poor consolation to the indignant citizen to think that the
people could not be fooled quite all the time, if the periods of
wisdom were so short as to be incapable of producing a new
habit of mind.

Faced with the union of the poorer elements of the population in support of political leaders who boasted of their financial
interest in the doubtful services they rendered to their cities
and, at worst, with a combination of the underworld with their
official enemies, the police and the courts, in support of politicians
who were barely concealed robbers, the reformers were horrified.
They turned first to machinery. The methods of election offered
to the machines means of keeping themselves in power, regardless of the opinion of the electorate. They had been planned
in the belief that the representatives of the two parties would
watch each other with partisan vigilance. That theory assumed,
however, that there was partisan feeling involved, that in fact
there was any politics in politics. There was, and is, none.
In most cities, the minority party, far from being an enemy of
the dominant party, is its ally, if not merely a branch under
a different trade name. The two parties live together in a
symbiotic relation ; the greater allots to the lesser all the duties
that law or tradition forbid it to carry out itself ; as for real
opposition, that is an appearance hardly worth keeping up. Of
course, the party that is in a minority in a city may have powerful
friends elsewhere. The Republican party usually has federal
support, so is not merely an appendix of Tammany in New
York, but its position in the city is so helpless that it has adopted
a live-and-let-live attitude. It is, in fact, one of the chief obstacles
to reform, one of the surest shields of Tammany. Again and
again the unity of the Anti-Tammany front has been broken by
hopeless Republican candidatures. Sometimes these were the
result of real party feeling, absurd but not necessarily disgraceful,
but at other times the benefit to Tammany was so obvious that
the blindness of the Republican machine was indicative of more
than party stupidity. It was a dummy Republican candidate,
Joel Erhart, run by J. J. O'Brien who brought about the defeat
of Abram Hewitt and one of the most disconcerting of Tammany
triumphs, the election of Hugh Grant as Mayor. There is no
general belief that things have changed much to-day in New
York, or that New York is exceptional. It is believed that
Mr. Koenig, the boss of the Republican machine in New York
City, is no more implacable an enemy of Tammany than were
" Johnny " O'Brien and " Steve " French in Kelly's day. Each
machine has something to trade with the other. " They daily
exchange hostages with their enemies. This is natural, since

each organization desires to offer its customers a full line of governmental goods."[1]

The folly of trusting to the Republican party in New York to do anything about corruption, even when Tammany is for the moment on the defensive has recently been displayed. The chairman of the state committee of inquiry into Tammany sins, State Senator Samuel H. Hofstadter, considered by some of the more gullible or partisan New Yorkers as a light shining in darkness, was rewarded, *by Tammany*, with support for election to the Supreme Court of the state ! The services which earned this favour can be guessed at if not proved, and to anyone with a working knowledge of New York political history, it must seem highly probable that the old spirit of bargaining between the two machines has had a new lease of life and that the victim, in this case, is the Supreme Court of New York.

In other cities, the minority party is often so weak as to be negligible except by the law. In Pennsylvania where machine politics reach their greatest perfection, the union of all power in the hands of one party and, until recent distressing years, in the hands of one section of one party, makes the bi-partisan system look as silly as it is. With a united Republican party in union with the federal and state governments, the task of a great Republican city machine, like that of the Republicans in Philadelphia, is almost too easy. It is there that whole wards throw their votes to the candidate of the boss with a unanimity that is unknown in any other human activity. It is there that the Democratic party has existence only by the courtesy of the machine. If it did not exist it would have to be invented. To-day there are not many simple enough to believe that in the play of regular opposition is to be found any effective check on corruption or inefficiency. That lesson has been learned, but there are still many in the second stage of illusion, in the stage that sees in the improvement of the political personnel, in the development of non-partisan governments carrying out a " business man's policy ", the key to the citadel of civic corruption.

Such an illusion it was easy and comforting to adopt and it would doubtless have arisen in the nature of things in America, for the identification of their interests and standards with the laws of Nature and of Nature's God, comes easily to the middle classes everywhere, but an initial bias was strengthened by the influence of two very remarkable spectators and actors on the American stage, E. L. Godkin and James Bryce. The *Nation*, the *Evening Post*, the *American Commonwealth*, were the bibles of the right-thinking man who was not to be taken by the sophistry

[1] Joseph McGoldrick, " The New Tammany ", *The American Mercury*, September, 1928.

of Whitelaw Reid's *Tribune*, the demagogy of Pulitzer's *World*, the cynicism of Dana's *Sun*. To escape from the divine ordinances of the Republican party, even for the best of causes, took so much out of the well-meaning American, that he had no energy left for further adventure and sank into an unorthodox orthodoxy. Much zeal, ability, and hard work was wasted for want of a little humility ; the greatest of the reformers, Godkin, had a humorous appreciation of corruption as an art, but less time spent in thanking God at the front of the temple and more at the door, interviewing publicans and sinners, would have improved his temper—and his aim. Godkin lived through the Tweed régime, saw " Honest John " Kelly out and saw the approaching retiral of Croker. He fought the good fight with great wit and courage, all without ever appreciating the real nature of the problem. It was axiomatic with Godkin that the good people were in the majority, that their interest lay in good and economical government and that, could they once be converted to independent voting, that is, voting as they were advised to vote by the *Nation*, instead of blindly following party labels, graft and the boss system would have short shrift. That the heart of the people was sound was never doubted. There were black patches, to be sure, but they were confined to the great cities or to special areas such as the southern states, plagued with a race problem that prevented any independent political thinking or action. The great enemy was apathy and party fidelity. In New York, Godkin pointed out that the city could not continue to exist as a great centre of industry and commerce if the qualities that make for commercial prosperity were not widespread. Yet Philadelphia and New York were governed by corrupt rings and the public conscience, occasionally roused by some particularly outrageous piece of public robbery, was always ready to fall asleep again.[1]

One remedy to which great hopes were attached was the abolition of the spoils system. If there were no prizes for the corrupt, the honest men would find the coast clear, and when reform of the Civil Service made some progress in New York, and in other cities, the reformers saw the dawn. Bryce thought that the machine would be fatally weakened when civil service reform became effective and, in the spread of the reform, saw the beginning of the end for the boss. Get rid of the spoils and get better men, representative of the better elements, into politics. Bryce devoted a famous chapter of his book to explaining why

---

[1] The guileless Richard Watson Gilder proposed to consolidate a temporary victory over Tammany, by starting a weekly which would circulate among the ignorant voters of the East Side and show them how foolish they had been in the past in supporting the machine.

the best citizens did not enter politics. There were many reasons, but chiefly they feared to touch politics and be defiled. Godkin pointed out that the deferential elements were insufficiently developed in America. " The habit of considering conspicuous inhabitants as entitled to leading municipal places must be regarded as lost." [1]   It was too true that the poor were not so good at recognizing their betters as they were in England, and the call to public service in America could not have the siren quality it had in a land where Alderman was a title of dignity and Mayors might hope to become knights and, if their cities were big enough, or they had no male children, even baronets. The office of Mayor could hardly have much dignity after it had been held by Oakey Hall, the " wise-cracker " of the Tweed régime, and as for the Aldermen, it was news in New York when they were suspected of honesty. In such circumstances it was Roman virtue for young men of good families to leap into the mire and fight for better things and the heroism of Messrs. Henry Cabot Lodge, Theodore Roosevelt and Boies Penrose was noted with hope. If more young men of wealth, education and family could be induced to enter the arena, it would be possible to create a tradition of unselfish service such as had recently been created in England ; the transition from the age of Walpole to the age of Gladstone might, in America, be cut down to a good deal less than a century and a half. There was an increasing section of the population, at any rate in the East, exempt by its wealth from the vulgar struggle for pelf and with a public educated up to appreciating the merits of this class and as successful a transplantation of English standards in politics as had been achieved in sport, the evils of corruption would be in a way to be cured. In some parts of the country it would take more time, for, Bryce thought, the newer states could hardly be expected to supply many Roosevelts or Lodges. In California, for example, " the most active minds are too much absorbed in great business enterprises to attend to politics ".[2]

The solution to the problem was naïve, but, even had it been a deeper answer, it would have suffered from the defect of being an answer to a non-existent problem. He would have been a severe judge who would have denied to Senator Leland Stanford of California a right to rank among the more active minds of his state and yet, *pace* Lord Bryce, the political activities of Stanford were numerous, and being a United States Senator was among the less important of them. The Southern Pacific Railroad was the Senator's chief occupation in life and critics who knew California a good deal better than Lord Bryce, saw in the

[1] E. L. Godkin, *Unforeseen Tendencies of Democracy*, p. 149.
[2] J. Bryce, *American Commonwealth*, vol. ii, p. 385 (1889).

Southern Pacific a political machine much better deserving of study and reform than the San Francisco " sandlotters " who fill so large a place in *The American Commonwealth*. The fight to transfer the effective government of California from the offices of the railroad in San Francisco to the state capitol in Sacramento, was the centre of Californian politics for twenty years after Bryce wrote, and a living United States Senator laid up enough capital as a political reformer in that struggle to last him a lifetime.

Even in Philadelphia, the good citizens whose apathy so alarmed Mr. Homer Lea, were not as indifferent to the issues as he assumed. Not all plunderers of the public were so maladroit as was Frank Cowperwood [1] and when he got to work in Chicago, he had allies and rivals from Philadelphia who, unlike himself, had never been caught in minor picking and stealing. It was, in fact, much harder to find men of wealth and standing who had nothing to gain from machine rule than was innocently assumed.

Though Godkin and his friends were unaware of it, they approached the problem of municipal reform without sufficient scepticism of the virtue of themselves and of their class. It was easy enough for Godkin to draw up a plan of municipal efficiency. The city was bound to clean the streets, light them, provide for certain rather meagre charities and a certain minimum of education, above all it was bound to have an effective and honest police force. If this municipal creed was, in fact, the civic religion of all sensible men, it was odd and disgraceful that the American cities paid so little heed to it, so odd that Godkin could only assume that blind party spirit and ignorant apathy kept the good citizens who were, of course, the vast majority, from doing their duty. Yet in fact, they did it seldom and never did it long, so that New York was hardly out of one spree before she was off on another ; the periods of sobriety being too rare and too short to effect a cure. Godkin ignored the possibility that a municipality could do far more, for good and evil, than was contained in his meagre programme. His politics were the politics of the rich man and they assumed that what benefited the rich man, benefited the poor as much or more. With all his evangelical fervour for political purity, he never understood that there were many thousands of American citizens, almost as good as his own readers, who, consciously or unconsciously, expected a good deal more from democracy than the reformers could offer and that a good deal of what they expected was supplied by Tammany and the other machines. The means,

[1] See Theodore Dreiser's novels, *The Financier* and *The Titan*. They are based on the career of Charles Yerkes.

in this case, half-justified the end. The Tammany boss was like Robin Hood, a robber who gave half his spoils to the poor ; the reformers would not rob, but gave nothing but counsels borrowed from Samuel Smiles.

If Godkin was blind to the strong side of the machine, he was equally blind to the weak side of the reformers. Godkin thought of the city too much in terms of the spoils system, too much as an office-giving institution whose value to the dishonest lay in the patronage. He did not understand that the city was a prize worth buying and selling, regardless of who held the offices, that Tammany's chief crime was in its readiness to betray its trust for the city, not merely to brothel-keepers or saloon-keepers, but to the wealthy, to far more powerful forces which could pay far more for Tammany's services than could the humble wrongdoers who most excited the reformers' wrath.

It was natural that when young Theodore Roosevelt went as a member of the New York legislature to Albany, he carried with him the fashionable illusions of the wealthier elements of New York and Harvard.

" In the America of that day, and especially among the people whom I knew, the successful business man was regarded as pre-eminently *the* good citizen. The tangible rewards came to him, the admiration of his fellow-citizens of the respectable type was apt to be his, and the severe newspaper moralists who were never tired of denouncing politicians and political methods were wont to hold up ' business methods ' as the ideal which we were to strive to introduce into political life." [1]

Roosevelt soon learned the reality that lay behind the façade, that the business man who was to redeem politics was an important element in the corruption of politics, that if the business man objected to the methods, and still more to the manners, of the bosses, it was because he thought he was entitled to get what the bosses had to sell at a lower price or for nothing, in that happy day when the people would be content to give the business man whatever he needed to make money for himself, that being the chief aim of the American political system. But the moral trimmings of the better elements were easily detachable and, at a crisis, all pretence of devotion to reform would be cast aside.

The constant firing at the politicians, the bosses, the ignorant foreigner who was inclined to vote for the grafters, and the disreputable Irish or Jewish politicians who traded on the ignorance of the urban voters, was directed on a dummy target,

[1] Theodore Roosevelt, *Autobiography*, p. 86.

sometimes with conscious attempt to deceive, more commonly, in all good faith. William Allen White drew a neat distinction when he called the Irish politicians of New Jersey, " the governing classes", and the great business interests who used them " the ruling classes ". The governing classes in every state were fair game for the moralist in pulpit, or university chair, or in the press, they might not suffer much from the assault, but the assailants had the sympathy of all right-thinking men. Very different was the fate of those who, learning their lesson, fired on the real target. Mr. Fremont Older and his millionaire friends, Messrs. Spreckels and Phelan, attacked in the great San Francisco graft prosecutions, not merely the obviously wicked " Labor " boss, Abe Ruef, but his employer and corrupter, the aristocratic Southern traction magnate, Patrick Calhoun. They then learned, that reform is all very well, but that it cannot be allowed to interfere with business, that no good citizen could deny that it was desirable to send a little Jewish grafter to jail, but that the public opinion of the best circles would never damn a man of Calhoun's quality —Ruef went to jail, but all efforts to convict Calhoun failed.

A naïve enthusiasm for the principles of reform taught him as a student and a resolution to carry them out induced Frederick Howe to enter the Cleveland City Council, and to learn that he was expected to be a reformer with the proviso that he should do nothing to hurt the gas company which had, in fact, planted the usefully innocent young man in the council. What he learned from this experience, was reinforced by the teaching of the notorious Mayor of Cleveland, the rabble-rousing demagogue, Tom Johnson. Johnson was a millionaire, he had been a great traction magnate and knew the inside story of business and politics as only a magnate or a boss could know it. He knew that he, and his friends, had never let any scruples stand in the way of financial profits to be gained by corruption, and that certain branches of big business were based on an experience-tested belief that honesty was no policy at all. The public utilities, the gas companies, the electricity companies, the tram-way companies, never tried to persuade a city council that they could buy. An honest Mayor or council stood in the way of the easy and speedy profits that could be made by promoters with a " pull "—and no cities had such good and reliable " pulls " for sale as those which were thoroughly boss-ridden. There were many simple business men who really believed they wanted a clean and honest city government, but there were far fewer who really knew and would pay the price which was the support of a city authority that would neither be bought by saloon-keepers, nor brothel-keepers, nor bankers, nor corporation promoters.

It was not for nothing that Johnson was a citizen of Ohio

and an old business rival and acquaintance of Mark Hanna in Hanna's own city. Cleveland was a political laboratory far more scientific and practical than the library of the Johns Hopkins University, where students were trained to go out and convert the better elements to playing the part their brethren played in England ; giving service to the nation and city, with no reward but honour. Johnson was no college man, he knew better than that. He knew how the better elements lined up behind Mark Hanna when their interests were threatened, and he had no illusions that those interests were those of the public ; they might be, but, whether they were or not, the private interest of the magnate was seldom sacrificed in any quixotic spasm of public spirit. Such conduct would have been a betrayal of the shareholders, if nothing worse. " The watered securities of franchise corporations [1] are politics capitalized." [2] There were, of course, business interests which had little or nothing to gain from a weak or corrupt government, but Johnson held that those were the businesses which made least money and ran most risks, and all business men believed that business should rule, even if it were not their business that was gaining thereby. " The city government belonged to the business interests generally, but as the public utility companies had more use for it than the other kinds of business enterprises had, they paid most attention to it." [3] It was the same story everywhere. Folk in St. Louis found what limits of decency were when he tried to get at the real powers behind the politicians, and the situation in Chicago moved Mayor Carter Harrison I to protest against the throwing of the odium of corruption on the aldermen while " ' the virtuous and moral railroad men who are or who seem to be patterns of piety and virtue do not appear to think their chances for a happy eternity at all jeopardized by letting someone spend their money to corrupt legislation ' ".[4] Young men of zeal and public spirit, reporters who had learned their trade under Godkin on the *Evening Post* like Lincoln Steffens, college-trained experts like Frederick Howe, learned that all was not what it seemed and that there were very disconcerting visions about. It was easy enough to get up enthusiasm against a corrupt machine that did little jobs for petty grafters, but when the trail ran into the best sections of the cities, into Fifth Avenue and Euclid Avenue and Nob's Hill, it was no longer so easy to follow it—and get support. Newspapers nominally battling for the right found it convenient to let their cartoonists, the creator of " Mutt and Jeff ", and the assailant of Mark Hanna, turn their talents to

[1] Privately-owned water, gas, tramway, etc., companies.
[2] Tom Johnson, *My Life*, p. 26.   [3] *Ibid.*, p. 114.
[4] W. J. Abbott, *Carter Henry Harrison*, p. 225.

ridiculing the inconveniently successful exposures of the employers of the machines.

The premisses on which the earlier reformers had worked were found to be at best irrelevant, and too often entirely misleading. They had concentrated on symptoms as if they were the disease. To-day it is still true, that it is not by shielding petty lawbreakers that a machine grows rich and secure ; low-grade and dirty graft is incidental. Nor were the business men hampered in their political activities by any of that blind party feeling that, to the first reformers, had seemed so great an obstacle to reform. Most "big business men" were Republicans, but they were quite ready to do business with Democratic politicians when the latter had anything worth while to sell. No party prejudice kept the rulers of the Southern Pacific from dealing with the Democratic boss of San Francisco, Christopher Buckley, and though they were good Democrats, William Whitney and Thomas Fortune Ryan were willing to placate Platt's agent at Albany, Lemuel Quigg. As Jay Gould put it, he was for the Republicans in a Republican county, for the Democrats in a Democratic county, but everywhere for the Erie Railroad.

To the leaders of the "muck-raking" crusade of the first decade of this century nothing seemed more important than to cure the illusion "that politics in America would be improved by turning all the public offices over to business men ":[1] that American politics were suffering from a neglect by "business". What they were suffering from was too close attention from business. Mr. Lincoln Steffens, the most noted exposer of municipal corruption in that era, gave his verdict that "the typical business man is a bad citizen ; he is busy. If he is a 'big business man' and very busy, he does not neglect, he is busy with politics."[2]

The intrusion of big business into politics was, of course, no new discovery of the early twentieth century. Bryce noted the evil influence of the railroads in New York state, but attributed the possibility of such sinful doings to the presence in the legislature of corrupt city members returned by the machines ; presumably if the city boss could be overthrown, the incorruptible rural members would make railroad intrusion a waste of time. Yet railways played an important part in the politics of rural states, as we can gather from abundant testimony :

"The curse of rail-roading, down to the decision of the United States Supreme Court in the Louisville and Nashville

---

[1] G. J. Nathan, *An American Credo*, Article 583.
[2] Steffens, *The Shame of the Cities*, p. 5.

case in 1917, was politics. For this the carriers [the railways] were partly to blame. In the early days they certainly reached out for everything in sight which was to be had through favour of the Congress of the United States or of the state legislatures." [1]

Even the most optimistic observer of the political scene could not ignore the fact that respectable men, perhaps even men who had passed the test of good citizenship by bolting the Republican party to vote for Cleveland, were corrupters of state legislatures. An explanation that satisfied the older reformers was offered by one unnamed railroad President to Bryce. He asserted that the popular dislike of railways in the West was so great that only by constant vigilance and financial arguments could the legitimate interests of the railroads and their owners be safeguarded. The validity of this defence depended largely on what one thought were the legitimate interests of the railroads, and to the rich those interests included a practically complete immunity from public control.

Though the chief offenders against political morality were the railroads, they were not the only sinners. If the Baltimore and Ohio fought the Pennsylvania Railroad for control of Maryland, the Pennsylvania had to fight other corporations for New Jersey. In that state, we are told:

" Every election was, in the last analysis, a solemn referendum upon the question as to which corporate interest should control legislation—whether the Pennsylvania Railroad, whose master mind was the Republican leader of the state, United States Senator Sewall, or the Public Service interest, whose votaries and friends were Senator Smith of New Jersey and Milan Ross, Sr., of Middlesex County." [2]

In New York, the great insurance companies were zealous defenders of their interests and kept on good terms with the corrupt elements in the state legislature, elements not confined to the Tammany members from New York City. The insurance companies were among the key positions of New York finance, their assets were prizes that the lords of Wall Street coveted, and which the heads of the insurance companies let them have, at a price. The continued neglect, to put it no lower, of the policy-holders' interests, was purchased from the legislatures of New York and of other states by generous libations offered to the great machines. The *New York Life* paid out in ten years $1,300,000 through an agent who could keep his mouth shut.

[1] W. Z. Ripley, *Main Street and Wall Street*, p. 234.
[2] J. P. Tumulty, *Woodrow Wilson as I Know Him*, p. 24.
As P. T. Barnum put it, New Jersey was " the State of Camden and Amboy ".

In alliance with another company, it maintained in Albany a central corruption office which came to be known as the " House of Mirth ".   A regular retainer kept the Republican machine under Senator Platt in good temper.   Not even the most hardened Republican had many illusions about Platt, but his colleague in the Senate, Chauncey Depew, if he differed from Platt in most things, was at one with him in his readiness to accept a retainer from the insurance companies for services that it took some ingenious word-spinning to describe without giving scandal to the innocent.   The great Democratic state boss, David B. Hill, was also on the pay-roll, but at a lower rate.   A last revelation of the intertwining of politics and business was the belief that it was useless to expect any of the leading lawyers of the state to undertake the investigation, as to do so would be to incur the wrath of the great corporations who had every interest in maintaining the old régime.   It was taken for granted that real legal eminence lay in being to the great corporations what the police-court lawyers were to the prostitutes and gamblers and crooks, useful allies in the war against the law !

The insurance magnates did not deny, beyond the point of credibility, that they did pay out money to legislators and that for that money they expected and got political service.   Their defence was the standard one.   To leave the legislature to its own devices was to invite blackmail ; bribery was legitimate self-defence.   It was the consensus of opinion, then and since, that the managers of the great insurance companies had not contented themselves with buying off raids on the companies' treasuries, they had used their hired bravoes to knife bills of all kinds, bad bills and good bills, bills to rob the companies and bills to protect the interests of the policy-holders from the malpractices which enabled the managers of the companies to build up fortunes out of other people's property and to be such useful allies of the great magnates of Wall Street.   In the war against the abuses of the insurance companies, Mr. Hughes became Governor of New York, thanks largely to President Roosevelt, but the better elements did not give any permanent sign of regarding Mr. John McCall of the *New York Life* as another dangerous Irishman in politics ; it was one thing to sell public power like Croker, quite another to buy it.

In contemporary America, it is not the insurance companies, or the railroads, that disturb the sleep of the reformer, but the public-utility companies, especially the " power trust ".   In every state the power companies exert their influence to keep down any too inquisitive spirit in the breasts of legislators.   In New York, the question of the utilization of the great resources of water power in the state has been an issue for ten years, an

issue in which the majority of the people of the state, led by
Governor Smith and by Governor Roosevelt, have fought the
rural Republican minority entrenched in the legislature, resolved
to block any attempts at public ownership.   In other states even
effective control has been resisted.   In Connecticut, the Republican boss, Mr. Roraback, nullified the efforts of the Democratic Governor to nominate as Public Utilities Commissioner,
Professor R. J. Smith, because his views were suspected of not
being as sympathetic to the companies as was desirable.   In
state after state, the companies have been at work, influencing
or buying outright machines, and feeding public opinion through
press and college with suitable information on the power problem.

The most famous intrusion of the power companies into
politics was furnished by the great Chicago senatorial primary of
1926.   A Senate Committee learned that the " Angel " of the
Frank A. Smith campaign was Mr. Samuel Insull, then the great
power magnate of Illinois, and that Smith had also been supported by other power financiers in a way that gladdened the
heart of his manager and made it useless for his millionaire
opponent to try to compete in expenditure.   The feature of these
contributions that attracted the uncharitable, was that at the
moment of his choice as Republican candidate, Mr. Smith was
head of the " Illinois Commerce Commission ", a post which
involved the duty of judging between the consumers and the
suppliers of electricity.   It was asserted, and widely believed,
that the power companies were paying for favours received.

There is no reason to be surprised at such a connection
between business and politics.   In a society whose tone is set by
business, it would be surprising if political standards were much
above or below the prevailing business standards, and in the
United States the two activities have been so closely united that
a difference would have been almost miraculous, for, as an
eminent politician reminds us : " Business and government are
so closely related that the atmosphere of one pervades the other.
If the standards of trade are low, the standards of government
will not be high." [1]   Even the great Tweed debauch was merely
an aspect of the general collapse after the Civil War and there
has never been a governmental scandal that has not had its
business counterpart.   Moreover, political corruption was a
useful weapon in the ruthless war of American business and one
that few dared to neglect.   At every stage of the political process
business was to be found asking for favours or worse and, for a
long time, business was almost the only buyer of the wares offered
by one important branch of the political organization, the state
government and the state machine.

[1] Calvin Coolidge, in the *New York Herald* (Paris), April 2, 1931.

Chapter VIII

THE STATE MACHINE

FROM the point of view of the " invisible government ", the state is the vital organ to be controlled. The federal government has its uses, the tariff is, in itself, sufficient reason to induce the great manufacturing interests to pay attention to politics. In the great days of railway building, when grants in money and lands were to be had for the asking, Congress, and those who led Congress, were worth the attention of a serious lobbyist and a serious politician. Then could politicians like Colfax, Blaine and Ames help business and themselves. Normally, however, the state is a convenient unit of operation. In the state legislature are passed most of the laws that help or hurt the interests ; there charters can be obtained that made such complaisant commonwealths as New Jersey, New Mexico and Delaware rotten-boroughs for the more predatory corporations ; there is the material for a political machine that can really be relied on. Moreover, it is difficult to get unified control in federal government circles ; except for Mark Hanna, no real national boss has adorned the American scene, and even Hanna had not the secure control of the system that is possible in a state.

The city can, of course, offer machines of marvellous efficiency and often, for the spoilsmen, offer pickings which the state cannot compete with ; what is even New York State compared with New York City as a prize of war ? But the city has no independent life ; legally, it is the creature of the state, no mere city organization can promise to deliver the goods as a state machine can. Within its own sphere the state is supreme, it has ownership and sovereignty to sell, and that is what the ruling classes want to buy. The strongest state machines have been based on a control of the state government, combined with control of the local government, or alliance with the ruling forces in this field, and support by the federal authorities. In consequence, the most effective machines have been Republican machines in Republican states. When all was well in Pennsylvania, the unity of action was delightful to the spectator and customer. Within reason, what Senator Cameron, or Senator Quay or Senator Penrose, were willing to sell would be delivered

whether the actual operating unit was at Washington, Harrisburg, Philadelphia or Pittsburgh. The " Keystone " state was
always a power with a Republican President ; the tariff, with
a grip of steel, united it to the Republican party in all its sections,
so that there was none of that intrusion of political issues into
politics which politicians have such reason to dislike. A squabble
over the spoils, some excessively bold piece of stealing, might
result in an independent or even a Democratic seizure of some
part of the machinery, but the break has hitherto always
been repaired, before any lasting damage was done. In consequence, the leader of Pennsylvania has been first prince of the
blood in any Republican dynasty ; no other state has a record of
sixty years of rule by first-class bosses and, until someone is
found to fill Senator Penrose's shoes, the American political
system will lack one of its most striking features.

The state boss and the state machine have not the uniformity
of character that applies to the city bosses and machines, but
their origin, their working and their place in the economic and
political life of the nation are at least as interesting and a good
deal more important. Addicks in Delaware ; Mr. Roraback in
Connecticut ; the great Pennsylvania bosses ; the legislative agents
of the Southern Pacific in California, whether they were the
employees of Senator Stanford, or were transferred, with the
railroad, to Mr. Harriman ; Dryden in New Jersey ; these were
men more formidable than Tweeds or Butlers— and playing a
more important economic rôle.

The powers and the personnel of the American state government are or were of such contradictory character that efficiency
and honesty were too much to ask of them—even if the question
would have been heard. Each state is sovereign, subject, indeed,
to an unpredictable degree of judicial control, but in itself a key
to part of that judicial power. Immense powers are entrusted
to a government artfully made as disjointed as possible, deprived
of all constitutional coherence and manned by politicians who
think a few months' pay at the dismal villages which in most
states serve for capitals, reward enough for the neglect of their
normal avocations. In short, the state legislatures are for the
most part filled with the nominees of city and county machines—
and not usually by the best members of the professional political
class at that. The work done by these fourth-rate politicians
has the character one might expect :

" The financial and economic legislation of the state has
usually shown incompetence and frequently dishonesty. In
their relations to the corporation they have occupied the
positions alternatively of blackmailers and creatures." [1]

[1] H. W. Croly, *The Promise of American Life*, p. 319.

The mere bulk of legislation and projected legislation makes reasonable policy almost impossible. In a good year in the New York legislature, the bills introduced number between three and four thousand, many are harmless, more are perhaps silly,[1] but in the mass, the legislative blackmailer gets his chance and Clarence Darrow's description of the Illinois legislature in which he served, could be applied to many others : " Every session was opened with prayer, and then a large part of the assembly proceeded to look around to find someone to hold up ',[2] and the existence of the " strike bill " and of the " black horse cavalry " is no myth invented by the interests to put reformers off the trail. The justifiable, or natural, suspicion of corporation action created a situation that resulted in the justifiable, or natural, defensive action of the companies. If a railroad company could not rely on local juries—or judges—to do anything like even-handed justice in claims against a corporation, it was strongly tempted to tamper, if not with juries, at any rate with the law which juries were to administer. Corporations which were liable to be deprived of their property by hasty legislative action, were more inclined to rely on a bought legislature than on informed public opinion. On this situation, the promoters of " strike bills " based their tactics. A " strike bill " is one designed to frighten a company into buying its death or disappearance. It has to be plausible, to be ostensibly legitimate legislation protecting the public interest, regulating street-car or subway fares, or the conditions of use of public telephones, or some other issue popular with the rank and file. If it is possible to induce some honest and naïve member to take the matter up, so much the better. The " striker ", having induced the introduction of the measure, offers, for a consideration, to have it lost in committee. If he is not bought off at once, the measure is given publicity, opinion mobilized behind it and the expenses of killing it go up. It is hard to blame the head of a corporation for taking the easy and cheap way out of these difficulties !

One product of the state government which blessed both parties to the bargain, the politicians who gave and the business men who received, was the charter of incorporation of what we should call limited liability companies. Any state in the Union can incorporate a company to do business all over the Union on any terms or no terms. Pennsylvania, indeed, once incorporated a

[1] " There ought to be a law about it " is no idle threat in American mouths, for in the state legislatures it is not very hard to find sponsors for any legislation, however silly. It is said that Indiana nearly enacted a statute declaring that in that state Pi should be 4, not the inconvenient 3.14 of other commonwealths.

[2] Clarence Darrow, *The Story of My Life*, p. 119.

company to do business in any state *except* Pennsylvania. It was the smaller states, however, who profited most by this power, since it was highly convenient for many business magnates to be able to hold such annual meetings as were necessary in Portland, Maine, or Phœnix, Arizona, while conducting all the real business of the company from New York. If English company meetings could be called for Stornoway or Lerwick, instead of the Cannon Street Hotel, some English directors would look forward to the annual ordeal with less trepidation !

There was little choice of evils ; if there was no boss, there was a " lobby ", a collection of agents of various interests buying or cajoling legislators into action, not necessarily bad action, but into action of some kind.

This was a situation not long endurable by the vigorous minds that were building up the great corporations. Enterprises that involved millions, activities that the dominant public opinion of the nation regarded as the most useful to the community and the most attractive to the individual, were not to be held to ransom indefinitely by groups of venal or fanatical farmers clothed with a little brief authority, out of all proportion to the economic forces they represented. The legal blackmail must be put on a tolerable basis, and the community made safe for big business. From this situation arose naturally the great state boss and the state machine.

The boss was a co-ordinator, a result of the careful separation of powers in the state constitution ; of the incoherence of the legal government of the state ; of the impossibility of any individual guaranteeing, in virtue of his *official* position, either positive or negative aid to the seeker after help, for the Governor was usually helpless and never omnipotent, the legislatures full of politicians who could not even reach the Pennsylvania standard of honesty by staying bought, when bought.

The boss might be the ally of a great politician as was Thurlow Weed in New York, or a Senator as were Conkling, Hill and Platt in New York, Gorman in Maryland, the Camerons, Quay and Penrose in Pennsylvania, Aldrich in Rhode Island, or a minor official as in modern Georgia. In some states, the business interests were so homogeneous that they naturally fell under the lead of one family or firm—such were California under the Southern Pacific, Montana under the Anaconda Copper Company and Delaware under the great industrial dynasty of the Du Pont de Nemours family. Whatever the character of the rule, it resulted in a centralization of power which undid the careful separation planned by the framers of the constitutions, and based its authority on the proved inability of the state officials to give efficient service to business, or even a moderate degree of protection. As a means to an end the boss was far better than any sporadic assaults on legislative virtue, his services were better planned to please and by keeping a permanent hold over the legislators he was able to cut down overhead. The boss " decasualized " corruption and the economic benefits that flow from such a change need hardly be emphasized.

To the control of the nominating system the state boss, like all other bosses, is indebted for the foundations of his power. The ability to give the party label to his nominees assures him a nucleus of support in the legislature, and denies it to opponents, whatever their merits, who lack the stamp of party regularity. In a great many states, the party label ensures victory in the elections, and in control of the state government the boss has only to fear the revolt of his troops in the legislature, or a revolt of the party voters in the nominating conventions, or now, in the primaries. The first is a test of his authority that most bosses can meet. Only a suddenly active conscience or a powerful financial inducement can lead a legislator to endanger his seat by turning against the controller of the party machinery. The member has little reason to expect his faithfulness or independence will be rewarded by his constituency. In all probability, he has been returned simply because he is the party candidate, not on any merits or strength of his own. His constituency expects to have its interests looked after, and the share-out of the revenue, which is what is expected of the legislator, is dependent on the good will of the boss. A revolt of individuals is useless, for their constituencies can be starved into revolt by the refusal of the boss to let any of the state plunder reach the districts represented by the rebels. A revolt of the majority of the party is another matter, but what reason is there for a general revolt ? There are few cases where party lines in the state reflect any division in policy, and it is probable that if some action of the boss becomes so widely unpopular that a majority of the electoral districts of the state are affected by the spirit of discontent, the beneficiary will be the opposition party, not the dissidents in the party in power.

Thus Platt was able to keep his control of the Republican party in New York state unshaken, despite a record series of defeats at the hands of his Democratic " opposite number ", David Hill. Hill's own control over the Democracy of up-state New York lasted long after he lost control of the state government. Steady adherence to the controllers of the party machine in the state is the way to preferment, as is shown by the careers of President Harding in Ohio and President Coolidge in Massachusetts. A leader of great personal force, like the elder La Follette, may defy the ruling machine, but for permanent or

even lengthy success in reform, it is necessary to build up a
machine which in its turn creates the problem, when is a boss
not a boss. A reformer may have a long career in and out of
office, he may do a good deal in office, but as long as American
politicians and American electors remain what they are, he can
have only transitory victories unless he can seize the existing
machinery of one of the parties or build up his own. The most
practical reformers, then, try to set up their own organization,
and we have anomalies like the " anti-machine " La Follette
machine in Wisconsin.

If, by a machine, we mean the uniting of political effort under
the command of one man or of a few men, the attribution of
political orthodoxy to one group, then the Progressive Republicans
in Wisconsin enrolled under the banner of the La Follette family
are part of a machine. " Don " Cameron did not succeed more
certainly to the family senatorship, than did " Young Bob " La
Follette. There is no evidence that the people of Pennsylvania
were less fitly represented by the Cameron dynasty, than the
people of Wisconsin by the La Follettes, and Mark Hanna had
as much claim to be the representative of a point of view, as had
the elder La Follette. In fact, there is an impalpable shading
off, we can see the difference between a pure politician, open
to hire in the market and the leader who incarnates a point of
view. But what gave all these men their power was their capacity
as masters of practical politics. No eloquence, no fidelity to
duty, no power of incarnating the passions of a section, would
have enabled La Follette to play the part he did, had he not
secured his rear by good management. This power may survive
its real justification ; there are critics who assert that " progres-
sivism " in Wisconsin is being emptied of meaning. To Champ
Clark, it seemed that the Bryan family in Nebraska had seized
the Democratic machine there and were using it purely for
personal ends. All this may be true, but one remains convinced
of the essential difference between the machine run by a Platt
and the machine run by a La Follette or a Bryan. However,
blindly or irrelevantly, the Western radicals do appeal to passions
and hopes that do not require the stimulus of direct bribery and
can command enough disinterested enthusiasm to do without
the more indefensible of the practices of the conservative machines.
They profess to exist to serve a policy, no one can convince the
average voter that the machine in Pennsylvania exists for any
serious purpose other than the aggrandizement of its owners and
the enrichment or insurance of *their* owners. When Oregon, as
Woodrow Wilson put it, had two governments, one at Salem
and the other under the hat of Mr. U'Ren, all the elements of
machine rule were in existence, but the spirit was lacking. The

appeal of Mr. U'Ren to the people of Oregon was, however misguided, an appeal to some ideal of the public good ; the real machine has in fact, and often in form, only the character of exploiters selling the authority they have acquired to the highest bidder. To create another tightly disciplined political organization may be an unfortunate necessity, but it is a necessity in the war against merely mercenary politics in which so many Americans are engaged.

The state machine is, of necessity, a federal structure. There are usually some political units which can, for a time, at least, defy the anger of the ruler or rulers of the state machine. This is especially the case when there are large cities in the state, for the city machine has always more money and usually better discipline than the corresponding rural unit. In many states there is a party difference ; Democratic cities like New York and Boston learn how to make terms with the Republican rulers of the state but are not, in the nature of things, assimilable to the same discipline as the rural counties. In any case, the boss of New York City is too great a figure to take orders from anybody. Platt and Croker made treaties ; Platt had power and Croker had money. No doubt the state boss had moments when he dreamed of using his legal authority to attack Tammany at the heart of its power, but courage went or wisdom came.

Nominal party unity is, however, no guarantee of effective co-operation as the troubled history of Pennsylvania shows. The allotment of power between the two great city machines, Philadelphia and Pittsburgh, and the state machine, has never been an easy problem. Even Simon Cameron had his difficulties with Philadelphia, when McManes dared to resist him, after the " Stalwart " rout in the Convention of 1880. As Pittsburgh grew, its bosses became more and more daring and were found difficult to handle even by Quay. " Chris " Magee quarrelled with Quay over his share of federal patronage and actually supported a Democrat. Twenty years later, the situation repeated itself and the Pittsburgh machine defied Penrose and supported Roosevelt, turning " Progressive " for this purpose—with the result that, for the only time since 1860, Pennsylvania did not cast her electoral vote for the Republican candidate. At the same time, Penrose had to face a more dangerous exhibition of independence in his own city of Philadelphia, where the Vare brothers raised the standard of revolt and forced terms on the great boss. Although there was peace of a kind till Penrose died, the question was far from being settled and the subsequent attempts to unite Pennsylvania under one command have hitherto failed. There seemed to be an obvious chief, or at any rate, an obvious centre on which all good men could rally, the great political and financial forces represented by Mr. Andrew Mellon of Pittsburgh, but the power and the pride of the Philadelphia machine revolted against such a transference of authority to the West and the resulting civil war with its unsatisfactory truces is a poor substitute for the unity of command which, in the old days, made the Pennsylvania machine powerful, and respected.

Corresponding problems afflict the state boss everywhere and make his job less easy of attainment and of tenure than that of the city or county boss. The difficulties that have kept the United States from knowing more than one national boss are at work in the state field. There are few Mark Hannas and even few Platts and Penroses, for even if the state is more or less united, the means of keeping it so are not lavished on the boss of the state as they are on his city brother.

To run an effective machine of the more commercial type, a boss must have means of rewarding individuals as well as sections or communities and the payment of his troops, apart from the direct legislative pickings, is not always easy. A good deal can be done by the use of the federal patronage which a boss can claim with authority if his party is in power, for a strong boss can make terms with Washington as long as the President or his advisers have no one in mind to replace the incumbent or cannot afford to quarrel. A boss who is also a leading Senator is in a position to defend himself as did Conkling and Gorman, for, though they collapsed in the process, the Republicans in New York, and the Democrats in Maryland, had reason to regret the internecine war. The bigger the state, the bigger the assets of the boss. Professor Gosnell points out the importance of Platt's control of the Republican delegation in Congress from New York, a control that made him far more important than his own comparative obscurity as a Senator did. The Indiana delegation under the orders of Tom Taggart, the New York delegation under Murphy, the Illinois delegation under Roger Sullivan, then under George Brennan, the New Jersey delegates under Frank Hague, had for years an important negative control over the Democratic national convention and the weight of the owner of the Pennsylvania machine in the opposite camp was so great, that it was exaggerated by popular romanticism which looked on the dying (and weakened) Penrose as a wizard. Yet his weight *was* great and if Mr. William Vare had managed to get into the Senate and had manœuvred from it the members for his Philadelphia pocket boroughs—and the hundreds of thousands of docile Philadelphia votes—his power in national party councils would have been vast.

It is one of the main difficulties of a third party that it has to work without this nucleus of machine support in the great states. The only state carried by La Follette was that run by his own machine. It was to the support of a section of the Pennsylvania machine that Roosevelt owed his victory in that state in 1912—and a decisive event in the history of the young and ailing Republican party in Pennsylvania was the conversion of Simon Cameron.

As a rule, only Democratic bosses have to support themselves. Some, like the masters of the machine in New Jersey or New York, have abundant city patronage to pasture on,[1] but so famous a state boss as Tom Taggart often had to go on very short commons in Indiana—whose politicians are even more voracious than their brethren elsewhere.[2] On the other hand, Republican machines can usually appeal to the federal administration to come over and help them in their missionary work. Indeed, the help of Washington is almost a necessity for a Republican state boss, but that help has its dangers, for to make it the basis of one's power is to give hostages to fortune, since its transference is often the means of replacing one boss by another. The history of the Republican bosses of New York remains to show the dangers of trusting to the fount of jobs in Washington. In Ohio, it is also possible to illustrate the power of the federal patronage. Foraker, as Governor, could and did give his most valuable piece of patronage to Boss Cox of Cincinnati ; he made him state oil gauger, but when Hanna entered the field with his special influence over President McKinley, Senator Foraker could not compete with his junior. In the matter of patronage, the state machine was hampered, in the past, by the meagre list of activities open to the state government. The state as such had little to give and the skilful boss had to amalgamate county and state patronage and make what terms he could with the city machines within his territory. There were exceptions, of course. In the Erie Canal, New York had for a century a great source of spoils and corruption. There was a succession of scandals in the distribution of work along the canal, in the expenditure of public funds on it, in the contracting for it.

[1] Tammany had a hard time between the inauguration of Wilson and the defeat of Mayor Mitchel in 1917, for the city patronage was shut off and Wilson gave a very meagre share of federal patronage to Fourteenth Street. Almost the only plum given to the " braves " was the nomination of Mr. Gerard to the Berlin embassy.

[2] The difficulties of feeding the hungry sheep in a backward commonwealth with little state (and no federal) patronage at the disposal of the Governor, has recently been illustrated by the Bilbo régime in Mississippi. In order to provide for his followers, the Governor made over to them the state university and kindred institutions, getting rid of the politically useless incumbents without any hesitation. The only seats of learning which escaped were those devoted to the education of Negroes, for there were no black Bilboites to be placated, so the black teachers were left alone !

Labour on the canal was a privilege of the faithful who were on good terms with the local bosses, to whom the canal patronage was farmed out by the state bosses. Expenditure of money on canal repairs " sweetened " the counties through which the canal ran—though it sometimes had the undesirable effect of annoying the counties which were off the line of the canal. There were not many comparable institutions. Thaddeus Stevens, in the days when Pennsylvania was in the canal and railroad business, showed great talent in the handling of the patronage, but in most states, the friends of the machines, the railroads, etc., had to provide the jobs. When all else failed, the boss could do a little in the way of public and private graft to oblige his friends. There was the state printing and advertising, the withdrawal of which from Daniel Manning by Cleveland was so annoying to the heir of Tilden, that printing which, a generation later, was one of the chief perquisites of the Albany Republican boss, W. T. Barnes. And even legislation might, indirectly, put money in the pockets of the faithful, as happened in the case of the Raines Law.

There has been, however, a marked increase in the amount of patronage at the disposal of the state authorities and civil service has not proved a serious impediment to the political use of it in such states as pay even lip-service to that reform. There is an accompanying danger, however, for the patronage is legally in the hands of the Governor and that officer is becoming more important and active, partly because the office has been given increased powers. A Governor is now in a strong position to set up for himself as Governor Len Small did, or to make himself the centre of the state organization as Governor Al Smith did. In such hands the patronage, the pardoning power, the veto, the publicity powers of the state executive may be concentrated on objectives of more importance to the Governor than to the party workers, on keeping out of jail in the case of Governor Small, on matters of public policy such as state reorganization in the cases of Governors Smith and Lowden. Generally faced with a hostile legislature, Governor Smith had to rely on the pressure of public opinion and on the referendum, but Governor Lowden induced the reluctant Republicans of Illinois to reform themselves, slightly, by withholding the patronage. This meant that the appointees of Governor Dunne stayed on and the spectacle of Democrats in jobs converted the legislators to the Governor's reforms.

Relatively, as well as absolutely, the rise in importance of the Governor's office has made the position of state boss harder to fill. In the old days, the importance of the state government was largely legislative, the boss, as legislative agent, was of supreme importance. Now, it is at least as much administrative, so that the Governor must be in the hands of the boss or the machine may fail to run smoothly. The ending of legislative elections of United States Senators has diminished that party loyalty which the bosses prized and the direct primary has worked powerfully in the same direction. Whatever the reasons, there can be no doubt of the fact that it is harder to-day to locate individuals running states with the old efficiency. It is possible that the scarcity is only temporary and that the job still awaits the man. Even now there may be a mute inglorious Penrose or Brayton or Gorman in some minor job, but already at work climbing up the ladder of power. When he at last displays himself, all who seek power or office, politicians or business men, will learn to apply to him with the same regularity that, a generation ago, men went to French Lick to see Tom Taggart or joined the faithful of Platt's " Amen Corner ".[1]

[1] This was the name applied to the Sunday morning meetings at which Platt gave out his orders to the " Yes Men " of his machine.

Chapter IX

THE PROSPECTS OF REFORM

THE obstacles to a reform of the American political machine have been, it is hoped, sufficiently suggested in the previous pages, but a recapitulation of the achievements and difficulties of the modern reformers will illustrate the position with more force than a mass of detail makes easy.

It has long been obvious that only by a joint capture of state and city machine can any permanent overthrow of the old-fashioned mercenary army of politics be hoped for. Yet it is extremely difficult to run, together, a campaign for the double reform of city and state. The necessary drive for reform is exhausted by the war with either city or state machines ; the double objective means dispersal of interest and it means attacking the least reformable political units in America, the rural counties. Moreover, the forces of reform often lost heart when they were called on to make victory secure by attacking the state machine. Joseph Choate was a vigorous opponent of Tammany and worked with enthusiasm for the election of Mayor Strong in 1894, but as he worked, at the same time, for a state victory for the Republican, that is the Platt machine, he was securing that there should be no permanent defeat of Tammany, for, at the last ditch, the two machines would work together. Platt would have dearly liked to seize as much of New York City's plunder for himself as he could, and any measure that would achieve that end, without weakening his control of the state machine, had his effective support. But any measure that threatened both machines, was fought, openly or covertly, by both. Dog does not eat dog and there is no politics in politics.

A machine can only be overthrown by the action of a majority of citizens who think it worth their while to sacrifice, to that end, their party prejudices and, if necessary, their private interests, and it has been proved almost impossible to command either, or both, of these conditions. It is true that party lines in state politics are usually meaningless, that the party principles, granting them any reality they may have in the nation, are usually quite pointless in state or city politics. Why does a good citizen who is a good party man support his party nominees, even when they are the tools of a Platt or a Gorman ? The answer is that the state machines are the real fighting units of the national parties. The Republicans who, normally, are in control of the federal government, have a " federal gang " in every state which is often an important unit, but even it cannot dominate the party in the state except by supporting, or creating, factions in the state organization. As for the Democrats, their national organization is inevitably a parasite on the state parties, that is to say, on the state machines. So it is a serious matter for a party man to desert his party in a state or city issue, for he may be weakening an essential part of the national party strength. This consideration is strengthened by the working of the presidential electoral system, for it has happened often enough in the past that a thousand votes or so have turned the election in a state, and that has turned the election in the whole country.

The importance of the great doubtful states and their machines intimidates the ambitious individual and the reforming group. It was in furtherance of his own ambition to succeed President Hayes that John Sherman supported Alonzo Cornell for Governor of New York, though he had shortly before removed him from his post of Collector because he was a corrupt spoilsman. After denouncing Platt as an incarnation of machine politics with whom no decent man could associate, Cornelius Bliss switched over when Platt had to be conciliated for the good of the party in New York, as Roosevelt, running for Governor, had to gloss over the great canal frauds. In the days of his power, Boss Cox of Cincinnati had some of the most respectable Republicans of Ohio on his string ; the vote of Hamilton County was too important for its owner to be lightly antagonized. The relations of respectable Democrats with Tammany have been a subject of comedy for a century past. Tilden was a silent associate of the Tweed gang long before he attacked them as a reformer. Cleveland's hostility to Tammany was an asset in the country at large, but his friends, the County Democracy of William Whitney, went for a ride with the Tiger when it suited them. David Hill was a politician of the stamp that was an offence to all right-thinking men, but President Cleveland had, at any rate, to play in with him in a formal fashion. Democratic Presidents like Cleveland and Wilson could win applause by giving Tammany little or no recognition, but they could not assert this high standard of probity all over the country. Wilson entered politics as the nominee of the Smith machine in New Jersey and one of the forces behind his presidential nomination was the Sullivan machine in Illinois—and neither James Smith nor Roger Sullivan differed much from Charles Murphy.

It is not a question of conscious or unconscious hypocrisy. As Roosevelt pointed out, if he antagonized Platt he might prevent some evils, but he would lose his chance to do any good. As Governor he could veto some of the more outrageous " steals ", oust some of the more notorious public robbers, but he could do nothing positive, for that required the assent of the legislature—which was in Platt's pocket. In the great industrial states, at least, it has only been possible to get very far in person or in policy by making terms with the machine. To devote all one's energy to destroying the machine is to undertake a difficult task with the lesson of experience very plain, by the time the reforms of machinery are completed, the reforming zeal of the electorate is likely to be exhausted and the new-made government is turned over to the old firm. A practical politician of the highest type is tempted, not always by unworthy motives, to make friends of the Mammon of Unrighteousness, to shut his eyes to evil, that some good may be done. It is possible that if the machine had friends only in the criminal classes, only among ignorant and venal foreigners, it might pay to attack it boldly, but the friends of the machine are more numerous and more faithful than its enemies.

There have, of course, been real successes in administrative and legal reforms. In the states, the adoption of various devices of " direct government ", the initiative, referendum and recall, has made it easier to appeal over the heads of the bosses to the people. An awakened public opinion can make itself more effectually felt than it could in the past. The direct primary has lessened the machine control of state government if only by making discipline harder to enforce ; it may not have improved government in the process, but it has made harder the position of a modern Aldrich or Penrose.

Various reforms of accounting, of election, even more fundamental reforms of political machinery have been tried in great variety. Illinois, it is odd to recall, was, under Governor Lowden, a pioneer in administrative reform, with a consequent strengthening of the powers for mischief of a Governor like Len Small. In city government, even more far-reaching reforms have been carried out. Authority has been concentrated ; the elaborate and cumbersome two-chambered city governments have in many cases been simplified and authority has been centred in the Mayor and as few other elected officials as possible. Yet the fate of the " Bullitt charter " in Philadelphia illustrates the weakness of mechanical reform. A citizenry resolved on good government could get it, even if with difficulty, through the old order and to-day indifferent or corrupt cities permit the machines to twist the reforms to their own ends. Thus the " commission " form of government, which entrusts power to a small non-partisan body, chosen to carry out the city's business efficiently with as little "politics" as possible, works as long as the reforming spirit is strong. Crooks, however, are not changed by a change of title, and if the authority of the city is in the hands of the machine it matters little what the ruling body is called.

The last, and from the administrative point of view the most successful, mechanical reform is the " City Manager " constitution. In this the executive control of the city is put into the hands of one man, not a politician, but an expert in administration. The City Manager may be a stranger like an Italian *podestà* ; he is a professional administrator and, as he succeeds, moves up in his profession from a small town to a larger. Given ordinary probity, he has none of the political inducements that beset the reform Mayor ; his professional pride and knowledge is a better equipment than any mere assemblage of principles, but, after all, his power depends on the forbearance of the masters of the popular vote. If they are interested in efficiency the Manager may go ahead, but he works on a rope the end of which is in the hands of the voters—or of those who control the voters. The reform of the frame of government of Kansas City (Missouri) by the adoption of a city manager system did little to shake the power of the leader of the Democratic organization, Mr. T. J. Prendergast, since the Manager was a sound Democrat who "played ball " with the machine. A very energetic City Manager in Cleveland was able to keep on top of the situation by humouring the Republican boss, Mr. Maurice Maschke, and by taking an active part in municipal politics himself, for he saw, rightly, that there was no such thing as good administration apart from policy. Untimely zeal, such as a raid on a politically protected brothel in Sacramento, is punished as quickly as in the old days—unless the citizens are "strong for " the Manager. Mere efficiency will not enable a Manager to handle the problems of discipline among municipal employees created by the rise of the Ku Klux Klan. It may be necessary to defend the manager system against a Socialist assault by introducing irrelevant issues such as the War—as was done in Dayton, Ohio, in 1918, and tax-policies may be the grounds for very legitimate differences of opinion in any city, no matter what its constitution—and from such differences politics spring.

The reformers who concentrated on this reform were not wrong, but expected too much from mere administration. They assumed, as the earlier reformers had done, that there was something tangible and non-political called good government, or clean government, apart from definite policies as to the purposes of city government. Is there any common ground on

which all men of good will can meet and which will offer
something more obviously attractive than what the machine
can give the poor, that is to say, the majority of voters ?
A possible answer is indicated by the history of Milwaukee,
the best-governed city in the Union, which owes its long immunity from graft and its present financial stability to a
Socialist administration. Will the rich abandon their prejudices
and privileges, or the poor theirs ? Until one or other section
changes its attitude very profoundly, and permanently, municipal
efficiency will be a series of white patches against a grey background. Only cities in which such reforms as the manager
system are luxuries, though desirable luxuries, can work them, for
the cities that need reform most are least capable of attaining or
keeping it. The grosser scandals may have been made less
frequent, though Chicago was never worse ruled than she has
been for the last few years. But no mechanical reform has got
to the heart of things. A very competent witness has told us
what happened in New Jersey after the famous revolt against
the machine which Woodrow Wilson led and capitalized so well :

> " Frank Hague, who has had himself elected and twice
> re-elected mayor of Jersey City, has a completer control over
> the state Democratic machinery than Smith or any old-line
> boss ever enjoyed. . . . The forms have changed, but the
> master politicians in both parties still pilot the government." [1]

Yet the lesson learned by the " muckrakers " has not lost its
force. The fruits of corruption are not always reaped by the
sowers. The franchises bought from the New York aldermen by
the despised Jake Sharp were the basis of the great corporation exploits of William Whitney and Thomas Fortune Ryan.
To attack the machine is one thing, to attack the Pennsylvania
or Erie Railroad, or the Mellon or Insull interests [2] is quite
another. In the old days of the great Louisiana lottery, the
politician of that state took his life in his hands if he resisted
the wishes of its managers, but the time came when the moral
sentiment of the people of the state was roused, backed by the
moral sentiment of the whole country, and the lottery went
down in ignominious defeat. The machine will go down just
as soon as public opinion *really* reprobates the control of great
states by big business, in its own interests, or in its own defence.
That time has not yet come. Yet American business men are
not more indifferent to public opinion than the rest of their
countrymen and their political connections often put them in an
odd light. Why do the rulers of the great businesses risk this

[1] James Kerney, *The Political Education of Woodrow Wilson*, pp. 129–30.
[2] This was written before the (financial) fall of the House of Insull.

alienation of the public? For much of the villainy of the machines with which they do business the magnates are not responsible, they would like more respectable machines, but they have to put up with what they are given. In most states they cannot afford to dispense with the services of the general broker who is the boss and even when the business interests are consolidated, as they used to be in California, the machine has to be given its head. Lincoln Steffens was told the reason, that even the Southern Pacific Railroad could not afford to carry the whole cost of maintaining the machine in California, that like some reluctant captain of mercenary troops, it had to allow its satellites to forage for themselves, to eke out their pay at a serious loss in discipline and efficiency. But a great deal of the attitude of the business interests is the fruit of a serious conviction that nothing that stands in the way of business has a right to exist, whether it is the law of the state or mere honesty. The business man has acquired all the psychology of an absolute monarch with a good deal less than the restraint imposed by custom and public opinion on an absolute monarch in Western Europe. He sees no contrast between his sincere dislike of tolerated prostitution and petty graft, the pillaging of the Treasury or the maiming of the schools, the hiring of the police and the selling of pardons, and his support of the alliance between machine politics and business.

A generation ago the business men and their lawyers were sincere in thinking that the law was on their side, that, in fact, the fourteenth amendment did, despite Justice Holmes, enact " Mr. Herbert Spencer's Social Statics ". Opposition to governmental interference of any kind was their right and the means were forced on them by the wickedness of the crooked politicians and the folly of naïve reformers. The most famous expression of the attitude of the ruling classes was the achievement of a minor Pennsylvania coal magnate, George F. Baer, who rebuked outside interference in a coal strike.

" The rights and interests of the labouring man will be protected and cared for—not by the labour agitators, but by the Christian men to whom God in His infinite wisdom has given the control of the property interests of the country, and upon the successful Management of which so much depends." [1]

This was a little too much even for the class which felt about it that way. " Divine Right Baer " was a handicap who had to

[1] Mark Sullivan, *Our Times*, vol. ii, p. 426. The Baer letter was so explosive a missile in the anti-corporation war that strenuous efforts were made to deny its authenticity, but Mr. Mark Sullivan, whose text I quote, and who is now no radical, believes it to be authentic.

be disowned, but there was little real difference in the points of view of Baer and the greatest masters of the ruling classes. So enlightened a specimen as Henry Lee Higginson of Boston declared that " the Nation and our legislation can safely trust the ruling Wall Street men ".[1] Interference might bring into the great corporations men of less marked honesty—this being written at a time when some of the magnates were described as being " so crooked they could sleep comfortably on coils of rope ".[2] Such faith in their own rights and righteousness was necessary to the peace of mind and energy of the great American magnates, there was nothing in their own experience or in their surroundings to shake their creed. They were no more trammelled by petty bourgeois morality than were Napoleon or Lenin. Yet their strength would not have sufficed them, if they had outraged really strong passions or principles among the mass of their countrymen. But, in fact, they did not " outrage the American conscience, they expressed it ".[3] When business booms, when the crumbs from the rich man's table are plentiful, the reformer has a hard time. Thus, when, as a result of the exposures of the Walsh investigation, the sad truth about the oil scandals was made public, John D. Rockefeller, Jr., exerted himself to depose Colonel Robert Stewart from the presidency of the Standard Oil Company of Indiana, the attempt to purify that famous corporation met with but moderate approval from business men and when Mr. Rockefeller, reversing a precedent created by his uncle William, made no bones about appearing before the Senate, the only comment in some circles was a jest that he could not be as rich as had been thought. Twenty years before, E. R. Chapman had been a martyr to business honour when he refused to testify in the sugar graft investigation —and his heroism had been widely approved ; now the flight or silence of so many magnates of the oil industry, like the bad memory of the movie censor, Mr. Will Hays, evoked, if not open approval, at least kindly tolerance from the business world.

To make honesty, the separation of politics from private interests, the only issue, is too much to expect of human nature. To appeal to the American to sacrifice everything, including in many cases, hard cash, to an abstract idea of the state's objective authority is asking too much. We all, when driven to it, defy state authority—German Catholics in the *Kulturkampf* ; English Conservatives at the time of the Ulster Covenant in 1913 ; the English Labour party at the time of the General

[1] Bliss Perry, *Life and Letters of Henry Lee Higginson*, p. 446.
[2] J. K. Winkler, *J. Pierpont Morgan*, p. 126.
[3] Walter Lippmann, *Preface to Politics*, p. 195.

Strike ; all demonstrated how lightly the authority of the great Leviathan can weigh on the minds of men. What happens occasionally in Europe, happens perpetually in America. There the individual state, and often the United States, is only one competing authority among many ; only one force among others and not always the one commanding the greatest power or prestige. All American history has been a record of state action resisted, often with success. The American Revolution was a revolt against an authority that was not tyrannical by European standards, but was not susceptible of the endless adjustment of the law to local needs that was demanded by the nascent American spirit. To expect the American state to have the unquestioned authority of a sovereign political society on the European model, is to disregard the historical processes behind the two types of society. History has allowed Americans the luxury of pluralistic practice. Disorder and war have not yet intimidated American energies as they have ours : order and efficiency in government is a luxury that America has been able to do without so far and perhaps cannot yet afford.

There was and is no special sanctity attached to the state's property or activities. Defrauding a political unit was quite compatible with complete peace of conscience, even with a reputation for exceptional respectability. Mr. Willis Phelps, in the God-fearing city of Springfield, could be a notable manipulator of traction franchises without losing caste in the eyes of his fellow-citizens or of his brother Methodists—and the authors of " Middle-town " have told us what a broad and flexible interpretation is given to the term " good man " in the case of public officers in that sound " Anglo-Saxon " town. Not merely is the state one among many authorities, there are some associations that claim more powerful loyalties than the colourless appeals of " good citizenship ". The loyalty of the Knights of Columbus to their assailed brother Mr. Joseph Pelletier in a famous Boston " graft " case could be paralleled in other countries, but in few could it be as natural as it was in America. At times, the American people, or a section of it, decides on a house-cleaning, descends on some not especially vicious politician and sends him to jail, threatens Chicago aldermen with hanging or chases the corrupt Speaker of the Illinois House of Representatives out of his chair as an effective protest against public plunder, but, as a rule, these outbursts are short-lived.

Yet the situation reached in many cities, the dominance by the machine racket, is exacting such a toll that business may be converted to the point of view that honesty and law-obedience are the best policy :

" Direct bribery of law-enforcement officers, the payment of ' protection ' by criminals, alliances between corrupt municipal politics and organized crime, if not common, are far from unknown. . . . The economic aspects of racketeering are important in this connection, since it is only because of the large profits of organized crime that the funds necessary for wholesale corruption became available." [1]

But would a state strong enough to restrain the gangs and their political allies, be strong-minded enough to keep its hands off the chartered licence of American business ?   Would the power trust as well as the beer trust suffer from a sudden return to law, order and honesty ? Would Illinois welcome rigorous honesty from an Altgeld ? Is business ready to pay the price of an honest government, a government not suspect of being under the control either of Mr. Capone or of Mr. Insull ? Nor is it only big business which is anti-social at times. Organized labour—whether more sinned against or sinning matters little here—has put off the mentally painful task of working out either a political or revolutionary policy in favour of mere bargaining— and sometimes of mere violence. To get pardons for colleagues in jail may have been a great temptation to labour leaders in Illinois to support Len Small, but that way no hope lies for the led and Debs was right when he attacked the labour racket, under its old name of " sabotage " and " direct action ".

The realists on both left and right may argue that abandoning violence and corruption as weapons is abandoning all hope of temporary victory or even survival in the American jungle. But even a Communist historian, like Mr. Anthony Bimba, has to admit the futility of the methods of violence of the fighting American labour unions. " Only with clearer political insight gleaned from bitter experience, does the working class learn that its struggle is not against this or that individual—who for a moment may typify the system it is fighting—but against the bourgeoisie as a class." [2] If the American labour movements learn this lesson from Communist preaching of the " dialectic process of history ", the lesson will have had powerful if unconscious teachers in many of the leaders of big business, whether the business is that of the employers or of the Union magnates.

It is difficult to refuse sympathy to any actors in the comedy of American machine politics. For any individual caught in the machine to live up to the standards of the reformers would not merely be heroic, (and American politics has had and still

[1] National Committee on Law Observance and Enforcement (The Wickersham Report) : Report on Cost of Crime, p. 411.
[2] Anthony Bimba, The Molly Maguires, p. 126.

has as many heroes as most other political systems), it would
often be so disconcerting as to provoke not unjustified resentment. An incorruptible Governor of Palestine in Turkish times
was a phenomenon unmanageable by the inhabitants and they
sighed for the old days when governmental power was for sale ;
in that world they could move, but in this new honest world
they were lost and life was paralysed. A Mayor, free from all
machine entanglements and all interested pressure, enforcing
all laws may be a brake on progress : there is no general system
of ethics or of political administration which an official or group
of officials can rely on, nothing approaching the German ideal
of an " objective state authority ". Yet a Mayor whose devotion
to the financial rulers of his city may be reasonable, finds himself
tempted to get a little for himself on the side. In using all his
powers to make Pittsburgh safe for the Mellon dynasty, Mayor
Charles H. Kline may have been actuated by public spirit or
a conviction that political power should go with financial power.
Yet the methods necessary to carry out this policy involve the
use of delicate casuistry and are apt to blunt the sensibilities
of the workers. But the law in unfriendly hands makes small
allowance for the difficulties of such a dangerous trade and
Mayor Kline has recently had to endure the indignity of a
conviction for malfeasance.

To create a rigid system of political morals and to insist at
all times and all places on judging public men by its standards
requires a faith which would move mountains ; so, naturally,
good men of all parties, all sections, and all kinds of legitimate
aspirations, have preferred to go round the mountains or to
tunnel them or to find passes over them. The faith of the
reformer in the essential importance of honest government must
be made manifest in works, works on a strikingly large scale.
It was possible for the corrupt, soldier-selling German princes
of the eighteenth century to display their complete indifference
to all public policy and decency and yet to command from their
docile subjects, loyal, competent and honest service. There is
no hope of such an attitude being bred in the common American.
" The better elements " will have to wear virtue permanently,
not put it on and off, whenever they find it convenient. It is
a little too much in these days of popular education to expect
the poor to behave with a self-restraint that their betters give
no indication of showing. Law and order in America have to
acquire prestige with all ranks of society, with none more than
the rich. But freedom from corruption and racketeering can
only be purchased at a great price, and it is fitting that it should
be paid by the section which has profited most manifestly by
the old order. A plundering soldier told General Sherman,

" You can't expect all the cardinal virtues for thirteen dollars a month." No more can you expect the highest civic virtue from the poor, if it is manifestly beyond the power of the rich.

Where politics are cleanest in the United States is where real political issues are fostered and in modern times such issues must be economic, must be open to the dangers of demagogy and give a chance to " radicalism ", that nightmare of the be- lievers in the divine rights of business men. Real politics in New York might defeat Tammany, not once in a way but again and again, if that city had two really antagonistic parties or theories of government in opposition as has the admirably governed " Socialist " city of Milwaukee. Brisbane Hall is the real reply to Tammany Hall. The state government of Wisconsin for all its faults is, we are told, honest in a way which makes it shine like a good deed in a naughty world. And this purity is owing to the political education of the state of Wisconsin. That commonwealth is pure " because the people—or most of them —have been taught to take an interest in their government, a continuing interest, not merely at election times ".[1]

If this is so, may not the assaults on the vested rights of capital be the price of purity ? What chance is there of American society being willing to pay this price ; of real politics with all its drawbacks and dangers being welcomed as a means of ending the power of the political rackets ?

There is, to-day, at any rate, more chance of purity being adopted as an ideal than there has been since the end of the Great War. As long as the autonomy of business was regarded as self-evident, as long as it was permitted to adopt its own set of values and to expect and be right in expecting all other values to give way to these, there was little chance of permanent reform. No mere adjustment of the machine could do the trick ; no commission government or city manager system if the commis- sion was, or seemed to be, a committee of the Chamber of Commerce and the manager merely another employee of the prosperous better elements. But to-day faith in the values of business, in its power of self-adjustment, is ebbing. Even if politics, as yet, reflect it only imperfectly, there is an increasing scepticism as to the present validity of such shibboleths as " busi- ness is business " ; in politics business is not business, but an intrusion whose contribution of suggestion should never have the force of a command or escape the constant challenge of criticism which it needs as much as any other human activity. On the depth of the current disillusionment, and the permanency of the present scepticism, depends the future status of American

[1] Elmer Davis, " Wisconsin is Different ", in *Harper's Magazine*, October, 1932.

local and national politics. Something like a change of heart is needed. It may take the comparatively simple but possibly dangerous form of a resort to distributive socialism, as vigorous and uncritical as was the former worship of what was fondly believed to be individualism. That menace to the rich, to the prosperous, may be avoided, but only by the development of a new self-restraint, a new limitation on the " rights " of business and property accepted, if not with good temper, at any rate without the present determination to sabotage a government that is not in friendly hands. It will mean more rigorous taxation, with less accommodation for the rich ; less buying of privilege and of immunities ; possibly, even, the deliberate acceptance of technical inefficiency in order to remove the apparently irresistible temptations to corruption which privately owned public utilities seem to offer the business world. Then, and only then, will it be possible to preach " good government " to the poor ; to attack the trade union racketeers as well as those owned by the great corporations ; to have a more honest police force and a less suspect court system. The temptation to " put away " such enemies of the dominant business order as Tom Mooney will have to be resisted ; the silencing of criticism in press, in university, on the platform, on the soap-box, will have to be regarded as disgraceful, as it is, on the whole, in Western Europe, for only when the effort to silence dissenters has been officially renounced, will it be possible to convince the poor that their masters have nothing to conceal. To abandon the privileged position he has assumed for himself and for his ideas may be, for the American business man, as difficult as corresponding sacrifices have been to other privileged classes in the past. Now, when the system, badly shaken as it is, still holds together, is the acceptable time for the American people as a whole to adopt an attitude to government that will make it more than a racket. In such a change, if it is not only, it is chiefly the first step that counts. *Que messieurs les riches commencent !*

PART NINE

CONVENTIONS AND CANDIDATES

Thou great democratic God! who in all Thy mighty, earthly marchings, ever cullest Thy selected champions from the kingly commons.

Moby Dick.

Chapter I

THE TASK OF THE CONVENTION

THE Conventions of the national parties are the nearest approach the American system permits to a parliamentary type of government. The decision of the Convention is final and the responsibility is put on the shoulders of the delegates ; their interest is assumed to be in a national victory for the party and not in an aggregate of local successes. Of course, the Convention is a parliament of a very unusual kind. It only meets once every four years, for a very brief period, and it has even less natural organization and coherence than Congress. Nevertheless, it commits the party to a platform, which means little, and to a candidate, which means much ; there are none of the buffers of the division of powers between a decision and its result and, in consequence, parliamentary talents of the English type have at least as much scope in the Conventions as in Congress. Oratory and diplomatic talents have each had brilliant successes in them and few days in the life of Congress have the dramatic interest attaching to crises in the Conventions. It is right that this extra-constitutional body should have its own importance and tradition, for it is, in many ways, a more representative body than Congress can be. The Democrat who is, for all practical purposes, disfranchised in Vermont, the Republican who is equally helpless in Georgia, have their brief day in the Convention. Both parties are sectional, but both pretend to be national and there are in both Conventions, great blocks of delegates who cast their votes for candidates who will not receive an electoral vote from the state or section whose support may have been indispensable to nomination. If the sole business of the party is to represent

297

its dominant section, this is an anomaly, but in a system that discourages any national issues, the choice of the one national official is none the worse made, on the whole, because the indispensable preliminary of nomination has been performed by a body which is more truly national than are most American institutions.

It is an axiom that a Republican President, if he really tries, can insist on a second nomination, no matter how unpopular he is or what feeble chances of election he may have. Andrew Johnson was, of course, an exception ; he could never have got the nomination of the party which had tried to impeach him, but the only comparable case since the Civil War is that of President Arthur in 1884. He was merely an accidental President, succeeding the murdered Garfield ; he belonged to a beaten faction in the party and he was in notoriously poor health. In these circumstances he could not compete with the immensely popular Blaine, the more that the opposition to Blaine was unwilling to rally round Arthur. Nevertheless, he polled a respectable number of votes and might have polled more if he had fought harder.[1] More to the point is the case of Benjamin Harrison who was known not to be a strong candidate, who had to face Blaine and other rivals while labouring under the unpopularity his cold manner earned him and which made Speaker Reed compare him to a dripping cave. Yet he was able to force his nomination in 1892 and take his party down to defeat with him. Taft, likewise, was able to win the nomination over the immensely popular Roosevelt, although his success in the 1912 Convention condemned the party to certain and ignominious defeat.

It is usual to attribute this presidential control to the black office-holders from the South and there has long been resentment of the part played by these mercenaries, whether they are bought with offices or spot cash. The scandals associated with the nomination of Taft in 1912 forced reform on the party and the weight of the South in the Republican Convention has been cut down, although it is still excessive from the point of view of voting strength. But the strength of a President asking for a re-nomination is not based merely on bought black votes. If we had more examples of Democratic Presidents to go on, we should probably find that they, too, could force the party to re-nominate them. The party, little as it may like it, is usually identified with its President and to renounce him, as the Democrats did in 1896, is a risky business. The President, in the eyes of the public, *is* the party ; to disavow him is to disown the party's record

[1] Out of the 278 first-ballot votes for Arthur, 196 came from the South, that is, from federal office-holders.

and play into the hands of the opposition. The death of President Harding doubtless was a relief to the G.O.P., but it may be hazarded that, scandals or no scandals, he would have been re-nominated in 1924.

In a doubtful Convention, where the nomination is not " in the bag " from the start, the preliminaries of the Convention have a symptomatic value to leaders looking for a candidate and a platform that will appeal both to the Convention and to the country. In the fight to elect the permanent chairman of the Convention is an indication of the movement of opinion among the delegates. In 1912, the early successes of the Taft managers disheartened the Roosevelt forces, demonstrating the futility of their hopes of a regular nomination, but the powers behind Bryan in the same year were more potent than the first skirmishes indicated. In 1932 the strength of the Hoover machine was so great that no real fight could be made, but the Democratic Convention was a series of tests of strength, disheartening for the Roosevelt forces when the attempt to alter the rules failed, heartening when their nominee, Senator Thomas Walsh, defeated the Smith leader, Mr. Jouett Shouse.

The preliminaries of organization over, the Convention settles down to speeches, the formal importance of which is greater than their content or effect would indicate. The " keynote " speech, like the platform at a later stage, is rhetorical history, devoted to the past glories of one party and the infamies of the other. This is usually delivered by some party hack like the late Mr. Harding, whose vaguely impressive appearance and capacity for meaningless rotund oratory were his chief political assets. A long eulogy of the past, present, and future of the party and a severe examination of the claims of the other party to respect, or even tolerance, is all that is required. The delegates get a chance to warm up in the blast of hot air from the orator and there are possibly voters naïve enough to pay some attention to this performance worthy, as a rule, of a " barker " for a third-rate circus.[1] Normally the Republican keynoter can point with pride to the achievements of his party and shudder to think what would have become of the nation if it had entrusted its destinies to the Democrats. The Democrats have usually only the resource of denouncing corruption or lamenting inaction. In 1932, the task of the Republican keynoter was harder and that of his opposite number easier. Senator L. J. Dickinson was given the ungrateful task and wisely he devoted more attention to the past iniquities of the Democrats than to the recent achievements of the G.O.P. What, he asked with

[1] Mr. Frank Sullivan has written an excellent " keynote speech " which can be used by either party, in *The New Yorker* (May 7, 1932).

indignation, were the Democrats doing, " as Hoover poured out his tremendous energies and abilities upon the altar of public service ? For two long years they have hampered the President at every turn. . . . Upon his shoulders the anvil chorus of the Democracy placed the responsibility of every ill at home and abroad." In Congress the enemy flouted their own leaders and threatened the gold standard—as they had done at Chicago in 1896. Then Representative Bertrand H. Snell took up the tale and saw in President Hoover " an engineer president solving stupendous problems as did the first engineer president, George Washington ". Can we wonder that the delegates, largely federal office-holders, saw in these orations excellent arguments against entrusting the government and the jobs to the Democrats ? When his turn came, the Democratic " keynoter " had an easier task than usual and Senator Barkley took his chance.

> " There is nothing wrong with this Republic except that it has been mismanaged, exploited and demoralized for more than a decade by a leadership incomparably shortsighted and bereft of statesmanship, incapable of dealing with fundamental causes, incapable even now in the midst of fearful havoc, and not understanding the extent of its own mischief. . . . We must apply to a hopeful but misused patient the recuperative processes of Democratic government to which in a century and a half it has responded in the emergencies which have always beset us at the end of every period of Republican control."

The Democratic Convention, with its share of prospective office-holders, applauded these stirring words.

It is even more in the keynote speeches than in the platforms that the emptiness of modern American parties is illustrated and the large section of the Republican Convention which walked out while Senator Dickinson was barn-storming was, if unconsciously, passing a verdict on the whole preposterous performance.[1]

With the inevitable preliminaries over, the Convention settles down to serious work, that is, to choosing the presidential candidate, a task which is made more difficult from the absence of strict rules or regular methods of approach. Each convention is anxious to pick a winner, but it seldom, except in the case of

---

[1] The model keynote speech was that delivered at the state convention of the New York Democrats in 1861, at a moment when the future of the country—and of the party—was being put to the ordeal of battle. The speaker devoted his time to a defence of the Sub-Treasury law of 1840 and the tariff of 1846 !

a President demanding re-nomination, has a very clear idea of how to achieve this end. The Convention has, in fact, a far more difficult and delicate task than any corresponding European body, for of all great offices in the modern world, the American presidency is that whose attainment owes most to luck and least to planning. Though, as has been shown, the President is *ex officio the* leader of the party in power and, from many points of view, the only leader in the whole world of politics, the office has seldom been filled from even the second rank of politicians. In the early days of the Republic, the President was designated by as effective a method as that which made Disraeli and Gladstone the heads of their parties. Washington was theoretically above party, but his successor, John Adams, was the inevitable, if unpopular, choice of the Federalists. Still more was Jefferson the leader of the Republican (Democratic) party. Under his skilful hand it acquired a doctrine, cohesion and office. He was leader of the party before he was President, he might have, had he so chosen, been leader after he left the White House. He was able to nominate his successor, Madison, but though Madison owed his practically undisputed election to Jefferson's choice, that choice fell upon the obvious candidate. Madison was the most eminent of the younger generation of American statesmen, the chief author of the constitution, the leader of the Jeffersonian Opposition in the House of Representatives and, for eight years, Jefferson's Secretary of State. He was, at least, the Hartington of a Gladstone who had really retired. Madison's successor, Monroe, had comparable though lesser claims. He was the leading Virginian politician of the old school, of varied if not always brilliant public service, and he, like Madison, had been Secretary of State to his predecessor. John Quincy Adams, after a brilliant career in diplomacy and politics and eight fruitful years as Monroe's Secretary of State, succeeded him in office. So far the line of succession had been regular and normal from an English point of view. The practical limitation of an administration to two presidential terms and the consequent necessity of providing a new chief executive, and a new party leader, every eight years was a consequence of the presidential system, making impossible the long reigns of Gladstone or of Lord Liverpool, but the first six Presidents of the United States had claims to that office which, *mutatis mutandis*, would have made them Prime Ministers in England.

The election of General Andrew Jackson in 1828 was in this, as in so many other respects, a revolution. Despite a brief term in each House of Congress, Jackson was even more a soldier statesman than his contemporary, the Duke of Wellington. His election ended the parliamentary phase of the presidency.

The " caucus ", composed of the majority members of both houses, had, up till 1824, chosen, or ratified, the presidential candidate. The nomination of Crawford in that year by the caucus had been a futile gesture. Now a President had been chosen whose political claims were almost nil. The consequences of this election on the relations between the executive and Congress were profound and are discussed elsewhere. It is to be noted, however, that Jackson, if hardly a politician himself, was surrounded by politicians of great eminence and skill. Calhoun, the Vice-President, had reason to hope that Jackson, an old, and believed to be a fragile man, would serve only one term, if that, and a President Calhoun would have restored the tradition of long and distinguished service in Congress and the Cabinet, culminating in the presidency. But Calhoun discovered that Jackson was stronger, physically and mentally, than he had hoped. A quarrel, whose details need not concern us, ended all hopes of an easy inheritance and Calhoun registered his disillusionment by resigning the vice-presidency and returning to the Senate. Jackson, in eight crowded years, was able to ignore practically every important politician in Congress and, for a part of his term, to defy the Senate, while his compeer, the Duke of Wellington, saw his power collapse under him at the first shock. Jackson was able to nominate his successor and that successor, Van Buren, was a politician if not a statesman. But being a politician was not enough : there was no career like Peel's open to President Van Buren. The old hero in retirement could not save his protégé from defeat in 1840 at the hands of General Harrison, a lath painted to look like hickory, a parody of Jackson. One part of the secret of empire was now known, a President need have no training or probable fitness for the office, and Presidents, like Roman Emperors, could be better made on the frontier than in the capital. The second secret was learned in 1844, when Polk, the first " dark horse ", was nominated over Van Buren and defeated Henry Clay. It is true that Polk was not such a dark horse as rash or embittered commentators have asserted. He was a leading politician of Jackson's own state, Tennessee, and the wit who asked, " Who is Polk ? ", might have jested later with more plausibility, for the candidate had been Speaker of the House of Representatives. Still, if not obscure, Polk was not an inevitable candidate : he was what was now to be more valuable, an " available " candidate. A politician of the second rank had defeated in the Convention of his own party an Ex-President, and defeated in the election Henry Clay, who ranks among the first half-dozen American popular leaders. Yet, compared with some later " dark horses ", Polk was a light grey. His successor, General

Zacchary Taylor, was chosen as the hero of the Mexican War. He had never held any political office or opinion, he had never even voted. The descent from Jackson to Harrison is steep, from Harrison to Taylor steeper. In the year he lived Taylor turned out to be a good President, as Jackson had been a great one ; the American public could be pardoned its growing fondness for leaps in the dark ! By 1850, the presidency had become a prize in a lottery for which the more tickets one had, the less chance of a prize.

For nearly a century past the American parties have looked for presidential candidates in the ranks of the safe, the pliable, sometimes even the obscure. The more a politician has displayed energy, leadership and willingness to take responsibility, the more likely it is that he has made formidable enemies, alienated important sections, in brief made himself less " available " than the sound party hack. Thus Stephen Douglas, the most formidable leader the Democrats had in the generation following the retiral of Jackson, the man who set the pace for his own and all other parties, was passed over for a second-rate soldier like Franklin Pierce, and then in an election in which the Douglas policy was the sole issue Douglas was again passed over in favour of James Buchanan, not so much a dark horse as a lame one, whose chief claim to eminence was that he had been Minister to London during the controversies which convulsed the Union and were a prelude to the Civil War. It was as if, in 1880, Mr. Gladstone had been passed over in favour of Lord Hartington *because* the election had been fought on the Midlothian issues.

So it has been since. The most eminent Republican in 1860, Seward, was superseded by the comparatively obscure Abraham Lincoln and again and again the obvious leader has had to step down in favour of the second-rater on whom the fates (or the party-managers) have decided. The party squabbles or personal difficulties which from time to time project such figures as Mr. Baldwin or Mr. Bonar Law suddenly into the seats of the mighty are always operative in America—and the claims of Mr. Bonar Law in 1911 or Mr. Baldwin in 1923 were almost dazzling compared with those of Mr. Harding or even of Mr. Hayes. Only twice since the Civil War has the Republican party nominated what we should call a " front-bench man ". Blaine in 1884 was undoubtedly the leading Republican—and the first Republican candidate to be defeated since 1860—and in 1896 McKinley was, roughly, the W. H. Smith of a party which had in its ranks a Sir William Harcourt in the person of Speaker Reed.

If the American presidential candidates are not chosen from among the political leaders, from whose ranks are they chosen ?

From those of the minor politicians or, when the " ticket " has
to be strengthened, from men whose eminence has not been
gained in politics at all, or, at any rate, in national politics.
Soldiers above all have been the darlings of the peaceful Republic.
There was a long gap between Washington and Andrew Jackson,
but after that the man on horseback became the favourite raw
material of the president-maker. Harrison, Taylor, Pierce,
before the Civil War, and then, after the Civil War, a long and
unbroken line of Republican soldier-Presidents testify to the
fondness of the American people, or the American politician,
for military heroes. Every Republican candidate from 1868 to
1904 save one owed a good deal—in some cases all—of his
availability to his military services, real or imaginary. It is
also worth noting that the only Republican candidate in this
period who never entered the White House was also the only
civilian candidate. This tradition has upset not only politics
but war, for Generals have been assumed to fight the foe with
one eye on the White House. Presidents in office have received
the news of victory with some of the mixed feelings of a Roman
Emperor hearing of the triumphs of a Corbulo or a Julian,
or French ministers scanning the ranks of commanders for
Renan's " General X " and rejoicing that General Sarrail, at
least, would never desert the Republic. Even during the Civil
War the administration did not know whether to fear or to hope
for an overwhelming victory by McClellan, and during the
Spanish War it was suspected that the dispatch of General Miles
to Porto Rico where laurels would be less easily culled than in
Cuba, was not unconnected with the dangers of a rival to
President McKinley arising in 1900. Nevertheless, fate was
not baulked, and the Spanish War produced a military President
Theodore Roosevelt, whose attack on San Juan hill was transformed, with the aid of its leader, into another charge of the
Light Brigade or *Todenritt* of Mars la Tour. When the late
War came, one of President Wilson's worries was what to do
with General Leonard Wood who was suspected of having an
eye on the White House which was to be reached *via* a victory
on the western front, and another was the problem of how to
handle the farcical project of Roosevelt's private army which
was to rescue the hard-pressed Allies—and, perhaps unconsciously
make straight the path to a nomination in 1920. It was among
the greatest of General Pershing's merits that he devoted himsel
to his professional business and he is the only successful American
General whose presidential aspirations have been suppressed
not merely by himself, but by his friends.

Next to being a General, it pays to be a Governor, for one can
acquire strength and even fame in that sphere without committing

oneself to any view of national politics and often enough a prominent aspirant for the presidency, or for that matter a President, has
been trained in no wider a sphere than that of a Chairman of
the London County Council.

Congress has provided a good many Presidents, usually not
the most eminent, but although several Presidents have been
Senators at some time or other in their careers, only one serving
Senator has ever been elected, and he, the late Mr. Harding,
can hardly be counted a happy precedent. The lower house
has been luckier, but Congress as a whole has to compete with
too many rival nurseries ; it has no monopoly as has Parliament
in England.

In addition to the legal barriers, that is to say birth in
the United States and a minimum age of thirty-five, there
are certain conventional barriers. No Negro and, it is highly
probable, no Catholic or Jew, need apply for a very long
time to come. Indian blood, however, is no handicap
whether in a very dilute form in the numerous descendants of
Pocahontas *et al.*, or in more generous quantities such as flow
in the veins of Mr. Charles Curtis, who might have been first
in a Kaw tribe instead of being second in Washington. Mr.
Curtis's presidential ambitions encountered many obstacles, but
his ancestry was not one of them, and had he become President
the spectacle of the Great Red Father in Washington perhaps
attempting to pacify the warring Palefaces of Chicago, would
have added to the American stock of innocent amusement.

Then it is necessary to pick one's state. It is no use coming
from a small state which is not worth conciliating. Not since
1852 has a citizen of a small state been elected. But even large
states fall into two classes, the doubtful and the certain. The
doubtful states, Ohio, Indiana, Illinois, New York, these it is
whose sons the party-managers delight to honour, but the faithful
states that can be relied on, Pennsylvania and, in the old days,
Texas and Massachusetts, put forward their favourite sons in
vain. Why nominate Mr. Philander Knox, for example, when
the party-managers were certain that Pennsylvania will swallow
any insult to her pride in defence of her pocket ?

What applies to the President applies to the Vice-President.
He is not chosen, because he is believed to be fit for the
presidency should fate call him into the White House ; indeed
there have been times, and not very remote times, when each
party has nominated a vice-presidential candidate, the thought
of whose accession to the presidency would have caused a shudder
even to the most faithful party devotees. How little thought is
given to this side of the vice-presidential nominees is illustrated
by the fact that this candidate is not younger than the presi-

dential candidate as a rule and, indeed, the Democrats once went to the length of nominating a wealthy Senator who was eighty-one. This nomination is used to pacify sections within the party, to conciliate " runners-up " like Mr. Garner and, in general, to paper over the cracks of the party structure. The list of Vice-Presidents is, consequently, a grave of very ephemeral reputations. What is suggested by the names of Daniel D. Tompkins, Hannibal Hamlin, William A. Wheeler, Adlai E. Stevenson, or Garrett A. Hobart ? Yet accident might have made them as well known as Millard Fillmore or Chester A. Arthur. That, it may be replied, is not saying much, but it is much more than the sponsors of these gentlemen ever expected. With no duties but to preside over the Senate, with little power or respect, waiting for a death which may elevate him from obscurity to power, a Vice-President is a melancholy figure. It is not surprising that the office seldom attracts anyone of real eminence, that Roosevelt had to be forced into it, that one term of it was enough for General Dawes, and that Senator Borah refused the nomination. It is true that Mr. Curtis was willing to give up a Senate seat and Mr. Garner the speakership for this office, but no Senator or Speaker who really felt sure of himself would consider accepting a vice-presidential nomination unless his running-mate were obviously a " bad life ". Bored, worn out by the summer heat, and indifferent to the claims of the various aspirants for this mildly honorific office, the Convention picks a candidate in what is sometimes almost a state of coma. After all, if the President lives, it hardly matters who is chosen. The most successful incumbent of the office in modern times, Thomas M. Marshall, said that what the country needed was a good five-cent cigar ; it is a man at about that level who is wanted for the vice-presidency. If fate throws him into the White House, it is hoped that the party press-agents will be able to " sell " him to the country as a Corona Corona. It has been done in the past and the Convention sees no reason to doubt that it can be done again.

It is on principles like these that the Convention works in choosing the national ticket. It may do very odd things. The Republicans, in 1856, nominated Frémont, " the Path-finder ", a candidate whose claims, such as they were, resembled those of Lord Baden-Powell. In 1896, the Democratic Convention was in revolt against President Cleveland and the " Gold Democrats ". The Convention was the " Carlton Club meeting " of the Democrats, as indignant at the alliance of their nominal leader with Wall Street, as were the revolting Tories in 1922 at the alliance of their nominal chiefs with Mr. Lloyd George. Of that revolt, " Silver Dick " Bland, of Missouri, was the leader, the parliamentary spokesman and the weightiest representative, yet he was passed over in favour of a young and little-known orator from Nebraska. Had English politics run on American lines, the result in 1922 might have been the premiership of Mr. Clary whose victory at Newport had set the ball rolling !

The career of President Hoover adds the last example to our collection. The first elective office Mr. Hoover ever held was the presidency. In this odd distinction, his only rivals are Generals Taylor and Grant and, like them, his political career is a fluke of war service. Those services were similar in kind, if not in quality, to those of the numerous " captains of industry " and other non-political organizers of victory so lavishly imported into public office by Mr. Lloyd George, but where are they now, the Geddes Brothers and the other old familiar faces ? Back at their old jobs, while the country is run by those whose business it is to run it, the professional politicians !

Having shown the unpredictable character of the presidential lottery, it remains to be seen what constitutes availability in a would-be President, for that is all that can be described. A contest for the presidency is a game in which there are more possibles than in corresponding games in other countries, but no probables.

The Convention is a race open to all ; no one can foresee the winner ; it is possible that he will be an outsider, and it is certain that the favourite, except in the rarest cases, will have two or three formidable rivals. The task of the ordinary delegate is to pick a winner ; of the expert riders among the bosses and leaders to steer their mounts to victory. It is usual to distinguish two classes among the rulers of a convention. The " bosses " are the leaders of the machines, men whose weight is solely due to the blocks of votes they are believed to have at their disposal. The knowledge that their favour can give disciplined legions of delegates to the lucky candidate makes the temptation to buy their support very great. If these men are themselves politically ambitious, they may be promised, or think they have been promised, high office. Thus Simon Cameron became Secretary of War ; thus Tom Platt thought he should have entered Harrison's Cabinet in 1889 ; thus Roger Sullivan thought he had earned support from Woodrow Wilson when he attempted to enter the Senate in 1914. The less ambitious bosses, like Kelly and Murphy, want more for their organizations or their friends than for themselves and in such cases the bargain is less obvious and so more easy to honour.

Beside the bosses rank the " leaders ". It is not always easy to distinguish one from the other. Quay, Hill, Conkling, Pen-

rose are marginal cases, but in general the leaders are men who
have weight in the country at large as well as in their own
states, men who represent a powerful block of party opinion, if
not always what we should call a policy. The support of such
men is even more indispensable than that of the bosses, for the
latter, as a rule, fall into line with the majority, reluctant to defy
party discipline with its consequent loss of patronage while the
former have their own reputations to consider and manage to
justify what in lesser men would be called " knifing the ticket ".
It is important, then, not to give them grounds for disloyalty, and
a candidate who can only win at the cost of estranging some
dominant figures in the party, finds his support melting away.
Normally, the business of the Convention is not to pick an
individual but to pick a winner, and it is sometimes impossible
to determine who will be a winner till the Convention has revealed
the feeling within the party. It is this feeling that the leaders
of the party set themselves to interpret or to dominate.

The game is never as easy as romantic observers think. It
is possible that if all the leaders and bosses combined together,
they could " put over " any candidate they liked, but whatever
may be the power of enlightened self-interest in the case of the
bosses, the leaders, most of whom are Senators, are men of great
self-esteem and slow to surrender their own or their nominee's
hopes. The union of the rulers is never complete and never
firmly soldered and, consequently, the last word lies with the
mass of delegates, all of whom are politicians, but most of whom
have few ideas in common and have no time in the brief life of
the Convention to acquire the coherence of even a militia. A
Convention is always a mob, ready to be stampeded by an adroit
leader, with one desire dominating all others, to back the winner
early ; to " get on the band wagon " before it is uncomfortably
crowded and so acquire merit in the eyes of the candidate. To
have the appearance of winning is, nine times out of ten, to
win and the first duty of the manager of a candidacy is to give
an appearance of inevitable victory to the troops under his
command ; if the illusion is complete, the enemy will desert.
The tactics of convention war are decidedly Chinese, not least
in the fluidity of loyalties and the importance attached to
noise.

Since it is taken for granted that the Convention will try to
pick a winner, it is desirable to show as unmistakably as possible
that the party is with the candidate proposed. Hence the
apparently absurd ritual of cheering. When the candidate's
name is presented, his supporters cheer and it is a point of honour
with them to out-cheer the supporters of candidates nominated
earlier. From this point of view, it is an advantage to be

fairly far down on the list.[1] There is then a definite mark to shoot at. In 1912 at Baltimore, the applause which started with twenty-six minutes for Oscar Underwood, rose to an hour and five minutes for Champ Clark, and then came an hour and a quarter of applause following the nomination of Woodrow Wilson. Next to the cheering, is the marching : this ritual is designed to sweep doubters off their feet, is accompanied by the waving of banners, the showering of badges on the delegates and spectators and the blaring of tunes designed to break down the audience's sales resistance in the fashion of a revival meeting. It is an art in which Americans excel, and though it is now dulled by mechanical repetition, it is not ineffective. A slogan or a song is a help. In 1912 the supporters of Champ Clark made great play with a simple ballad of Missouri :

> " ' I don't care if he is a houn' [*anglice*, mongrel]
> You gotta quit kicking my dawg aroun'.' "

> " This strenuous objection to the kicking of hound dogs was shouted, screamed, whispered and cat-called until the air quivered with its echoes. It was silly and meaningless, of course, but if you think it was ineffective, you would change your mind if you ever watched a political convention. . . . We [the Wilson men] had nothing in the way of a battle-cry that was the equal of the ' houn' dawg ' in noise." [2]

In the Democratic Convention at New York in 1924, the song of the Smith forces was the " Sidewalks of New York ", inspiring to them, but infuriating to the southern delegates, for most of whom those sidewalks (pavements) pointed to " where New York's seduction, the Broadway, leadeth to destruction ". At the same Convention a natural, but disastrous error in the choice of a tune further embittered the embattled Democrats of the South. As a compliment to the " Empire State of the South " a Tammany band struck up " Marching Through Georgia ", to the fury of the Southerners, who had been brought up to regard Sherman as a baser Attila and received the song as an Orange Lodge would " The Wearing of the Green ".

But not all the time, even of a Democratic Convention, is devoted to songs and cheers. There are the speeches. It is impossible to evaluate the effect of convention speeches. In

---

[1] Candidates are nominated in accordance with the alphabetical order of their states. Thus, Democratic conventions were for long familiar with the nomination of Oscar W. Underwood by Alabama. A state which has no candidate of its own may yield its place to a state which has. In 1912 Delaware yielded to New Jersey to permit the early nomination of Woodrow Wilson.

[2] W. G. McAdoo, *Crowded Years*, p. 143.

1880, Garfield's speech nominating John Sherman helped to secure his own nomination, and in 1896 Bryan made the most famous of all convention orations :

"Having behind us the producing masses of this nation and the world, supported by the commercial interests, the labouring interests and the toilers everywhere, we will answer their demand for a gold standard by saying to them : You shall not press down upon the brow of labour this crown of thorns, you shall not crucify mankind upon a cross of gold ! "

The Convention adjourned in hysterics, and for once a speech had won a nomination. An embittered " sound-money " delegate might whisper " confusion now hath made her masterpiece " and another critic declare later that Bryan was like the Platte River of his own Nebraska, " six inches deep and six miles wide at the mouth ", but the Democrats had given themselves a master whose authority had had no rival since the days of Stephen Douglas.

Next, although at a long distance, ranks the effort of Colonel Robert Ingersoll in the Republican Convention of 1876 when the widespread suspicions of Blaine's probity were repelled, if not cured, by a famous image. " Like a plumed knight, James G. Blaine marched down the halls of the American Congress, and threw his shining lance full and fair against the brazen forehead of every traitor to his country and every maligner of his fair reputation." However, the Convention decided that there were too many chinks in the armour of the " Plumed Knight " for Blaine to be a safe candidate in a very doubtful year.

Even if the orators do not win votes in the Convention, they may win votes in the campaign, for slogans struck off in the Convention play an important part in the election. When Roosevelt and his followers left the Republican Convention in 1912, the speech of protest delivered that night at a mass meeting, if it left the Taft rump unmoved, was responsible for the very effective campaign slogan, " We stand at Armageddon and we battle for the Lord " and the epithet, " the Happy Warrior ", with which Mr. Franklin D. Roosevelt presented the candidacy of Mr. Al Smith at the Convention of 1924 lasted until the differences between the two statesmen made its use tactless.

A power which is difficult to assess is that of the galleries. Conventions are held in vast halls, sometimes built for the purpose, and the galleries are full of spectators who take an active part in cheering, singing, shouting, banner-waving and badge-wearing. As the delegates have all a strong desire to back a winner, the voice of the galleries is sometimes taken for the voice of the people. It is thus, normally, an advantage to have the

Convention held in one's own state. It was the opinion of Blaine and other good judges that to this Lincoln owed his nomination in 1860. The most formidable opponent of the Republicans was sure to be Stephen Douglas of Illinois and the politicians and spectators from that state were able to assure wavering delegates that only Lincoln could defeat the " Little Giant " in his own state. When the Republican Convention of 1880 was held in Chicago, it was thought to be an augury of success for Grant who was technically a citizen of Illinois. There is another side to this, however, for good judges think that the vociferous support of Al Smith by the galleries at the New York Convention of 1924 did him more harm than good. When it had become practically certain that he would be the nominee in 1928, it was prudent to fix the Convention in the South since the great problem was to hold that section loyal, but despite the compliment paid Texas by the choice of Houston, that state went for Mr. Hoover.

Nevertheless, the voice of the people is heard from the audience at least as much as from the delegates, if the sections of the people are not equally represented. A Republican orator, at the Chicago Convention of 1932, was so ill advised as to tell the galleries to shut up as they were not delegates, laying himself open to the ominous retort, " We are voters." If the delegates represented any definite policy or had a personality of the first rank to lead them, they might disdain the galleries, but seeking a winner above all, they would be more than human if they were not influenced by their surroundings. But party strategy is not the only factor in the choice of a convention city. A Convention is an expensive business and the honour of receiving the delegates is bid for by the shopkeepers and hotels of the various cities, for it is deemed a good advertisement to house the Convention. The convenience of the delegates has also to be considered, and consequently the Convention normally meets in the Middle West, and no city can rival Chicago in the number of times it has been honoured by the national parties.[1] In 1932 both parties met in that city, in the same hall and using in these hard times a good deal of common material in the way of seats, flags, decorations as well as the customary common stock of perorations and images.

Although the general structure of the Conventions is similar, there are marked differences between the Democrats and the Republicans in the rules and in the spirit of their assemblies. One of these differences is due to the very different prospects of the two parties. The Republican nomination is, as a rule,

[1] The Democrats travel farther than their rivals. They have gone to San Francisco (1920) ; New York (1924) ; Houston (1928).

equivalent to election. It is a great prize which the party confers on one of its members and it matters little who gets it, victory follows as a matter of course. The nominee, then, is chosen less for his appeal to the country at large than for his availability, for his appeal to the ruling forces within the party. A Republican convention is, consequently, duller than a Democratic one ; its nominee may be impossible to foresee, but the kind of nominee easy to guess. If there is one strong figure in the party his enemies will combine to beat him, if there are several, they will eliminate each other as Johnson, Lowden and Wood did in 1920. The only really lively Conventions of the dominant party in recent times have been those of 1912 and 1916, and in each case this was due to Roosevelt, who had a great body of personal supporters whose adherence was necessary to ensure Republican victory. In each case the rulers of the party thought victory not worth the price.

A Democratic Convention is a very different kind of assembly. It knows that its chances of victory depend very largely on the candidate it nominates. The candidate must be stronger than the party, he must have, or appear to have, the power of winning over dissident Republicans in sufficient numbers to give the minority party a fighting chance. For this reason a Democratic candidate once chosen is, as long as the campaign lasts, much more definitely in control than is his Republican opposite number. The one has to go all out to win, the other, normally, has merely to avoid egregious blunders and allow the normal Republican majority to register its will. It is for this reason that the average Republican candidate is of lesser calibre than the Democrat. The Democrat could, perhaps, have nominated a Harding ; they could never have elected him, except, possibly, in 1932.

There are, in addition, important procedural differences between the two Conventions. In the Republican Convention, a bare majority nominates ; in the Democratic Convention the candidate must have two-thirds of the votes cast and those votes are usually in the beginning, cast according to the " unit rule ". The two-thirds rule dates from the days of Andrew Jackson, who invented it to aid his nominee, Martin Van Buren, and Van Buren was its first victim, for, in 1844, he had a majority of the delegates but was held up by the two-thirds rule and the nomination went to the first dark horse, Polk. Only once since then has the rule kept a candidate who had a majority of the delegates on any ballot, from the nomination. In 1912 Champ Clark had a majority but could not get two-thirds and Wilson was chosen. It is impossible to limit the effects of the rule to these two instances, for there are other cases where it is possible, or probable, that a candidate would have got the majority of delegates, if a majority would have made him the candidate. Such was the possibility which the rule denied Mr. W. G. McAdoo in 1924. The effect of the rule is to give a minority of the party a veto on the candidate. The Democratic party to-day, more than ever, represents two hostile sections, held together by old associations. The control of the party by one section is made difficult by the two-thirds rule and has thus a pragmatic justification, for a candidate who cannot rally two-thirds of the delegates has no chance of winning the election. The attempt of the Roosevelt forces at the Democratic Convention of 1932 to repeal, by a majority, the two-thirds rule failed and it was a confession of weakness and doubt to attempt it. A Convention which was willing to overthrow the century-old rule would be willing to give two-thirds of its votes to the candidate who was seeking the alteration—or a nomination got in this way would be worthless.

A corollary of the two-thirds rule is the " unit rule ". If the party in the state has so decided, the whole vote of the state is cast for the candidate supported by a majority of the delegates from that state. Otherwise it might be difficult to muster a two-thirds majority for any candidate. This produces some paradoxical results. As a delegate from New York, Mr. W. G. McAdoo was forced to vote with the rest of the delegates for Harmon, although he was one of the Wilson leaders. Bryan, even after his breach with Clark, had to vote for him with the rest of the Nebraska delegation. The unit rule strengthens the hands of the bosses and leaders and in a Democratic convention, the leaders of Tammany Hall in control of all the ninety New York delegates—or even of two-thirds of them—are continually watched by the other delegates who have a deep respect for the power and skill of the Tiger.

Nevertheless, from the point of view of the western delegates, the Tammany support is often a handicap. The Wigwam's frequent differences of opinion with leading Democrats in its own state are reflected in the Convention where a candidate may wilt under the assertion that he *cannot* carry New York—an assertion that the Convention often takes as a threat that Tammany will see that he *does* not. In 1884 the threat was used against Cleveland, but the Convention was resolved to pick a candidate who could win over dissident Republicans and, as General Bragg put it, loved Cleveland " for the enemies he had made ". In 1892 the same threats were uttered in an impassioned oration by the " Tammany Demosthenes ", Bourke Cockran, but the Convention was again faithful to Cleveland. The most brilliant handling of the Tammany dictatorship was the work of Bryan in 1912. Resolved to stop the nomination of any conservative candidate, whether from disinterested zeal or because of a lingering hope that a deadlock would force the Convention to run " the perpetual candidate " for the fourth time, he rallied the radical delegates to oppose any candidate who was supported by the powers of Wall Street, present in the persons of August Belmont and Thomas Fortune Ryan, and the powers of Tammany Hall, represented by the ninety delegates from New York under the orders of Charles Murphy. Breaking the unit rule which bound him to support Champ Clark, he refused to support any candidate who was also supported by Tammany. This bold stroke practically disfranchised the New York delegates, ended Champ Clark's chances and gave the Democratic party a new dictator in the person of Woodrow Wilson, for that master politician had defied the advice of his timid manager, McCombs, and declared himself for Bryan's side of the battle. In every Democratic convention the battle has to be fought out, shall the party lean to the East or the West, to Tammany or to the embattled farmers ? As a rule the lead is given by the Republican Convention : if it has gone one way, the Democrats must go the other, or throw up the sponge. For this reason, the Democratic is held after the Republican Convention ; the candidate and the platform are dissenting reports.

In normal times, the Republican nominee is the choice of the bosses and leaders ; there is much that is cut and dried about the whole proceedings and the popular belief that the whole affair is " in the bag " has some justification. The nomination of Harding, especially, was the subject of all sorts of legends, and in popular belief the choice of the man who was to lead America out of the European morass was made by a handful of Senators and bosses in a Chicago hotel bedroom.[1]

Corresponding action by Democratic bosses could only make a candidate, and if there were no popular support behind the candidate, all the art would be wasted. The Democratic Convention has to decide whether it will retain its historic character of the party of the dissidents and appeal to the West to join the South or whether it will cater to the East and let the West go. It has tried both ways with success. Cleveland was successful as a conservative " business man's " candidate, Wilson as a radical promising deliverance from Wall Street. Every Democratic Convention among other squabbles has to settle this one. The decision is hard to make, for it may not be at all certain which policy will pay or whether the paying policy is open to the

[1] " That President Harding was nominated at Chicago as a result of a clever trick arranged by Col. George W. [sic] Harvey, and that Harvey was made ambassador to England as a reward " (G. J. Nathan, An American Credo, Art. 1016).

party. But the objective of cheers, speeches, songs, gallery demonstrations, is the same, to convince the delegates that the favourite of the moment is going to win the nomination and the election. Get that idea into the heads of the delegates and the battle is half-won. The balloting then takes on the character of a poker game. An immense show of strength at the beginning may overawe opposition—or it may concentrate hostility on the most formidable candidate. When it was realized that Hanna had his pockets full of Negro delegates in 1896, the nomination of McKinley was assured, for the Whites hastened to follow the lead of their astute coloured brethren, but it takes a keen judge to decide when a candidate has a royal flush and when he is bluffing. To know when to release one's delegates, and to whom, is important for a leader who has despaired of winning with his own man. At Baltimore in 1912, McCombs, Wilson's manager, was ready to abandon the game, when he was given a tip by Roger Sullivan that the opposition was cracking.

The test of resourcefulness in a manager comes when the tide is running strongly in favour of one candidate ; if in favour of his candidate, how is he to maintain the impression that fortune has now declared herself ; how to avoid the painful moment when the tide hesitates and then begins to ebb? If another candidate is winning, the problem is even more difficult. His own legions may be held in line, but the auxiliaries from the other states who have been won over, or are in the process of being won over, are only too ready to desert to the winner. In the first case, it is all-important to keep the balloting going on. The weather may help. Conventions are held in June ; it is usually very hot ; the delegates are increasingly uncomfortable and anxious to have it over ; they pay their own expenses and have no motive to linger. Before now, the choice of a convention has been as much due to the heat as to anything else ; this is especially true of the nomination of the vice-presidential candidate, and some hold that it was mere impatience that induced the Convention of 1920 to put Mr. Coolidge in the way of becoming President. On the other hand, if the Convention is *very* hot and weary, it may adjourn to the next day to get some sleep and other refreshment, and such an adjournment, it was thought, stopped the tide which was flowing strongly for Seward in 1860 and thus made Lincoln President. Another adjournment, which proved fatal to the ambitions of Blaine, occurred in 1876, when the gas went out and the Convention had to postpone the possibly decisive ballots till the next day, when enthusiasm for the " Plumed Knight " had waned beyond recovery. Convenient darkness of this kind was an old Tammany trick, but on this occasion the accident, so helpful to the enemies of Blaine, was suspected to be connected with the presence of that Pennsylvania master, Matthew Quay. But as one candidate approaches a decisive majority, the resistance of the minority candidates begins to crack. All manner of temptation is put in the way of the leaders who are still holding out, promises or half-promises of patronage or the second place on the ticket. At last the delegates of some favourite son are released. In 1932 in the Democratic Convention, it was the acceptance by Speaker Garner of the nomination for the vice-presidency which, probably, represented the reward of the throwing of the vote of Texas and California to Governor Roosevelt and the collapse of the resistance to the nomination of the New Yorker.

Indeed, the reasons advanced by one of his chief supporters for the nomination of Mr. Harding illustrate, at their lowest, the motives which guide some of the delegates, or their leaders, all of the time and all of them some of the time :

" ' There was ', said Harvey, afterward, ' no popular explosion for Harding. There was little spontaneity. He was nominated because there was nothing against him, and because the delegates wanted to go home. The delegates had become convinced that neither Wood nor Lowden could be or ought to be nominated, and they could not see anybody who would serve better as a candidate than Harding. There was no compromise about the matter. It was a fresh selection of the man whom the delegates considered the best in sight.' " [1]

It is not often, if ever, that a national party reaches the level of the 1920 Convention, but the natural drift is towards putting down the mighty from their seats in favour of the docile.

There is a last-minute rush to aid the victor ; the fatal announcement is made and, with what grace they may, the representatives of the beaten aspirants agree to make the nomination unanimous, save when an embittered leader refuses to pay this lip-service to party harmony, as Roscoe Conkling did in 1880 and Mr. Al Smith in 1932. The Convention has done its real business and interest is abruptly switched to the candidate, normally many hundreds of miles distant, playing the part of a Cincinnatus ready to be called from his plough or, in one case, from the river where he was ostentatiously bathing.

Coming before the nomination in time, but far behind it in importance, is the " platform ". The planks in this necessary piece of party furniture are as variegated as possible, and, in many campaigns, the alteration of a few words would have made the platform of one party available for the other. Since neither

[1] *George Harvey*, by W. F. Johnson, p. 278.

party is attached to any body of doctrine, the Convention has to decide for four years what line, if any, the party is to take on the current issues. It has to combine two possibly incompatible objects ; to adopt a policy and a candidate who will appeal to the country and, at the same time, to reflect the dominant opinion of the party. If, as frequently happens, there is no dominant section in the party, at any rate as far as policy is concerned, all hands can be turned to selecting a winner in the country. If there really are issues, the unpleasant task of finding a *via media* between the extremes of " yes " and " no " devolves upon the party strategists and is sometimes beyond them.

It is, happily, seldom that a plank, much less a whole platform, is of sufficient importance for a fight to be made over it, and when there is a fight it is a sign that the part is dangerously rent by dissensions. In 1860, at Charleston, the Democrats of North and South could not agree on a compromise and the party split. Despite all the manœuvres of Mark Hanna, the Republican Convention of 1896 could not find a formula that would mean silver to the silver men and gold to the gold men, so the silverites, with a great deal of dignity, left the Convention and were soon supporting Bryan. In 1924, the bitterest fight of the long Democratic Convention was fought on the desirability of making the Convention denounce the Ku Klux Klan by name, but the fight was made on that point by the resolute leaders of the opposition to Mr. McAdoo, as a means of putting that candidate's supporters into a corner. Normally, the platform is a series of platitudes and of vague promises, interspersed with denunciations of the opposite party and fervent appeals to past glories. The less it has to say on current issues, the better the party leaders are pleased :

> " The more issues a party meets, the less votes it is likely to poll. And for a very simple reason : you cannot keep the citizenship of a nation like this bound to its allegiance to two large parties unless you make the grounds of allegiance very simple and very obvious." [1]

The final result of so much carpentry is at last turned out and the traditionally necessary job is over.

If the contents of the platforms do not differ from party to party there is a difference in the spirit of the two documents. The Republicans, as the party in office, have usually an opportunity, if no particular reason, for " pointing with pride " to their achievements ; the Democrats have to attack this claim, and in normal times the American people loves a " booster ", not a

[1] Walter Lippman, *Preface to Politics*, p. 257.

" knocker ". The difference was more marked a generation
ago than it is now, but there was an unmistakable note of legitimate authority in Republican platforms that has not yet wholly
disappeared and which is, apparently, beyond Democratic
power to imitate. " When, in the economy of Providence, this
land was to be purged of human slavery, and when the strength
of government of the people by the people and for the people
was to be demonstrated, the Republican party came into power." [1]

A generation later the note is the same. In 1904, the happy
exclusion of the traitors and rascals from office, " is not due to
chance ". It is a demonstration that:

> " the Republican party has commanded the confidence of the
> American people for nearly two generations to a degree never
> equalled in our history, and has displayed a high capacity for
> rule and government which has been made even more con-
> spicuous by the incapacity and infirmity of purpose shown by
> its opponents : "

and in 1924 :

> " The tasks to which we have put our hands are completed.
> Time has been too short for the correction of all the ills we
> received as a heritage from the last Democratic administration,
> and the notable accomplishments under Republican rule
> warrant us in appealing to the country with entire confidence."

The Democrats could in 1880 " execrate the course of this
administration in making places in the civil service a reward
for political crime ", and demand " a reform by statute which
shall make it for ever impossible for a defeated candidate [Hayes]
to bribe his way to the seat of the usurper by billeting villains
upon the people ", but these complaints and somewhat remote
achievements could hardly have the appeal of the Republican
proclamations. In 1916, indeed, the success of the first Wilson
administration offered a chance which was gladly taken ; the
initiative was taken out of Republican hands with gratifying
results, but normally the Republicans are smug and the Democrats plaintive.

After these general proclamations come the specific proposals.
They are vague and remote and are, as far as possible, incapable
of precise application ; farmers are promised relief ; law is
promised enforcement ; economy is combined with hints of
generosity in the proper quarters, and on all really controversial
questions the candidate is committed to being on both sides of
the fence, if not actually perched on it.

[1] Platform of 1876.

This programme of pious opinions and pious hopes is some-times not enough. In 1896 the Democratic platform did take a determined stand on free silver, taking over the stock-in-trade of the Populists whose million votes of 1892 they were angling for.[1] In 1904, the Convention nominated a Gold Democrat on a money plank open to two or more constructions, but the candidate, Judge Parker, threw the platform overboard and the Convention had to swallow the insult. In 1928 the Democrats nominated a " wet " candidate on a dry platform, but Governor Smith refused to sail under false colours. The platform is a concession to the superstition that the American national parties are parties of opinion ; that they must have a common political belief and programme. Since this is false, the platforms must be mostly nonsense. They were put at their true worth by Senator Aldrich who, when taxed with neglecting the party platform, admitted, with no appearance of discomfiture, that he had never read the document.[2]

The damage wrought by the Prohibition controversy to the old party ways was illustrated, in 1932, by the conflicts in both parties over the planks dealing with the most controversial of questions. It took all the pressure applied from the White House to induce the Republican Convention to accept the " straddle " on this question. The compromise " wet-dry " plank which was adopted was put over by the votes of states in the South and West. The plank was an attempt to be all things to all men ; to hold at the same time the votes of those who think prohibition an experiment noble in more than purpose and the rampant eastern wets of the school of Dr. Nicholas Murray Butler who must be given an excuse for sticking to the G.O.P. Almost inevitably, the Democrats had to take a more definite stand. In another year they might have gone " dry ", but the Republican party is the party of the *status quo* and the Democrats naturally join the attacking side. Prohibition and the Republican party were in possession and on the defensive ; the Democrats had to give up the game or attack. They attacked, by coming out for repeal of the amendment, gambling, that is, on the drift away from the drys and successfully playing on party discipline holding the South, hitherto the great dry stronghold.

But it is rare that an issue is so frankly made and the rest of both platforms consists of vague generalities of the traditional

[1] The only modern platform of any intrinsic merit or interest is the powerful manifesto drawn up for the Populists of 1892 by Ignatius Donnelly.

[2] Lord Snowden, once a member of a party that was supposed to take its programme seriously, was not ashamed to admit he had not read the Labour programme on which, in theory, the party had fought the election of 1929 which restored him to office.

kind. It is not only the Democrats, as the Washington corre-
spondent of *The Times* has suggested, who should go forth to battle
under the banner of Joseph's coat ; both parties, whenever they
can manage it, offer a platform and a candidate who can stand
on it comfortably, announcing :

> " Ez to my princerples, I glory
>   In hevin' nothin' o' the sort ;
> I ain't a Wig, I ain't a Tory,
>   I'm jest a candidate in short."

In the great reforming wave of 1904–16, it was natural
that the Convention system should be attacked. Although the
most indefensible of presidential nominations was still in the
future, there had been, in the past, performances which took
a good deal of explaining away and it was natural that there
should have arisen a demand for the extension of the primary
system to the national Conventions. A number of states did
adopt the presidential primary and the election of 1912 tested
the efficacy of the system. In such states as had primaries,
Roosevelt ran far ahead ; nevertheless, the Republican Convention nominated Taft ; in the Democratic primaries, Wilson
was a good deal ahead of Clark, but his nomination owed more
to skilful handling in the Convention than to the will of the
people expressed at the primaries. These experiences seemed,
to the reformers, to justify a complete overhaul of the system and
a universal presidential primary was one of the proposed reforms
of the Wilson administration. It has got no further and there is
little sign, at the moment, of any enthusiasm for the further
extension of the primaries or for giving them more than a moderate
moral weight. To-day, the primaries merely serve to sort out
the leading contenders for the nomination ; to give a lead to the
Convention in the all-important question of availability. Thus
the defeat of Governor Roosevelt by Mr. Al Smith in the Massachusetts primary was important, not because it was any final indication of how the Massachusetts vote would go, but as interfering
with the apparently easy victory of Governor Roosevelt since that
victory depended, as is usual, on the belief that it was inevitable.
Even more acute than the anxiety of the Democratic delegates to
pick a winner among the contenders in the Convention, is the desire
to pick one who will also appeal to the country and so a primary
vote serves to indicate what appeal a candidate will have in the
various sections. If it had been decided to cater to the industrial
East, it was important to have some idea if any other eastern
candidate would appeal to Massachusetts, for instance, as
strongly as the primary indicated Governor Smith would. If
it had been decided to cater to the West, it was important to

reflect on the strength shown by Governor Murray in so typically discontented a rural state as North Dakota. In this calculation it is important not merely to find out who appeals most, but to how many he appeals ; thus the high Democratic vote in the Democratic primary in North Dakota had a value as an indication, not to be attached to Speaker Garner's victory in California in a poll which in itself gave deceptively little hope of detaching that state from Mr. Hoover.

A candidate may be far stronger with the politicians than he is with the voters of the party, far stronger with the unattached than with the faithful. From 1896 to 1912, there was no doubt that Bryan was the idol of the rank and file of the Democrats and little doubt that he could not carry an election. Unfortunately when in 1904 Parker was nominated in an effort to appease the conservative East, he lost far more disgusted Bryanites than he won Republicans or Mugwumps. The Convention has a task of great complexity, a task fundamentally diplomatic, and unwieldy and ill-organized as it is, it is far more fit to do its job than any substitute yet suggested. It is with wisdom that the American people have refused to extend the primary system to the nominating of candidates for the presidency. Most of the arguments in favour of the primary in the state lose all force when applied to the primary in the nation. The local primary has restored reality to local parties and local politics ; it has given a meaning to empty names, but it is the essential character of the national parties that they should be empty bottles, which can be filled with whatever contents the immediate necessities of the case demand. To ask of the parties that they should have a permanent policy is to ask of them to commit suicide, unless at the same time politics can be effectually nationalized. The convention system with its compromises, its vague platforms and its often vague candidates is, like the parties themselves, a pragmatic acquiescence in the main fact of American politics, its sectionalism.

In these questions of party strategy, the primary can give useful information, but it cannot and should not do more. The verdict to be given must be given by such a jury as a Convention ; the voters in the primary are only witnesses. The present national parties and the national Conventions stand or fall together. The chief task of the national parties is to induce the heterogeneous mass of the American people to act as two units once every four years for the object of electing a President. It is a task of great difficulty, calling for diplomatic management, a task for which the Convention may be ill fitted, but for which the primary is not fitted at all.

Chapter II

THE TICKET

THE considerations governing party strategy in the first manœuvres of a campaign are most easily illustrated in a study of a presidential nomination, but fundamentally, the rules are the same for all offices. In the choice of a candidate for any office from the presidency down, availability is one of the chief, certainly the most regularly marketable asset. Will a nomination strengthen the ticket, or if the ticket does not need strengthening, will the nomination be a reward to the deserving and docile or breed discontent in more formidable figures who are passed over, or worse still, reveal unsuspected ambition in the favoured one? There are practical politicians who believe that such radicals as the late Senator La Follette could have been kept " regular " if they had not, by untimely severity on the part of the bosses, been forced to strike out for themselves. There are others who believe that it is well to teach the aspiring that there is only one way to success, " to play in with " the rulers of the party and take what they choose to give. For this school, the late Murray Crane of Massachusetts was the master politician and the career of Mr. Coolidge an encouragement to the well-disciplined politician who, in contemplating it, may be led to believe that all comes to him who bides his time and does his duty in the stations to which it pleases the party rulers or ruler to call him.

The two parties have, in the main, two different approaches to this problem. As with the presidency so with minor offices, the Republican nomination is usually an asset to be given to a deserving member, the Democratic nomination an opportunity for a fight offered to a candidate who must bring his own strength to the ticket to have a sporting chance. There are areas, outside the Solid South, where this is not true, especially in local politics. In New York and, in normal times, in Boston, it is the Republican candidate who is fighting a forlorn hope, and so the nomination is given to a candidate who carries weight for his name, such as Theodore Roosevelt, Jr., or to a vigorous fighter like Mr. Ogden Mills who was later rewarded with the reversion of the Treasury for the strain of having stood up to

Al Smith at the height of his popularity. As a rule, however, the Republican nomination is the more valuable, as may be seen by comparing the kind of Senator who can carry Ohio on the G.O.P. ticket with the timber the Democrats have to employ in the same position. A Democrat of great personal popularity is in a stronger position for forcing a nomination on his party than is a Republican. If Theodore Roosevelt had been a Democrat and, making the very large assumption that he had become President all the same, he would in all probability have been able to force his own nomination in 1912. The mere party assets of the Democrats are in most states not enough. Thus Mr. Al Smith was stronger than his party in New York and was able to make his own terms in 1922, notably he was able to refuse to run on the same ticket as Mr. W. R. Hearst. Carter Harrison I was much stronger in Chicago than his party, and even his son, Carter Harrison II, though not such an irresistible campaigner as his father, was an asset that the Democrats had reason to regret discarding. In normal times, it takes a Democrat of wealth, family and respected public spirit like Mr. James Phelan to make a real fight for the Democrats in California and a man like Senator Bulow in South Dakota runs far ahead of the rest of the Democratic ticket. In such circumstances what can the minority party do but cater to the tastes of the electorate? For the same reason, the Democrats have to welcome and use very recent recruits to the party while the Republicans, except in such crises as that of 1896, can afford to be offhand with these eleventh-hour labourers. The career of " Ben " Butler in Massachusetts fifty years ago illustrates this point, for the Republicans would hardly have welcomed so recently returned a prodigal with the eagerness displayed by their rivals. In the same state, twenty years ago, the Democratic acceptance of Mr. Eugene Foss revealed the same diffidence. If Mr. Foss could carry over his personal following to his new party, he could get on the ticket at once. It is a natural and perhaps a paying policy, but the labourers of the first hour have always been a little resentful of the fact that when there is a chance to win, the honours are in danger of going to a new recruit without even a decent interval of probation.

In making up the ticket, whether that ticket has to be put over in a primary, or to be announced through a hand-picked Convention in the good old Connecticut fashion, what material is available to the party chiefs? At least a century old is the complaint that American politics have no place for a gentleman. The picture of the resentful better classes, paying lip-service to the democratic system which debars them from their due place in the state, has not much altered from the days of Tocqueville. Yet the picture is less true now than it was a century ago, less true relatively, that is. Compared with England, the America of Jackson's time was a levelling community. In England, Jackson himself could no more have come to the top in politics than in war ; instead of duplicating the career of Wellington, he would have remained a sergeant and, at most, a political publican. But in the century that has gone past, England has changed more than has the United States and there is less to pick to-day between the two sets of politicians than is popularly supposed. Such differences as do exist are due far more to the general social structure of the two countries than to any specific democratic prejudice in the one country or aristocratic reverence in the other.

In the present House of Commons, there are over a hundred Etonians ; it is impossible to imagine a corresponding flooding of Congress by Groton and St. Paul's, but then it is impossible to imagine that Groton or St. Paul's are Eton. It is not merely the locality rule that prevents the flooding of districts all over the country with elegant young men, but the whole social structure of the country which hinders the creation of such a type. The English aristocratic class sets the tone for all aspirants through its centralized character, through the handful of first-class schools, through the two ancient universities, through the reduction of all standards to the London standards. In this sense America has no capital, no unified aristocracy ; it has not and cannot have a class which takes to politics naturally, as it does to sport, but with less seriousness and less permanent devotion. But it is not the exclusion from politics of Mr. Bertie Wooster and the rest of the " Drones Club " that the critics of American democracy profess to lament, but the obstacle presented by the vulgarity and baseness of American politics to the young man of wealth who would serve the state. This obstacle is, if existent at all, far less formidable than it is fashionable to believe. The theory that what politics need is more attention from the rich has already been discussed, but it is worth noting that even those who shared the fundamental illusion that business neglected politics, did not always share its collateral belief that politics were impossible for a gentleman. Godkin briefly dismissed this superstition :

> " I am unable at this moment to mention a single man who, being qualified by culture or character for a political career, has been shut out from it by popular dislike of his mental, moral or social excellencies." [1]

[1] Rollo Ogden, *Life and Letters of Edwin Lawrence Godkin*, vol. i, p. 314.

What was true in 1867 is still true to-day. Men of wealth, education and leisure enter American politics at no disadvantage ; they enter it at an advantage.

It will not surprise anyone who knows the sacred place of genealogy in American life, to learn that the politician who gets in on his father's reputation, or even of his grandfather's, is common enough. When the *Springfield Republican* declared nearly fifty years ago that " ' there is no further-going ancestry in America than that of Henry Cabot Lodge ' " [1] it put its finger on one of the chief assets of that eminent politician. The long life of the Frelinghuysen name, if not of the family, in New Jersey ; the four generations of Bayards in the Senate testifying to the loyalty of Delaware ; the ramifications of the Saulsbury clan in the same state, ending in a typically eighteenth-century English alliance with the Du Pont family ; these examples recall the Herbert-Clive connections in Shropshire and the Blackett-Trevelyan connection in Newcastle whose importance we have learned from Professor Namier. Even the vast polyglot state of New York has, in the Wadsworths of Geneseo, a political family of the first rank.

These are cases of political families based on local economic and social prominence, but they can be paralleled from families which have not this solid foundation for their ambitions. The Adams family with its long list of public men down to Mr. Hoover's Secretary of the Navy ; the Harrisons, who numbered in their clan a " Signer of the Declaration ", two Presidents and, still more remarkable, two Mayors of Chicago, are hard to equal, but they are not alone. The political careers of the sons of Lincoln, Grant, Roosevelt, were certainly not impeded by the shadows of the founders of the family and even though the Democrats objected to the Republicans running Fred Grant as an attempt to introduce a peerage system, they did the same thing when they made George B. McClellan II, Mayor of New York, and Tammany, in recent times, was pleased to show its respect for one of the great names of the Democratic party by employing a Gallatin as a Park Commissioner.[2]

[1] Quoted in F. Curtis, *History of the Republican Party*, vol. ii, p. 119.

[2] It should be remembered that in America pedigrees are not necessarily proof of wealth. The American Durbeyfields do not forget their D'Urberville origin, no matter how poor they may be, and such a tribune of the plain people as " Alfalfa Bill " Murray of Oklahoma may live like a Poor White, but he boasts his descent from Pocahontas and has even written a book on genealogy.

It should also be remembered that the claims of aristocracy may differ in different countries. A Chinese who reverenced a descendant of Confucius might be ashamed at a robber-baron pedigree which would have dazzled Proust, and it is childish to laugh at such a boast of aristocracy as that made by a southern Senator who married into the " first family to cross the Yadkin on wheels ".

It may be said, however, that these cases are comparatively rare, that it is hard to parallel the centuries-old political importance of the Stanley family round Liverpool. It is, but it is also hard to parallel the economic importance of the Derby estate round Liverpool over so long a period, and does anyone imagine that the political weight attaching to the Earldom of Derby would have long survived the loss of the wealth or even of the transference of the wealth out of South Lancashire ? Political power accrues to economic power in America just as easily and inevitably as it does in England. The moment he put out his hand to take it, the political dominance of the Pittsburgh areas fell to Mr. Andrew Mellon as a function of his financial power, as it did to the rulers of the Anaconda Copper Company in Montana, of the Southern Pacific Railroad in California, of the Du Pont de Nemours Company in Delaware. As long as the Mellon family are dominant in western Pennsylvania, they can have as much political power as they want to pay for ; as was true of the Russells, Cavendishes and the rest of the Venetian oligarchy in eighteenth-century England. Of course, in both countries, the rise of a popular movement with real vigour in it may put the magnate in the position of having to make terms with the new political powers or of having to give way. Even in this case, it will often be found that there is a weakening in the relative economic power of the millionaire or corporation involved. The California revolt against " The Octopus ", the defeat of the Anaconda Copper Company in Montana, were, from one point of view, reflections of the relative weakening of the great corporations concerned, as well as being results of a popular upheaval. The success of demagogues like Tillman against aristocrats like Wade Hampton in South Carolina was not merely a belated Jacksonian revolt, but a result of the economic decay of the planter class, a decay whose political results had been delayed for a generation, but could not be delayed for ever.

To the other privileged classes of the American political scene must be added the kin of recently dead statesmen. When Senator Caraway of Arkansas died, the Governor of the State appointed his widow to serve out the rest of the unexpired term on the grounds, publicly stated, that it was her right to succeed her husband in the office which had belonged to him. The lady members of Congress have been almost all relicts of dead members, or daughters of such men of might as Mr. Bryan, and the only woman who has been a formidable contender for a Senate seat, in her own right, was Mrs. Ruth Hanna McCormick, widow of Senator McCormick of Illinois and daughter of the great Mark

Hanna.[1] The succession of Robert La Follette, Jr., to his father's seat is more a sign of the establishment of a new political dynasty in Wisconsin than a mere sentimental tribute, but Congressman Paul Kvale of Minnesota would have had a harder time in getting into Congress if he had not succeeded his father ; just as, before any adventitious aids became unnecessary, Colonel Lindbergh might have made a fight for a seat from the same state on the strength of his father's political service. The election of 1932 has sent Mr. Bennett Champ Clark to the Senate, a tribute to the loyalty of Missouri to the memory of its favourite son as well as to the talents of the new Senator. Nor are other claims than those of wealth and family without political weight. Every American machine or group recognizes the need for at least one or two presentable figures. It was not, in all probability, mere gratitude for forensic services that induced Mr. William Vare to present Mr. James M. Beck to one of his Philadelphia " pocket boroughs ", or Tammany to rejoice in the eloquence of Bourke Cockran. The rulers of the machine feel that in politics there are different gifts and a place for him that exhorteth in exhortation, as for him that ruleth with diligence ; although it is important not to confuse the ministries.[2]

A man of education and good family, if he has any political talent, will not want for bidders. He will be able to start higher up than if he had neither, but if he does not keep up with his proletarian rivals, the fault is likely to be his own. The rules of the game will not be altered for his benefit, but none of them really prejudice the issue against the gentleman. It was not because he had been educated in the Fulton Street Fish Market that Mr. Al Smith beat Mr. Theodore Roosevelt II or Mr. Ogden Mills, while it is possible that neither of these gentlemen would have gone so far in politics as they have, had they not had the aid of wealth or of a great name.

There remains a third class of gentleman politician ; the " fat cat " whose sole claim to office is that he is willing to pay his own expenses—and more than his own expenses, to get the nomination. This type is probably rarer in the United States

[1] One Congresswoman was sent to take the place of her husband who was serving a term for a liquor offence. The mountaineers of eastern Kentucky, good Republicans as they were, would not let this stigma rest on the victim of official zeal and promptly returned the grass widow to Congress, a palpable hint to President Coolidge to restrain his agents.

[2] That startling specimen of the " gentleman and scholar " in politics, Senator Boies Penrose of Pennsylvania, had a clear view of the place of the orator and spokesman in a party machine. " ' I'm not against statesmen. Every party's got to have a few. They're the kept women of politicians. They come in handy when the people get tired of you ' " (Walter Davenport, *Power and Glory*, p. 189).

than in England.   Every House of Commons contains its share of
" fat cats ", chiefly, although not exclusively, on the Conservative
benches.   It is doubtful if any American machine would be as
frank as are the Conservative Associations of English " safe
seats " which openly demand from the prospective candidate
contributions far in excess of his salary and this in constituencies
where there can be no normal election expenses, since there is
never a real contest.   There are " fat cats " in the other English
parties, too.   The old Irish Nationalist party had its share and
every party which has to help out its candidates with election
or living expenses, is tempted to adopt docile men of wealth
who can be relied on to give with simplicity.

The United States has had many such generous givers in all
ranks of the political hierarchy.   Some become Ambassadors,
many become Senators, sometimes Senators with real political
ability and principle like Senator Couzens of Michigan and
Senator Cutting of New Mexico, sometimes just Senators.   Others
become Governors like the two rival " barrels ", Roswell Flower
of the Democratic party and Levi P. Morton of the Republicans.
Indeed, the career of the latter, with its vice-presidency and its
dreams of the presidency, is probably the most remarkable example
of how far money can eke out political ability in American history.
Nevertheless, it is notable that where there is real fighting to be
done, money is not sufficient ; it is a decided help, but no President between Washington and Mr. Hoover could have been
reasonably called a rich man and the long and futile pursuit of
office and political influence by Mr. Hearst is an object-lesson
to those who think that America worships money as such.

Nothing, then, keeps the wealthy classes out of American
politics but incapacity for successful political action, and this
incapacity is not induced by any moral, æsthetic, or intellectual
superiority.   The American millionaire or even the professional
man has no special handicap of this kind to overcome that
does not equally bar poor men of equal delicacy.   The real
reason why American politics do not attract more men and
women of leisure, is that it is not an occupation for people
of leisure but a whole-time job.   There are few or no opportunities for passive membership such as the House of Commons
offers, where a member may do very tolerably on a nominal
attendance, unless his neglect is so palpable that even Bath
awakens in protest.   As has been explained, a Congressman is
never idle or he ceases to be a Congressman.   On the other hand,
there is very little reason why anyone should want to be a
Congressman, even if the work were lighter or more pleasant.
Parliament may no longer be the best club in Europe, but it is
still a club in the capital.   It involves no separation from the

social life of the upper classes, no exile in a country town, such as
Washington is and even if it is only moderately agreeable, it
promises real rewards to those who take it seriously. Congress
may provide an amusement for a Nicholas Longworth or a
stepping-stone for Mr. Ogden Mills, but it is a dead-end for
most of its members. The Senate is another matter, but there
has never been any difficulty in getting candidates of wealth,
breeding and education to go to great, one can almost say any,
lengths to enter it.

If there is still a place kept at the American political board
for the man of family, there is a still better one kept for the
representative of the older stocks who allies himself with the
politicians, especially if he supports the Democrats. There are
first of all, the Southerners, or the sons of Southerners, who find
their hereditary allegiance to the party not much of an asset,
unless they care to turn it to political advantage. Then, it is
asserted, they do very well. It was such a family membership
of the Democratic party that opened the way to Woodrow
Wilson, to Mr. McAdoo and to many others, somewhat to the
annoyance of the representatives of the stocks that supplied most
of the voting and fighting strengths. Not only Southerners
benefit by such considerations. It is only in this generation
that the leaders of the Democratic party in the North-east
have been largely drawn from the Irish who are its chief
supporters. Governor David Walsh in Massachusetts, Governor
Al Smith in New York, are among the conspicuous specimens, but there is still a belief in the drawing power of representatives of the old stocks such as Governor Ely of Massachusetts and Governor Cross of Connecticut. The policy may
be unpopular with the professional Democrat, but it pays.

But if for the more ornamental offices there is still a bias in
favour of candidates of " American " origin, there is also a high
degree of sensitiveness in the other racial blocks that must be
catered for. When " Big Bill " Thompson attacked King George
and exalted the heroes of the American Revolution, he won the
hearts of hundreds of thousands who had no ancestral connection
with the Revolution and no traditional hostility to King George,
but who saw in him the " King of the Nordics ", of the " better
elements " which they distrusted as the French radical distrusts
the " gens bien ". To secure party success there must be a
higher synthesis of all these hates and fears, and it is the making
up of lists of candidates to cater to all these factions and sections
that tests the tact of a politician and was one of the soundest
reasons advanced by politicians for opposing the direct primary.
Under the primary a candidate may be imposed on the party
who represents one racial section but has no outside strength ;

such, it was asserted, was the explanation of the nomination of
Fiorella La Guardia to run against " Jimmy " Walker in 1929,
with disastrous results.   In the same way, there have been
Democratic candidates in Massachusetts and New York who
represented the centres of party strength, Boston and New York
City, but had little appeal to the rest of the state.   Such blunders
impress upon the managers the desirability of cultivating tact
in dealing with all voting groups and using both the platform
and the ticket, to win over blocks of voters held together by
sympathies that have little or nothing to do with the current
American political issues—if any.[1] This takes two forms : in
the choice of candidates and in the use of the platform to
win racial support.   The latter is the easier of the two methods,
since it costs little.   It reached its height in the period between
the rise of Parnell and the establishment of the Irish Free
State.   Congress permitted " The Chief " to address it and the
recognition of his power in America was an important asset
in Parnell's campaign at home.   Weaned from revolutionary
methods by Parnell, full of national zeal, deeply involved in
politics and numerous enough to be worth conciliating, the
Irish-Americans were for long enough the classical example of
the racial group in politics.   From the days when the Fenian
raids on Canada upset the nervous politicians who had to enforce
neutrality, till the establishment of the Irish Free State, the Irish
vote was catered for with great earnestness, in words if not in
deeds.   The Democrats had the advantage of the natural
adherence of the Irish and in the main they have kept it.   Again
and again the Republicans have attempted to win the Irish, but
they have been more fortunate in seducing leaders than rank and
file.   There was a time when it seemed that Blaine, himself of
Irish origin, would manage to win over his kin, but despite the
zealous aid of Messrs. Patrick Ford and Patrick Egan, the
manœuvre was only partially successful.   In the campaign of

[1] In Britain such considerations have to be borne in mind in many areas.
A Liberal organizer who forgot that the last remnant of the faithful are the
undaunted Nonconformists of the West Country, so far as to take the name,
Liberal, in its literal sense, would soon be out of a job.   In Liverpool, the Conservative party has to consider whether it loses more by antagonizing Orange-
men than it gains by winning Catholics.   Two Catholic M.P.'s of old family
and landed wealth have found that their religion makes them impossible
candidates for otherwise safe Conservative seats.   In the East End of London
and in the Gorbals Division of Glasgow, candidates and programmes are alike
chosen with an eye to the Jewish vote.   To run a Catholic Conservative in
the Ogmore Division of Glamorgan and to induce the withdrawal of an
Independent Protestant candidate in East Stirlingshire are all in the day's
work for the Conservative machine, while the Labour party has to try to
conciliate several brands of religion in order to hold the working classes
together.

1884 Cleveland had to call on all the strength of his party to reassure voters normally Democratic who were being misled by the " Blaine Irishmen"; prominent Irish-Americans like John McCall and Patrick Collins spoke and wrote in defence of Cleveland's religious impartiality and the war was carried into Blaine's camp by such victims of coercion in Ireland as Daniel McSweeney, who assured large audiences all over the land, that Secretary Blaine had done little or nothing for himself and other American citizens when they lay in British dungeons.

For forty years, the platforms of both parties were profuse in vague sympathy for the Irish cause, especially after Gladstone's conversion to Home Rule had made the issue more respectable, but not much good—or harm—was done by such kind words. A Mayor of New York learned that St. Patrick's Day was a public holiday that it was politically unhealthy to slight, and another had reason to fear for the effects on his future of the discovery made by his enemies that he had dined in the British Embassy on the Queen's birthday. In Boston, the happy coincidence that the British had evacuated the city in 1776 on the 17th of March made it easy to cater to two different emotions. The Great War with the executions of the leaders of the 1916 rebellion embittered Irish feeling to an unprecedented degree and cemented their alliance with the Germans. This alliance turned against Wilson in 1916 and its aid was not despised by *all* Republicans, but on the whole it probably did Mr. Hughes more harm than good. The last fling of the old-style Irish-American politician occurred at the Republican Convention of 1920, where various politicians attempted, in vain, to persuade Mr. De Valera (who was present) to take something less than a recognition of the Irish Republic in exchange for the votes he was supposed to control. But although the Convention would not go as far as that, the opponents of the League of Nations had stressed the dangers to Irish freedom involved under the covenant and the picture of the American soldier being sent to keep the land of his fathers under English rule was used with great effect to seduce normally Democratic voters from Wilson's party. The issue is now dead or so near it as makes no difference, to the regret of those citizens to whom it was *the* issue and to others to whom it was a livelihood.[1]

" The German vote " was less constantly to the fore, but it was incensed in 1870–71 by the sale of arms to France, a rehearsal of the great blockade grievance of 1914–17. The services to Germans stranded in Paris rendered by Elihu Washburne when

[1] In England the same results have followed the establishment of the Irish Free State. The " delivery " of the Irish vote to credulous candidates was of considerable benefit to persuasive talkers who have now no visible assets to cash in.

he was minister to France during the Franco-Prussian War, were supposed to have increased his political importance and the parties congratulated both Germany on the new empire and France on the new republic with the greatest good will. For many years the German vote was largely concentrated in Carl Schurz, whose influence over his countrymen was his chief asset. Unlike the Irish leaders, Schurz had no crippling party loyalties ; he worked for the Democrats in 1872, for the Republicans in 1876, served in a Republican Cabinet till 1881, went back to the Democrats from 1884 to 1896 when he joined the G.O.P., returning to the Democrats in 1900 ! As he was believed to carry many thousands of votes back and forth, his support was worth winning and as his political standards were high, he was a stimulating force for good. The hysteria of the World War told hard on the German-Americans and embittered them, not unnaturally. The German-Americans have not forgotten : " Big Bill " Thompson in Chicago, Senator Reed and Senator Hawes in Missouri, have all benefited from German gratitude for their moderation when the Hun hunt was on and when Governor Philip La Follette told the Wisconsin legislature that the people who refused to vote any more money for the relief of distress had " ' squandered $40,000,000,000 of American money in the most wasteful and futile war of modern history ' " [1] he was not merely justifying his father's opposition to the war and defending his own policy, but gratifying the feelings of the Germans of the most German state in the Union.

With the increasing variety of immigration, the difficulties of the politicians grew. It is no great trouble to make the 12th of October a public holiday, and call it Columbus Day. The Italians like it, but it is quite another thing to imply that America was discovered on that day in the year 1492—if you have many Scandinavian voters. Then it is as well to call a street after Leif Ericsson and let the rival claimants to the honour of having produced the discoverer fight it out between themselves. With the coming of the Poles, politicians acquired a much readier sense of the services in the Revolution of Kosciusko and Pulaski, and it is a poor group that cannot work up some claim to recognition. These unimportant exercises of political diplomacy are of no great moment, but it is a more serious matter that Woodrow Wilson's attitude on Fiume should have influenced thousands of Italian voters in the United States ; that Germans should have avenged their wrongs on him and that every diplomatic effort after the war has had to face a barrage of interested criticism. The only palliation is that the various sections tend to cancel each other out and that no section has a clean record. Mr.

---

[1] Quoted in *The Nation*, Dec. 9, 1931.

Mencken does not approach questions of foreign policy without a Germanophil bias, but Wilson and Walter Hines Page approached them with an English bias. Most Americans feel, in their hearts, that they cannot trust each other to handle these questions from any objective standpoint and that the isolationist has some wisdom on his side.

An operation requiring much more skill was the " salting " of the " ticket " with a minimum of candidates who were supposed to have a useful hold on their kinsmen. This device shows no signs of losing its attraction, although it is conceivable that the ending of immigration will in the long run render it unprofitable. Sometimes a party is locally dominated by one group or dependent on it for success. Thus in Rhode Island, if the French-Canadians had no other reasons for being Republicans, the fact that their Irish brethren in the faith are Democrats would be enough to rivet them to the G.O.P. It is not surprising, therefore, that the leaders of the Republican party in the state should often bear names that suggest Quebec. The Scandinavian complexion of all political parties in Minnesota, however, merely reflects the general ethnology of the state as does the Germanism of politics in Wisconsin.

Where there is more than one great block to be catered for, the art of the manager is called in. He will play up to one section by many minor offices ; to another by an important office for a dominating figure. It was complained that in Cleveland justice was tribalized by filling the office of the District-Attorney by representatives of every nationality which could persuade Mr. Maschke that it was worth conciliating. The bench, the public offices in New York to-day illustrate Tammany's conviction that if the Irish can still hold on to the really worthwhile jobs, the Jews and the Italians have won the right to very handsome recognition. So it is in Chicago ; in Pittsburgh ; the clannishness of the immigrant is exploited by the politician, or, to look at it from a more kindly view-point, the rapid ascent of the leaders of racial groups to office is an example of the Americanizing force of politics.

Not all racial sections are interested in foreign politics all the time and some are purely indigenous. Long fidelity to the Republican party brought the rank and file of the Negro people little enough, but their drift to the North of recent years has increased their political importance, for in their new homes they have votes, and as such are cultivated, getting a share, if a meagre one, in the jobs. The value of the vote as an asset has thus been convincingly displayed. In New York, the solid Democratic mass of Manhattan is broken by the Negroes of Harlem, but Tammany has hopes of winning over this enclave and by a judicious use of patronage and the cultivation of leading lights among the coloured people, it is making some progress. This catering to the black vote aroused ire in the South and one of the charges against Governor Smith that incensed that section was his association with this policy. It is believed that, for the period of the election of 1928, a halt was called to this process, but with the defeat of the presidential candidate Tammany had no further reason to cater to southern prejudice and resumed the siege of Harlem. A similar concentration of black voters in Chicago has given Congress its first black member for forty years in the person of the Honourable Oscar De Priest of the First District of Illinois. It also put Mr. Hoover in a hole, for he had either to invite Mr. and Mrs. De Priest to the White House and so infuriate the South which he was hoping to win over, or to break with the traditions of the Republican party— and alienate important blocks of coloured voters in northern and border states. Mr. De Priest was invited and the storm raged, but Mr. Hoover afterwards acquired so many other handicaps that this one could be neglected. But the Negro voter is cultivated in every state where he is numerous and allowed to vote: the official sponsors of the race are worth conciliating and are put on lists of candidates of all parties and sections of parties, and such a figure as Mr. W. L. Cohen, an important federal office-holder in New Orleans, was naturally called on to hold the coloured voter true to the administration candidate in Chicago in 1926.

Of recent years there has arisen another important block of voters who are free from any suspicion of interest in European affairs, but who are susceptible to racial appeals. All over the South-west are important blocks of Spanish-speaking voters, either survivors of Mexican rule, or sons of immigrants from across the Rio Grande. Hitherto these peons have been voted *en bloc* by their masters, whether these were descendants of the old Spanish gentry or Anglo-Saxon overlords. With the rise of a " Mexican " middle class there has come to be a competition between the great landed magnates of the border counties of Texas and the aspiring politicians of the towns. There are " Latin American " unions and societies and more than once a cattle king has seen his human flock revolt with the same dazed surprise with which the gentry of Clare saw their tenants vote for O'Connell instead of for Vesey-Fitzgerald.[1]

---

[1] If we may accept the authority of Mr. Harvey Fergusson's novel, *The Blood of the Conquerors*, political strength among the Spanish-speaking population of New Mexico was one object of ambition for a young gentleman and membership in that strange religious organization, the *penitentes*, a means comparable to the use of the Elks, Shriners, etc., in other states.

But the patriotism that pays is not only that of European countries or races : local patriotism has been the safe refuge of many a harassed politician. The spirit that keeps the " locality rule " alive is ready to be used by any adroit practitioner to cover up his own defects or exaggerate those of his opponent. The claims of southern as against northern California in allotting offices, of the " Eastern Shore " of Maryland against Baltimore, of Chicago against down-state Illinois, all these can be used by even an average practitioner. Suspicion of interference with local autonomy is also a sure card. Did not John F(aithful) Hylan [1] defend the " five cent fare " against the dangerous machinations of Governor Miller and earn (and win) the suffrage of every New Yorker who could fight his way into the Subway ? But localism goes further than mere city or county loyalty. Wards and districts have their own character which must be preserved against intrusion and corruption from the outside. " ' Do you want our district to be represented by that Pole, Wolleck, from the other side of Ashland Avenue ? ' " [2] The Chicago politician who directed this rhetorical question at his followers knew his business. The manifest inferiority of the lesser breeds across the avenue made every red-blooded voter on the right side of it resolve, " They shall not pass." And so it goes on : administrative reforms are fought on the cry of " Philadelphia jobs for Philadelphia men " : the free hand in appointments which is a feature of the city manager system is developed to a horrified Oakland (California) audience as making possible Japanese or Chinese officials. The nation is but the ward writ large. While Mr. Thomas O'Grady is defending his ward from the neighbouring enemy, Mayor Thompson is defending Chicago from the King of England. What was the Stevenson rubber control but a subtle English scheme to wreak vengeance for the Revolution ? Who will remember that the vastly important franchise question could be settled more agreeably to the wealthy interests concerned by the mercurial " Big Bill ", than by a duller executive like Mayor Dever ? King George was kicked out of Chicago and various people from obscure gangsters to great business magnates had reason to rejoice, while King George, it is believed, was not a penny the worse. When enemies of Senators Watson and Robinson in Indiana asserted that they were being supported by the Ku Klux Klan, it was a good stroke to retort that the enemy was the agent of those dread forces, the " international bankers ". The Non-Partisan League was the tool of the Germans, or so conservative Republicans

[1] This epithet was coined for the Mayor of New York by some ingenious employee of Mr. Hearst.
[2] Quoted in Woody, *The Chicago Primary of 1926*, p. 206.

thought, and when a more effective bogy appeared, it was Bolshevism. In a political system poor in general ideas, such general conceptions as nationalism and its antitheses are only too useful. Patriotism is the first, not the last, refuge of a great many American politicians.

The varied origins of the candidates on an American party ticket ought not to hide the essential uniformity of its class and economic status. In all offices above the lowest, the American politician is a middle-class man, and it is at the lower, not at the upper end of the social scale, that the personnel of American politics is most markedly different from that of the English system. It is not in its comparatively cold welcome to the mere gentleman, but in its decidedly hostile attitude to the mere proletarian that the American system seems strange to one familiar with modern English politics. The stress on humble origins for political purposes should not blind us to the fact that there is less place for a man of obscure origin, *who has not risen into the middle class*, in American than in English politics. We are familiar with the average Labour Member of Parliament who is strong in his poverty, representing the poor and weakened when he loses contact with their life. The English working man doubts whether one who does not live his life can understand his wants and so is anxious to have his class represented by men who have not merely been born in it, but who have stayed in it. He is not as suspicious of the sincerity of the bourgeois politician of the Left as is the French Radical, but his class politics are sufficiently deeply rooted to fill a large part of an average parliament with really poor men. There is little or nothing of this in America because, as yet, the American working man has not reconciled himself to a permanently proletarian destiny and so has no reluctance to support poor men who have escaped from poverty—as he proposes to do himself. Whether he will change when the shades of the prison house have definitely and obviously closed over his class remains to be seen. At present there is no real fear of or hope from the " labor vote ".

Politicians play up to it, when they can do so without offending more potent blocks of opinion, but few, indeed, are the careers that have been mainly made possible by trade-union support. There is little political fame or profit to be got out of a career in labour activities ; there are the chance of being Secretary of Labor, a number of minor jobs of the same kind and some cash or other tangible reward when the organized labour vote is wanted in a critical moment—cash or other reward that may very probably come from the agents of big business. Few, indeed, are the politicians who see much for themselves in labour politics, and a remarkably high proportion of those who do, have had their view of things distorted by European birth and upbringing. The native-born American who wishes to make a career in politics instinctively knows better than to try to make it through an apprenticeship in the average American trade union.

The reasons which make labour support of comparatively little use to a candidate are still more powerful in freeing a party from any real fear of incurring labour displeasure by its programme or past conduct. At times the American Federation of Labour was compelled to throw itself into the political arena, but when in 1908, the year of the boldest judicial attacks on the unions, Mr. Gompers and his allies tried to throw the union vote to the Democratic candidate, Mr. Bryan, the demonstration of power was a miserable fiasco. Yet from this point of view, Mr. Bryan's opponent, Mr. Taft, was an excellent politician of whom to make an example, for he had been an eminent " injunction " judge and to his dying day never recanted his simple judicial faith. When the Democrats won in 1912 they paid for labour support by an " Anti-Injunction act " and some other favours, but their victory was not due mainly to labour support and no administration has ever felt it necessary to cultivate the unions as much as it has felt it necessary to cultivate, for instance, the old-soldier vote. A " good " record on railway legislation is a help in most states where the industrially powerful railroad brotherhoods are strong and, in Pennsylvania, Mr. Pinchot has cultivated the coal-miners with success, but over the union the views of organized labour are only taken into consideration after more potent organizations have been pacified.

Indeed, the importance of labour support is only that of an agglomeration of individuals, it is not that of a class. It is true that special causes may embitter local feeling and, by 1926, it was no longer an asset in Arizona to have been a party to the Bisbee deportations which in war-time had taught labour its place. In the main, however, the great trade unions count for far less than they do in Europe, possibly no more than do the great fraternal orders. In the United States, it is possible that Senator James J. Davis has owed as much to being the Supreme Organizer of the Order of Moose as to being " Puddler Jim ". The Moose, the Elks, the Eagles, the Lions, the Nobles of the Mystic Shrine, have all their political members who do their best to cash in on the order's good will and, in the United States, eminence in a great order is a proof of the possession of the qualities that make a " regular fellow " and so a good candidate.[1]

---

[1] President Harding was an Elk, a Moose, a Mason, a Shriner and a Tall Cedar of Lebanon. Senator Cole Blease of South Carolina tells us in the Congressional Directory, that he is the only South Carolinian who " has represented three of the State fraternal bodies in national grand bodies.

It follows then, with barely enough exceptions to relieve the monotony, that the personnel of American politics, except in local offices, is more like that of the old Liberal party than that of either the Conservative or Labour parties. At one end of the Liberal party was a group of aristocrats, of blood or wealth, preferably of both, at the other was a group of working men, like Joseph Arch or John Burns, but the bulk of the party was middle class, counting in that class all grades from Joseph Chamberlain and Campbell-Bannerman down to minor lawyers, doctors and small business men. Both American parties are recruited in that stratum of society. It matters little what they started at ; it is the destination that counts and the most convenient place to stop is about half-way up the ladder. There is neither the recognized place of the " gentleman ", the retired officer, the class which provides the traditional Tory member, or the professional working man of the Labour party. One nominal and one real profession are the only ones granted a traditional respect in politics. It is still believed that the average American is a farmer or ought to be and so politicians cultivate a direct interest in things of the soil. More politicians than Ike Stevenson have put themselves down as farmers because they owned " twenty banks and one cow ", for a farmer is one of the two classes of men who are entitled to enter politics with a sense of having a claim on the suffrages of their fellows. But farmers, real or political, are not the staple supply of candidates and office-holders, for although there are politicians who have no other profession, some who have been business men, doctors, jockeys, soldiers, even more than in England the average active politician is a lawyer. On the other hand, the American political lawyer is a different animal from the English type. His law has been a starting-point, not his politics, an investment which he hopes to cash in on later. The lesser importance of the trial lawyer in the American system and the wide diffusion of the courts over the whole country, makes it hard to combine the rôle of leading lawyer and leading statesman. Lawyers of great eminence, Messrs. Root, Knox, Kellogg, have sat in the Senate, but their legal eminence was not increased thereby. Senator Borah, for example, deliberately sacrificed his career as a lawyer when he entered the Senate, and an eminent Senate lawyer is usually one who, like the late Senator Thomas Walsh, is so styled because he is

Great sachem and great representative Improved Order of Red Men ; grand master, grand patriarch, and grand representative of grand encampment and grand lodge to sovereign grand lodge, Independent Order of Odd Fellows ; dictator Loyal Order of Moose, and representative to supreme lodge ; past chancellor commander Knights of Pythias ; member benevolent and protective Order of Elks and Woodmen of the World ".

learned in the law, not because he dashes from court to Congress
and back again. The American system offers poor rewards to
the legal talent which is so adequately catered for in England ;
a few jobs for " lame ducks " ; the chance of being Attorney-
General at a low salary and moderate prestige ; the faint possibility of a seat on the Supreme Court. There is not enough in
this to attract the talents of a first-class jury lawyer or the skill
of a great corporation lawyer. If, then, the legislatures are full
of lawyers, they are so because in the lawyer-ridden American
system, some knowledge of law is necessary before any positive
political achievement is possible ; a lawyer starts on his political
career with a slight advantage over the layman.

One legal qualification for high office that is peculiar to
America is the importance attached to a successful record as
district or state's attorney. Among the many politicians who
have owed their start in English politics to legal eminence, few,
if any, have been noted because they snatched some notorious
evildoer from the shielding arms of Sir Edward Marshall Hall.
A record of convictions won is not, in itself, much help in winning
the suffrages of a people which still takes it for granted that,
when a prosecution is started, the prosecution will manage to
get its man. In the United States, even politicians who have
reached the front rank point with pride to the days when they
were winning popular gratitude by filling the gaols. His record
as District Attorney of Kansas City (Missouri) remained still a
bright memory to Mr. " Jim " Reed, if we may rely on the
biography he contributed to the Congressional Directory while
he still adorned the Senate, and even a radical like Senator
Robert M. La Follette was inordinately proud of his achievements as a district attorney : " I believe I broke the record for
convictions in Dane County." [1] A little more reasonable is the
importance attached to political convictions, that is to say, cases
whose origin or development reveal connections with machine
rule—and these are not infrequent. Merely to get convictions
may be a result of machine co-operation, as well as of public
spirit, but the direct assault on graft has always been a way to
popular favour, for a time at any rate. Such a reputation
made Tilden, Gaynor, Hughes leading figures in New York
politics and the conviction of Lieutenant Becker for the murder
of Rosenthal made Mr. Whitman, for a moment, a political
figure of importance and Governor of the State. His share in
the San Francisco graft prosecutions made Senator Hiram Johnson a successful aspirant for the governorship of California and,
in more recent times, the prosecution that filled Stillwater with
grafting Minneapolis aldermen made the prosecutor Governor

[1] *Autobiography of Robert M. La Follette*, p. 41.

of Minnesota. In a country where the law is enforced in a very patchy fashion, the public admiration for a successful manipulator of the complicated machinery of justice is less unreasonable than in a land where the chances of an accused person are less, and public sympathy is as likely to be with the poor wretch feebly defending himself against the power of the state as with the well-paid officers whose duty it is to prosecute him.

By the time the state, the city, the county ticket have added their quota of " available " candidates, the final list in a well-compiled ticket represents a chain of compromises, of calculations, of bargains, that is the fruit of diplomatic talent of a very high order. Race, social position, religion, profession, character, popularity, party fidelity, oratory, even policy, are all represented on it, each contributing, it is hoped, an element of strength or neutralizing some element of danger. But one thing all the candidates must be prepared to do or pay the price, they must play politics.

The statesmen, the orators, the " fat cats ", must all look after the fences or find someone who will. Andrew D. White might urge the election of Roscoe Conkling to the Senate on the ground that New York needed a voice, but the view of the practical politician was better represented by the orator who defended the re-election of Simon Cameron to the Senate. " ' Ingalls and Evarts are orators and I would like to know what they ever got or ever did except blow off their mouths ? Pennsylvania gets everything she wants through her senators.' " [1] But if politics in Pennsylvania are supremely political, the Pennsylvania point of view has its spokesmen in other states. When Senator W. B. McKinley was striving in vain for the Republican nomination in 1926, his claims on the politicians of Illinois were cogently set forth.

> " ' They allowed that they had been treated pretty well by McKinley, that they had had fairly good picking at the federal patronage table, that Brother Grossman had pulled down a pardon from the White House, that McKinley's law enforcement [Prohibition] employees had not unreasonably molested the water-carriers, and that on the whole, McKinley was safe and sane.' " [2]

Of such is the political heaven, and the statesman in the big states who neglects this side of his job will not stay in office very long. He may be as much of a statesman as he likes, but he must not neglect the chores. Matthew Quay and Henry Cabot Lodge both realized this truth, and while all politics and no

[1] H. J. Ford, *Rise and Growth of American Politics*, pp. 223-4.
[2] C. H. Woody, *The Chicago Primary of 1926*, p. 79.

statesmanship was enough for Pennsylvania, all statesmanship
and no politics would make a poor candidate even in Massachusetts. Some there are who think they are above it, but their
careers, as a rule, are short. Even a representative from a
" silk-stocking " district, like Mrs. Ruth Pratt, had to learn her
lesson and promise the district leaders " to play ball "—just as
if she were a Tammany nominee instead of a member of the
" party of moral ideas ". For behind each candidate for office
are the workers who seek no elective office, being better employed
in getting out the vote for others—and they insist on having their
reward. For they are the makers of candidates and their electors.
The elected office-holders may have as much glory as they like,
even as much power as they like, but they must keep the implied
bargain.

At bottom it is this necessity for placating the machine owners
and workers that hampers the political aspirant with principle,
whether he be poor or rich, and accounts for the moderate worth
of most candidates. Only by an increasing and permanent
interest in politics in the average citizen will the hold of the
machine be shaken and then the improvement in political
personnel may be attempted. Till then the good citizen will
often have to say with " Abe Martin ", " We'd all like t'vote
fer the best man, but he's never a candidate."

PART TEN

THE CAMPAIGN

So they march in percessions, an' git up hooraws,
An' tramp thru the mud fer the good o' the cause,
An' think they're a kind o' fulfillin' the prophecies,
Wen they're on'y jest changin' the holders of offices.

The Biglow Papers.

Chapter I

THE PLAN OF CAMPAIGN

SOME weeks after the Convention has nominated him, the news is formally broken to the Candidate by a notification committee and the formal speech of acceptance is officially the first gun o the campaign. Of course the Candidate has not been idle and he has already laid down the general lines of his fight, notably by the appointment of a Chairman of the National Committee of the party. This official is chief of the working staff of the party which is chosen by the national Convention and holds office till the next Convention meets. The Chairman is the Chief Whip and, much more than that, the personal representative of the Candidate and the ruler of the national party organization. The rise in importance of the Chairman is comparatively recent, the first politician to win fame in that office being Senator Gorman, whose activities were generally believed to have had much to do with the election of Cleveland in 1884. But all other Chairmen pale into insignificance compared with the great Mark Hanna who put McKinley into the White House and, with a little more luck and longer life, might have put himself there too. The importance of the national Chairman depends a good deal on the character of the Candidate, on whether he is a figurehead or his own manager. A President in office, seeking a second nomination, is inevitably his own manager and the national Chairman may have a rival in the chief political officer of the Cabinet, the Postmaster-General. In Mr. Hoover's administration the Postmaster-General, Mr. Walter Brown, was suspected of being a more potent aid to his chief than was Senator Fess, the Chairman of the National

GOVERNMENT OF THE PEOPLE

Committee.[1] A Candidate on his way to the White House—or

Committee.[1] A Candidate on his way to the White House—or
to defeat—has, however, reason to be very careful in his choice
of a chief of staff, for a tactless or injudicious national Chairman
may do immense damage. Yet once the Candidate is committed
to one man, it is almost impossible to drop the pilot, even if he
be steering the ship perilously near the rocks. Wilson had to put up
with McCombs in 1912, despite his many defects ; in any case there
was little that McCombs could do to stop the progress of Wilson
to the White House, but in the far more difficult task of 1916,
Mr. Vance McCormick did a much better job, and much of the
credit for Wilson's re-election should go to him. The election
over, the national Chairman does not sink back into obscurity
but, with his committee, remains in charge of the party machine,
and every Convention thus starts its life under the control of a
committee chosen by its predecessor. Occasionally this has very
odd results. The domination of the Republican Convention of
1912 by the Taft committee of 1908 rendered hopeless all efforts
of the Roosevelt delegates to nominate their hero, for it fell to
the " Old Guard ", who were supporting Taft, to decide the
contested elections on which the control of the Convention
turned. As a Convention is often the scene of internal feuds
representing permanent schisms within the party, the " hold-
over " system is one of the prizes of victory, since it enables the
victorious faction to start the next Convention fight from an
advantageous position. Thus Governor Smith in 1928 was able
to demonstrate his control of the party by nominating as Chairman a complete new-comer to politics, whose previous party
affiliations, if any, had been Republican. Mr. Raskob at once
took command and remained in a position of commanding
importance in his new party up to 1932, an exercise of power
beyond the dreams of a Prime Minister. By making his friend,
Mr. W. M. Butler, Chairman, President Coolidge gave another
demonstration of the dominance of the party machine by the
standard-bearer in the presidential election. In each case, a
new-comer was promoted to the seats of the mighty, without
any effective protest being possible.

To the National Committee and, above all, to the Chairman
falls the direction of the strategy of the campaign, the decision
that one state shall be fought for to the end, another abandoned
as hopeless, that Senator X shall be used in the west and Congressman Y kept east of the Mississippi, that such a faction shall
be conciliated even at the cost of alienating another. All the
daily decisions that have to be made on the spot and which may
turn out to be decisive, are made by the Chairman, subject, of

[1] Senator Fess was succeeded in the campaign of 1932 by Mr. Everett
Sanders.

course, to the control of the Candidate. The most experienced politicians in the party may wring their hands and exhaust their eloquence in pleas ; once the battle is on, the Candidate and his manager are in complete control, and even defeat does not always relax the grip.

Above and beyond all other duties of the national Chairman is that of putting money in his purse. The cost of a nation-wide campaign has risen steadily, partly through the growth in population, partly through the decay in spontaneous political interest, partly through the falling off in the revenue from assessments of office-holders, partly for the intangible reasons that make things dearer and dearer. It cost the Republicans $100,000 to elect Lincoln and $3,500,000 to elect McKinley ; a measure of the change in party methods in thirty-six years. The money collected by John Wanamaker in 1888 to elect Harrison, and by William Whitney in 1892 to defeat him, was a subject of comment, but the first great demonstration of the financial possibilities of politics came with Mark Hanna's management of the McKinley campaign of 1896. Faced with the menace of Bryan and " Free Silver ", the " interests " were chilled by panic until Hanna took command and, scorning mere requests for contributions, assessed the threatened plutocrats on a proportional basis. The banks, which had most to lose by a currency upset, were assessed at $\frac{1}{4}$ of 1 per cent of their capital ; insurance companies, railroads, the trusts, were all levied on in a business-like fashion ; no one was encouraged to give more or permitted to give less than his share of the cost of :

Pouring out the long green to a million workers,
Spondulix by the mountain-load to stop each new tornado,
And beat the cheapskate, blatherskite,
Populistic, anarchistic,
Deacon-desperado.[1]

In 1896 the Democrats were even poorer than usual, for all, or almost all, the wealthy Democrats had been alienated by the nomination of Bryan, and such magnates as John McCall were handsome contributors to Hanna's war-chest, providing abundant funds drawn from the coffers of the corporations they controlled. Faced with the menace of inflation, all big business, whatever its nominal party affiliations, imitated that nominal leader of the Democracy, President Cleveland, and hoped and helped to elect McKinley. The silver barons, led by Marcus Daly of the Anaconda Copper Company, did their best for Bryan, but they were a handful compared with the embattled millionaires who were enrolled by Hanna.

[1] Vachel Lindsay, " *Bryan, Bryan, Bryan, Bryan.*"

The success of Hanna's drive seemed to the politicians to teach a great lesson ; they had tasted blood and their demands would have surprised the most practical politicians of the previous generation. Indiana methods were generalized, but although there was lavish expenditure in 1900 and 1904, there was no longer the great fear of 1896 to stimulate generosity, and there was an increasing temptation to ask for specific, as apart from general reward, from the party which was being so handsomely supported. The energetic agent of the Panama Canal promoters, Mr. Cromwell, gave Hanna $60,000 in 1900 and wanted, but did not get, definite promises in exchange, while the contributors of 1904 were convinced that Roosevelt had, by his anti-trust policy, shown base ingratitude in biting the hand that had fed his party.

The Democrats, who had very little chance of getting hold of the cash, protested more and more loudly. Judge Parker had been nominated in 1904 to win conservative support, and the sight of corporation money going to his radical opponent was too much. The objections of the Democrats were shared by many Republican opponents of Wall Street and, re-enforced by an unfortunate dispute between Roosevelt and Harriman as to the reasons which had led the railroad magnate to contribute so handsomely, public opinion was won to the conviction that a time had come to stop this purchase of the presidency by the rulers of the great corporations. Mr. Perry Belmont, a member of one of the few wealthy Democratic families, grew tired of attempting to match the floods of money that poured into the Republican campaign chest. He set himself to build up a public opinion for the compulsory publication of contributions, and there was increasing agreement that contributions made out of corporation funds ought to cease. 1908 was the first election fought under the new conditions, for the candidates ordered the publication of contributions and statute had forbidden the acceptance of corporation gifts. Since that date, the legal regulation of campaign contributions has gone to what, to a British politician, would seem extraordinary lengths. The sums that may be spent on congressional and senatorial elections are regulated on principles similar to those of our own laws, but the side of party finance that is almost entirely neglected by the British law, the origin of contributions, is highly regulated in law, if not in practice. In almost all states, political organizations are bound to furnish lists of contributions and contributors and, where the law was doubtful, the Senate has investigated at great length and helped to create a public opinion that proscribes political success that has been too openly bought. There have been many difficulties to face and many of them have not been got round. What is a political body ? Is the Anti-Saloon League bound to reveal its finances to the public because its members are advised how to vote ? It has been forced to do so, but there are other ways of getting round the statutes. Should individuals or groups be barred from contributing to buy advertising space in the newspapers ? If they are not, the candidate with rich supporters is at an advantage, but is there not force in the complaint of " Poor Swede " Lundin that the candidate who commands newspaper support is usually a rich man and unless a poor man buys space he gets none ? At what time does a campaign begin ? Very effective expenditure can be made long before an election is " on ".

How far is it possible to distinguish between the action of General W. W. Atterbury as a member of the Republican National Committee and his action as President of the Pennsylvania Railroad ?—and how far are the interests of the Pennsylvania Railroad distinguishable from or opposed to those of the other taxpayers of Pennsylvania ? It is impossible to be certain whether the motives which induced one member of the Du Pont family to contribute handsomely to the campaign chest of Mr. Smith and another member to contribute to that of Mr. Hoover are public or private, legitimate, illegitimate, or neutral. Are campaign contributions which are followed by appointments or other rewards *ipso facto* suspect ? And in any case what is the use of limiting contributions or insisting on publishing them if a party machine can get into debt and have its accounts settled, after the election, by kind friends whose public support might have been embarrassing if the public had got wind of it in time ? One of the most alarming discoveries of the long-drawn-out investigations of the Harding régime was the revelation that it was Mr. Harry Sinclair who had been one of the chief liquidators of the debts incurred in putting Harding over in 1920. The connection between this generosity from a man who did not know whether he was a Republican or a Democrat, and the leasing to him of the Teapot Dome oil-lands, was not inevitable in fact, but likely to seem inevitable in the public mind.[1]

A comparable situation arose in the Democratic party in 1928. Deficits were, indeed, normal in that party, but the party credit was not high enough to make it easy to incur really heavy liabilities. The campaign of 1928 was an exception ; for once,

[1] Senator Borah was so shocked by this discovery that he started a fund to pay off the debt and clear the party's honour. Republicans were, it proved, no more anxious to do this than Liberals in England were to escape, by personal contribution, from the shame of dependence on Mr. Lloyd George's mysterious fund. Mr. Sinclair had contributed $260,000 to a total deficit of $1,350,000.

the Democrats had something like an adequate supply of money. Mr. Raskob and Mr. Raskob's friends contributed handsomely and bore the burden of a very heavy deficit. In the past four years, some of that deficit has been paid off, but all the while there has been a lavish and, politically speaking, remunerative expenditure on propaganda. The attack on President Hoover was boldly planned, but it was very expensive, and the Democratic party had to meet in Convention to choose a Candidate with the knowledge that the manager and friends of the late Candidate, Mr. Al Smith, had what punctilious critics called a mortgage on the party. The first skirmishes of the pre-Convention campaign took place in the bosom of the National Committee between the Smith " hold-overs " and the delegates who were supporting Governor Roosevelt and the defeat of Mr. Jouett Shouse was a blow to the anti-Roosevelt forces from which they did not recover. Mr. Raskob and Mr. Shouse retired and put in a claim for their money.

No country is in a position to throw stones at the United States on this question. The Comité des Forges is an old bugbear of the French " Left " and the reasons which induce the " Left " itself to run so many wealthy candidates are not very obscure. In England, the existence of secret party funds is taken as the most natural thing in the world and the manner in which a Conservative majority in 1927 proceeded to make it as hard as possible for its opponents to draw their normal revenue from the Trades Unions, was a measure that Americans could have scarcely credited even had it been sponsored by a Pennsylvania senator. If the American public has not managed to control the power of money in the making of public opinion, it has, at any rate, got to the point of seeing that it *is* a power and a problem. Again and again, candidates have discovered that too obvious a use of money may be a handicap. General Leonard Wood was ruined as a presidential possibility by the lavish expenditure that preceded the Convention of 1920. The expenditures of Senator Newberry to defeat Mr. Ford in 1918 passed the courts, but the Senators who seated him paid dearly for their defiance of public opinion. Despite the ingenious argument for constitutional propriety with which Mr. James M. Beck bombarded the Senate on behalf of Mr. Vare, the lavishness of the Pennsylvania primary of 1926 resulted in a refusal to seat the winner of the orgy. Mr. Smith of Illinois might ask, with reasonable curiosity, why it was any worse for him to receive contributions from Mr. Samuel Insull than it was for Mr. Coolidge to run on a fund largely collected from manufacturers protected by the high Republican tariff. No answer was provided, but Mr. Smith was barred all the same.

It was with his usual talent for expressing the mind of the average man, and more than his usual wit, that Bryan, in 1912, pricked the bubble of Roosevelt's independence of " the interests ". George Perkins, one of the rulers of the Harvester Trust, was Roosevelt's chief " angel ". " ' If Roosevelt ' ", said Bryan, " ' thought he was the Moses of the Progressive movement, he must have mistaken the voice of Perkins for the voice of God.' " [1] The shot went home in a country where there is a suspicion that rich men who contribute handsomely to party funds, may get something more for their money than an ambassadorship or other equivalent of a peerage. Yet, however suspicious the American people may be of money in politics, money is a tremendous political force in America. Veteran politicians point out that the Democrats have always less and, usually, much less money in a national campaign than the Republicans. They go on to assert that it is to this that the Democrats owe their feebleness, but it is as likely that it is to their feebleness that the Democrats owe their poverty. If they were stronger, if they had more than an off-chance of winning, they would find money more easily, for the owners of that money spend it to buy or to placate power. It is natural that they should pay over their millions to the party which is likely to be in a position to deliver the goods.

At last the whole party machine is ponderously set in motion, and the complicated task of electing a vast mob of officials from the President down to small-town aldermen or county officials is begun. All the candidates, from highest to lowest, are bound together in mutual dependence. A minor blunder in a rural county in New York may defeat a presidential Candidate ; a masterly use of money in a senatorial election may change the complexion of the Senate for reasons that have far more to do with Michigan politics than with the League of Nations and the Treaty of Versailles and, at the other extreme, a career of party fidelity and carefully cultivated local popularity may be ruined by upheavals starting from Headquarters and inspired there by momentous events in world politics. The whole chain, with its hundreds of thousands of candidates, may prove no stronger than its weakest link and that link, from one point of view, may be the presidential Candidate whose tactlessness upsets a scheme for stealing or saving the waterworks in Sycamore Ridge, or it may be the candidate for Mayor of Winesburg, whose failure to capture the support of the local Campbellite church loses the county and the presidency. In the 1916 campaign, Colonel House told Daniel C. Roper, who was in charge of the Democratic organization, " ' We must run the

[1] Merriam and Gosnell, *American Party System*, p. 321.

President for Justice of the Peace and not for President ; we need not consider the disposition of sixteen or seventeen million voters, but the disposition of the voters in individual precincts ' ".[1] Care should be taken to find out " ' what argument we are using appeals most to the voters of each community. This enables us to soft-pedal in some directions and push harder in others ' ".[2] It is, indeed, sometimes necessary, when a national issue has been rashly raised, to say *something* about it ; it was foolish of Mr. Hughes to attack the Wilson foreign policy and then, when asked what he would have done had *he* been President when the *Lusitania* was sunk, to have merely " cleared his throat ", as a wit put it. But the politician is much happier when he has merely to " soft-pedal ", when he can emulate the great example of Senator Allison of Iowa, who was said to be so discreet that he could walk on the keyboard of a piano from New York to San Francisco without striking a note.

[1] C. Seymour, *The Private Papers of Colonel House*, vol. ii, p. 359.
[2] *Ibid.*, vol. ii, p. 364.

Chapter II

LOCAL AND PERSONAL ISSUES

SINCE a few votes may carry or lose a state and that may turn the whole presidential election, the Candidate must be exceedingly adroit in his dealings with local issues. Sometimes he is helpless ; for some reason or other, the local party has alienated part of its normal support on issues which have no relevance to the national election, but for which the national party must pay.[1] At times it is necessary for the candidate to cater to sectional issues, and often he and the state or even the national party with him fall over concealed strings in the political long grass. In Kentucky, it may be the fight over the place of the pari-mutuel in the great local industry of horse-racing ; in Chicago, the legality of boxing ; in the state of Washington, the opposition of the cinema proprietors to the sabbatarian activities of that Christian Senator, the late Wesley L. Jones ; every State has its own problems which have little enough to do with national issues, but too often the state and national tickets are inextricably mixed up and an election fought on local issues or local factions may incidentally involve such, politically, minor questions as the World Court or war debts, ingredients added to the seething pot of local issues to give it flavouring.

The issues may of course be largely personal and in such faction fights the Candidate, if he cannot avoid taking sides, should at least try to choose the stronger. In 1916, the Republican Candidate, Mr. C. E. Hughes, would have been elected, despite his failure to equal Wilson's popular vote, if he had carried California. He visited that proud state, failed to call on the Governor, Mr. Hiram Johnson, who was running for the Senate, was at a lunch served by " scab " waiters during a

[1] Vice-President Marshall tells of a Democratic meeting in Indiana which listened dutifully to senatorial eloquence on the great issues of the day and was then addressed by a local light as follows : " ' My fellow-citizens, I hope you won't leave. I want to say something to you touching the dog law that is in force.' Every man returned to his seat with his coon dog at his side, and I am not sure that the Democratic majority of the county that fall did not come more from the local candidate's opinion of the dog law, than from the senatorial candidate's opinion of the tariff " (*Recollections*, pp. 135–6).

waiters' strike in San Francisco and was surrounded by the
leaders of the Crocker faction of the Republicans of the state.
California had gone for Roosevelt in 1912 ; the Crocker Republicans were merely a handful ; it was indispensable to win
over the former Progressives of whom Governor Johnson was
the chief.   Everything was done by the Democrats to win them
and Mr. McAdoo, ably aided by his Treasury officials, carried
the state for Wilson in 1916 by a few thousand votes and the
campaign was won and lost.

Similar factions split the Democrats in New York in 1904.
The nomination of Parker had no justification if he failed to
carry his own state, but whatever slight chances he had were
lost because of the antagonism between D. Cady Harrick and
David B. Hill.   Twenty years before, it was the turn of the
Republicans to suffer, for Cleveland was elected by his majority
of a thousand in New York—and it is strongly suspected that his
majority had in its ranks many Conkling "Stalwarts" who were
taking their revenge on Blaine.

Party factions are bad enough, but the task of conciliating
sections of the population whose displeasure is formidable, taxes
all a candidate's ingenuity.   Then his enemies rejoice that he
has written a book.   In his *Life of Benton* Roosevelt had expressed
his poor opinion of Quakers ; this was a luxury he had to repent
of and explain away when he ran as the candidate of a party
which enrolled most of the Quakers in its ranks.   Woodrow
Wilson had written a severe judgment on the quality of Italian
immigration ; he had to tone it down when he left the chair for
the forum.

The friendship or enmity of religious bodies is important for
all classes of candidates.   In rural America, as in Portadown,
the Pope has a bad name, but in the great industrial states the
candidates of all ranks will go to great lengths to conciliate Catholic feeling.   It may be guessed that a Protestant candidate would
not have incurred the disastrous risk run by Mayor John Purroy
Mitchel, of New York, in encouraging awkward investigations
of Catholic public charities with an election at hand.   Generally,
in Massachusetts, Rhode Island, New York, it pays to lean over
backwards in cultivating the Catholic vote.   To incur Protestant
hostility is, in itself, an asset and one recent Democratic candidate
for Governor of Massachusetts is said to have acted up to the
spirit of the epigram : there was no Ku Klux Klan in the state,
so he invented one.   He was preceded and attached, in his tour of
the western part of the state, by fiery crosses and inflammatory
inscriptions which, it was hoped, would drive the normally
Republican French-Canadians into the Democratic camp.   This
manœuvre deserved more success than it achieved.   Religious

difficulties sometimes make strange alliances and are thus a nightmare to the politician. The notorious case of the Bennet Law in Wisconsin, forty years ago, has not been forgotten. The old temptation of the Republican party to cater to its Puritan element was succumbed to ; a law was passed hindering the work of private schools ; it united Catholics, Germans and Scandinavians in a formidable alliance which delivered the State over to the Democrats and led to an investigation of the state treasury that cost Republican leaders dear, both in credit and in cash. On the whole, it is safer to let sleeping dogs lie ; to distribute, as Boies Penrose used to do, cheap Bibles in rural areas, and favours to cardinals and lesser lights in the cities. The support both of the Ku Klux Klan and the Knights of Columbus is the ideal to be aimed at and it is sometimes almost achieved.

Candidates, however discreet, have to pray to be saved from their friends, as many accidents testify. The most famous of these occurred in the close campaign of 1884. The secession of the " Mugwumps " threatened the fortunes of Blaine, but it was hoped to offset that defection by the aid of the " Blaine Irishmen " who had been carefully cultivated by the Republican candidate. Alas ! on the eve of the election, the tired " Plumed Knight " received a deputation of clergymen of Evangelical connections whose spokesman referred to the rival party and Candidate as the agents of " Rum, Romanism and Rebellion " Blaine was not ready-witted or attentive enough to protest. Too late, he protested that he could not be suspected of hostility to the religion of his mother ; the damage was done. Eight years later, another Republican candidate, Benjamin Harrison, incurred Catholic hostility because his Indian commissioner had shown what was interpreted as a bias against Catholic missions, and his defeat was believed, by some observers, to be in part due to the resentment of Catholic voters.

The American Protective Association, the " A.P.A." of bitter Catholic memory, was a force to be reckoned with in the " ninetics ", but the Republican party had, in the not very long run, reason to regard it as a handicap. The post-war revival of the Ku Klux Klan put both parties in an awkward position but, on the whole, hurt the Democrats most, revealing their internal dissension and, in a doubtful state like Indiana, proving a powerful, if not always acknowledged aid to the Republicans.

In the election of 1928, despite semi-sincere disclaimers, religion played a great part and it was an unacknowledged weapon of the Republicans. They calculated, probably wisely, that they had little Catholic support to lose and it was impossible to keep the one issue that stirred the country out of the campaign. Whispering never reached such heights and many of the whispers

were so loud that they were inconveniently overheard. Verse
of a kind more stirring than the usual campaign balladry was
poured on to a receptive market :

> Alcohol Al for President,
> I stand for whisky and bad government ;
> My platform is wet and I am too,
> And I get my votes from Catholic and Jew.
>
> .   .   .   .   .
>
> I'll take down the flag from the public schools
> And put up the cross for the ignorant fools,
> The Bible in the schools shall not be read.
> But instead we'll say masses for the dead.[1]

The Pope was kept out of the White House and it is improbable that any direct attempt to introduce him into it will be made
by a major political party for some time to come.

Another Church that was for long under grave suspicion was
that of the Mormons. The suppression of polygamy was one of
the original Republican planks and the failure of attempts to
suppress such un-American practices provoked the same reactions
that to-day are associated with Prohibition enforcement. This
immunity was attributed to adroit political management, but
the time came when polygamy had to be abandoned and the
Church which was the great scandal of all right-thinking men,
is now one of the chief bulwarks of righteousness, being simply
a more romantic version of American evangelical religion. If
it was ever true that the Latter Day Saints were deliberately
sent in to permeate both parties, it is no longer so. The faithful,
not only in Utah, but in the other mountain states where they
are strong, are generally reckoned among Republican assets ;
as is fitting in a body which has, as one of its most exalted rulers,
so important a Republican as Senator Reed Smoot, and Utah
was one of the two states that went for the orthodox Republican
candidate in 1912. Alas ! in 1932 even Utah deserted both
President Hoover and Senator Smoot, but the victor over the
veteran Senator is himself a leading Mormon.

All over the Union religion is a useful political asset. In
Pennsylvania, the fact that Senator Pepper had written little
books of devotion helped him somewhat, though not enough to
overcome the arms of the flesh wielded by the Vare machine.
In Massachusetts, the political opinions of Cardinal O'Connell
are as well worth considering as are those of the Reverend
" Bob " Shuler in Los Angeles, or of Bishop Cannon, the
" Methodist Pope ", in the " Bible Belt ". The constitution may

---

[1] Quoted in Michael Williams, *The Shadow of the Pope*, pp. 250–1.

not mention God and the state may be officially secular, but American politics consists in satisfying groups and no Church which has a useful block of votes at its real or assumed disposal, need complain of not having friends at court.

One concession all parties must make to the churches and the organized moralists. The candidates for at any rate the more conspicuous offices must be good men—or the enemy will make a frank appeal to the " moral " vote. The advantages and disadvantages of scandal in democratic politics have been illustrated abundantly from the days of Alcibiades. In every country there are taboos, not strictly relevant to the political issues, that are more than a candidacy can bear. Even the tolerant land of France regards certain derelictions which are tolerable in a Prime Minister, as a handicap to one who proposes to be President of the Republic, but it is in the English-speaking countries that the " morals ", that is, the sexual morals, of the politician have been most strictly scrutinized since the democratization of the franchise. In the United States the standards are even higher than in England and chastity is stressed, sometimes to the exclusion of other moral qualities more strictly relevant to the character of a public servant. It is especially the woman voter to whom the player on " moral issues " appeals, for politicians, it is asserted, " know that no matter of expediency will induce her to vote for a man of immoral life or a dishonest man. They realize that of two candidates, she will choose the upright one, even if his ability is less than that of the other ".[1]

But even in America not all politicians are chaste and the history of the country has some famous examples of political probity and sexual irregularity. Franklin is a case in point, but Franklin has never really won the approval of the more respectable sections of his countrymen, in his lifetime, or later. Alexander Hamilton is an example of more force, for he is one whom modern Americans of the better classes have resolved to honour. Yet Hamilton defended himself against a charge of public peculation by admitting private adultery, a defence that was accepted then, but would now prove as dangerous, if not more dangerous, than the offence charged. There are many Americans who think the revelation that the late President Harding had an illegitimate child, is likely to cause more disrespect for the presidency than the discovery that he had put more thieves and liars into his Cabinet than any President since Grant. The standard of public morals, in both the United States and Britain, is kept high by the severe penalties visited on such politicians as are found out, but it is not the thing in England to point out the sins of the opposing candidate, there is a gentleman's agreement

[1] Mary Roberts Rinehart, in *The Ladies' Home Journal*, October, 1931, p. 31.

not to raise the question. The Dilkes have, or, at any rate, had, to be above suspicion, but it was nobody's business to raise it.[1]

The higher standards of America have been reflected in the numerous partisans who " private dirt in public virtue throw ". When the Democrats assailed the honesty of the Republican candidate in 1884, the defenders of Mr. Blaine's honour did not content themselves with the exegesis of the Mulligan letters and the casuistry of congressional finance, they revealed to a shocked world that the Democratic candidate, Mr. Cleveland, the honest man of the Mugwumps, had acknowledged an illegitimate child. This discovery threatened the Democrats with defeat, for it introduced a new and, emotionally, more powerful moral issue into a campaign already well stocked with such material. It made many of the Mugwumps ashamed of their candidate and it might have alienated many of the Irish Catholic supporters of Mr. Cleveland, but most Cleveland supporters stood their ground, notably Mr. Godkin, who wrote one of his most effective articles on this theme. Thus heartened, the Democrats returned the attack, with less force because of the difficulty of getting hold of scandal of a suitable kind, but with ingenuity they did a good deal and the campaign descended to a level not reached again till 1928 :

" We are here plunged in politics funnier than words can express. Very great issues are involved. . . . But the amusing thing is that no one talks about real interests. . . . We are afraid to discuss them. Instead of this, the press is engaged in a most amusing dispute whether Mr. Cleveland had an illegitimate child, and did or did not live with one or more mistresses ; whether Mr. Blaine got paid in railway bonds for services as Speaker ; and whether Mrs. Blaine had a baby three months after her marriage." [2]

Despite his admitted sin, Cleveland was thrice the choice of the people for President, but it is by no means certain that to-day, with the women's vote and the growing delicacy of the public mind, he would survive such an ordeal.

The Cleveland case got into print, miles of it indeed, till one might have thought a presidential election was a competition for a prize of virtue, but later elections have seen less print and

[1] The Parnell case is not, perhaps, on all fours with the Dilke case. The motives or forces which suddenly and conveniently prompted Captain O'Shea to defend his household's honour have never been completely accounted for.

[2] Henry Adams to C. M. Gaskell, September 21, 1884, *Letters of Henry Adams*, p. 360.

more whispering. What can be done by an excited public in
this way is indicated by the stories about the habits of the late
Lord Oxford and his friends, the innumerable degenerates of the
Pemberton-Billing case, and such rumours had a considerable
share in the overthrow of the Asquith ministry. The fever of
war is a palliation, but no such excuse can be found for the
Republicans who were so free in their verbal criticisms of President
Wilson's private life and made the election of Mr. Hughes in
1916 as much the remedy for the Capri-like degradation of the
White House as the solution of the problem of relations with
Germany and the Allies. In 1920, the Democrats, provided
with so many reasons for not electing Senator Harding to the
presidency, or to any office, thought fit to rely on his alleged
Negro descent as likely to arouse more feeling than the mere
charge of unfitness for any responsible office.[1] These charges
are not made in public by responsible people, but they are
extremely effective with electors, and there seems no sign of any
decay in the belief that a " whispering campaign ", for all its
dangers, cannot be neglected as a political weapon. If it does
nothing else it arouses interest that otherwise might slumber.
" Such popular discussion of campaign issues as is in fact incited
is mostly of the nature of gossip about the personal character
and habits of candidates, and the politicians cater to such tastes
by systematic calumny." [2]

There is another side to this medal and if good candidates
have been beaten on irrelevant issues, bad ones have won on
their chastity, orthodoxy, sobriety, etc. It is deemed a good
answer to political charges to assert that the candidate or
office-holder is a good man and woe betide the controversialist
who gives his opponent a chance to invoke the home, family, etc.
Thus Mr Al Smith annihilated Mr. Ogden Mills by an appeal
to his opponent " ' to lay his private life alongside of mine ' ".[3]
This challenge was not strictly relevant, but it " went over big ".
In the same way, the numerous and not unjustifiable charges
against Mr. William Vare and his machine in Philadelphia were
made, as his champion bitterly complained, " ' forgetful of the
fact that his family life is the most beautiful thing I know of ' ".[4]
Unfortunately Mr. Mackey was addressing a Senate Committee,

[1] " I think it amused him to realize, as he did and I did, that the scandal
that came up in the presidential campaign of 1920 in which Mrs. Arnold's
name and his were linked very frequently, was for us the source of greatest
protection, for while the Democrats who were ' slinging mud ' played with
Mrs. Arnold's name they were not looking for mine or any other." Nan
Britton, *The President's Daughter*, p. 102.
[2] H. J. Ford, *Representative Government*, p. 285.
[3] P. Odegard, *American Public Mind*, p. 161.
[4] *Reed Committee Hearings*, p. 559.

not a jury or a public meeting, and Mr. Vare was unseated with no more compunction than if he had been Brigham Young.

Attacks on other aspects of the lives of presidential or other candidates are old enough, but many important statesmen survived a good deal of notorious high living, until, with the growing importance attached to moral issues after the Civil War, it became necessary to cater to the susceptibilities of voters. It was with wisdom, as well as humour, that Blaine said he wanted his gout announced as rheumatism and resented his Washington house being described as of " palatial grandeur ", and Roosevelt never showed so much anger at an attack as when he was rashly accused by a Michigan editor of heavy drinking.[1]   It is fairly safe to say that no candidate who had the habits of Daniel Webster could reach the heights not merely of popularity, but of respect, that Webster attained.   The moralists of to-day would not have waited for a political sin to write him down as a fallen angel.

Another change which may be permanent is the importance attached to humble origins.   " From log-cabin to White House " was for two generations a well-travelled road, but of recent years there has been marked in widening areas a respect for polished rather than rough diamonds.   With the exception of Harding, every President since McKinley has been a college product and there was widespread fear that Governor Smith and his wife would " let down " the social tone of the White House.   How far these fears were rationalizations of deeper emotions it is not easy to determine.   The objection to the New York speech of the Democratic candidate was in marked contrast to the tolerance, not to say admiration, granted to President Coolidge's New England drawl.   The appreciation extended to " cow " pronounced as a word of four syllables by Mr. Coolidge and the horror registered when Mr. Smith pronounced " radio " as " raddio ", probably signified no more than the fact that the dialect of New York is to the average American a foreign, second-class dialect, not yet admitted to the full civil rights allowed to the speech of New England or of Iowa.

Yet the American middle class has decidedly forgotten its origins and is not anxious to have political leaders who behave with less social grace than the average reader of the *Saturday Evening Post*.   It may be doubted if Kansas would admire to-day the courage of the famous demagogue who rejoiced in his title of

---

[1] Roosevelt was, innocently, the means of damaging badly a promising career.   He visited the home of his Vice-President, Charles M. Fairbanks, at Indianapolis.   There cocktails were served and Fairbanks was a leading layman of the Methodist Episcopal Church !   The resultant row not only ruined Fairbanks but was a factor in a split of the Republican party in the state that revived the dormant Democracy of Indiana.

"Sockless Jerry" Simpson, but wherever the social conditions
that bred the Sockless Jerries and the "Wool Hat" boys who
followed "Pitchfork Ben" Tillman exist, too great insistence on
the correct thing may be a political handicap.   In a rash moment,
a woman working against "Alfalfa Bill" Murray in the still
frontier state of Oklahoma, asserted that the Sage of Tishimingo
"'lived for years in a house without a bath-tub.   He never
wears a coat unless the weather chills him, and habitually
appears in a dirty shirt.   The story of how Murray and his
family lived contentedly for years in a house with a sod floor
will be broadcast to the nations.'"   It was, at any rate, effectually
broadcast to the majority of the citizens of Oklahoma, who saw
that Mr. Murray was very like themselves and triumphantly
elected him.   In these hard times the number of voters in the
agricultural states who, from necessity if not choice, have to
live in the manner of Governor Murray is so great that it is not
surprising that he became a formidable contender for the
Democratic nomination in the rural states, but even in southern
states a politician whose heart is indubitably with the suffering
poor may be excused for not living like them.   That popular
tribune, Senator Huey P. Long of Louisiana, makes a point of
canvassing the poverty-stricken farmers of his state in a good car
and in good clothes.   With the generosity of the poor, they bear
him no ill will for his prosperity.

It is, indeed, very hard to fix upon a brand of scandal that
will do equally well for all areas or offices.   An authority tells
us that in the old days of indirect election, a Senator or would-be
Senator could get away with a good deal.   Thus Platt "did not
require in his work of political management such a spotless
record of domestic tranquillity as Roosevelt possessed",[1] and Mr.
Boies Penrose stayed in the Senate as long as he liked, but owing
to the existence of certain inconvenient photographs, was unable
to indulge his real ambition of being Mayor of his good city of
Philadelphia.   Even the human inclination to damn for sins one
has no mind or means to, is not uniformly potent.   A group of
Chicago reformers ran a worthy bricklayer against a dishonest
alderman, pointing the contrast of the life of useful toil against
the life of graft, cigars and champagne, but the voters admired
the grafter both for his ability to get hold of the good things of
life and for his open enjoyment of them and the honest toiler
had to go on toiling.[2]   But such mistakes in the difficult city

[1] H. F. Gosnell, *Boss Platt*, p. 330.
[2] There is a corresponding story of a candidate for an English constituency
who was accused, justly, of having had a horse "pulled".   His opponents
spread the story, but found that the voters thought the sporting man one
after their own heart.   He romped home.

of Chicago are not confined to the reformers. Even the professionals slip. When Mr. Charles E. Merriam was running for Mayor on a reform platform, his opponents passed round the word that he was always to be called " Professor " Merriam, for such was his profession and the calculation was that such a title would damn him in the eyes of red-blooded men. It was fortunately discovered, before it was too late that, in the less thoroughly Americanized parts of the city, the voters thought the title of Professor one of honour and an asset, and the word had hurriedly to be passed round that the title was only to be used in the " Anglo-Saxon " wards.

Of the minor taboos that a candidate must not break there is no end. Even as late as twenty years ago, it was a handicap to President Taft that he played golf, and laughter split the welkin twenty years before that when it was discovered that a candidate for office in New York played *tennis* ! Both these games have risen in popular estimation : was not the support of Al Smith by " Bobby " Jones political news ? But the consecrated sport of Americans is still fishing. It is the rural sport and the political tradition still insists that the leader of the nation must be a countryman in his work and his play.[1]

---

[1] Even fishing has its political dangers. Cleveland was charged with fishing on Decoration Day, the commemorative festival of the Civil War— in which he had not served. It did him the same kind of damage as the story that he had gone to the theatre on the night that the news of the death of General Gordon arrived, did Gladstone.

Chapter III

ADVERTISING

THERE is an acute difference of opinion as to the wisdom of making a speaking tour in a presidential campaign. To say nothing at all is the ambition of the prudent politician who has painful memories of what Winfield Scott and Winfield Scott Hancock did to themselves in rash moments of candour, and the lesson of 1896 seemed to be that oratory did not pay. McKinley sat on his front porch at Canton, received carefully shepherded deputations and issued carefully worded statements. Bryan swept all over the land, speaking everywhere, to hostile audiences in New York, to ragging students at Yale and then in his own country inflaming the farmers at great meetings and with brief exhortations wherever his train stopped. Bryan was the most powerful public speaker in American politics since the Civil War and his campaign of 1896 was the most brilliant of all time, but he was beaten. It is far from certain that Bryan had any option. He was engaged on a forlorn hope ; when he was nominated few thought he had the ghost of a chance ; if, in a month or two, he galvanized the Democrats into action and terrified his enemies, he did it by speech. The campaign lasted too long : his audiences no doubt contained an increasing number of sensation seekers, but the huge poll that Bryan achieved was an army won by speech. If he had stayed at home in Lincoln, issuing careful statesmanlike messages, the campaign would have been dead-born. McKinley could stay within his Torres Vedras, he had only to hold on to win, but Bryan had to take the initiative or be impotent from the start.

But not all candidates are Bryans, able to stir any group, if only for the moment, with burning, powerful, empty words Among the many causes of the defeat of Mr. Hughes in 1916, his speaking tour seemed to some observers one of the most potent. According to custom, President Wilson remained at his country house at Shadow Lawn : it was not fitting for a President of the United States to indulge in an oratorical contest. Mr. Hughes, despite the doubts of some of his supporters, covered all the country in an attempt to make himself more than a name. But a manner lacking in superficial attraction, and the habits of a judge, were inadequately covered by a mask of energetic vagueness. The speeches palled and the tide which had seemed to be flowing with the Republican Candidate, ebbed after he had been seen and heard. A natural orator, one who is inflamed by an audience and inflames it, a Bryan, a Theodore Roosevelt, an Al Smith, for all the differences of their styles, is wasting his talent if he does not use it to sink the impression of his personality into the public mind, but few presidential Candidates are of this stamp and they are well advised to leave the synthetic portrait manufactured by their publicity man to go before the country with as little contradiction from the facts as possible.

The fate of Mr. Hoover's speaking campaign in 1932 seems to reinforce the belief that it is both undignified and unwise for a President to go on the stump on his own behalf. The demoralization of the Republican ranks which followed the Democratic victory in Maine in September made drastic measures necessary and Mr. Hoover abandoned that close attention to executive business in Washington which was to have been his rebuke to the demagogic speaking tours of his rival. Mr. Hoover displayed much more political pugnacity than the public had credited him with, and he " swung round the circle " predicting doom and disaster if Mr. Roosevelt were elected, seeing in prophetic vision the grass growing in the streets of a hundred cities if he were not kept in the White House. It is possible that Mr. Hoover's speaking tour had no effect either way, but there was nothing to show for this descent from the dignity of the office or for the great effort involved in speaking frequently (Mr. Hoover spoke fifteen times in twenty-four hours) and ruling the country at the same time. On the other hand, Mr. Roosevelt had reason for speaking frequently and over a wide area. The physical energy thus displayed was a more effective answer to the whispers of ill-health than any number of pictures taken in swimming-baths or on board yachts. In addition it was possible to make an open and successful bid for support by speeches such as that delivered at Los Angeles, which no doubt helped to win the President's own state away from him. The chance to show tact, sympathy, diplomatic ambiguity and rhetorical skill made Mr. Roosevelt's speaking tours a model to presidential aspirants as Mr. Hughes's performance in 1916 was an unforgettable lesson in what to avoid.

The radio is a new force in politics whose importance it is as hard for politicians to assess, as it is for advertisers. It is probable that it had a great negative effect in 1924, that whatever chances the Democrats had were thrown away by the time the listeners had been infuriated with the apparently endless squabbles and flaring up of tempers in the Madison Square Garden. The newspaper reports had a far less irritating effect on the average man and woman than had the long procession of ballots and the accompaniment of noise, coming over the radio to listeners who had less and less confidence that a party which obviously could not rule itself, was fit to rule the country. The horror with which Governor Smith's accent was listened to in millions of homes was a handicap, which might have been forgiven had these listeners seen the "Happy Warrior" face to face. In a local election radio has told with great effect. The possession of his own radio station enabled Mr. Henry Field to persuade the Republicans of Iowa that Senator Brookhart had put too many of his own family on the national pay-roll, but in a national election, except that it has added the expense of a "hook-up" to the worries of the managers, no one can be certain what its influence has been or will be. It is probable that it has diminished the importance of the old flamboyant oratory; "spread-eagling" was going out of fashion in any case; the old style of tearing a passion to tatters is less and less acceptable, although it has its practitioners still, especially in the ranks of the southern statesmen to whom rhetoric is nature. But speech is little; to the politician, it is one of many forms of propaganda, dangerous as well as useful, liable to upset the careful combinations of party strategy. The most successful of modern American politicians, Mr. Coolidge, brought to an unequalled pitch the art of saying little in words and less in meaning. His resolute ignoring of all that his opponent had to say in 1924 was immensely successful. Gone, possibly for ever, are the days of debates, of attack and rejoinder, and the ideal speech should combine Spartan brevity and Delphic obscurity in nicely planned proportions.

It has so often happened that the candidates for the presidency were unknown to the country at large that the art of "selling" a skilfully manufactured personality to the country has had to be brought to a pitch of virtuosity which makes the hurried explanation of Mr. Baldwin in terms of pigs and pipes very crude work. The rails which Lincoln was supposed to have split, and which had been providentially preserved, were very useful in giving the public of 1860 *some* idea of what manner of man the Republican candidate was. Grant's past spoke for itself and so, in a different fashion, did Blaine's, but Garfield, Hayes, Hancock, and, most of all, Cleveland, needed presentation to the country. This is the function of the campaign biography which tells a far from unvarnished tale about the Candidate. The essential rightness of his early upbringing and his present tastes is stressed. In his dress and manner, Roosevelt always managed to suggest that he had just either come off a ranch, or back from a war, but not many can rival his versatility and usually it is desirable to give an appearance of rustic peace ; it is a far greater asset to have learned swimming in the " Ole Swimmin' Hole " of James Whitcomb Riley's poem, than in the East River which was Governor Smith's equivalent. Mr. Coolidge was wise in cultivating the appearance of a shrewd Vermont farmer with a general background of " The Old Oaken Bucket ", but soon learned by public laughter that in a " ten gallon " hat of the Wild West model he was a subject for laughter. To be a farmer's boy, unspoiled by long years abroad, was the campaign ambition of Mr. Hoover and one which his publicity managers achieved with much success.

Not only is it still an asset to have rural origins ; the Candidates appeal to the farmers for support with a vehemence and earnestness apparently undiminished by the decline in political importance of the rural population. No Candidate, as yet, has had the heart, or the courage, to ignore the farmers and to appeal frankly to the urban majority. It is still a law of political nature that the farmer is entitled to help—if only one knew how to help him. How far farmers are taken in by the sudden solicitude of politicians for their welfare every four years is doubtful, but the semblance of courting the rustic vote must be gone through, even by so patently urban a Candidate as Al Smith. " The candidate knows that what the farmer wants, more than any debatable plan, is a sympathetic government. Therefore, what the candidate says about his plan really is less important than his way of saying it." [1]

Of course no candidate can afford to appear unsympathetic to any large group which, unlike the Negro in the South, can vote. It is always necessary to pacify the farmer since he has had grievances since the memory of living man, but in these bad times it has been necessary to assure large numbers of usually content urban Americans that the heart of a candidate was with them as well as with the farmer. It was necessary in 1932 to revamp the publicity man's picture of President Hoover ; the " engineer in politics ", the great organizer of prosperity was no longer saleable, so the innate kindness of the President, his freedom from the numerous faults alleged by his now very numerous enemies, had to be stressed. Books had to be written to refute the flood of criticism and slander and the country was to be reminded, not of the great executive who had built up a great industry, but of the poor boy who had been unable to comprehend how one man could eat seventy-five cents' worth of food at a meal.

[1] Garet Garrett, " Notes of these Times : The Farmer ", in *The Saturday Evening Post*, November 12, 1932.

In any case the candidate, rural or urban, must be made human. The grimness of his features was a handicap to Wilson who prudently made a jest of a disability by a limerick. As his academic rank was also a handicap, his reputed skill as a football coach at Wesleyan University and as a pinch hitter at baseball, when he was a student at Davidson College, North Carolina, were dwelt on. There was no need to sell Mr. Harding as a "regular fellow"; he was "nothing else but". Mr. Coolidge's dry Vermont wit, economy of speech and clothes were all stressed as far as was safe. Mr. Hoover presented a more difficult problem, for he had fewer political friends than most Presidents when he took office and he made none afterwards. His friends had a whole corpus of legend to fight against and some showed real skill in the forlorn hope.

The Muses are called in and there is a campaign song; either one manufactured for the occasion, or a popular ditty adopted by the supporters of the candidate, with more or less relevance. Bryan had the Sousa march "El Capitan" and Al Smith "The Sidewalks of New York", but these were exceptionally appropriate. The song is usually a very poor affair. Mr. Al Jolson, probably, does not pride himself especially on "Harding, You're the Man for Us" which he contributed to the campaign of 1920. In some campaigns there have been "theme songs" which had symptomatic importance. "Sheridan's Ride" was a campaign document of 1864, for it made dramatic that Battle of Winchester which was one of the blows which wrecked the Democratic platform, "the War is a failure". In 1916, "I didn't raise my boy to be a soldier" was a heart-cry whose popularity indicated how the voter's mind was moving in the West and how far from certain it was that the country at large shared the hysteria of Roosevelt and the New York clubs. It was a hint that "He Kept Us Out of War" was a slogan more popular than any melodramatic pictures of the unavenged victims of the *Lusitania*.

In a national life almost devoid of pageantry the American political parade played a great part; it was a safety-valve for emotions which, apart from orgiastic religion, had no other legitimate channel. In a country where politics had to be regarded in their naked crudity, with none of the gloss cast on them in older countries by association with other, more æsthetic aspects of society, the mass hysteria of a hotly contested presidential campaign had its value. Failing a great personality, there had to be stimulated artificially the emotions bred naturally by a really potent demagogue. The parade, the bands, the slogans, all were so many cheer leaders to intoxicate the mob and distract its attention from the emptiness of the "issues".

In the Lincoln campaign, the " Wide Awake Clubs " marched under their broad-brimmed hats singing of the merits of the " rail-splitter " who had " come out of the Wilderness, down in Illinois "—a song that was to be parodied a few years later when Lee's army taunted " Fighting Joe Hooker " in the Wilderness of Virginia, soaked in blood because Lincoln had been elected. Twenty years later it was " Tow-path clubs ", for had not Garfield been a canal boy ? He had afterwards gone to college, but he was an example of that American democracy of which the Republican party was the providential guardian. The last great campaign of the old style came when the Republicans had to counter the magic of Bryan's oratory with some equally potent appeal to the emotions. Money might buy many and argument win others, but there were masses, which might prove decisive, to be won through the eye and ear ; to be convinced that the incendiary *was* going to be beaten and so induced to join the winners—and yet persuaded that he might *not* be beaten and that the end of all things would be then at hand. In the panic that shook the complacency of the rich, the reserve that is traditionally supposed to keep American business men out of politics was cast aside and they poured into the streets to convince the wavering that the men who knew, the men whose opinions counted, had really their hearts set on the defeat of this miscreant. A startled English observer saw the great Chicago parade.

" Between them, now eight abreast, shoulder to shoulder, now four abreast in open order across the whole street, advanced battalion after battalion of marchers. . . . A hundred thousand men ! More than thirteen miles of procession ! Capitalists worth two hundred million dollars ! . . . ' If M'Kinley gets all of that votes out of this county,' said the lift-boy, . . . ' he'll be our next President sure '." [1]

That was the object ; the average American like the average Englishman is a believer in the big battalions ; few are the Spartans who are not intimidated by the myriads in the enemy's ranks ; the zealots may stand firm, but the large body of the undecided have often their minds made up for them by ingeniously fostered beliefs that one side is sure to win. It was the mark of a good campaigner that he gave this impression. [2]

[1] G. W. Steevens, *The Land of the Dollar*, pp. 189 ff.
[2] Hence followed the remarkable contradictions between the reports of the size of meetings and processions in papers of opposite opinions. A Democratic procession in Indiana was announced as " the greatest torchlight procession that had ever marched in the city of Crawfordsville ; that it was so large that it took two hours to pass a given point. The evening Republican

In the torpor of the Coolidge years, politics was an intrusion on the public's concentration on private affairs, for the nation took the President's dictum to heart, " the business of the United States is business ". The bitter personal and religious issues of 1928 and the desire to " take a crack " at the administration so widespread in 1932 stimulated public attention, but the American public is still less politically minded than are most European peoples and only on exceptional occasions do the party agents find willing hearing for their oratory and other arts of persuasion or illusion.

paper quoted this statement, confessed it was true, and then added that the given point was Mike Mulholland's saloon " (*Recollections of Thomas M. Marshall*, pp. 137–8).

Chapter IV

"VOX POPULI"

IT has to be remembered that a presidential year is also a year full of other elections and if the public eye is concentrated on the main campaign, the many eminent politicians running for other offices are not all in a self-sacrificing mood, nor is the victory of the presidential Candidate a complete substitute for local triumph. It is true that, as a rule, a successful presidential Candidate can pull up the total vote and especially in the case of a Republican victory, drag into office many minor candidates whom the electors would never have chosen in cold blood. Yet a great presidential triumph may have little effect on local or congressional victory. Wilson's triumph in 1916 was marked by an ebb of Democratic strength in the congressional and state elections and even the great Hoover sweep of 1928 only carried eight Democratic Congressional seats with it. The union, in time, of a series of elections that have little else in common, produces more effect than it deserves, in the way of producing a nominal uniformity of political decision in the country at large, but the strength of American parties is, as a rule, too sectional, too much divorced from any current national controversies, for there to be anything like our " swing of the pendulum ". There have been elections which inflicted humiliating defeat on one party all along the line. The Republicans suffered in this way in the congressional election of 1890, after the McKinley tariff, and the force of popular resentment was not spent in 1892. The Taft administration was " rebuked " in 1910 and destroyed in 1912, and the unanimity with which the United States disowned Wilsonism in 1920 left little to be desired by the spectator. But most American elections are " no decision " contests, fought at times fixed by the calendar and decided on lines laid down sixty years ago. The record size of the poll in 1932 only represented the anxiety of millions to register their sense of deception, not their positive political philosophy, if they had any. But in more normal years, not only has politics to face the competition of other and more dramatic sports, it has to suffer under the indifference of a sport-loving public to a " set-up ". Few can get excited over a certainty.

Since the destruction of the old Democratic party in 1896,

there has been only one really doubtful election, that of 1916. All the others, despite panic on one side and vain hope on the other, were fights with only one possible result and that result obvious long before the election. Since 1896, the majority of the American people, in presidential years, is Republican. Unless a new alignment of sections can be made, there is no reason to suspect that this will change and indeed, the parties being what they are, there is no reason why it should. The only cause that can induce the people to oust the present board of directors is the passing of the dividend or a division among the directors themselves. Such a division did the trick in 1912 and the Democratic administration was able, narrowly, to carry on over 1916, but in 1920 the old rulers were reinstated and the election of 1924 showed that nothing could shock the people enough to induce them to unseat the party which was delivering the goods. Since 1896 the Republicans had successfully claimed to be the party of the "full dinner pail", and right down to 1928, the fundamental claim of the G.O.P. was prosperity, reaching its height in that year with the imminent abolition of poverty by the party. For this reason, as well as for others, the Republicans have been able to rely on "consumer acceptance", while the most eloquent and popular Democrats encountered an unbreakable "sales resistance". In good times, then, the election is a formality. It was in vain that, in 1900, Champ Clark tried to rouse the indignation of Missouri farmers at the scandals of imperialism in the Philippines. The political philosophy of the average American was expressed by the voter who told Clark, " ' Well, I guess we can stand it as long as beef-cattle are seven cents a pound on the hoof'." [1] The Republican party and the tariff were together responsible for the plenty that marked off the United States from less favoured lands.

"Perhaps your husband is a carpenter earning $10.16 a day [£2 at gold parity]. You own a home, a phonograph, or a radio. There's enough in the savings bank and in insurance policies to assure those fine children of yours a high-school education, possibly college if they are ambitious. In the garage there's a tidy car into which the whole family piles for a ride at the end of a hot day. The children belong to the school orchestra, your husband and you to a card club, and you all go to the movies when there's a picture worth seeing. . . . Behind the prosperity of the American woman stands the protective tariff . . . the tariff for which the Republican party has stood squarely for generations." [2]

[1] Champ Clark, *My Quarter Century of American Politics*, vol. ii, p. 196.
[2] Anna Steese Richardson, *What Every Woman Wants to Know About the Tariff*, issued by the Republican National Committee, Washington, D.C., 1928.

AA

In a moment of painfully expiated rashness, some Republican orators promised in 1928 " a chicken in every pot and a car in every garage ".   A long and prosperous life for the legend of Republican rule and resultant prosperity was paid for at last.   In vain had Democrats protested in the past that, for instance, the Wilson tariff of 1894 could not have been responsible for the panic of 1893 ; that the slump of 1920 was inevitable after the war boom ; the facts seemed to be on the Republican side.   But these pleasant inventions of controversy returned to plague their inventors.   It was painful for Republicans to see Democrats wearing badges rashly issued in 1928 bearing the image of President Hoover and the legend, " Good for four years more of prosperity."   It was vain to point out that President Hoover had as little to do with the depression as his predecessor had to do with the boom.   The American people has been trained to regard the President and his party as witch-doctors and, like an African tribe, is ready to kill the magicians who cannot or will not work the traditional fertility rites effectively.   The lesson of the past is only too plain ; bad times mean destruction for the party in office.   That party has usually been the Democrats, but in 1932, in the worst of times, the party of prosperity had to explain why its old tariff magic, used in increasing doses, failed and what it hoped to put in its place.   The panic of 1837 shook the Democrats, the panic of 1857, as much as the Dred Scott decision, tided the young Republican party over its delicate first years.   1873, 1893, 1907, each exacted its political price. Mr. Robert Marshall has worked out an ingenious correlation between bad rainfall and a party upheaval.   When the rains are below normal, the party in power goes out.   " ' In 22 cases out of 25 the quadrennial rainfall predicted the next President.' " [1] The series of droughts of the late eighties that stopped the western advance of the grain farmer, bred the Populist party and ended the political careers of many conservative statesmen, as an earlier plague of grasshoppers had given Nebraska a radical constitution, known since as " the grasshopper constitution ".[2]   But those were the days when a farmer was badly off and resentful only

[1] Quoted in P. Odegard, *The American Public Mind*, pp. 148–9.

[2] The defeat of Senator Ingalls of Kansas produced a poem by Mr. Eugene F. Vare :

> " . . . My
> District expects me to produce territorial
> Humidity, and divide the rain-belt with
> The sea-board states. Ingalls could not
> Accomplish it. He therefore failed to be a
> Statesman."

Quoted by Mr. J. D. Barnhart in " Rainfall and the Populist Party in Nebraska ", in *The Political Science Review*, vol. xix (August, 1925).

if, as Solon Chase of Maine put it, "his grass grew backward ";
now with the advance of civilization, he is just as surely ruined
if he has a good crop and it is harder and harder to satisfy him
politically.   It is a sad problem for the Republican party which
has kept going by inducing the farmer to believe that it was
his sure shield.   As they sang in the bad times of the nineties :

>   " 'We voted with our party no matter where it went
>   We voted with our party till we haven't a cent.' " [1]

There is a great temptation to vote, if only in bad temper, for
the party which, if it promises little help, has, at least, not let
you down.

   With the growing industrialization of the United States, the
prosperity or misery of the farmers is not the only thing to be
considered, and since the great Bryan campaign the proletariat
of the towns have been promised everything from a full dinner-
pail to two cars in every family.   That dream has been postponed ; that paradise, if not lost, has at any rate been mislaid.
In 1932, the slogan which was certain to win was that announced
by " Alfalfa Bill " Murray :   " Bread, Butter, Beans and Bacon."
The outcome of the race was almost certain ; it depended on
the relative strengths of fear and hope, but there are moments
when all other emotions subside before hunger.   There are
rock-ribbed Republican states to-day where Lincoln would be
beaten by Jefferson Davis if the latter could make the farmers
believe he could raise the price of wheat to a dollar a bushel,
and General Sherman might beat General Longstreet in Georgia,
if he could perform a corresponding miracle for cotton !

   In good times the Democrats, no matter how hard they may
try, cannot make themselves into *the* party of business and the
status quo.   Since 1896 and the defeat of the Cleveland Democrats,
business has decided to stick to the G.O.P.   The election of
1904 was decisive.   Roosevelt might be a demagogue, Parker a
model of conservatism, but " the interests " supported the Republican candidate, saying, in the words of the *New York Sun* :
" Theodore, for all thy faults, we love thee still."   As M. Siegfried
puts it, despite all attempts to reform the Democratic party on
new lines, it remains, in the eyes of conservative Americans, a
spare tyre.   If the car runs smoothly, it will be left untouched.

   Prosperity is the Republican issue ;   the Democrats must
wait for that moment when they can say " We told you so ".
Then what no oratory on the crimes of the " Black Horse cavalry "
of plunder could do, is done by a panic or, its successor, a
" depression ".   At what are, for the Democratic politician, the
darkest moments:

[1] Quoted in J. D. Hicks, *Populist Revolt*, p. 167.

" they'se always wan ray of light ahead. We're sure to
have hard times. An' whin th' laads that arre baskin' in th'
sunshine iv prosperity with Andhrew Carnaygie an' Pierpont
Morgan an' me frind Jawn D. finds that th' sunshine has
been turned off an' their fellow-baskers has relieved thim iv
what they had in the dark we'll take thim boys be th' hand
an' say : ' Come over with ye'er own kind. Th' Raypublican
party broke ye, but now that ye're down we'll not turn a
cold shoulder to ye. Come in an' we'll keep ye—broke.' " [1]

The decision to continue to entrust the direction of the Union
to the old firm may mean very little, for the Congress that
is elected with every President may have next to nothing in
common with him or his ideas. It will usually, but not invariably, be of the same party composition, but with a much stronger
representation of the minority party than the figures of the
presidential popular vote would lead one to expect, for it may be
possible to invent some issue or other to justify the quadrennial
presidential orgy of oratory, but it is very hard indeed to extend
this issue to the congressional elections which are so often fought
on local issues, or to the senatorial elections which are so often
fought on personalities.

As the constitution provides, the elections occur at fixed times ;
every two years the lower house and a third of the Senate, every
four years the President, the House of Representatives and another third of the Senate run the gauntlet and on both occasions,
the issues and the ballot paper are complicated by the multitudi-
nous local elections. With us this regularity is a feature of local
elections, but Parliament can last five years or ten months. We
have had six general elections since the Armistice, twice our normal allowance, each precipitated at the initiative of the government of the day from necessity or choice, but, at any rate, with
as much regard to electoral possibilities as possible. No such
choice of the strategic moment is possible to an American administration. No sudden burst of popularity can be cashed in by
another election and a new vote of confidence ; there is no opportunity of making the enemy fight on impossible ground ; all is left
to the calendar. Disasters may come thick and fast, but the
election cannot be postponed. The life of the Republic was
once in grave danger because the Lincoln administration, in
the summer of 1864, had to look forward to fighting the presidential election of that year on the question proposed by the
Democrats to the electors, " Is the war a failure ? " It seemed
only too probable that the answer would be overwhelmingly
" Yes ", but Sherman captured Atlanta and Sheridan cleared

[1] *Mr. Dooley's Opinions*, pp. 97-8.

out the Shenandoah Valley and Lincoln was elected. Yet if
the South could have kept the war in a state of stalemate till
the election was over, the Republican party and possibly the
United States, would have been done for. Mr. Hoover, believ-
ing as he did, that the depression was nearly over in 1930,
would no doubt have liked to avoid an election in that
year, but he could do nothing but endure it, while the
country proceeded to wipe out his congressional majority.
Woodrow Wilson had to face a congressional election just before
the War ended and then had to see support for the League of
Nations ebb all through 1919 till it was drowned in November,
1920, by a tidal wave of hostility to everything connected with
the War. Not for him the timely appeal to the country by
which Mr. Lloyd George and Lord Younger got their tame
Parliament of 1919 !

There is a further complication caused by the six-year term
of the Senate. A third is elected every two years, but the third
that runs the gauntlet at any one time may not be a good sample
of the whole body. The system of rotation may result in an
election year which sees a great presidential and congressional
upheaval, leaving the Senate practically untouched, because
only the safest of safe seats have been contested. On the other
hand, it may exaggerate the drift by offering up to slaughter
Senators whose seats are marginal to the party strength. In
an upheaval so complete as that of 1932, it is impossible to
be dogmatic as to the party chances in any state, but the
dreadful losses suffered in the Senate elections by the Republicans
were possibly exaggerated by the type of states involved and
still more by the results of the previous primary elections which
had made the party nominees in some of the western states the
representatives of a party section which the electorate, as a
whole, was extremely anxious to have a chance to reject. The
chance of getting a decisive majority for or against any policy
is thus further rendered more difficult by the possibility that
the sections of the country where Senators are up for election
may be indifferent to the main issue or issues, or on the minority
side, and the result may be to maintain a Senate majority differing
from the House of Representatives and from the President not
only in party colour but, what is more important, in sectional
weight. If it is to its immunity from the hazards of a general
election that the Senate owes some of its power and prestige,
it is to that immunity that the American government owes some
of its spasmodic character in action.

But if the Senate's share of the election may falsify the popular
verdict on the issues of the election, it may do no more than
illustrate the very artificial character of the issues, such as they

are. It is the duty of politicians everywhere to persuade the electorate that something of importance is at stake in the current election, but this task, difficult in all countries at some times, is difficult at almost all times in the United States. The structure of parties, the interweaving of local and national issues, the undecisive character of any popular verdict due to the separation of powers and judicial review, all make it very difficult to persuade the average American that his vote will count for very much in the vast mass of personal, sectional, and national issues from which, in some mysterious way, the pure liquor of popular will is assumed to be distilled. To keep up the interest, to inject some animation into the election is not easy and is not made easier by the long-drawn-out campaign. A candidate may start off well and find his strength ebbing with every week. Bryan might have been elected in 1896, if the election had been held in September instead of November, but the pressure of business on the electors told more and more. Hughes in 1916 went from strength to weakness and in other campaigns, if the result would not have been very different, the shares of the popular vote would have been less unequal if the campaign had been shorter. But the interval between the nominations in June and the elections is too great. Five months of politics breeds boredom, reluctance to change and is thus in favour of the administration, that is, as a rule, of the Republicans. It makes things easier for the defensive. Attention is concentrated more and more on the marginal states and both sides live in hope and fear of accidents that will blast their foes or themselves. Reports come in from the states to the strategists. Roosevelt is driving off more Germans and Irish by his violent assaults on Wilson than he is winning old Progressives to the fold of the G.O.P. Don't let him go west. There is a fighting chance for the Democrats in New Hampshire, so back up the faithful and their Progressive allies in that state. Such were the considerations that moved the headquarters of the two parties in the last close election, 1916. In 1920 the word goes round among the Democrats, make it plain that Cox is the Democratic candidate, not Wilson ; the President's unpopularity is becoming more and more evident to both parties. In 1924, let Republicans stress the danger of the election being thrown into the House of Representatives if the vote is split evenly between Coolidge, Davis and La Follette. Is wheat going to go up or stay up long enough to take the sting out of the La Follette appeal to the farmers ? In 1928, would the Democrats ignore the " whispering campaign " ? Al decides to drag the skeleton out of the cupboard and does it in his invasion of Oklahoma. Will it pay the Republicans to ignore the aid they are getting from the Klan and its allies or try to hold some of the Catholic vote by renunciation of the Willebrandts and other organizers of Protestant sentiment ? There is more to be lost than gained by such a rejection of eagerly proffered aid and the assault on Rome continues. As the election gets nearer it is more and more obvious who *will* win, but the statisticians are busy calculating how, by carrying such and such states, the other man *could* win, no matter what popular majorities are piled up against him elsewhere. Reserves of orators and cash are sent to the threatened spots and there remains one last worry, the weather on election day, for that is a factor which no party has, as yet, managed to control.

Since the party strengths are distributed geographically, the rain does not necessarily fall on the just and unjust alike or with equal force. In a state like New York, the rural Republicans may be kept away from the polls by bad weather which will not be a serious impediment to the urban Democrats. The bad weather was one of the reasons advanced for the failure of Blaine to carry New York in 1884. So much was rain recognized as a Democratic asset that, on one occasion, a rain-maker offered his services at party headquarters ! On the other hand, rain in Oklahoma helps the Republicans by keeping the rural Democrats from the polls. The coming of the car and of good roads has lessened the importance of a factor which added to the worries of the candidate and of his sponsors.[1] But as there are many more natural Republicans than Democrats, i.e. thousands in every northern state who do not vote at all at state elections or vote Democratic, but who always vote and vote Republican at presidential elections, bad weather is a Democratic asset and a small poll is to their advantage.[2]

All political ears are kept to the ground and a remarkably large proportion of the prospective voters make themselves ready to vote for the ticket that seems likely to win. In the old days of narrow elections the voting in the local elections which were, in some states, held in advance of the federal elections, was carefully scrutinized. Was the Republican majority in Maine up or down ; which party had carried Ohio ? On the answers to these questions depended the party allegiance of many Americans. To-day the place of the " October states " has been taken by the " straw votes ", volunteer polls held by newspapers, the most famous of them being the vast enterprise of *The Literary*

[1] Too good weather may also be a handicap. The comparative smallness of the rural poll in the Pennsylvania primary of 1926 was suspected to be due to the reluctance of the farmers to waste a perfect ploughing day in voting.

[2] Both parties have their presidential voters on whom they cannot rely in local elections. Although Governor Roosevelt had only a majority of 25,000 in 1928, a presidential year, and one of 725,000 in 1930, his total poll was down by 460,000.

Digest. This straw vote has in the last three presidential campaigns shown the way the wind was blowing with a most impressive accuracy. Not only in the presidential campaigns, but in such controversial issues as Prohibition, it has been an invaluable guide to the politician and to the voter. As it is assumed that the American voter wants to be on the winning side, parties and causes which see a straw vote running against them, find ingenious reasons for arguing that there is something wrong either with the honesty or the competence of the managers of the poll which is annoying them. Democrats in 1928 whistled to keep their courage up as the evidence of a Hoover victory got clearer ; " dries ", startled by the wet sentiment revealed in the *Digest* prohibition poll of 1932, made wild charges of " wet " corruption and as the monumental majorities of the Democratic ticket and the evidence of a wholesale desertion of the Republican party by former members of it were registered, week by week, in the autumn of 1932, desperate efforts were made to deaden the popular impression of coming doom for the G.O.P. Arguments, not altogether fallacious, were found for distrusting the indications of the poll. The sentiment of the country was declared to have changed since the ballots were sent out ; one New York brokerage house sent out a mendacious circular to its clients asserting that Republican voters were writing in to correct the votes which they had given to the Democratic ticket ; one desperate politician tried to offset the impression made by recalling errors in the poll in 1916. The country was not convinced and when it was discovered that Mr. Hoover had carried Pennsylvania which the *Digest* poll had given to Mr. Roosevelt, there was a general feeling that the poll was probably right, but that Pennsylvanian politicians had been up to their tricks again. If, as is usual, the Pennsylvania elections are the subject of a Senate investigation, the failure of the official election returns to harmonize with the *Digest* prophecies will seem to many a good reason for inquiry into the causes of this discrepancy.[1]

At last the polling day comes and the inextricably mingled forces of local, personal, national sentiment declare their ambiguous verdict. The defeated Candidate sends his congratulations to the victor, bowing to the popular choice as to the will

[1] Maine still consoles herself for her electoral unimportance by having her state elections in September. The state, save in sad times of fusion or split, is uniformly for the G.O.P. It was, then, convenient for the Republicans to attribute importance to an irrelevant election, but in 1932 when the state went Democratic, the evidential value of the vote had to be hurriedly altered in the proclamations of the two parties. The public, however, had been so well taught by the Republicans, that it was too late to undo the mischief, and the Maine election sent a chill down the backs of the Republican parties and President Hoover out on the stump.

of God, and relapses into an obscurity that we find hard to
comprehend.   The President-elect sees power and all its difficulties before him in the rush of job-seekers and policy-moulders.
He begins to pick his Cabinet and to face the possibilities of an
armed truce with Congress.   The end of so much machinery
has been achieved : the United States has a new President.
In normal times it is impossible to be sure of more than that
Mr. X has been elected President instead of Mr. Y ; that one
party, usually the Republican, has carried the presidency and,
usually, has secured " control " of Congress.   Nothing more than
this can be assumed, for in an average election there is no real
programme, nothing at stake but the personal fortunes of the
Candidates.

To the spectator, cynical or indignant, starting from the
premiss that the main object of the election is to put into office
a responsible body of men, thinking alike concerning the main
problems before the Republic, neither the process nor the result
is likely to be edifying.   The campaign seems more and more
to become :

> " A chaos wild of friend and foe,
>   With party-cries of long ago
>   Still *bombinans in vacuo.*"

The result of the election is not to give form to chaos, but to
perpetuate it under a formal order which does not stand any
serious strain.   In more cities than Spoon River, the serious-
minded believer in democracy asks :

> " Can never contests of great moment spring
>   From worthy things, not little ? "

and the enthusiast for any particular measure can begin to indulge his talents for casuistry as did the eminent economist who
proved that the United States, in 1920, voted *for* entering the
League of Nations, while others maintained that the heavy
majority given to Harding was given as a final decision *against*
such an entrance.

When all allowances are made, there seems little reason to be
gratified by this ambiguity.   If it is hard to be sure that the
people have voted against a measure, it is even harder to be sure
that they have voted *for* anything.   In the long run an American
politician seldom suffers from being against anything ; it is
possible to be too conservative, but the risk the other way is
greater.   Timidity and passivity are encouraged and a system
that may have worked well enough in leisured times, when a
policy lasted a generation, is more and more expensive to-day.
The government is turned over to the President and Congress

with the vaguest indications of what the people expects them
to do with it. Differences of opinion between the various
sections of the government are inevitable and the one common
end all have left, after their political ideals have cancelled out,
is the catering to the sectional interests which are so much more
full of life than any general will that can be held to be embodied
in any branch of the government. If the United States is an
agglomeration of electoral districts, this may do very well, but
if it is, or should be, more than that, the muffling of the voice of
the people or the more than oracular vagueness of its words is
tragic for the democrat. It is then that he is most discouraged
and inclined to agree with Mr. " Ed " Howe that the " talk of
government by the people, for the people, etc." is meaningless,
for " that was one of Abe Lincoln's jokes ".

PART ELEVEN
CONCLUSION

Most schemes of political improvement are very laughable things.

DR. JOHNSON.

A CENTURY ago, the Viennese school of medicine was criticized because it was prone to regard its work as done when it had completed its diagnosis. Cure was a base, empiric matter, unworthy of the serious attention of a scientist. Something of the same criticism may be incurred by a student of politics who is content to enumerate weaknesses, without suggesting remedies for them. It has to be admitted that the picture of American politics painted in the preceding pages is not very flattering ; it may compare favourably with the picture that could be drawn of politics in many or most other large countries, but that is not enough. The oldest democratic government in the world faces what is undoubtedly an awkward moment and may be a turning-point in its history, with a system of government obviously illadapted to the necessities of contemporary life. Whatever its merits, the American government is slow, uncertain in its action, liable to have its approaches to a solution barred to it by the courts and, apparently, incapable not merely of a long view, but of a national view, however short.

Part of the weakness and diffidence that marks the American government also marks all other democratic governments. It is no longer possible to take it for granted that the methods of representative government are apt for all emergencies ; whether justly or unjustly, there has been a diminution of faith in the traditional processes of political democracy and a consequent loss of vigour in action. Democracy in the last century made its way not on its moral or intellectual claims, though they had some importance, but on the pragmatic test of success, in war and peace. Lincoln was right when he saw in the American Civil War a test of democratic government, for the public opinion of the world so regarded it. Even the late war, in its immediate results, seemed to justify the faith that had triumphed at Gettysburg. It was the democratic governments which triumphed and

379

the autocracies which, for all their strength in minor matters, were weak in the one thing needful, political sense.

But the problems of peace have proved more distressing than those of war. Faced with the task of liquidating its adventure and meeting, at the same time, the challenge of revolution, European democracy has not notably distinguished itself. It is unnecessary to labour the point. But in the United States, the problem was not so acute. Here was no case of administering the small and, possibly, diminishing assets of a bankrupt estate, but the easier and more cheerful task of declaring a dividend and even distributing a bonus. For this task, the American government was well fitted. It had brought to a high point of efficiency the relationship between political power and cash benefits. It professed to hold the balance even between sections and classes and, thanks to the natural resources of the country and the reign of prosperity, it was able to convince most of the citizenry that it was in fact doing so. But these happy days are over :

> " Dove sono i bei momenti
> Di dolcezza e di piacer ? "

The problems now facing the American government are of the European type, and they are problems which the American government is much less fitted to deal with than are most European governments. The problem facing all the democratic countries to-day is the reconciliation of political democracy with economic development. On the one hand, *laissez-faire* economics may be far better than the mixed system, if it can be called a system, that dominates the industrial countries of western Europe ; but, politically, *laissez-faire* is impossible. No solution based on disregard of this patent truth has any practical value, whatever its intellectual elegance ; it is a solution for a problem in dynamics with friction left out. It is possible that the practice of limiting an economic system based on free enterprise by various measures incompatible with its true character, *is* making the worst of both worlds, but, without adopting either Fascism or Communism, it is the experiment that the old industrial countries must try. Now ill as this compromise between what are, possibly, incompatible attitudes to social life works in Europe, and indifferent as is the technique we have developed, it is far better than anything the United States has developed or can easily acquire. This compromise requires a government which shall take a fairly long and a definitely national view. The American system does its best to make a government of this kind impossible. This system requires a tradition of bureaucratic efficiency and authority that is almost totally lacking in the United States, and a degree of professional autonomy which is not, as yet, present in more than a rudimentary form. This system requires a flexible government, ready to try social experiments and ready to abandon and vary them as necessity dictates. The American government is so organized that it is difficult to do anything at all, impossible to do some things and difficult or impossible to undo things once they have been done, without what may very well be disastrous delay.

The American government must be made more powerful, more united in action and given both a national viewpoint and a competent organ of that viewpoint. To this end there are a number of obvious reforms which are difficult, but not complex or startling. The spoils system, the locality rule, are abuses which have deep roots, but which might come up if there were a strong pull by a people setting its house in order. More difficult, and as necessary, is an attack on the system of checks and balances, on the separation of powers and the unalterable rights of the states and, of course, on their sure shield, judicial review. If sectionalism, slowness, and impotence are the great weaknesses of American government, they are fostered by the constitutional system.

The national government must be given more power in the " twilight zones " in which, at present, legislative power escapes the hands both of state and national government. It must be made easier to amend the federal constitution, as easy as it is to amend the average state constitution by referendum. Judicial review must be the first word, not the last. If the courts find a leak in the system, it must be made easy to stop it up. The present system is a result of that distrust of the state which is now so expensive a luxury for the American people. The customary seven years allotted to the passing of a constitutional amendment and the power thus given to state legislatures are intolerable in these quick-moving days. The American Isaac cannot afford seven years even for Rachel, much less for the Leah which the present amending process usually gives him—when it gives him anything. Even if the American is willing to wait, the problems of the new order may not be willing to wait with him.

It may be objected that the American citizen will not consent to trust Congress with new powers and that Congress has as much power as it deserves or can wisely use. Both of these objections are probably sound, but if the United States has definitely entered on the same stage of social-political development which has been endured in England and Germany since the War, she cannot struggle through with her present government.

If the powers of the national government are thus enlarged, how are we to ensure, or attempt to ensure, that they shall be used in a national spirit ? There seems to be only one answer, by

strengthening the presidency. The adoption of parliamentary
government would be no answer, for parliamentary government,
in a vast country like the United States, is a very different thing
from what it is in England, even if we assume that, in its English
form, it leaves little to be desired as a solution of the problem
of the relations of executive and legislature. It is surely easier
to develop the existing national institution, the presidency, than
to nationalize either House of Congress. The one is a development of an institution which has behind it what there is in the
way of a national tradition and so has the advantage of comparative simplicity. We can have some idea of what a stronger
presidency would be like, but little of what would be the results
of giving more power to Congress. How, then, shall we reform
the presidency ? It might be desirable to give the President the
power of dissolution, but that would involve tampering with the
character of the Senate and would produce an inferior form of
parliamentary government. But the existing powers of the
President should be strengthened. He should be freed from the
necessity of senatorial confirmation of appointments, not because
it is in itself of great importance, but as a means of weakening
the spoils system. " Senatorial courtesy " should die. He
should have greater positive and negative financial power. A
veto on items of bills would help to abolish the " pork barrel "
and over the disposal of the revenue, the President should have
very wide powers, Congress being reduced to voting general
appropriations. Nor should congressional control of financial
detail come in by a side door. Let Congress investigate as much
as it likes, but let its power be purely moral, except in the case
of such offences as deserve impeachment.

But the fundamental addition which is necessary to enable the
President to defy the pressure of local interests incarnate in
Senators and representatives, is the right to appeal to the nation
by referendum. This power has already raised the state Governor
from a figurehead to a public servant who can, if he wills, do
things worth doing. The President should have an absolute
veto over constitutional amendments proposed by Congress, until
the country has decided between them, and the right to propose
his own amendments and his own direct legislation to the country, whether or no Congress approves. If it is possible to make
national politics out of sectional politics, it can only be done
through the presidency.

But the presidency must be made more national in its origin.
The electoral college must go. It is not merely that it may,
as it did in 1876 and 1888 and, nearly, in 1884 and 1916, distort
the national will as expressed by the popular vote, but that it
makes a presidential election the sum of state elections, makes

the alliance with the state machines necessary to the national parties and concentrates attention, both before the nomination and before the election, on the doubtful states. If it is necessary to attack the locality rule in Congress—and it is—it is more important to attack the presidential equivalent. If the United States were one vast presidential constituency, the present bars to a candidate from either Pennsylvania or Delaware would break down, the power of " availability " be weakened, and a presidential primary would have more chance of working well.

It will be of little avail to nationalize the presidency, if that office is to be the creature of the present party system. The present parties have had their life drained out of them and are now mere shells ; collections of professional politicians trading on the irrational loyalties of the mass of the voters. It is difficult to see any way of improving the existing parties. The Republicans have all the faults bred by long success and the illusion that all is for the best in the best of all possible parties. The fidelity and success with which the G.O.P. served the dominant interest of the American economic system in the past two generations, makes the party, to-day, less able than ever before to meet the altered demands of the new society. *The* party of business, by its tariff policy, its farm policy, its lack of any rational foreign policy, is now an enemy of many forms of big business. The relationship between the party and business may have been symbiotic in the past, but it is now parasitic. The feeblest industries, the least hopeful activities of the American capitalist system are those which the Republican party is determined to foster.

Nor is the Democratic party any better. Much against its will, it has been unable to identify itself with the economically dominant forces of modern America and is therefore less committed to an obsolete politico-economic technique ; it has given fewer hostages to old fortunes. But what it gains in this direction, it loses by its internal incoherence. The victory of 1932 is probably meaningless in relation to party fortunes. The nation has given the ship of state a new master and a new crew and given them sealed orders. If by a miracle of political boldness and sagacity, a new orientation could be given to national policy and that were accompanied by a revival of business, the Democrats might dig themselves in, but such a new course would require a degree of boldness and coherence which the Democrats, no more than their rivals, have had any chance of developing. If they remain content to be " maintained by the business interests as a combined lightning rod and lifeboat ",[1] they will give way to the Republicans as soon as the major party has got its breath back. If

[1] Paul H. Douglas, *The Coming of a New Party*, p. 164.

they start on a really new tack, they will split or cease to be the old Democratic party.

If little or nothing can be done with the existing parties, what chances are there of a new party ? For the moment the third party hopefully planned by Professor Dewey and the academic liberals is impossible. If things get so bad that the existing parties break down, the new party, or parties, will not be made by professors. Yet the professors, whatever their defects as practical politicians, are intellectually on the right lines. The American sectional and classless parties are a delusion and a snare, and if they were tolerable in the good old days they are now a luxury that the United States cannot afford. It is necessary that the cards be put on the table, and that the sections of the population who believe in giving the rich their head, should be on one side and those who disagree should be on the other. It is often asserted that what the United States wants is a powerful Socialist or Labour party, but what is immediately necessary is a powerful and intellectually honest Conservative party.

The United States has had only one openly Conservative party and that short-lived. The Federalists, with some necessary political ambiguity, were frankly conservative ; opposed to aggression against property rights, denying the egalitarian theses of their opponents and attempting to hold up the American Revolution at the point most convenient to the upper-middle classes. Apart from the great successes of the constitution and the courts, the Federalists failed. Since their day the conservative case has been let go by default or defended by arguments at an intellectual level beneath contempt. To bring all kinds of pressure to bear and, when that failed, to indulge in the most violent abuse and rhetorical excess of language, has been the method of the American " better classes " when confronted with dangerous movements among the more numerous part of the population, the poor. Not until the possessing classes consent to fight in the open, with the usual allowance of mendacity, of pressure, of conscious hypocrisy, will American politics recover or acquire health.

A really powerful Radical party, basing itself openly on economic, not on sectional differences, would, of course, smoke the rich out of their holes in the old parties. Hopeful radicals have again and again seen a red sky at morning, but it has always been a false dawn. Yet the forces that should make for a new class party are getting stronger. The dominant American political theory asserts the existence of a republic which offers economic independence to all capable and industrious citizens. This was as true as such theories can be, a century ago when the present

political system took shape ; it is less and less true to-day. The
frontier is closed, no longer can the discontented make themselves
independent on the farm ; indeed, the farmer who is already
established is losing ground ; a serf of the banker when he is
not a tenant farmer or an outright employee. The farmer's
republic is dead. The average American to-day is a proletarian ;
the alleged " new economic revolution " which was to spread
property, in small doses, all over the land, was always a joke
and is now a joke in bad taste. If the present depression lasts
much longer, this truth will be forced into the heads of even the
most stoutly Anglo-Saxon of Americans. The ending of immigration is producing a fairly homogeneous labouring class and
economic pressure is curing millions of formerly hopeful citizens
of dearly-held illusions. A new boom will postpone this development, a prolongation of the present acute distress will accelerate
it, but the conviction that, for the vast majority of Americans,
there is no hope of deliverance from dependence on the possessing
classes can hardly be postponed indefinitely. Baseless hope is
the last infirmity of feeble minds, but the power of self-deception
must have a limit. When that limit has been reached, the party
system in America will suffer catastrophic changes. For, despite
all slogans to the contrary, few, if any, Americans are believers
in *laissez-faire* or rugged individualism. Everyone who thought
he would be heard, in every class of society, has been accustomed
for a century past to demanding from the government very
tangible economic benefits. The moment the poor American
thinks he will get more directly from the government, than he
will at second-hand from the rich, he will take the matter in
hand. For the task to which he will then address himself, he is
very ill prepared by his previous political experience. It will
be difficult to disabuse him of the idea that somewhere there is
a cornucopia on which he is entitled to draw. Prudence, foresight, accurate stock-taking, have not been features of American
political methods in the past nor will they be in the near future.
It is in such an emergency that the American rich may have.
reason to regret the absence of a frankly conservative party
which could appeal to a bewildered people with more force
than the palpably worthless parties of the old order. It is then
that the American rich may regret their neglect of the attributes
of a true oligarchy, self-respect, prudence and a minimum
standard of political decorum. It is possible that, if the American
rich were less given to panic and had a higher standard of class
responsibility, they might still induce the poor to let them take
over the state, as the Bank of St. George did the Republic of
Genoa. The American poor, however angry and disillusioned,
might have a very reasonable distrust of their own powers of

recasting society or keeping the industrial machine running. A firm offer from a class which had earned trust, might pacify the poor, but there is no class to make the offer with any chance of being believed. If then, the present crisis does not liquidate itself soon and that without intolerable suffering on the part of the poor, the dykes of the old party system may cave in sooner than most people expect—and after that the deluge. For, no matter what hopes one may have of the curative or palliative powers of the reforms suggested in these pages, one can hardly think their adoption likely except in the case of a breakdown so complete that the difficulties imposed by constitutional pro-prieties would be among the least of the national worries.

There is another possibility. These fears may be idle or exaggerated ; the long-promised corner may have been already turned or panic may induce the parties, like Tweedledum and Tweedledee, to drop their mock battle and do some hasty repairing which will keep the old ship afloat. If this be so, America's trust in the essential rightness of her political methods will be restored along with prosperity. The question whether the present system is an essential lubricant or mere sand in the machine of production, will not be asked or answered ; the importance of politics will again be personal and sectional, a way of " beating the game " and getting economic goods which otherwise would go to someone else. The weaknesses and abuses of the system will be humorously tolerated. Prudent men, politicians and private citizens alike, will put up with inconsistencies and abuses, submitting to unpleasant necessities lest worse befall them. For if the old system has really exhausted itself, the changes will take unpredictable forms and find unforeseen weapons and new men to wield them.

" If ", said Burke, " a great change is to be made in human affairs, the minds of men will be fitted to it ; the general opinions and feelings will draw that way. Every fear, every hope, will forward it ; and then they, who persist in opposing this mighty current in human affairs, will appear rather to resist the decrees of Providence itself, than the designs of men. They will not be resolute and firm, but perverse and obstinate."

Nothing less than such a revolution will discredit the old order and its defenders ; until then the American political system will stand in its ancient ways.

APPENDIX I

CONSTITUTION OF THE UNITED STATES OF AMERICA

(Italics and notes are the author's)

WE THE PEOPLE of the United States, in order to form a more perfect union, establish justice, insure domestic tranquillity, provide for the common defence, promote the general welfare, and secure the blessings of liberty to ourselves and our posterity, do ordain and establish this Constitution for the United States of America.[1]

ARTICLE I

Section 1.—All legislative powers herein granted shall be vested in a Congress of the United States, which shall consist of a Senate and House of Representatives.

Section 2.—*The House of Representatives shall be composed of members chosen every second year* by the people of the several States, and the *electors in each State shall have the qualifications requisite for electors of the most numerous branch of the State legislature.*

No person shall be a Representative who shall not have attained to the age of twenty-five years, and been seven years a citizen of the United States, and *who shall not, when elected, be an inhabitant of that State in which he shall be chosen.*

Representatives and direct taxes *shall be apportioned among the several States* which may be included within this Union, *according to their respective numbers, which shall be determined by adding to the whole number of free persons, including those bound to service* for a term of years, and excluding Indians not taxed, *three-fifths of all other persons.*[2] *The actual enumeration shall be made* within three years after the first meeting of the Congress of the United States, and *within every subsequent term of ten years,* in such manner as they shall by law direct. The number of Representatives shall not exceed one for every thirty thousand, *but each State shall have at least one Representative ; and* until such enumeration shall be made, the State of New Hampshire shall be entitled to choose three, Massachusetts eight, Rhode Island and Providence Plantation one, Connecticut five, New York six, New Jersey four, Pennsylvania eight, Delaware one, Maryland six, Virginia ten, North Carolina five, South Carolina five, and Georgia three.

When vacancies happen in the Representation from any State,

[1] Drafted in 1787, went into effect in 1789.
[2] " Three-fifths of other persons ", i.e. slaves, cf. Amendments XIV, XV and XIX.

the executive authority thereof shall issue writs of election to fill such vacancies.

The House of Representatives shall choose their Speaker and other officers ; and *shall have the sole power of impeachment.*

Section 3.—The Senate of the United States shall be composed of two Senators from each State, chosen by the legislature thereof, for six years ; and each Senator shall have one vote.[1]

Immediately after they shall be assembled in consequence of the first election, *they shall be divided as equally as may be into three classes.* The seats of the Senators of the first class shall be vacated at the expiration of the second year, of the second class at the expiration of the fourth year, and of the third class at the expiration of the sixth year, so that *one-third may be chosen every second year* ; and if vacancies happen by resignation, or otherwise, during the recess of the legislature of any State, the executive thereof may make temporary appointments until the next meeting of the legislature, which shall then fill such vacancies.

No person shall be a Senator who shall not have attained to the age of thirty years, and been nine years a citizen of the United States, and *who shall not, when elected, be an inhabitant of that State for which he shall be chosen.*

The Vice-President of the United States shall be President of the Senate, but shall have no vote, unless they be equally divided.

The Senate shall choose their other officers, and also a President *pro tempore,* in the absence of the Vice-President, *or when he shall exercise the office of President of the United States.*

The Senate shall have the sole power to try all impeachments. When sitting for that purpose, they shall be on oath or affirmation. *When the President of the United States is tried, the Chief Justice shall preside ; and no person shall be convicted without the concurrence of two-thirds of the members present.*

Judgment in cases of impeachment shall not extend further than to removal from office, and disqualification to hold and enjoy any office of honour, trust or profit under the United States ; but the party convicted shall nevertheless be liable and subject to indictment, trial, judgment, and punishment, according to law.

*Section 4.—*The times, places, and manner of holding elections for Senators and Representatives, shall be prescribed in each State by the legislature thereof ; but the Congress may at any time by law make or alter such regulations, except as to the places of choosing Senators.

The Congress shall assemble at least once in every year, and such meeting shall be on the first Monday in December, unless they shall by law appoint a different day.[2]

*Section 5.—*Each house shall be the judge of the elections, returns and qualifications of its own members, and a majority of each shall constitute a quorum to do business ; but a smaller number may adjourn from day to day, and may be authorized to compel the attendance of absent members, in such manner, and under such penalties as each house may provide.

[1] Cf. Amendment XVII.   [2] Cf. Amendment XX.

Each house may determine the rules of its proceedings, punish its members for disorderly behaviour, and, with the concurrence of two-thirds, expel a member.

Each house shall keep a journal of its proceedings, and from time to time publish the same, excepting such parts as may in their judgment require secrecy ; and the yeas and nays of the members of either house on any question shall, at the desire of one-fifth of those present, be entered on the journal.

Neither house, during the session of Congress, shall, without the consent of the other, adjourn for more than three days, nor to any other place than that in which the two houses shall be sitting.

Section 6.—The Senators and Representatives shall receive a compensation for their services, to be ascertained by law, and paid out of the Treasury of the United States. They shall in all cases, except treason, felony, and breach of the peace, be privileged from arrest during their attendance at the session of their respective houses, and in going to and returning from the same ; and for any speech or debate in either house, they shall not be questioned in any other place.

No Senator or Representative shall, during the time for which he was elected, be appointed to any civil office under the authority of the United States, which shall have been created, or the emoluments whereof shall have been increased during such time ; and no person holding any office under the United States, shall be a member of either house during his continuance in office.

Section 7.—*All bills for raising revenue shall originate in the House of Representatives ; but the Senate may propose or concur with amendments as on other bills.*

Every bill which shall have passed the House of Representatives and the Senate, shall, before it becomes a law, be presented to the President of the United States ; if he approve he shall sign it, but if not he shall return it, with his objections, to that house in which it shall have originated, who shall enter the objections at large on their journal, and proceed to reconsider it. If after such reconsideration two-thirds of that house shall agree to pass the bill, it shall be sent, together with the objections, to the other House, by which it shall likewise be reconsidered, and if approved by two-thirds of that house, it shall become a law. But in all such cases the votes of both houses shall be determined by yeas and nays, and the names of the persons voting for and against the bill shall be entered on the journal of each house respectively. If any bill shall not be returned by the President within ten days (Sundays excepted) after it shall have been presented to him, the same shall be a law, in like manner as if he had signed it, unless the Congress by their adjournment prevent its return, in which case it shall not be a law.

Every order, resolution, or vote to which the concurrence of the Senate and House of Representatives may be necessary (except on a question of adjournment) shall be presented to the President of the United States ; and before the same shall take effect, shall be approved by him, or being disapproved by him, shall be repassed by two-thirds of the Senate and House of Representatives, according to the rules and limitations prescribed in the case of a bill.

Section 8.—The Congress shall have power to lay and collect taxes, duties, imposts and excises, to pay the debts and provide for the common defence and general welfare of the United States ; but all duties, imposts and excises shall be uniform throughout the United States ;

To borrow money on the credit of the United States ;

To regulate commerce with foreign nations, and among the several States, and with the Indian tribes ;

To establish a uniform rule of naturalization, and uniform laws on the subject of bankruptcies throughout the United States ;

To coin money, regulate the value thereof, and of foreign coin, and fix the standard of weights and measures ;

To provide for the punishment of counterfeiting the securities and current coin of the United States ;

To establish post-offices and post-roads ;

To promote the progress of science and useful arts, by securing for limited times to authors and inventors the exclusive right to their respective writings and discoveries ;

To constitute tribunals inferior to the Supreme Court ;

To define and punish piracies and felonies committed on the high seas, and offences against the law of nations ;

To declare war, grant letters of marque and reprisal, and make rules concerning captures on land and water ;

To raise and support armies, but no appropriation of money to that use shall be for a longer term than two years ;

To provide and maintain a navy ;

To make rules for the government and regulation of the land and naval forces ;

To provide for calling forth the militia to execute the laws of the Union, suppress insurrections and repel invasions ;

To provide for organizing, arming, and disciplining the militia, and for governing such part of them as may be employed in the service of the United States, reserving to the States respectively, the appointment of the officers, and the authority of training the militia according to the discipline prescribed by Congress ;

To exercise exclusive legislation in all cases whatsoever, over such district (not exceeding ten miles square), as may, by cession of particular States, and the acceptance of Congress, become the seat of the government of the United States,[1] and to exercise like authority over all places purchased by the consent of the legislature of the State in which the same shall be, for the erection of forts, magazines, arsenals, dockyards, and other needful buildings ; and

To make all laws which shall be necessary and proper for carrying into execution the foregoing powers, and all other powers vested by this Constitution in the Government of the United States, or in any department or officer thereof.

Section 9.—The migration or importation of such persons as any of the States now existing shall think proper to admit, shall not be prohibited by the Congress prior to the year one thousand eight hundred and eight, but a tax or duty may be imposed on such importation, not exceeding ten dollars for each person.

---

[1] That is, the District of Columbia in which Washington is situated.

The privilege of the writ of *habeas corpus* shall not be suspended, unless when in cases of rebellion or invasion the public safety may require it.

No bill of attainder or *ex post facto* law shall be passed.

No capitation, or other direct tax shall be laid, unless in proportion to the census or enumeration herein before directed to be taken.[1]

No tax or duty shall be laid on articles exported from any State.

No preference shall be given by any regulation of commerce or revenue to the ports of one State over those of another ; nor shall vessels bound to, or from, one State, be obliged to enter, clear, or pay duties in another.

No money shall be drawn from the Treasury, but in consequence of appropriations made by law ; and a regular statement and account of the receipts and expenditures of all public money shall be published from time to time.

No title of nobility shall be granted by the United States ; and no person holding any office of profit or trust under them, shall, without the consent of the Congress, accept of any present, emolument, office, or title, of any kind whatever, from any king, prince, or foreign State.

Section 10.—No State shall enter into any treaty, alliance, or Confederation ; grant letters of marque and reprisal ; coin money ; emit bills of credit ; *make any thing but gold and silver coin a tender in payment of debts* ; pass any bill of attainder, *ex post facto* law, *or law impairing the obligations of contracts*, or grant any title of nobility.

No State shall, without the consent of the Congress, lay any imposts or duties on imports or exports, except what may be absolutely necessary for executing its inspection laws ; and the net produce of all duties and imposts laid by any State on imports or exports, shall be for the use of the Treasury of the United States ; and all such laws shall be subject to the revision and control of the Congress.

No State shall, without the consent of Congress, lay any duty of tonnage, keep troops, or ships of war in time of peace, enter into any agreement or compact with another State, or with a foreign power, or engage in war unless actually invaded, or in such imminent danger as will not admit of delay.

ARTICLE II

Section 1.—The executive power shall be vested in a President of the United States of America. He shall hold his office during the term of four years, and, together with the Vice-President, chosen for the same term, be elected, as follows :

Each State shall appoint, in such manner as the legislature thereof may direct, a number of electors, equal to the whole number of Senators and Representatives to which the State may be entitled in the Congress ; but no Senator or Representative, or person holding an office of trust or profit under the United States, shall be appointed an elector.

The electors shall meet in their respective States, and vote by ballot for two persons, *of whom one at least shall not be an inhabitant of*

[1] Cf. Amendment XVI.

the same State with themselves. And they shall make a list of all the persons voted for, and of the number of votes for each ; which list they shall sign and certify, and transmit sealed to the seat of the government of the United States, directed to the President of the Senate. The President of the Senate shall, in the presence of the Senate and House of Representatives, open all the certificates, and the votes shall then be counted. *The person having the greatest number of votes shall be the President, if such number be a majority of the whole number of electors appointed ; and if there be more than one who have such majority, and have an equal number of votes, then the House of Representatives shall immediately choose by ballot one of them for President ; and if no person have a majority, then from the five highest on the list the said House shall in like manner choose the President. But in choosing the President, the votes shall be taken by States, the representation from each State having one vote ; a quorum for this purpose shall consist of a member or members from two-thirds of the States, and a majority of all the States shall be necessary to a choice. In every case, after the choice of the President, the person having the greatest number of votes of the electors shall be the Vice-President. But if there should remain two or more who have equal votes, the Senate shall choose from them by ballot the Vice-President.*[1]

The Congress may determine the time of choosing the electors, and the day on which they shall give their votes ; which day shall be the same throughout the United States.

No person except a natural born citizen, or a citizen of the United States, at the time of the adoption of this Constitution, shall be eligible to the office of President ; neither shall any person be eligible to that office who shall not have attained to the age of thirty-five years, and been fourteen years a resident within the United States.

In case of the removal of the President from office, or of his death, resignation, or inability to discharge the powers and duties of the said office, the same shall devolve on the Vice-President, and the Congress may by law provide for the case of removal, death, resignation, or inability, both of the President and Vice-President, declaring what officer shall then act as President, and such officer shall act accordingly, until the disability be removed, or a President shall be elected.[2]

The President shall, at stated times, receive for his services, a compensation, which shall neither be increased nor diminished, during the period for which he shall have been elected, and he shall not receive within that period any other emolument from the United States, or any of them.

Before he enter on the execution of his office, he shall take the following oath or affirmation :

" I do solemnly swear (or affirm) that I will faithfully execute the office of President of the United States, and will to the best of my ability, preserve, protect, and defend the Constitution of the United States."

[1] Cf. Amendments XII and XX.
[2] The presidential succession is now regulated by an Act of 1887. Beginning with the Secretary of State, the succession goes *according to the seniority of the departments.*

Section 2.—The President shall be Commander-in-Chief of the army and navy of the United States, and of the militia of the several States, when called into the actual service of the United States ; he may require the opinion, in writing, of the principal officer in each of the executive departments, upon any subject relating to the duties of their respective offices, and he shall have power to grant reprieves and pardons for offences against the United States, except in cases of impeachment.

He shall have power, by and with the advice and consent of the Senate, to make treaties, provided two-thirds of the Senators present concur ; and he shall nominate, and by and with the advice and consent of the Senate, shall appoint ambassadors, other public ministers and consuls, judges of the Supreme Court, and all other officers of the United States, whose appointments are not herein otherwise provided for, and which shall be established by law ; but the Congress may by law vest the appointment of such inferior officers, as they think proper, in the President alone, in the courts of law, or in the heads of departments.

The President shall have power to fill up all vacancies that may happen during the recess of the Senate, by granting commissions which shall expire at the end of their next session.

Section 3.—He shall from time to time give to the Congress information of the state of the Union, and recommend to their consideration such measures as he shall judge necessary and expedient ; he may, on extraordinary occasions, convene both houses, or either of them, and in case of disagreement between them, with respect to the time of adjournment, he may adjourn them to such time as he shall think proper ; he shall receive ambassadors and other public ministers ; *he shall take care that the laws be faithfully executed,* and shall commission all the officers of the United States.

Section 4.—The President, Vice-President, and all civil officers of the United States, shall be removed from office on impeachment for, and conviction of, treason, bribery, or other high crimes and misdemeanours.

ARTICLE III

Section 1.—The judicial power of the United States, shall be vested in one Supreme Court, and in such inferior courts as the Congress may from time to time ordain and establish. The judges, both of the supreme and inferior courts, *shall hold their offices during good behaviour,* and shall, at stated times, receive for their services, a compensation, which shall not be diminished during their continuance in office.

Section 2.—The judicial power ·shall extend to all cases, in law and equity, arising under this Constitution, the laws of the United States, and treaties made, or which shall be made, under their authority ; to all cases affecting ambassadors, other public ministers and consuls ; to all cases of admiralty and maritime jurisdiction ; *to controversies to which the United States shall be a party ; to controversies between two or more States ; between a State and citizens of another State ; between citizens of different States ; between citizens of the same State claiming lands under grants of different States, and between a State, or the citizens thereof, and foreign states, citizens or subjects.*[1]

[1] Cf. Amendment XI.

In all cases affecting ambassadors, other public ministers and consuls, and those *in which a State shall be party, the Supreme Court shall have original jurisdiction. In all the other cases before mentioned, the Supreme Court shall have appellate jurisdiction, both as to law and fact, with such exceptions, and under such regulations as the Congress shall make.*

The trial of all crimes, except in cases of impeachment, shall be by jury ; and such trial shall be held in the State where the said crimes shall have been committed ; but when not committed within any State, the trial shall be at such place or places as the Congress may by law have directed.

Section 3.—Treason against the United States shall consist only in levying war against them, or in adhering to their enemies, giving them aid and comfort. No person shall be convicted of treason unless on the testimony of two witnesses to the same overt act, or on confession in open court.

The Congress shall have power to declare the punishment of treason, but no attainder of treason shall work corruption of blood, or forfeiture except during the life of the person attainted.

Article IV

Section 1.—Full faith and credit shall be given in each State to the public acts, records, and judicial proceedings of every other State. And the Congress may by general laws prescribe the manner in which such acts, records, and proceedings shall be proved, and the effect thereof.

Section 2.—The citizens of each State shall be entitled to all privileges and immunities of citizens in the several States.

A person charged in any State with treason, felony, or other crime, who shall flee from justice, and be found in another State, shall on demand of the executive authority of the State from which he fled, be delivered up, to be removed to the State having jurisdiction of the crime.

No person held to service or labour in one State, under the laws thereof, escaping into another, shall in consequence of any law or regulation therein, be discharged from such service or labour, but shall be delivered up on claim of the party to whom such service or labour may be due.

Section 3.—New States may be admitted by the Congress into this Union ; but no new State shall be formed or erected within the jurisdiction of any other State, nor any State be formed by the junction of two or more States, or parts of States, without the consent of the legislatures of the States concerned as well as of the Congress.

The Congress shall have power to dispose of and make all needful rules and regulations respecting the territory or other property belonging to the United States ; and nothing in this Constitution shall be so construed as to prejudice any claims of the United States, or of any particular State.

Section 4.—The United States shall guarantee to every State in this Union a Republican form of government, and shall protect each of them against invasion ; and on application of the legislature, or of the executive (when the legislature cannot be convened) against domestic violence.

ARTICLE V

The Congress, whenever two-thirds of both Houses, shall deem it necessary, shall propose amendments to this Constitution, or, on the application of the legislatures of two-thirds of the several States, shall call a convention for proposing amendments, which, in either case, shall be valid to all intents and purposes, as part of this Constitution, when ratified by the legislatures of three-fourths of the several States, or by conventions in three-fourths thereof, as the one or the other mode of ratification may be proposed by the Congress ; provided that no amendment which may be made prior to the year one thousand eight hundred and eight shall in any manner affect the first and fourth clauses in the ninth section of the first article ; and *that no State, without its consent, shall be deprived of its equal suffrage in the Senate.*

ARTICLE VI

All debts contracted and engagements entered into, before the adoption of this Constitution, shall be as valid against the United States under this Constitution, as under the Confederation.

This Constitution, and the laws of the United States which shall be made in pursuance thereof; and all treaties made, or which shall be made, under the authority of the United States, shall be the supreme law of the land ; and the judges in every States shall be bound thereby, any thing in the Constitution or laws of any State to the contrary notwithstanding.

The Senators and Representatives before mentioned, and the members of the several State legislatures, and all executive and judicial officers, both of the United States and of the several States, shall be bound by oath or affirmation, to support this Constitution ; *but no religious test shall ever be required as a qualification to any office or public trust under the United States.*

ARTICLE VII

The ratification of the conventions of nine States shall be sufficient for the establishment of this Constitution between the States so ratifying the same.

AMENDMENTS[1]

ARTICLES in addition to and amendment of the Constitution of the United States of America, proposed by Congress, and ratified by the legislatures of the several States, pursuant to the fifth article of the original Constitution.

ARTICLE I (1791)

Congress shall make no law respecting an establishment of religion, or prohibiting the free exercise thereof; or abridging the freedom of speech, or of the Press; or the right of the people peaceably to assemble, and to petition the government for a redress of grievances.

ARTICLE II (1791)

A well-regulated militia being necessary to the security of a free State, *the right of the people to keep and bear arms shall not be infringed.*

The Bill of Rights.

[1] The date of the adoption of each amendment has been inserted in brackets.

ARTICLE III (1791)

No soldier shall, in time of peace, be quartered in any house without the consent of the owner, nor in time of war, but in a manner to be prescribed by law.

ARTICLE IV (1791)

The right of the people to be secure in their persons, houses, papers, and effects, against unreasonable searches and seizures, shall not be violated, and no warrants shall issue, but upon probable cause, supported by oath or affirmation, and particularly describing the place to be searched, and the persons or things to be seized.

ARTICLE V (1791)

No person shall be held to answer for a capital, or otherwise infamous crime, unless on a presentment or indictment of a grand jury, except in cases arising in the land or naval forces, or in the militia, when in actual service in time of war or public danger ; nor shall any person be subject for the same offence to be twice put in jeopardy of life or limb ; nor shall be compelled in any criminal case to be a witness against himself, *nor be deprived of life, liberty, or property, without due process of law ;* nor shall private property be taken for public use, without just compensation.[1]

ARTICLE VI (1791)

In all criminal prosecutions the accused shall enjoy the right to a speedy and public trial, by an impartial jury of the State and district wherein the crime shall have been committed, which district shall have been previously ascertained by law, and to be informed of the nature and cause of the accusation ; to be confronted with the witnesses against him ; to have compulsory process for obtaining witnesses in his favour, and to have the assistance of counsel for his defence.

ARTICLE VII (1791)

In suits at common law, where the value in controversy shall exceed twenty dollars, the right of trial by jury shall be preserved, and no fact tried by a jury shall be otherwise re-examined in any court of the United States, than according to the rules of the common law.

ARTICLE VIII (1791)

Excessive bail shall not be required, nor excessive fines imposed, *nor cruel and unusual punishments inflicted.*

ARTICLE IX (1791)

The enumeration in the Constitution of certain rights shall not be construed to deny or disparage others retained by the people.

ARTICLE X (1791)

The powers not delegated to the United States by the Constitution, nor prohibited by it to the States, are reserved to the States respectively or to the people.

[1] Cf. Amendment XIV.

The Bill of Rights.

ARTICLE XI (1798)

The judicial power of the United States shall not be construed to extend to any suit in law or equity, commenced or prosecuted against one of the United States by citizens of another State, or by citizens or subjects of any foreign State.

ARTICLE XII (1804)

The electors shall meet in their respective States, and vote by ballot for President and Vice-President, one of whom, at least, shall not be an inhabitant of the same State with themselves ; they shall name in their ballots the person voted for as President, and in distinct ballots the person voted for as Vice-President, and they shall make distinct lists of all persons voted for as President, and of all persons voted for as Vice-President, and of the number of votes for each, which lists they shall sign and certify, and transmit sealed to the seat of the government of the United States, directed to the President of the Senate ; the President of the Senate shall, in the presence of the Senate and House of Representatives, open all the certificates and the votes shall then be counted ; *the person having the greatest number of votes for President, shall be the President, if such number be a majority of the whole number of electors appointed ; and if no person have such majority, then from the persons having the highest numbers not exceeding three on the list of those voted for as President, the House of Representatives shall choose immediately by ballot, the President. But in choosing the President, the votes shall be taken by States, the representation from each State having one vote ; a quorum for this purpose shall consist of a member or members from two-thirds of the States, and a majority of all the States shall be necessary to a choice. And if the House of Representatives shall not choose a President whenever the right of choice shall devolve upon them,* before the 4th day of March next following, *then the Vice-President shall act as President,* as in the case of the death or other constitutional disability of the President. The person having the greatest number of votes as Vice-President, shall be the Vice-President, if such number be a majority of the whole number of electors appointed, *and if no person have a majority, then from the two highest numbers on the list, the Senate shall choose the Vice-President ; a quorum for the purpose shall consist of two-thirds of the whole number of Senators, and a majority of the whole number shall be necessary to a choice. But no person constitutionally ineligible to the office of President shall be eligible to that of Vice-President of the United States.*[1]

ARTICLE XIII (1865)

Section 1.—Neither slavery nor involuntary servitude, except as a punishment for crime whereof the party shall have been duly convicted, shall exist within the United States, or any place subject to their jurisdiction.

Section 2.—Congress shall have power to enforce this article by appropriate legislation.

[1] Cf. Amendment XX.

ARTICLE XIV (1868)

Section 1.—All persons born or naturalized in the United States, and subject to the jurisdiction thereof, are citizens of the United States and of the State wherein they reside. *No State shall make or enforce any law which shall abridge the privileges or immunities of citizens of the United States ; nor shall any State deprive any person of life, liberty, or property, without due process of law ; nor deny to any person within its jurisdiction the equal protection of the laws.*

Section 2.—*Representatives shall be apportioned among the several States according to their respective numbers, counting the whole number of persons in each State, excluding Indians not taxed. But when the right to vote at any election for the choice of electors for President and Vice-President of the United States, Representatives in Congress,* the executive and judicial officers of a State, or the members of the Legislature thereof, *is denied to any of the male inhabitants of such State, being twenty-one years of age and citizens of the United States, or in any way abridged except for participation in rebellion, or other crime, the basis of representation therein shall be reduced in the proportion which the number of such male citizens shall bear to the whole number of male citizens twenty-one years of age in such State.*[1]

Section 3.—No person shall be a Senator or Representative in Congress, or elector of President and Vice-President, or hold any office, civil or military, under the United States, or under any State, who, having previously taken an oath, as a member of Congress, or as an officer of the United States, or as a member of any State legislature, or as an executive or judicial officer of any State, to support the Constitution of the United States, shall have engaged in insurrection or rebellion against the same, or given aid or comfort to the enemies thereof. But Congress may by vote of two-thirds of each house remove such disability.

Section 4.—The validity of the public debt of the United States, authorized by law, including debts incurred for payment of pensions and bounties for services in suppressing insurrection or rebellion, shall not be questioned. But neither the United States nor any State shall assume or pay any debt or obligation incurred in aid of insurrection or rebellion against the United States, or any claim for the loss or emancipation of any slave ; but all such debts, obligations, and claims shall be held illegal and void.

Section 5.—*The Congress shall have power to enforce, by appropriate legislation, the provisions of this article.*

ARTICLE XV (1870)

Section 1.—*The right of citizens of the United States to vote shall not be denied or abridged by the United States or by any State on account of race, colour, or previous condition of servitude.*[1]

Section 2.—*The Congress shall have power to enforce this article by appropriate legislation.*

[1] Cf. Amendment XIX.

Article XVI (1913)

The Congress shall have power to lay and collect taxes on incomes, from whatever source derived, without apportionment among the several States, and without regard to any census or enumeration.

Article XVII (1913)

The Senate of the United States shall be composed of two Senators from each State, elected by the people thereof for six years ; and each Senator shall have one vote. *The electors in each State shall have the qualifications requisite for electors of the most numerous branch of the State legislatures.*

When vacancies happen in the representation of any State in the Senate, the executive authority of such State shall issue writs of election to fill such vacancies : *Provided,* That the legislature of any State may empower the executive thereof to make temporary appointment until the people fill the vacancies by election as the legislature may direct.

This amendment shall not be so construed as to affect the election or term of any Senator chosen before it becomes valid as part of the Constitution.

Article XVIII (1918)

Section 1.—After one year from the ratification of this article, *the manufacture, sale, or transportation of intoxicating liquors within, the importation thereof into, or the exportation thereof from, the United States and all territory subject to the jurisdiction thereof, for beverage purposes, is hereby prohibited.*

Section 2.—*The Congress and the several States shall have concurrent power to enforce this article by appropriate legislation.*

Section 3.—This article shall be inoperative unless it shall have been ratified as an amendment to the Constitution by the legislatures of the several States, as provided in the Constitution, within seven years from the date of the submission thereof to the States by the Congress.

Article XIX (1920)

Section 1.—*The right of citizens of the United States to vote shall not be abridged by the United States or by any state on account of sex.*

Section 2.—*Congress shall have power to enforce this article by appropriate legislation.*

Article XX (1933)

Section 1.—*The terms of President and Vice-President shall end at noon on the 20th day of January and the terms of Senators and Representatives at noon on the 3rd day of January,* of the years in which such terms would have ended if this article had not been ratified ; and the terms of their successors shall then begin.

Section 2.—The Congress shall assemble at least once in every year, *and such meeting shall begin at noon on the 3rd day of January* unless they shall by law appoint a different day.

Section 3.—If, at the time fixed for the beginning of the term of the President, the President-elect shall have died, the Vice-President-elect shall become President. If a President shall not have been chosen before the time fixed for the beginning of his term or if the President-elect shall have failed to qualify, then the Vice-President-elect shall act as President until a President shall have qualified ; and the Congress may by law provide for the case wherein neither a President-elect nor a Vice-President-elect shall have qualified, declaring who shall then act as President, or the manner in which one who is to act shall be selected, and such person shall act accordingly until a President or Vice-President shall have qualified.

Section 4.—The Congress may by law provide for the case of the death of any of the persons from whom the House of Representatives may choose a President whenever the right of choice shall have devolved upon them, and for the case of the death of any of the persons from whom the Senate may choose a Vice-President whenever the right of choice shall have devolved upon them.

Section 5.—Sections 1 and 2 shall take effect on the 15th day of October following the ratification of this article, [i.e. October 15, 1933].

Section 6.—This article shall be inoperative unless it shall have been ratified as an amendment to the Constitution by the Legislatu.es of three-fourths of the several States within seven years from the date of its submission.

_____

The ratification of this amendment was completed by the adherence of Missouri, on January 23, 1933.)

APPENDIX II

APPORTIONMENT OF SEATS IN THE HOUSE OF REPRESENTATIVES [1]

THIS arrangement of states by sections is intended to make clearer the allusions in the text to the main blocks of states and is not intended to be rigidly descriptive of their economic character. The " border states ", it may be said, are the slave states which did not secede during the Civil War. Their importance as a separate group of states has steadily diminished but, as in local elections, they have not altogether lost all of their distinguishing marks, it has seemed best to group them together.

NEW ENGLAND [1]

Connecticut	6	(5)
Maine	3	(4)
Massachusetts	15	(16)
New Hampshire	2	(2)
Rhode Island	2	(3)
Vermont	1	(2)
	29	**(32)**

ATLANTIC STATES

New Jersey	14	(12)
New York	45	(43)
Pennsylvania	34	(36)
	93	**(91)**

THE SOUTH

Alabama	9	(10)
Arkansas	7	(7)
Florida	5	(4)
Georgia	10	(12)
Louisiana	8	(8)
Mississippi	7	(8)
North Carolina	11	(10)
South Carolina	6	(7)
Tennessee	9	(10)
Texas	21	(18)
Virginia	9	(10)

BORDER STATES

Delaware	1	(1)
Kentucky	9	(11)
Maryland	6	(6)
Missouri	13	(16)
West Virginia	6	(6)
	35	**(40)**

102 (104)

[1] The figures in brackets show the number of Representatives under the old apportionment and thus illustrate the change in population and political strength since 1910. As the strength of a state in the electoral college is equal to the sum of its Representatives and Senators, the electoral vote of any state can be found by adding two to the number of Representatives. No state can have less than three presidential Electors as no state can have less than one Representative or less or more than two Senators. The small states are thus over-represented. The dependencies of the United States, Porto Rico, Alaska, Hawaii, the Philippines, have each a Delegate in Congress who may speak but not vote.

The Middle West
(Industrial States)

Illinois	27 (27)
Indiana	12 (13)
Michigan	17 (13)
Ohio	24 (22)
	80 (75)

The Middle West
(Farming States)

Iowa	9 (11)
Kansas	7 (8)
Minnesota	9 (10)
Nebraska	5 (6)
North Dakota	2 (3)
Oklahoma	9 (8)
South Dakota	2 (3)
Wisconsin	10 (11)
	53 (60)

The Mountain States

Arizona	1 (1)
Colorado	4 (4)
Idaho	2 (2)
Montana	2 (2)
Nevada	1 (1)
New Mexico	1 (1)
Utah	2 (2)
Wyoming	1 (1)
	14 (14)

The Pacific Slope

California	20 (11)
Oregon	3 (3)
Washington	6 (5)
	29 (19)

Total . . . 435 (435)

The states shown shaded are those which have voted for the same party in every presidential election since 1916. Those in the North are the nucleus of Republican, those in the South, of Democratic strength.

APPENDIX III

PRESIDENTS OF THE UNITED STATES

George Washington . .	1789–1797	F.[1]	Virginia.[8]
John Adams . . .	1797–1801	F.	Massachusetts.
Thomas Jefferson .	1801–1809	R.-D.[2]	Virginia.
James Madison .	1809–1817	R.-D.	Virginia.
James Monroe . .	1817–1825	R.-D.	Virginia.
John Quincy Adams .	1825–1829	R.-D.	Massachusetts.
Andrew Jackson .	1829–1837	D.	Tennessee.
Martin Van Buren .	1837–1841	D.	New York.
William Henry Harrison .	1841–	W.[3]	Ohio.
John Tyler . . .	1841–1845 [4]	W.	Virginia.
James Polk . .	1845–1849	D.	Tennessee.
Zacchary Taylor .	1849–1850	W.	Louisiana.
Millard Fillmore .	1850–1853 [5]	W.	New York.
Franklin Pierce .	1853–1857	D.	New Hampshire.
James Buchanan .	1857–1861	D.	Pennsylvania.
Abraham Lincoln .	1861–1865	R.[6]	Illinois.
Andrew Johnson .	1865–1869	U.[7]	Tennessee.
Ulysses S. Grant .	1869–1877	R.	Illinois.
Rutherford B. Hayes .	1877–1881	R.	Ohio.
James A. Garfield .	1881–	R.	Ohio.

[1] F. (Federalist).

[2] R.D. (Republican-Democrat). The Jeffersonian party was called by itself the Republican party, by its enemies, the Democrats. It is usual to count the Republican Presidents of the Jeffersonian party as Democrats, but the first President to bear the name of Democrat was Andrew Jackson.

[3] W. (Whig). This party arose out of the split in the Jeffersonian party. It is usually considered, however, to have no claim on any of the Presidents elected before 1840.

[4] Tyler was elected Vice-President and as such succeeded Harrison, serving all of that President's term save one month. He is classed as a Whig, though with doubtful propriety.

[5] Fillmore succeeded Taylor on the latter's death (July 9, 1850).

[6] R. (Republican). Despite its adoption of the old Jeffersonian name, this party is generally assumed to begin its list of Presidents with Lincoln.

[7] U. (Union). At the election of 1864 the Republicans ran as the Union party and as such nominated the war Democrat, Andrew Johnson, for the vice-presidency. He succeeded on Lincoln's death (April 15, 1855), serving out the rest of Lincoln's second term. He was never officially a Republican, though usually classed as such.

[8] The states given are the states of official residence, not of birth.

Chester A. Arthur .	. 1881–1885 [1]	R.	New York.
Grover Cleveland .	. 1885–1889	D.	New York.
Benjamin Harrison .	. 1889–1893	R.	Indiana.
Grover Cleveland .	. 1893–1897	D.	New York.
William McKinley .	. 1897–1901	R.	Ohio.
Theodore Roosevelt .	. 1901–1909 [2]	R.	New York.
William H. Taft .	. 1909–1913	R.	Ohio.
Woodrow Wilson .	. 1913–1921	D.	New Jersey.
Warren G. Harding	. 1921–1923	R.	Ohio.
Calvin Coolidge .	. 1923–1929 [3]	R.	Massachusetts.
Herbert C. Hoover .	. 1929–1933	R.	California.
Franklin D. Roosevelt	. 1933–	D.	New York.

[1] Arthur succeeded on the death of Garfield (September 19, 1881).

[2] Roosevelt succeeded on the death of McKinley (September 14, 1901), serving the rest of McKinley's term, and a complete term of his own.

[3] Mr. Coolidge succeeded on Harding's death (August 2, 1923), serving the rest of that term and a whole term of his own.

INDEX

Abbot, W. J., 268
Adams, Brooks, 24
Adams, Charles Francis, III, 128, 325
Adams County (Ohio), 236
Adams, Henry, 356
Adams, John, 119, 301
Adams, John Quincy, 128, 301
Adamson Act, 152
Addams, Jane, 194, 219
Addicks, J. Edward, 274
Adkins Case, 22
Ailes, Milton E., 197
Alabama, 62, 112, 139, 309
Alaska, 203
Albany (N.Y.), 101, 257, 269, 271, 282
Aldrich, Nelson W., 41, 64, 149, 164, 165, 178, 180, 276, 286, 319
Alien and Sedition Acts, 33
Alleghany Mountains, 74
Allegheny County (Pa.), 73, 234
Allen, W. V., 178
Allison, W. B., 164, 178, 350
Altgeld, John P., 292
" Amen Corner ", 283
American Federation of Labor, 337
American Legion, 211
American Protective Association (*A.P.A.*), 353
Ames, Albert A., 243, 244, 260
Ames, Fisher, 42, 142
Ames, Nathaniel, 42
Ames, Oakes, 273
Anaconda Copper Company, 276, 326, 345
Andrew, John A., 245
Annapolis (Md.), 203
Anti-Saloon League, 104 ff., 115, 160, 347
Apollo Hall, 253
Arizona, 98, 159, 337
Arkansas, 326
Arthur, Chester A., 127, 189, 191, 298, 306
Asbury, Francis, 103
Atlanta (Ga.), 110, 228, 372
Atterbury, W. W., 347

Baer, George F., 289
Bailey, Joseph W., 154
Baker, Ray S., 134
Baltimore (Md.), 59, 108, 110, 130, 236, 245, 309, 335
Baltimore and Ohio Railroad, 270
Bancroft, George, 202
Bankhead, John H., 70
Barkley, Alben W., 99, 300
Barlow, F. C., 189
Barnard, George G., 30
Barnes, William T., 282
Barnhart, J. D., 370
Barnum, P. T., 270
Bayard *Family*, 59, 325
Bayard, T. F., 201
Beard, Charles A., 197
Beard, William, 197
Beck, James M., 99, 327, 348
Becker, Charles, 247, 339
Beecher, Henry Ward, 356
Belknap, W. W., 203
Belmont, August, 314
Belmont, *House of*, 60
Belmont, Perry, 346
Benett Law, 353
Benton, T. H., 352
Bilbo, T. G., 281
Bimba, Anthony, 292
Bisbee (Ariz.), 337
Black, Hugo, 112
Black, John C., 207
Blaine, James G., 54, 55, 126, 127, 147, 174, 188, 190, 273, 298, 303, 310, 311, 315, 331, 356, 358, 363
Blaine, Mrs. James G., 356
Blaine, John J., 86, 87
Bland, Richard P., 306
Blease, Cole, 131, 133, 229, 337
Bliss, Cornelius, 285
Blythe, Samuel, 71
Bonaparte, Charles A., 130
" Bonus Army ", 213
Borah, William E., 176, 177, 306, 338, 347

405

McClung 10-11-44